TOPICS OF THE TIME.

BY

JAMES PARTON.

BOSTON:
JAMES R. OSGOOD AND COMPANY,
LATE TICKNOR & FIELDS, AND FIELDS, OSGOOD, & CO.
1871.

UNIVERSITY PRESS: WELCH, BIGELOW, & CO.,
CAMBRIDGE.

CONTENTS.

UNCLE SAM'S TREATMENT OF HIS SERVANTS.

FIRST, as to the wages he pays them. It is not necessary for him to give high salaries, because there are two precious commodities with which a government can reward its servants, over and above the money it pays them. One is honor; the other is safety. These two things, honor and safety, are what the virtuous portion of mankind strive for; and so precious are they, that when, after years of honest toil, a man has attained them, most of us join in the acclaim which pronounces his life successful. Now a government can bestow these upon every person whom it retains in its service. It can reasonably ask a man, in the full tide of a victorious career, to relinquish his vocation, and devote his life to the public service, for a comparatively small sum per annum, provided that sum per annum is made securely his until justly forfeited. It can do this, because a decent and secure maintenance, with the honor properly belonging to a government office, constitutes an entire material success. No man can get any more material good than that, for the simple reason that there *is* no more to get. Mr. Astor was right in saying that he derived from his estate only the few thousands a year which it cost him to live; but those few thousands are so securely his that he can be deprived of them only by his own fault or folly. A government can place its higher servants in a position more desirable even than his, since to his safety it can add honor. There is no honor in owning a thousand houses, but it is highly honorable, under a properly constituted government, to be the trusted and faithful servant of the public.

Hence, on these terms, a government can usually have the choice of all the most suitable persons for any post.

If it happens to want a judge, it can usually have the best lawyer of the most distinguished court. If it wants a man of business, it can select the best executive talent known to exist. Why should it not? It can offer better wages than a man gets in a private station, — more honor, and equal safety. We have recently seen that one of the ablest business men in the country, already in the possession of a secure fortune, was willing to give up three millions per annum for the honor and satisfaction of serving the public.

I fear we must admit that Uncle Sam, with all his generosity and good intentions, pays to his upper servants the smallest wages a government ever paid, — wages so mean that it is wonderful he gets any faithful, efficient service at all. He does get a good deal; but he has little right to expect it. When he confers security he gives along with it a pinching, lowering, corrupting salary; and in the majority of cases, his servants enjoy neither safety nor abundance.

I will mention a few facts with regard to the Supreme Court, the judges of which receive six thousand paper dollars a year, and the chief justice six thousand five hundred.* When I was in Washington last winter, the daughters of the late chief justice were earning a scanty, precarious livelihood by copying documents in one of the public offices, at eight cents per hundred words. The father of those ladies, twenty-seven years before his death, lured by an honorable, long-cherished ambition, gave up a practice at the Maryland bar which in a few years would have enriched him, in order to accept the post of chief justice. Whatever his errors may have been, I know he accepted the seat from a proper human motive, — that of winning the esteem of his countrymen by interpreting justice to them; and he devoted himself wholly to the performance of its duties. I well remember hearing him, one evening, some years before his death, give a sketch of his daily and yearly round of work and travel. It was wonderful that a man of fourscore could get through an amount of labor only equalled by that of the active editor of a great daily

* The salaries of the judges of the Supreme Court have since been raised to $ 10,000 and $ 10,500. — PUBLISHERS.

paper. Except that he smoked like a steam-engine, his habits were regular and abstemious; but he died so poor that his family were destitute almost immediately after his last year's salary was spent.

Other facts: A justice of the same high court — the highest, considering all its duties, in the world — was paying exactly his whole salary, last winter, for the board and lodging of himself and his wife. They had one parlor and one bedroom. The judge, of course, gave up the parlor to his wife and her guests, and used the bedroom for an office and consultation-room. There was a great clearing away of papers at bedtime; for, the room being very small, the bed had to serve as an office-table. Another justice, who relinquished a practice of forty thousand dollars a year, being a Californian, had to sell his paper dollars during the war at from one third to one half their nominal value; and he spent a quarter of the year in laborious travelling. One eminent member of this court was compelled to resign his seat, — not because he could not live upon his salary, for no justice of the Supreme Court can do that, — but because he had not private income *enough* to eke it out. There is not a justice now sitting upon that bench who lives or can live upon his salary; although, fortunately, it is not etiquette for a justice of the Supreme Court to entertain.

Now, reader, it is no hardship for a man to spread his papers over his bed; nor is it much more painful for the daughters of a chief justice to do copying at eight cents a page than it is for the daughters of a chief cook. I never had six thousand dollars a year, and have managed to rub on pretty well without it, and expect to continue so to do. To me, to nine tenths of all my readers, and to nearly all the people in the world, six thousand dollars a year would be wealth. *I* cannot, therefore, consider it a hardship for men in general to be limited to such a revenue. But it *is* hard for a patriotic President to be limited in his choice for the office of Supreme judge to the very few lawyers who happen to possess an independent estate. It *is* a hardship to a great lawyer, formed by nature and circumstances for that sublime place, to be compelled to leave it to inferior men because he cannot live upon the salary.

It *is* a hardship to the generous people of the United States to see men of such exalted rank in their service — men intrusted with such difficult and important duties — cramped and pinched and anxious for a little money, unable to keep a secretary, and too poor to afford a ride on horseback before going into court.

To this, some will be disposed to reply that any sum per annum is too much for a court from which the Dred Scott decision emanated. But on that principle you must cut off supplies from the White House, starve Congress, and suspend nine tenths of all official and all private salaries. We were all misled or corrupted by slavery, except the few original, thorough-going Abolitionists, who alone of all the inhabitants of America have a "record" on that subject of which they need never be ashamed. Because Judge Taney was perverted and corrupted by slavery is no reason for degrading forever the Court over which he presided. It is worth mentioning, too, that if the Supreme Court had been decently compensated the Dred Scott decision would never have been written. Judge Taney was past eighty when he wrote it, and he would have retired some years before if he could have retained his ridiculous but indispensable little salary.

It is not necessary, I repeat, for the judges of this Court to be paid high salaries; because the appointment is for life, and the honor is immense. It is only necessary that they be paid such a sum per annum as will enable lawyers who have little property to accept seats on that bench without injustice to those dependent upon them. Judges of the same rank in England, if there were any, would receive a salary not far from equivalent to a hundred thousand of our dollars per annum. We can, and properly may, get the best lawyers at a lower rate; for the same principle should fix the compensation of a Supreme judge as regulates the wages of day laborers. The average of unskilled laborers being two dollars a day, if you want men of average quality you pay two dollars a day. If you want only the refuse of the streets, you pay a dollar and a half. If you want the pick of the whole town, you pay two dollars and a half. The question is, What grade of lawyer do we desire for a justice of the Supreme Court? If we desire the highest, and no other, we must give him an equivalent for what he is to surrender. A lawyer of the first rank, at the present time, earns an income ranging from thirty to sixty thousand dollars a year. Hence I presume that if the salary were fixed at twenty thousand dollars a year, with a proper retiring-pension, the government could look over the bar of the whole country, and get the best living man for every vacancy. Perhaps fifteen thousand would almost answer, which is about the sum it costs to keep house decently in Washington at present.

On almost any morning during the winter, if you take your stand at the front (which is the back) of the Capitol, you may see lawyers who practise in the Supreme Court driven up to the entrance in well-appointed carriages, while the justices before whom they are to argue get out of street-cars or trudge up the steep hill on foot. It is pleasant to see the judges in the cars, and to observe that the respect due to their place is manifested by all who ride in their company. Nevertheless, if *any* people about the Supreme Court are to have carriages, surely the justices ought to be among them. Uncle Sam can certainly afford to pay his highest servants as liberally as clients pay their lawyers; and it concerns both his dignity and his interest to do so. Of course, people can always be found to take any place at any salary; but the more able a man is, the more he can choose what he will do, and the harder he is to get. If it is desired to have truly competent persons in the public service, the public service must be made truly desirable.

What a wise thing Congress did, in 1855, in establishing the Court of Claims! The founding of that court was a step forward in the art of government. The late Sir Frederick Bruce, British Minister in Washington, who was an intelligent observer of men and things in America, used often to say that there was nothing in Washington which seemed to him more admirable or more original than that Court. "It is," he once said, "a grand and noble thought that any citizen can go before a legal tribunal, and maintain his rights against thirty millions. Nothing American in America has so deeply impressed me." When he met one of the judges of the Court, he was never weary of listening to explanations of its procedure and narratives of its cases. His appreciation of the value of this Court would have been still greater if he had lived in Washington before it was established, and had witnessed the bad lobbying and weary waste of time and resources which it has in some measure prevented. Before the Court of Claims existed, an honest claimant might well doubt whether *any* amount of money could compensate him for the intrigue, solicitation, and anxiety involved in the prosecution of a claim before Congress; and, at the same time, a dishonest claimant might doubt whether a claim could be so ill-founded that indomitable lobbying might not weary Congress into conceding it. A citizen can now go before this Court, present his claim, establish it by evidence and argument; and, if the court allows it, he has but to exhibit proof of the fact at the treasury, and draw the money. Very large claims and war claims are alone exempted from its jurisdiction; but probably the time is not distant when all disputed claims of whatever kind or amount will be submitted to it for adjudication. Not only does this Court decide upon claims, but it establishes principles. Its decisions are now a rule in the Departments for the guidance of heads of bureaus. The volumes containing reports of cases tried before it, prepared by Judge Nott and Mr. Samuel H. Huntington, show, even to the unprofessional mind, that this court contributes its share to the maintenance and elucidation of justice in this land.

The reader will observe that in constituting this Court Congress has nobly parted with a portion of its sovereignty. When it was first established, a claimant had to procure a decision in his favor from the Court, and then go to Congress and enter upon a course of lobbying to get the money appropriated. This was heart-breaking work to many a wretch; nor was the time of Congress always saved by decisions which had no effect until Congress ratified them. The Court was in fact no more than an adjunct to the Committee on Claims. At length, Congress wisely gave to the decisions of the Court a practical validity by empowering the Secretary of the Treasury to pay the sums awarded, — securing to the disappointed claimant a right of appeal to the Supreme Court.

Every reflecting person, I think, will feel that judges intrusted with powers so peculiar and so great, — judges singularly liable both to temptation and suspicion, — ought to be lawyers of very high rank and men of the highest character. In other words, they ought to be men who in private life can earn a liberal income. In 1855, when a dollar was a dollar, Congress fixed the salary of the judges of this Court at four thousand dollars a year. It was not enough then; but the salary has never been changed, except by the depreciation of the currency. Consequently, it now possesses about one half of its original value, and a judge who has no private income is in sorry case. Wealthy and powerful claimants come before him, some of whom are foreigners whose *only* care is to get their claim allowed. Thriving lawyers plead at the bar, gain large fees, go to luxurious homes, and enjoy every facility for the doing of their work; while the judges, if they have no estates and are blessed with families, will be in doubt sometimes whether they can really afford to ride in the street-cars.

Now, human nature being always human nature, ability and force will as a rule take the path in life that leads to a good front-door, with a nice saddle-horse tied to the post before it. Therefore, if a judge on the bench gets four thousand dollars a year, and the leading lawyers at the bar get twenty thousand, you will observe, *at last*, that the first-rate men remain at the bar, and the third-rate men are on the bench. Not at first, because the permanence of the appointment counts for much, and the honor for more. But in the course of time, if you persist in condemning judges to a lifetime of respectable pinch, the valuable men will resign and decline, until the peculiar honor once attached to the title of judge is gone. I say nothing of the temptation to which a poor judge in *such* a Court may be exposed, because we have not yet sunk to the point when an American judge permanently appointed can be thought of as subject to temptation. But keep judges' salaries as they are for a few years more, and there will be no justice obtainable in the United States, except by purchase. If a seat on this bench should become vacant to-morrow, the President might be driven half mad by the multitude of applicants; but if he were to offer it to each of the hundred most eminent lawyers in the country, it is probable that it would be declined by them all. Most of these would probably reply: "Mr. President, you do me great honor, but I really cannot afford it; the luxury is beyond my means."

Every senator, I believe, without exception, and nearly every member of the House, will own, in conversation, that the salaries paid to judges, heads of departments, some heads of bureaus, and other officials, are insufficient; but many senators hang back from increasing salaries, for fear of an imaginary fool of a farmer, who is supposed to begrudge the servants of the public a just compensation. Whenever I have been in the country lately, I have looked about in search of that narrow-minded agriculturist, but I have not been able to find him. The farmers understand this matter as well as senators; they know perfectly well that if the government wants a diamond or a man, it must go into the market and pay what the article will fetch from other purchasers. The only question is, what grade of diamond or man does it want?

Sir Frederick Bruce might well be interested in the Court of Claims; but there is something in Washington a thousand times more wonderful and more original than that. Like other wonders, however, it escapes observation because we are so familiar with it. Walk over the Treasury building; mark the thousands of persons employed therein; consider the nature of their employment; contemplate the magnitude and difficulty of the task imposed upon the head of that department; think of the wide-spread ruin that could result from an error on his part, and the lasting good that might come of one superior method. Consider the trust reposed in him, the ease with which that trust could be violated, and the absolute certainty we have that it never is, never has been, and never will be violated. Think of all this, and then reflect upon the fact that out of those inconceivable millions that pass under his control, we permit him to retain for his own use not enough to keep house upon. "How much rent do you pay here in Washington?" asked some one of Mr. Evarts last winter. "My salary," was the reply. This is the great wonder, not of Washington only, but of the world. The pyramids of Egypt are commonplace compared with it. The man that supplies the Treasury building with any one of the leading articles used in it would turn up his nose at eight thousand dollars a year. Fortunes were made in the mere erection of the edifice. Yet Secretaries of the Treasury, as they have gone down those granite steps in the afternoon, have doubtless often fallen into a deep meditation upon the ways and means of getting over the next rent-day. They have generally been men of small fortunes. Hamilton was obliged to resign and go home to earn money for his large family, and Gallatin was never in very liberal circumstances. Gallatin had an opportunity, once, of gaining a large fortune in Paris without dishonor. "No," said he to the representative of the great house which he had obliged, — "no; a man who has been intrusted with the finances of his country must not die rich." In this lofty spirit the office has generally been held.

The time has come, I think, for putting the members of the Cabinet a little more at their ease. The people do not want to be under an obligation to them of a pecuniary nature. They did not want Mr. Stanton to work during the war as no galley-slave ever worked, and yet live in part upon his private fortune; nor is it wise to subject human nature to such a staggering temptation. The man whose signature confers place and wealth ought not to be left to grapple with the embarrassments of an insufficient income. Uncle Sam has a large although not unencumbered estate, and he can well afford to maintain those who serve him in a style suited to the importance and dignity of their duties. To keep house in Washington on the scale adopted by Mr. Seward, who lived plainly enough and gave perhaps twenty moderate dinners a year, costs about fifteen thousand dollars per annum; which is about the present value of the salary which Hamilton found inadequate during the presidency of General Washington. Hamilton, however, had married a rich man's daughter, who had probably a rich man's daughter's ideas as to what are the necessaries of life. His vices also were expensive, or, to speak more exactly, his vice. The virtuous public men of the present day could probably retain the post of Cabinet Minister or Vice-President for a few years upon fifteen thousand dollars a year without seriously encroaching upon their private fortunes; and a salary of that amount would give the President a much wider range of choice. "Perhaps," said Mr. Wade last spring, "I should have taken office, if it had been offered me; but the pay is inadequate. I could not have held the position and kept house in Washington as Cabinet Ministers are expected to, for the salary. It would have taken five thousand dollars a year more from my private means, unless I 'd steal, and I 'm too old to begin to steal."

The grade of officials just below that of Cabinet Minister, the class represented during the war by Mr. G. V. Fox, Assistant Secretary of the Navy, are persons of great importance in Washington. The supposed necessities of party sometimes induce a President to fill a place in the Cabinet with any old figure-head that happens to be lying about. In any case, the person next in rank to the chief exercises great authority, and will generally be to his department what a first lieutenant is to his ship. It is admitted on all hands that the sudden expansion of the navy of the United States during the first years of the war, resulting in a real blockade of an immense line of coast, and in the immortal victories of Farragut and his comrades, was the *ne plus ultra* of administrative achievement. It is also admitted that this was chiefly the work of Mr. G. V. Fox. Now, it was no hardship to Mr. Fox, in those glorious years, to serve his country for less money than would pay for the board and lodging of a small family in a third-rate hotel. On the contrary, it was a sweet, a high, a priceless privilege. The meanness of the salary enhanced the glory and fascination of the post. It must have been delicious, sometimes, when he had signed contracts that would enrich half a dozen men, to contemplate the leanness of his own exchequer. It must have been a gratification bordering on the sublime, just after he had asked a creditor to wait till next quarter-day for his money, to read in a Democratic newspaper of the enormous sums he was making from his interests in navy contracts. But human nature cannot be kept at that pitch of exaltation in which we lived from 1861 to 1865; nor is there any need that it should be. In the long run, bread-and-butter, as Ex-alderman Johnson styled it, rules the world; and, when the war was over, Mr. Fox was more than justified in resigning his place in Washington, at thirty-five hundred dollars a year, to accept the superintendency of a manufactory at Lowell, at seven thousand. Seven thousand dollars a year at Lowell is about equal to eleven thousand dollars a year at Washington.

The simple question for us to consider is: Are men of great capacity wanted in government offices, or are they not? If they are, we must pay them what others find it worth while to pay them. Mr. Fox represents a class of able men, nearly all of whom were compelled to retire from the public service after the close of the war because the salaries attached to their posts were inadequate. I mention him by name, because he is well known to the public, and also because I have never seen him, and do not even know whether his was the creative mind of the Navy Department. *Some* mind was; and the principle is the same, whether it goes by the name of Fox or another. To this class of officials,—assistant secretaries, heads of important bureaus, and others,—Uncle Sam, it is to be noted, pays nothing but money. Their names become known to the public only by accident; for it is part of the etiquette of their place to see to it that the honor of what they accomplish shall be awarded to their nominal chief; nor is their appointment permanent. A man with sense enough to know wherein consists human happiness can accommodate himself to a narrow income, provided it is safely his own. But to an income of any magnitude whatever, subject to be taken away without notice and without cause, a man of sense and ability was never yet reconciled. To accept such a place, in ordinary times, is a confession of incompetency.

This brings us to the rotation-in-office question, to which attention has been powerfully recalled of late by the able and patriotic labors of Mr. Jenckes of Rhode Island. Still more powerfully has attention been called to it by the recent rebellions in the State Prison at Sing-Sing which were said to be caused by the sudden dismissal of Republican officers to make room for a number of Democratic politicians who had to be provided with places. That event, doubtless, aggravated the state of things existing in the prison; and probably the stanchest Jackson-Democratic father and housekeeper in that part of Westchester County has had doubts this year whether the system of rotation is quite applicable to the officials of an establishment containing thirteen hundred criminals. As that father made his rounds at night, locking up house, barn, and stable, and reflecting upon what might happen if that mass of ruffians were let loose upon an unprotected village, I fear he did not feel all that veneration for his departed chief which it is the pride of Jackson Democrats to exhibit. It perhaps occurred to him that to govern with firmness, humanity, and wisdom so peculiar a community demanded other qualifications than the single one of being able to "carry" a ward or a county, and that those other qualifications ought at least to be thought of in making prison appointments. "I don't see what is the *use* of having such men as John Clark here," said a high official in the Philadelphia custom-house, of one of its clerks. "Why not?" asked a bystander. The reply was: "He has been here six or seven years, and he has never carried his precinct."

We have now tried the Jackson rotation system forty years and six months. How has it worked?

I admit that there is something plausible to be said in its favor. I am writing this article on Cape Ann, part of the "stern and rock-bound coast" of Massachusetts, which is now getting sliced up into wonderfully long pieces of fine granite, and carried off in schooners to various Atlantic ports for building and paving. Fish and granite are the products of this rugged, romantic region. All day long, under the hot summer sun and in the cutting winter winds, the quarrymen swing the great hammer, or hold the perilous boring-tool, or manage the ponderous machinery that lifts and loads the huge masses, or yell like tragedians at the writhing oxen. The men of Cape Ann who do not work in the quarries go for codfish in schooners to the coast of Labrador, to the banks of Newfoundland, and elsewhere, not shrinking from the cruel tempests of February and March; or they cruise up and down the coast in search of the uncertain mackerel, coming in sometimes, after weeks of dangerous voyaging, without a fish; or else they court destruction in a little flat-bottomed boat called a dory, and gather the harvest of the sea within a few miles of the shore, supplying lobsters at four cents each for canning, and sending fresh fish to the Boston markets. Life on Cape Ann wears a serious aspect, and is maintained by fierce grappling with hostile forces.

But here and there on the Cape there is a man who walks serene, listening to the musical ring of the hammer which he never lifts, and viewing the boundless peril which he never shares. The whole fleet of mackerel-men and cod-men may come in empty; but it is naught to him, *his* salt pork and biscuit are secure. Nobody may want granite, and the music of the quarries may cease; but *he* surveys the scene with a tranquil mind, and draws his pay as before. As long as the President of the United States is a Republican, and the member of Congress who got him his place continues to be re-elected, and does not want the office for some one else, so long he remains a gentleman of leisure, in the midst of a most laborious people. Such are the lighthouse-keepers, the inspectors of customs, the postmasters, and a few others. How natural that the men of the Cape should think it right to take a turn, now and then, at these easy employments and this certain pay! Why, they ask, should Neighbor Jones *always* walk up and down, looking out for smugglers, catching one every year or two, and the rest of us *always* split the granite and hunt the mackerel? Turn about is fair play, they think; and there will never be wanting politicians to sympathize with them in this view of the subject.

Such is the light in which rotation appears upon the granite coast of New England. But none of these stalwart men would begrudge a lighthouse to a one-legged soldier or the widow of a drowned fisherman; and when the government is put once more upon a basis of common sense, lighthouses will invariably be reserved for persons whose circumstances and past services mark them out from all mankind for just such posts. Nor do the men of this Cape envy the lot of a certain postmaster, the slenderness of whose emolument exactly balances the more desirable circumstances of his place, and keeps him equal to the rest of the village. Still less would they be disturbed, if the incumbent of such an easy post were a woman. They *do* envy the case of some of the customs-officials; and well they may. Several of those gentlemen have very little to do, and that little is not arduous; while the pay is more liberal than it would have to be, if the appointment were permanent. Nor would the present salaries be deemed excessive, nor excite envy in the breasts of honest men, if they were the late reward of faithful service in lower posts, for which every man's son might compete. These hardy fishermen do not feel it a grievance that some of their neighbors own a share in a schooner, which gives them a double portion of the profit of voyages to the toil of which all hands equally contribute. But when Uncle Sam comes along and bestows sudden, unearned ease and honor upon one of their number, they feel that, the next time he looks in upon Cape Ann, he ought to put that man back into the quarry or the schooner and give some one else a respite from toil and trouble. But our respected Uncle ought not to bestow sudden, unearned ease and honor upon any man. This is one of the many wrongs of rotation; and, hence, I must reckon Cape Ann an argument for permanence.

This remote and stony Cape is representative on this subject. Having been for many years interested in the question, I have sought opportunities of learning how it appears to average voters, the owners of the United States, who will have finally to decide it. At present, the average voter is under the impression that we ought to take turns at enjoying what few good things Uncle Sam has to bestow. This feeling is *the* difficulty to be overcome.

Cape Ann, on the other hand, has afforded a pleasing illustration of the solid, enduring happiness which can result from a very small income, when it is not precarious. Yonder lighthouse, built in the year 1800, was occupied for forty-nine years by the same keeper. The salary was three hundred dollars a year; but a garden furnished the family with vegetables, and the ocean with fish. They were noted the country round for innocent cheerfulness and bountiful hospitality, and the old man, when at length the lamp of his own life went out, left an estate worth seven thousand dollars. Quiet, stable welfare like this *can* exist wherever there is a secure livelihood suitably bestowed. Lamb had it from his place in the India House. Hawthorne might have had it in the Salem custom-house. There are people in this world who possess high, rare, and exquisite qualities;

people who can render the most perfect service in posts the duties of which are fixed for them; and yet they are wanting in a certain audacity and energy that fit men to make a successful career of their own. How excellent a thing for a bank, a company, or a government to give permanent welfare to such in return for admirable service! It is idle to urge men to be moderate in their pursuit of fortune, so long as the possession of property is the *only* means of securing independence and dignity. In the United States a man is a fool who does not sacrifice to the acquisition of wealth everything except health and honor; since wealth alone gives a platform upon which a happiness can be established. Faraday might well decline to make a fortune of a hundred and fifty thousand pounds by doing chemistry for men of business; he had a secure eighty pounds a year, three rooms, fuel, and candles; and, having these, he could afford the ineffable luxury of spending his life in the discovery of truth.

I turn from Cape Ann to a scene which I witnessed in the White House a few days after the last Inauguration. If the Jackson rotation system appears endurable upon the sea-coast, it is entirely hideous at Washington.

About nine o'clock one morning, on going by the President's house, I observed a great number of men standing about the front-door, and many others walking towards it, as though something was going on and the public had been invited to attend. I joined the throng and entered the hall. The President's family had not yet taken possession, and several upholsterers were making wild efforts to take up the carpets; while parties were waiting for some one who had gone to find some one else who had the key of the East Room, which they were desirous of seeing. Meanwhile, they strolled about in the smaller show apartments, stumbling over rolls of carpet, inhaling dust, and viewing works of art. But most of those who entered this private residence of a respectable family went up stairs, where the President was supposed to be. Following the stream, I found myself in one of the suite of rooms of the east wing, adjacent to the apartment in which the President usually receives people who call on business. These large rooms were filled with men, standing in groups talking eagerly together, or sitting silent and anxious on the seats that lined the wall. The roar of conversation was like that of the Chicago Exchange when wheat is coming in freely, and the air was as pestiferous as at an evening party the giver of which keeps four stout colored men opening champagne, but forgets to let in a little inexpensive atmosphere. The men here assembled had a sufficient, capable aspect; many of them were persons of note in politics; many had distinguished themselves in the war. Strolling about among them, and passing from room to room, I came at last to the DOOR, — the door of doors, — which all of those present desired to enter. Some of them had crossed a continent to enter it; and there it was, tight shut, guarded by two ushers, and two hundred people were waiting to go in. It was not necessary for any one to be told that this door led to the President's office. There was a lane of men, terminating at the door, and extending back into the middle of the room, each man of which looked at the door as though it were beef and he had tasted nothing for three days and three nights. I saw then what the poet meant who first spoke of people *devouring* objects with their eyes. These men had a hungry look. With their eyes they were eating up that dingy-white door. So intent were they upon it that they were unconscious of themselves, of their attitude and expression; and, when at last the door opened, it was awful to see how they scanned the face of the messenger, and watched his movements. And so they waited, hour after hour. Failing to get in one day, they would try again the next. Some of those then present had been trying for four days for admission, and had still no expectation of getting in very soon. Many had given up the attempt to see the President, and were waiting there in hopes of speaking with their senator or member, who would convey their wishes to him.

A scene similar to this, but on a smaller scale, was going on wherever there was a person in Washington who had easy access to the President. A member of Congress who was supposed to have any particular influence with him would have a hundred applications a day for the exertion of that influence. One member, who was not on the best terms with the President, would have twenty callers in one evening, asking his aid in procuring a favorable presentation of their "claims." Washington swarmed with office-seekers. At the Capitol, when a messenger arrived from the White House with a packet of nominations, the rush of men toward the Senate wing of the building was like the thundering tramp of buffaloes across a prairie.*

I might dwell upon the waste, the anguish, the indecency, the degradation, of this scramble. I might speak of men coming to Washington with high hopes and full pockets, who begin by living at Willard's and treating with champagne, then remove to a less expensive hotel, afterwards to a cheap boarding-house, and finally, after subsisting awhile at "free lunches," borrow money to go home, where they arrive haggard and savage. I might speak of the impossibility of making good appointments in such circumstances; of the much better chance that brazen importunity has at such a time than merit; of the greater likelihood that a noisy eleventh-hour convert will get an office than a man who has borne the burden and heat of the day, but has omitted to come to Washington; or of the infernal cruelty of working a President to within an inch of his life in the first six weeks of his term. But all things cannot be said in one short article. The great evil of the system, as it is seen at Washington, is, that it compels the chief persons of the government to expend most of their time and strength upon a matter that properly belongs to subordinates. When President Grant came into office, there were several matters of great importance which

* A Washington letter of April 2, 1869, has the following: "To-day the hundreds of office-seekers now here flocked to the Capitol. At about two o'clock General Porter made his appearance, and after depositing with the Senate his sealed packages of appointments he repaired to the Secretary's office, and there placed a list of the same for the public. In an instant a grand rush was made for this office, and soon there was scarcely standing-room therein. The reporters of the afternoon papers tried in vain to secure copies of the names on the list, but the hungry, anxious, and eager crowds rushed in pell-mell. It was amusing to see the expressions of the faces of these people after the list had been read. Of course none of the successful candidates were present, and all were disappointed. The score or more persons seeking the same office sought their Congressmen, and each demanded explanations of the why and wherefore. Profanity raged among all. . . . . The 8.40 train for New York was packed with the most dejected, pitiful, profane, and demoralized crowd of men that ever left this city."

demanded his attention and that of his Cabinet; such as Cuba, the Alabama claims, reconstruction, and the adoption of a financial policy. The consideration of such subjects is the high duty which the Constitution assigns to the heads of the government, and in order to get *that* duty done the people gave General Grant their votes. But during the first week of his term he was worn out, day after day, by listening to the claims and settling the differences of people whose existence would naturally be known to a President or a Cabinet Minister only through the Blue Book.

And this, let me add, is the chief labor of a President all through his term. "What is it to be President?" I once asked of a gentleman who had filled the office; "what is the principal thing a President does?" The reply was, "To make appointments." A mere lounger about Washington can see that this is true; and it is manifest to all who look over such documents as that containing the testimony taken by the Covode Committee in 1860. The reader of that choice volume perceives that Mr. Buchanan wrote long letters and spent laborious hours in forcing upon the Philadelphia Navy-Yard an incompetent head-carpenter. The authorities of the yard sent back word that the man could not pass his examination. No matter; the President of the United States would have him appointed, and he was appointed; for he had rendered services in the Presidential election which a Buchanan could not overlook. The following is a portion of the man's sworn testimony: —

"*Question.* Do you mean to say that you gave [naturalization] papers to parties who subsequently used them in elections without ever going before a court to make the necessary proof [of five years' residence]?

"*Answer.* I have given a few.

"*Ques.* Well, how many did you distribute yourself?

"*Ans. Two or three thousand.*" *

This was the man — Patrick Lafferty was his name — whom the President of the United States put over the heads of American mechanics. I do not adduce the fact to illustrate the corrupting tendency of rotation, but to show

* Covode Investigation, p. 396.

the petty nature of the employments to which it reduces the head of the government. I am not sure that Mr. Buchanan was aware of the kind of service which his Irish friend had rendered him; but the assiduous Lafferty swore that when he failed to pass his examination he went to Washington and conversed with the President upon the subject for an hour and a half. We also find the President, upon the pages of this huge volume, meddling in the pettiest details of the pettiest ward elections, and superintending the division of the vulgarest portion of the spoils. He arranged the division and subdivision of the profits made on the public printing, and he parcelled out among three of his Pennsylvania neighbors the percentage allowed on the price of the coal purchased for the government. Do we elect a President for such work as this? Mr. Lincoln, too, was immersed in the most trivial details of administration. I think he must have spent more than half his time, and a full third of his strength, in arranging affairs of which, in a properly constituted public service, he would never have heard; and this, with a million men in the field, and the existence of the nation at stake. That the same system prevails to-day I have a hundred proofs before me; but they are needless, for every one knows it to be the case. We have even read lately a printed notice, signed by the commandant of a navy-yard, in which it is stated that "no person hostile to the present administration will be employed in the yard," and that "the Secretary of the Navy particularly desires" the enforcement of this rule.

Now, human nature being what it is, we may be sure that nine Presidents out of ten will make nine appointments out of ten with an eye to their own re-election, or the election of their candidate. They will generally make haste to have the fifty thousand office-holders active agents in their behalf; and since "power over a man's support has always been held and admitted to be power over his will," an ambitious and able President can easily convert all that large army of men from servants of the public into personal retainers. John Tyler, of precious memory, for example, employed *his* postmasters in circulating copies of a campaign Life of himself. They were called upon by a circular letter, franked, to subscribe for and spread abroad "fifty or sixty copies," which would be furnished "at the low price of fifty dollars a hundred." This circular letter was accompanied by a note penned in the President's own office by his son and secretary. The following is a copy of the note: —

"(Private.) PRESIDENT'S HOUSE, 1st Dec., 1843.

"SIR: As it is considered of importance, *in justice to the President,* to circulate among the people the work spoken of in Mr. Abell's letter accompanying this, you will confer a favor on the undersigned by taking such measures for that end as Mr. A. suggests.

"Prompt attention and a liberal subscription will render your services still more useful.

"I am, very respectfully, your obedient servant,

"JOHN TYLER, JR."

This letter, I believe, correctly represents a system which time has not materially changed. As a rule, we shall not have in the Presidential chair such blundering people as Tyler and Johnson, who let their clumsy hands be seen from behind the curtain of the show; but no President who could be nominated by the present style of politicians can be reasonably expected to refrain from using his power to perpetuate his power. Rotation belittles, personalizes, and disgraces the government in its every department and grade. From peculiar circumstances, I am thoroughly familiar with the working of the system, and I am convinced that Mr. John Stuart Mill's recent utterance on this subject is the truth. He well says that rotation is *the* evil of our government,* and that

* "I have long thought," wrote Mr. Mill, a few months ago, to a friend in New York, apropos of Mr. Jenckes's bill, "that the appointments to office without regard to qualifications are the worst side of American institutions, the main cause of what is justly complained of in their practical operation, and the principal hindrance to the correction of what is amiss, as well as a cause of ill-repute to democratic institutions all over the world. If appointments were given, not by political influence, but by open competition, the practice of turning out the holders of office, at every change in politics, in order to reward partisans, would necessarily cease, and with it nearly all the corruption and larger half of the virulence of mere party conflict. I have been delighted to see that Mr. Jenckes's measure meets with increasing support from disinterested opinion, though it will have to encounter the utmost hostility from the professional politicians, who are the great perverters of free government."

professional politicians are the great perverters of free government. Rotation has created professional politicians, and by rotation alone they are kept in being. The order did not exist before Jackson debauched the government: it will cease to exist when Mr. Jenckes has reformed it.

At the penitentiary upon Blackwell's Island, near New York, the superintendent once pointed out to me a young man (not more than twenty-eight) who had been in the prison fifty-seven times. Other young men there had been "sent up" thirty times, twenty times, eighteen times, ten times; and, I think, comparatively few were serving their first term. This led to the disclosure of the fact that most of the crime in the large cities of the world is committed by a small number of professional villains, who pass their short lives between the prison and the streets; not unfrequently getting themselves arrested and convicted when times are hard. Thus the Tombs in New York has, like the Astor House, its regular customers; and Blackwell's Island is, like Newport, a place of resort; and the virtuous portion of the people pay three or four millions per annum for the support, arrest, and entertainment of a few thousand individuals who have adopted stealing as a vocation. We support them out of prison and we support them in prison. Rotation in office has called into existence an order of politicians as distinct as the order of thieves; and the inhabitants of New York do not need to be informed that between these two orders there is an affinity, such as that which we suspected between Buchanan and Lafferty. If anything is certain, it is this: the rotation system is developing this affinity into an alliance. In the city of New York, we all see this; but the country at large is so sound, and there are still so many respectable men in office and so much of the public business is tolerably done, that the tendency is less apparent to those who live out of the large seaports. But the tendency exists. Honorable men, who are still occasionally sought for office, instinctively perceive it, and shrink from contact with a class who seem to have something in common with men of prey which easily develops into an understanding, into a partnership.

That coal agency, already referred to, may serve as an

example of the way in which political transactions shade off into criminal ones. Half a dozen applicants for the agency were in Washington, all of whom had spent money and wind in the preceding election, and all neighbors or friends of the President. Some of the applicants and their adherents met and talked the matter over, and they agreed at length that one of their number should be appointed agent, and that the emoluments of the office should be equally divided between him and two others. It is hardly necessary to add that neither of the three knew anything particular about coal, or even took pains to inquire; one of them being a physician, another an editor, and the third an omnibus proprietor. The business was "turned over to Stone, Tyler, & Co.," who "became at once the purchasers for, and the sellers to, the government." I am happy to be able to add, that when Mr. Getz, editor of the Reading Gazette, came to understand the arrangement, he declined to take any share of its profits; so that the doctor and the omnibus man had the whole fourteen thousand dollars a year to divide between them. I do not say that this was as bad as picking pockets, but only that it was akin to it.

It is ludicrous to observe sometimes how entirely the public service is lost sight of under this insensate system, and what absolute puppets the lower officials are in the games of the higher. If a member of Congress, for example, bolts on an administration measure, the President turns out of office the postmasters, lighthouse-keepers, custom-house clerks, and navy-yard laborers who owed their appointments to him. There is something about this so exquisitely absurd, that it is provocative of laughter rather than horror, as when we read of those usages of barbarous tribes which have the peculiarity of being both deadly and silly. We are so constituted that murder itself becomes laughable if a Chinaman is hung up by his pigtail; and suicide excites mirth when we read of a Japanese nobleman going aside and quietly ripping himself up. So, when we read of Buchanan turning a mechanic out of his shop because a New York member voted against Lecompton, we can hardly resist the comic incongruity of the transaction. I cannot read seriously such a passage as the following from the Covode Report, although I know that precisely the same system prevails to-day, and that it is as monstrous as it is ridiculous: —

"The division of patronage among members was well known in the Brooklyn navy-yard. Each master workman understood to whom he and each of his fellows owed their places. Thus the constructive engineer, the master plumber, and the master block-maker represented Mr. Sickles; the master painter represented Mr. Learing; the master sparmaker, master blacksmith, and timber-inspector represented Mr. Maclay. . . . . Lawrence Cohane was appointed master carpenter upon the nomination of Mr. Haskin, in the general division of patronage. *He was removed on account of Mr. Haskin's course upon the Lecompton Constitution.*"

Each of these representative master mechanics selects and discharges the men of his shop, and he is expected to do this with the most implicit deference to the will and political interest of the member who caused his appointment. But to this, it seems, other members sometimes object. Thus, Mr. Haskin procured the appointment of Master Carpenter Cohane; but we find the Hon. John Cochrane addressing the unfortunate Cohane thus: "I *will* have my proportion of men under you; if you do not give them, I will lodge charges against you. . . . . I will make application that you be turned out. The bearer will bring me an answer." The master painter, about the same time, took the very great liberty of discharging a man for habitual drunkenness. The man's member of Congress made the following remark to the master painter in consequence: "You may set it down as a fact that I will have you removed if I can, if you don't put that man back again." The drunkard was not put back again, and the master painter *was* removed. Another member writes to the master of one of the shops: "As a general thing, Hugh McLaughlin, master laborer, knows who my friends are, and he will confer with you at all times."

In these absurd contentions the Secretary of the Navy himself did not disdain to mingle, and of course we find him siding with the aggrieved member and adding the weight of his positive order to effect the member's purpose.

Equally, of course, it was the refuse of the mechanics of New York and Brooklyn who usually came to the yard backed with a member's demand for their employment; and thus the Brooklyn navy-yard, once the pride of ship-builders, to be employed in which was formerly a coveted honor, was "reduced to a mere political machine where idleness, theft, insubordination, fraud, and gross neglect of duty prevailed to an alarming degree." Of course! An employer who treats his workmen thus deserves to be served so, and always will be. The wonder is, that any ship built in the yard kept afloat long enough to reach Sandy Hook.

A noteworthy circumstance is, that members of Congress of any intelligence, who employ this system, are as keenly alive to its absurdities and its ill consequences as we are who pay the cost and suffer the shame of it. That very John Cochrane who *would* have his share of the navy-yard carpenters has solemnly declared that the system is an unmitigated evil, injurious to the purity of elections, injurious to the mechanic and his work, and a frightful nuisance to members, who are beset at every turn by applicants. Another member has testified: "My house was run down. I was addressed upon the subject in the street; when in the lower part of the city on business I would be pursued; and I really could find no rest by reason of the great number of such applications. . . . . This whole system tends, in the first place, to the demoralization of the laboring class to their serious detriment, and, in my judgment, to the degradation, personal and political, of members of Congress." As men and citizens they all comprehend this; while as politicians they insist on having their share of its supposed advantages.

"We shall be broken up," said Senator Trumbull of Illinois, in April last, "unless some administration will set the example, or some legislation will compel it, of making the price of office good behavior only. The scenes and the scramble of the last month have been disgraceful, as you know. But you do not probably know the effect of this periodical rotation upon Congress. For example, I want the Secretary of the Treasury to give my man an office. I go up to the department and wait there for an audience, long or short, as the case may be. The Secretary speaks encouragingly. Next day I go up again, and he is not quite so sanguine. It is by this steady persistence that offices are obtained here. Not merit, nor recommendation, nor impulse, but dingdonging, obtains the offices. Well, the Secretary has a financial policy, perhaps. How can I, as a senator, speak independently of his policy, while my man is in a state of suspense? Thus the executive part of the government paralyzes in a great degree the legislator's independence."

A striking case in point, which clearly illustrates the working of the system, was furnished by a late collector of the New York custom-house, who desired to represent the United States at the court of St. Petersburg. The Senate frustrated his ambition, and he took his revenge by turning out of the custom-house thirty clerks and porters whom a New York senator had recommended for appointment. A gentleman who was present when the thirty new men were sworn in asked the collector whether the vacancies had been created in order to retaliate upon the senator for his adverse vote. He did not deny the soft impeachment, though he pretended that the thirty dismissed were "incompetent." He concluded his answer to the question in these words: "Blood is thicker than water. If a man cheats me I am going to pay him off for it. I did not want the mission to Russia particularly. It would have cost me ten thousand dollars a year to go there. But then, when a man makes up his mind to do a thing he don't like to be cheated out of it. There have not been more than thirty new appointments made." Thirty men suddenly deprived of their means of living, and thirty more lured perhaps from stable employments, in order to gratify the spite of a person whom it had been an affront to Russia to send thither as a representative of the United States! How foolish it is for us to complain of the alleged peculations of custom-house officials! Has it ever been possible, in any age or country, to get decent and capable men to serve on these terms; to be the puppets and instruments of such a person for a hundred and fifty dollars a month? You can get thieves on such terms. You can get fools on such terms. You can get necessitous honest men for a short

2

time on such terms. But Uncle Sam will never be well served so long as he can stand by with his hands in his pockets while his servants are thus treated.

"You don't do work enough to earn your salary," said a chief of bureau, in this same custom-house, to one of the clerks. "Work!" exclaimed the young man, "I worked to get here; you surely don't expect me to work any longer."

This anecdote, which sums up the system in a sentence, is one of the hundreds of good things collected by the indefatigable industry of Mr. Jenckes. He relates another story, to show the marvellous carelessness with which men are selected even for situations requiring special or professional knowledge. The chief clerk of the Office of Construction in the Treasury Department being requested to give the "full particulars" of his examination, thus replied: "Major Barker commenced the 'examination' by saying: 'You are from New York, I believe, Mr. Clark?' I replied that I was. He then commenced a detailed narrative of his first visit to New York, and gave me an interesting and graphic account of the disturbance created in his mind by the 'noise and confusion' of the great city. The delivery of this narrative occupied, as nearly as I remember, about half an hour. I listened to it attentively, endeavoring to discover some point in his discourse which had reference to my (then present) 'examination.' I failed to discover any relevancy, and therefore made no reply. At the close of his narrative, without any further question, he said to his associate examiners: 'Well, gentlemen, I presume there is no doubt but that Mr. Clark is qualified.' Whereupon they all signed the certificate, and my 'examination' closed."

Is it not one of the wonders of the world that the Treasury building stood long enough to get the roof upon it? But the erection of an edifice ever so huge is an easy task compared with other tasks less conspicuous. A building is open to the inspection of all the world; few men would apply for employment upon it who were wholly incompetent; and it was easier to build it tolerably right than obviously wrong. But you cannot collect a whiskey-tax on rotation principles. I have quoted Thomas Benton's maxim that power over a man's livelihood is power over his will. Now, who *has* power over a tax-collector's livelihood? Mr. E. A. Rollins, Commissioner of Internal Revenue, answers this question for us in one of his reports. The whiskey-tax, he assures us, can never be collected until "the combined and active hostility of all those against whom the law is enforced *shall be insufficient for the removal of any officer opposed to their plunderings.*" He says further: "The evil is inherent in the manner of appointments, and lies deeper than the present supremacy of any political party. . . . . Their tenure of office when secured is uncertain and feeble, seeming *to be strengthened rather by concessions to wrong than by exacting the rights of the government.*" That tells the whole story. They naturally obey the power which gave and can take away their places. Uncle Sam, to use the language of the ring, "goes back" on those who carry his commission; does not stand by his servants when they do their duty. He treats his servants vilely; and, as a natural consequence, many of them are exceedingly remiss, or worse, in their duty. This error costs him, it is computed, in the collection of the revenue alone, a round hundred millions per annum in mere money, without reckoning the injury to the morals of the people, and the bad example set to other employers. "I can't get a man of talent," said one of the architects employed by the government, "to help me here; because, first of all, the salary is too low; secondly, no degree of merit in a man can get him an appointment; and lastly, no degree of merit can keep a good man in a place if he should happen to get one."

Let no one hug the delusion that the system is changed under President Grant. He cannot change it. I have no doubt he is as fully alive to its absurdities and its impolicy as any man living; but, like Mr. Lincoln, he feels that he must run the machine as he finds it. He is, indeed, a victim of the system, which may yet cost him his life, as it cost the lives of two of his predecessors. His appointments show that he practically accepts the doctrine that to the victors belong the spoils, and that he is even exceptionally insensible to the peculiar claims which politicians occasionally respect. In fact, he is worried out of his life with the endless succession of importunate applicants. I used to wonder in Washington that he did not give it up, and fly to parts unknown, leaving us without any Uncle Sam. In all probability, too, he desires re-election. Every President desires it. It is human nature. The politicians would drop him in an instant, and set "party organs" at work creating odium against him, if he were to pause and make appointments on any other principle than the one which politicians recognize; and when the nominating convention met, in 1872, his name would not be mentioned among the candidates.

Nothing will ever touch this evil short of restoring to the public service that element of permanence which it once had, and which all successful private establishments possess. In the lower grades of the persons employed in our great houses of business, there are frequent changes. Young men come and go, as they ought, trying themselves and the places they fill. Sometimes the person resigns the place and sometimes the place rejects the person; and it is seldom indeed that a man goes on for life as he begins. But in the higher grades there is, there should be, there must be, a degree of permanence. Twice a year, for fifteen years, I have gone to a certain bank to receive a dividend for a person who cannot conveniently go herself. Invariably I find the same paying-teller, well-appointed, self-possessed, counting out the money with that careful rapidity that never permits a mistake; the same excellent cashier, who learned his Latin Reader at my side at school no end of years ago; the same serene and agreeable dividend-clerk, and the same nice young man helping him. All goes like clock-work; all is efficient, vigorous, and successful. The young men, as is just, work hard, get little, and are not yet certain of keeping their places; but they know that if they finally choose to trust their future to that bank, there are places in it for the deserving which will give them a decent livelihood and all the security needful for peace and dignity. So it could be at the custom-house round the corner, if only two men in it were fixed in their places during good behavior; namely, the collector and the appraiser. Give just those two men a fair compensation, say thirty thousand dollars a year and no fees; put it out of the power of politicians to remove them; give them the right to select their assistants; and hold them responsible for the faithful collection of the duties, — and we should soon have a customhouse that would afford as pleasing a scene of tranquil and efficient industry as the bank. The principle of permanence should be carried much farther; but even this little would lay the axe at the root of the evil, and give Uncle Sam better work and more revenue at two thirds of the present expense.

After a trial of forty years, rotation stands condemned as a wholly unmitigated evil, hurting everybody and blessing nobody, helping nothing that is good, and aggravating every evil. Uncle Sam will never be better served than he is until he learns to treat his servants with a liberality and consideration that seem at present far from his thoughts.

THE YANKEES AT HOME.

THOSE horrible Yanks! I have seen them in their native haunts. The most dreadful creatures become interesting when, regarding them only as objects of natural history, we creep up near their den, and watch them as they devour their prey, caress their cubs, and gambol in the sun. Perhaps a busy universe, which has heard already a good deal about the mean, low, cheating, infidel, and entirely odious Yankee, may yet be willing to lean back in its arm-chair for a short time, and learn how he looks to a stranger's eyes, and how he comports himself amid his own hills and rocks, in that unique organization of his, a New England town.

There was published, a year or two since, an article upon Chicago, which chanced to attract the notice of a young gentleman then residing among us, a citizen of the Argentine Republic, which is the United States of South America. He was so much struck with the exploits of the people of Chicago, that he translated the article into Spanish, and caused it to be published as a pamphlet in his native land, with a Preface calling upon his countrymen to imitate the spirit, energy, forethought, and patriotism displayed by the men of the prairie metropolis. It was well done of him; for, indeed, the creators of Chicago have performed, and are performing, the task assigned them in a manner unexampled in the history of the world; and the record of what they have done and are doing will for ages be a chapter in our history honorable to this nation and instructive to others. But perhaps one of those quiet towns sleeping among the umbrageous hills of New England is a triumph of man over circumstances and over himself not less remarkable than the more striking and splendid achievements of the Chicagonese. And what is Chicago but a New England town in extremely novel circumstances, that was forced to undertake enormous enterprises, and compelled to expand, in thirty years, into a high-pressure Boston? If I could only succeed in revealing to mankind the town of New England, — its defects as well as its merits, — I should have produced something worth translating into every tongue.

It is evident that the Yankee system, with modifications, is destined to prevail over the fairest parts of this continent, if not finally over the best portions of the other. It prevails already in the West as far as San Francisco, the famous Vigilance Committee of which was a veritable town meeting. Wherever the Yankee soldier has tramped the Yankee schoolmarm will teach. Noble and chivalric gentlemen may throw stones at her windows, burn her schoolhouse, drive her from their neighborhood; but she reappears, — she or her cousin, — and the work of Yankeefication proceeds. First Julius Cæsar, then Roman civilization, then Christianity. The soldier must always go first, and open the country. In this fortunate instance, the gentle and knowing schoolmarm quickly follows the man of war, and she is preparing the way for the gradual reorganization of the South upon the general plan of New England towns. It is hard for the noble and chivalric gentlemen to bear, but it seems inevitable. The Carolinas may object, and Georgia expel; Texas may slay, and Louisiana massacre, — it will not avail; *this* is the fate in reserve for them. The Yankee schoolmarm is extremely addicted to writing long letters home, which go the round of the village, are carried into the next county, and are sent at last to circulate by mail over all the land. Most graphic and powerful some of her letters are, and New England knows her new conquest in this way. The schoolmarm's lover has thoughts of settling there, when the land itself is "settled." Her uncle the capitalist has long had an eye on those rich lands, those unused watercourses, those mines and quarries. She is merely one of the first to tread the path worn by the army shoe stamped U. S. A.

A New England town, the distant reader will please take note, is not a town, though it may have a town in it, and two or three villages besides. It is a subdivision of a county, or, to use the language of the law-books, it is "an organized portion of the inhabitants of a State, within defined limits of territory, within the same county." It may consist of only three or four hundred people, or of several thousands. Perhaps two thousand may be an average number, which gives about three hundred voters; and the average circumference of the territory may be about ten miles. Every five years the selectmen are required to "perambulate" the boundaries, to see that the boundary-stones and guide-boards are right; and this work, I believe, is generally done in one day. The inhabitants of this area are an association for the performance of certain duties imposed upon them by the State. They are, says the law, a "corporate body," which is intrusted with powers defined and limited. It can fine you a dollar for driving over a bridge faster than a walk, or twenty dollars for declining a town office. It can itself be fined fifty dollars for not having a cattle-pound, five hundred dollars for not electing town officers, a thousand dollars if a person falls through a rotten bridge and loses his life, and three thousand dollars for sending to the legislature more members than it is entitled to. It is responsible — as much so as a railroad company — for any accidents happening through its fault, and can claim damages for an injury done to itself. It can sue and be sued as though it were one man. It can hold, hire, buy, sell, let, lease, or give away real estate. It can tax and be taxed, — both, however, for purposes named in the law, and for no others. For example, it can raise money by taxation to pay for schools, public libraries, the support of the poor, guide-boards, burial-grounds, bridges, roads, markets, pounds, hay-scales, standard weights and measures, public clocks, houses destroyed to stop a conflagration, the prosecution and defence of suits. Such of these things as concern other towns, or the county, the State, the United States, or the universe, each town is compelled to provide, — bridges, pounds, roads, and schools, for example. But the towns may or may not vote money for hay-scales or a public library. The schools are a necessity; the library is merely desirable in a high degree. The cattle-pound protects neighboring towns from devastation; but it is a question for each town to decide, whether or not it will have a public clock or a soldiers' monument.

The governing power of a New England town is the whole body of voters in town meeting assembled. Speaking generally (for all the States of New England have not yet quite come up to the standard of the most advanced), we may say that every man, white or black, is a voter, who can read the constitution of his State in the English language understandingly, and who is not an alien, a lunatic, a pauper, or a convict.

The exclusion of paupers is of small consequence, because in most of the towns there are no paupers able to go to the polls, and in many there are no paupers at all. At the time of the first cable celebration, Mr. Cyrus Field, desirous that all the world should rejoice, sent orders to his native village in New England that a banquet should be provided at his expense for the paupers of the whole town. The selectmen sent back word that there were no paupers; and there are none there now. Your mean Yankee is a stickler for justice; and it would offend his sense of justice, that a man who had contributed nothing to the fund raised by taxation should have a voice in directing its expenditure. He is beginning to think, too, that it is hardly fair to tax a widow or an independent spinster and refuse her a vote in town meeting. Here and there there is a bold Yankee who goes further than this, and pronounces it unwise to exclude such women as Miss Sedgwick, Mrs. Stowe, Miss Catharine Beecher, and Mrs. Horace Mann, while admitting to the franchise every male citizen who can be trusted alone out of doors, and who can boggle through a paragraph of the Constitution. In some towns, where a few crusty old farmers can always be depended on to defeat a liberal scheme, the votes of the ladies, it is thought, would give a lift to the library and a blow to the grog-shop, and help all the civilizing measures. The necessity of women's assistance becomes more apparent as the towns advance in wealth and refinement; and the Yankee would long ago have seen this, and sought the aid of the decorative sex, but for a few words in an ancient epistle.

The exclusion from the polls of men who cannot read

works nothing but good.* It is a measure absolutely necessary in the peculiar circumstances of the United States; and I will venture to predict that every State will in time adopt it, or, like the city of New York, become a prey to the spoiler. This law, however, excludes very few natives of the soil. If, in a New England town, there chances to be a native who cannot read and write, he is regarded as a curiosity, and is pointed out to strangers as one of the objects of interest in the place. There is one such man near Stockbridge, in Massachusetts, who was pointed out to me last summer as the only native of New England in all that region who could neither read nor write. The people appeared to be rather proud of him than otherwise, as though he had given no slight proof of an ingenious mind in having escaped so many boy-traps and man-traps, baited with spelling-books, as they have in New England. The reading law merely keeps away from the polls the grossly ignorant among the foreign population, who, being unable to read, are dependent upon other men's eyes and minds for their political information, and who can be driven in herds to the polls by the party having the least scruples.

Major De Forest, in one of his valuable and entertaining articles on the "Man and Brother," has intimated an opinion that the black man will never associate in this country on equal terms with the white man. *Never* is a long time, and we cannot even see into the next century; but I should say that the condition of the colored people in New England supports the gallant Major's conjecture. There are not more than twelve or fifteen thousand negroes in Massachusetts; but they are so unequally distributed that you may occasionally find a considerable number of them in one town. They stand before the law equal to the white man; their children sit in the public schools side by side with his; they are treated with consideration and respect;

* "No person shall have the right to vote, or be eligible to office under the Constitution of this Commonwealth, who shall not be able to read the Constitution in the English language, and write his name; *provided, however*, that the provisions of this amendment shall not apply to any person prevented by a physical disability from complying with its requisitions, nor to any person who now has the right to vote, nor to any persons who shall be sixty years of age or upwards at the time this amendment shall take effect." — *Constitution of Massachusetts.*

they have the same opportunities to acquire property as the white man; they go with him to the ballot-box and vote on the same terms and conditions, — nevertheless, their social position is precisely the same in New England as it is in North Carolina. They usually live in a cluster of cottages in the outskirts of the village; the men are laborers or waiters, and the women take in washing or go out to service. They live in peace and abundance, but they are no nearer social equality with the whites now than they were thirty years ago. They seldom get on so far as to own a farm, seldom learn a trade, and never run a factory or keep a store. In the free high schools — one of which nearly every town in New England supports, or helps support — a colored youth is rarely found. In and near Stockbridge, for example, there is a colored population of two hundred, and they have been settled there for many years; but no colored boy or girl has ever applied for admission to the high school, though it is free to all.

But the negro is an indispensable and delicious ingredient in the too serious and austere population of New England. They appear to be the only people there who ever *abandon* themselves to innocent merriment. What a joyous scene is one of the negro balls so frequently given in some of the New England villages! In the morning, the stranger notices upon the lordly, wide-spreading elm that shades the post-office a neatly written paper, notifying the public that an "entertainment" is to be given that evening for the "benefit" of some afflicted person, — perhaps a woman whose husband a ruthless constable has taken off to jail. "All who wish to enjoy a good time are respectfully invited to attend, — admission, twenty-five cents," for which a substantial supper of pork and beans and new cider is furnished. Soon after eight in the evening the village resounds with the voice of a colored Stentor, who calls out the figures of the quadrille, and all the world is thus notified that the "entertainment" has begun. The scene within the ball-room might make some persons hesitate to decide which destiny were the more desirable in New England, — to be born white or black. The participants seem so unconsciously and entirely happy! An ancient uncle, white-haired and very lame, stands near the entrance, seizes the new-comers with both hands, and gives them a roaring and joyous welcome; and there is a one-legged man with a crutch, and four mothers with infants in their arms, who go through a quadrille with the best of them. The mothers, however, when they grow warm with the dance, hand the blessed baby to a passing friend to hold. The band, which consists of two male fiddlers and a woman who plays the accordion, is seated upon a platform at one end of the long room, and plays with eyes upcast, ecstatic, and keeps a heel apiece going heavily upon the boards. The room itself seems to be quivering. There is no walking through a quadrille here; but each performer, besides doing his prescribed steps, cuts as many supplementary capers as he can execute in the intervals. A dance begins, it is true, with some slight show of moderation; but as it proceeds the dancers throw themselves into it with a vigor and animation that increase every moment, until the quadrille ends in a glorious riot and delirium of dance and fun. No Mussulman would ask *these* people why they did not require their servants to do their dancing for them. On the contrary, that famous pacha, catching their most contagious merriment, would have sprung upon the floor, and dashed his three tails wildly about among those shining countenances. Nevertheless, there was not the smallest violation of decorum; all was as innocent as it was enjoyable. As the room was lined with white spectators, perhaps we shall some day learn the trick of cheap, innocent, and hearty enjoyment. One thing was very noticeable, and would certainly be noticed by any one familiar with the South, — the purity of blood exhibited in the faces of the company. Among the one hundred and fifty dancers, there were perhaps ten who were not quite black; and this was an ancient settlement of colored people, dating back beyond the recollection of the present inhabitants. The only fault with which their white neighbors charge them is, that one or two in a hundred has not yet got the old plantation *steal* out of their blood. A person interested in the health question would observe the roundness and all but universal vigorous health of these children of the tropics, which is another proof that human nature in America does not dwindle necessarily.

"In town meeting assembled." Once a year, and oftener

if necessary, the voters of this small and convenient republic meet to elect town officers, consider proposed improvements, and vote taxes. The town meeting is a parliament, of which every voter is an equal member, and the authority of which is final so long as its acts are legal. It is a public meeting clothed with power.

I will here respectfully invite the attention of the Argentine Republic, France, Italy, Austria, Russia, and all countries supposed to be groaning under the yoke of the oppressor, and hoping one day to throw off that yoke, to the following truth, now for the first time given to the world: —

THAT PEOPLE IS FIT FOR FREEDOM WHICH CAN HOLD A PROPER PUBLIC MEETING.

To us how easy! to a great part of the rest of mankind how impossible! Before a community reaches the stage of development which admits of the public meeting, there must exist in it considerable ability and knowledge, and there must be a certain prevalence of what may be styled the virtues of maturity, — self-conquest and self-control. Men must respect themselves, but respect one another also, and, along with a proper confidence in their own opinions, have a genuine tolerance for those of their neighbors. With an ability to convince others, there must be in the people the possibility of being convinced, as well as of frankly submitting to a decision the most adverse to that for which they had striven. A strong, keen, and constant sense of justice must be tempered by a spirit of accommodation, an aversion to standing upon trifles, and a disposition to welcome a reasonable compromise. There must be in many of the people a true public spirit, and in some a very great and deep love of the public welfare, and a capacity for taking a prodigious amount of trouble for a public object. The desire to shine, so natural to immature persons and races, must have been by many outgrown, or, at least, exalted into a noble ambition to be of service, and *thus* to win the approval of the community. An insatiate vanity in only two or three individuals might render profitable debate impossible; nor less harmful is that other manifestation of morbid self-love which we call bashfulness.

The horrible Yanks, with all their faults, do actually possess the qualities requisite for holding a public meeting in a higher degree than any other people. They have governed themselves by public meeting for two hundred years or more. It seems now instinctive in them, when a thing is to be done or considered by a body of men, to put it to the vote and be governed by the decision of the majority. The most curious illustration of this fact that has been recorded is the one related by Mrs. John Adams in one of her letters of 1774 to her husband. The men of Braintree and neighboring towns, alarmed lest the British general should seize their store of powder, assembled on a certain Sunday evening to the number of two hundred, marched to the powder-house, took out the powder, conveyed it to a place of safety, and secreted it. On their way they captured an odious Tory, and found upon him some still more odious documents aimed at the liberty of the Commonwealth. This man they took with them, and, when the powder was disposed of, they turned their attention to him and his documents. Readers familiar with the period do not need to be reminded that these men, marching so silently and seriously on that Sunday evening, were profoundly moved and excited. All New England, indeed, was thrilling and palpitating with mingled resolve and apprehension. Nevertheless, instinct, or ancient habit, was stronger than passion, even at such a crisis, in these two hundred Yankee men, and therefore they resolved themselves into a public meeting. Upon the hostile warrants being produced and exhibited, it was put to the vote whether they should be burnt or preserved. The majority voting for burning them, the two hundred gathered in a circle round the lantern, and looked on in silence while the offensive papers were consumed. That done, — and no doubt there were blazing eyes in that grim circle of Puritans as well as blazing papers, —"*they called a vote whether they should huzza; but, it being Sunday evening, it passed in the negative.*"

The reader who comprehends the entire significance of that evening's performance knows New England. If I were a painter, I would try and paint the scene at the moment the blazing papers flashed light into the blazing eyes. If I were a king, I should think several times before going to war with people of that kind.

After a practice of two centuries the Yankees would be

able to hold a very good town meeting without assistance, and yet everything relating to it is prescribed and regulated by statute. The people must be notified in just such a way; the business to be done must be expressed in the summons; and nothing can be voted upon or discussed unless it has been thus expressed. In case the selectmen of a town should unreasonably refuse to call a town meeting, any ten voters can apply to a justice of the peace, and require him to issue a call. Every possible, and almost every conceivable, abuse or unfairness has been anticipated and guarded against by the legislature, and yet the town meeting is absolutely unfettered in doing right. It may also do wrong if it chooses, provided it does wrong in the right way, and the wrong is of such a nature as to harm nobody but itself. And I will here observe, that, if any one would know how deeply rooted in the heart of man is the love of justice, and would inspect the most complete system of fair play mankind possesses, let him buy, keep, and habitually read the volume containing the Constitution and Revised Statutes of Massachusetts. Most of the standard law books are interesting and edifying, but this one is the most instructive and affecting of them all. It shows, in a striking manner, how much better the heart of man is than his head; for the community which wrought out this beautiful system of justice and humanity believed, *while it was doing it*, in the doctrine of total depravity! Delightful inconsistency! Would that all the head's mistakes could be so gloriously refuted by the other organ!

The principal town meeting of the year generally occurs in the spring, when the town officers are elected by ballot. The town officers are: Three, five, seven, or nine selectmen, who are the chief officers, and take care of things in general; a town clerk; three or more truant officers; three or more assessors; three or more overseers of the poor; a town treasurer; one or more surveyors of highways; a constable; one or more collectors of taxes; a pound-keeper; two or more fence-viewers; one or more surveyors of lumber; one or more measurers of wood and bark; a sealer of weights and measures; a gauger of liquid measures; a superintendent of hay-scales. Here is a chance for office-seekers! But, unfortunately, the emoluments attached to these offices are as small as the duties are light; and it has been found necessary to compel men to serve in them, if elected, under penalty of a fine of twenty dollars, — a sum much larger than the usual amount of the fees. But then no man can be made to serve two years in succession. These officers being elected, the town parliament proceeds to consider proposed improvements and appropriations; and you may frequently hear in the town hall excellent debating, very much in the quiet and rather homely manner of the British House of Commons, when country members get on their legs to discuss country matters. There is usually a total abstinence from all flights of oratory, for every man who speaks or votes has a personal and pecuniary interest in the question under debate. He who advocates a stone bridge in place of the rickety old wooden one knows that he will have to pay his share of the expense; and he who opposes it knows that he will have to cross the rickety structure, and will have to pay his part of a thousand-dollar fine when it lets a pedler through to destruction.

In the list of town magnates just given the reader may have noticed "truant officers." They must be explained.

There is one thing upon which these mean Yankees are entirely and unanimously resolved, and it is this: That no child, of whatever race, color, or capacity, shall grow up among them in ignorance. In the oldest of their records we find the existence of the school-house taken for granted. When there was no church in a town, no court-house, no town-hall, there was always a school-house, which served for all public purposes; and ever since that early day the school system has been extending and improving. Very pleasant it is of a summer day to ride past the little lone school-houses, and peep in at the open door, and see the schoolmarm surrounded with her little flock of little children, whose elder brothers are in the fields; nor less pleasant is it to mark in every village the free high school, where the pupils who have outgrown the common school continue their studies, if they desire it, to the point of being prepared for college, and snatch a daily hour for base-ball besides. Indeed, it is an excellent thing to be a child in this land of the Yankees. If you are a good boy or girl you have these common and high schools for your instruction; if you are a bad boy, they send you off to a reformatory school to be made better, or to a ship school to be changed into a good sailor; and if you are a bad girl, there is a girls' industrial school for you, where you will be taught good morals and the sewing-machine. And they do not leave the bad boys and girls to go on in their evil ways until they are developed into criminals. The towns in Massachusetts are now authorized to appoint the truant officers before mentioned, whose duty it is to take care that every child between the ages of six and sixteen shall avail itself either of public or private means of education. No miserly parent, no hard master, no careless guardian, can now defraud a child of his right to so much instruction as will make it easy for him to go on instructing himself all his life.

By way of showing how much in earnest the Yankees are in this matter, I will insert upon this page certain "by-laws concerning truants and absentees," which I had the pleasure of reading last summer on a handbill displayed in the post-office of a small village in New England. It seems to me that these by-laws may convey a valuable hint to the Argentine and other republics. The following selection may be sufficient for our purpose: —

"2. Any child between the ages of six and sixteen, who, while a member of any school, shall absent himself or herself from school without the consent of his or her teacher, parent, or guardian, shall be deemed a truant." (Penalty, a fine of twenty dollars, or a term not exceeding two years in a reform school.)

"3. Any child between the ages of six and fifteen, who shall not attend some public school or suitable institution of instruction at least twelve weeks in a year, six of which shall be consecutive in the summer term, and six of which shall be consecutive in the winter term, shall be deemed an absentee.

"4. Absentees of the Second Class. — Children between the ages of seven and sixteen years of age, wandering in the streets or loitering in stores, shops, or public places, having no lawful occupation or business, and growing up in ignorance, are hereby placed under *supervision* of the *truant officers*, so far as the law provides. The first offence shall be reported to parent, guardian, or master of said child by a truant officer, and, in case of the failure to secure said child the requisite amount of schooling or instruction elsewhere, he shall be fined twenty dollars; for the second offence of the same person, the child shall be sent to the almshouse or to the State Reform School, or the nautical branch of the same, or State Industrial School for girls, for a period agreeable to the statutes, as the justice of the court having jurisdiction of the same shall decide."

"6. It shall be the duty of every truant officer to inquire diligently concerning all persons, between the ages aforesaid, who seem to be idle or vagrant, or who, whether employed or unemployed, appear to be growing up in ignorance, and to enter a complaint against any one found unlawfully absent from school, or violating any of these by-laws.

"7. It shall be the duty of every truant officer, prior to making any complaint before a justice, to notify the truant or absentee child and its parents or guardian of the penalty for the offence. If he can obtain satisfactory pledges of reformation, which pledges shall subsequently be kept, he shall forbear to prosecute."

In one of those country towns of New England, a person likely to be elected a truant officer would have some knowledge of all the inhabitants. Hence it is now almost impossible for the most perverse or neglected child to avoid getting a little schooling. Each town, I should add, pays for the maintenance of children sent from it to a reformatory school, provided the parents or guardians cannot. The female teachers employed in the common schools receive now from five to eight dollars a week, and the master of a country high school from eight hundred to two thousand dollars a year. Twelve hundred dollars is very frequently the salary. Now, in a New England village, an active man who has a saving wife and an ordinary-sized garden, can live decently upon the salary last named, send a son to college, and give his daughters lessons on the piano.

I suppose that in New England there is a less unequal division of property than in any other region of a civilized country. I chanced to be in a country bank there last

July, about the time when the coupons due on the first of that month had been mostly paid, and the money for each individual had been done up in a neatly folded small package. The village was small, and remote from any important centre; and these packages of greenbacks belonged to the farmers, mechanics, and manufacturers of the neighborhood. I think there must have been half a peck of them, — perhaps a hundred packages. There are country towns in New England where nearly every respectable house has some United States bonds in it, and the Savings Bank will wield a capital of half a million dollars besides. Reason: *diversified industry.* These Yankees, finding themselves planted upon a soil not too productive, were compelled at a very early period to become good political economists; and while the fathers scratched the hard surface of the soil for a few bushels of corn, the sons rigged small schooners, and fished off the coast for cod. By and by they got on so far as to build ships, in which they sailed to the coast of Guinea, brought thence a load of slaves and a few quills of gold-dust, sold the slaves to the West-Indians for molasses, brought the molasses home, distilled it into rum, took the rum to Guinea for more slaves, sent most of the gold-dust to England for manufactured goods, and made the rest into watch-chains and gold beads. Thus Newport was enriched; thus was founded in Rhode Island the manufacture of jewelry and silver-ware which has attained such marvellous proportions. This infernal commerce is now regarded by the people of New England as wise and honest Catholics regard the Inquisition and the Massacre of St. Bartholomew; that is, they wonder how their forefathers could have been guilty of it, and attribute it chiefly to the general barbarism of the age.

But the diversified industry remains, and it has enriched New England. Those streams which wind about the wooded hills and mountains of this region, useless as they are for navigation, shallow, winding, rocky, and rapid, frequently have such a descent that there can be a factory village every mile or two of their course for many successive miles. Travellers by such railroads as the Housatonic know this to their sorrow; for these villages are so frequent along the banks of the Housatonic River, that there is a stopping-place, at some parts of the line, every mile and a half. Among the glorious, wood-crowned hills of Berkshire I have passed in an afternoon ride the following manufactories: an iron-smelting furnace; two very extensive manufactories of the finest writing-paper, the linen rags for which are brought from the shores of the Mediterranean; a large woollen mill; a small factory of folding-chairs and camp-stools; a manufactory of something in cotton; a mill for grinding poplar wood into material for paper; and some others, at a little distance from the road, the nature of which could not be discerned. All these may be seen in a ride of ten miles along the Housatonic, and all are kept in motion by that little bustling stream.

So much of this diversified industry as is legitimate (i. e. unforced by a stimulating tariff) is beneficial; the rest is excessive and hurtful. It is excellent for the farmer to have a market near his barn, but it is bad for him to have to pay such a price for labor as neutralizes that advantage. These numberless factories absorb female labor to such a degree that I have known a family try for four months to get a servant-girl in vain; and the few girls in a village that will go out to service are often the refuse of creation, and rule their unhappy mistresses with a rod of iron. The factories, too, are attracting to some parts of New England Irish and German emigrants much faster than they can be assimilated. I read in a religious Report: "The mountain regions [of Massachusetts] are continually drained of a large part of their most enterprising population; the furnaces buy up the farms for the sake of their wood, and, having 'skinned them,' — in the expressive language of the region, — sell them out at low prices to foreigners, who are thus, in a number of places, coming into possession of hundreds of these mountain acres. This transfer of population, while apparently beneficial both to those who go and those who come, throws new burdens on the churches, and adds new embarrassments to the already difficult problem of a general popular Christianization. Considerable numbers of the Canadian French are now coming into Berkshire, turning its forests into fuel for the mills and founderies."

This is partly owing to the tariff stimulation of the factories, and tends to show that stimulation is no better for the body politic than for the corporeal system of man. The truth remains, however, that diversified industry is one of the chief secrets of a country's prosperity and progress. The most desperate and deplorable poverty now to be seen on earth — so I am assured by an intelligent and universal traveller — is in some of the sugar and coffee districts of Cuba, where Nature has lavished upon the land her richest gifts. There is room there for the planter, the slave, and the importer of manufactures; all others cringe to the plantation lord, as toadies, beggars, or white trash.

It is curious to see how the emigrants, who arrive in the country at the rate of a thousand a day, distribute themselves over the land, and settle just where they are wanted. These obscure factory villages of New England swarm with Irish people and Germans; but no Yankee sends for them. They come. If they do well, they induce their relations and friends to join them; if work is scarce, if the factory closes, they either scatter among the farmers to subsist, and wait for the reopening, or a band of them moves off to Iowa, Wisconsin, or Minnesota. In the back country, employers will make considerable sacrifices to avoid closing their works during the long, snow-bound winter, partly from benevolent feeling, partly from their unwillingness to create a destitution which it will fall to them to relieve. Here, as elsewhere, it is only about one third of the workmen who save their money and improve their position in the world; another third about hold their own, or can get credit in dull seasons sufficient to carry them over to the next period of superabundance; another third live in such a way that, if work ceases this week, they must go hungry the next, unless more provident people help them. Some of the factories in odd, out-of-the-way nooks of New England are of such antiquity that men who went into them as boys are now gray-headed foremen or partners. Upon the whole, I must confess that some of the factory villages, with their rows of shabby cottages close together, their tall factory buildings humming with machinery, and all the refuse of manufacture lying about, do not leave an agreeable impression upon the mind of the visitor. But whatever in them is merely unpleasing to the eye admits of easy and inexpensive remedy.

The time was when very few men would be farmers in New England who could help it, and farming there is still far from being an attractive or popular occupation. The dearness of labor compels most of the proprietors of the soil to work with their hands from the rising of the sun to the going down of the same; and, so long as this is the case, the more capable of our idle species will extol the noble occupation of the farmer, and avoid it. But the business is rising in dignity. It is beginning to detain the superior sons of farmers from the city, and now and then lures from the city a volunteer who brings to the soil a highly trained and sure intelligence. The railroads go everywhere, and enable the farmers of the most northern town of Vermont to send to New York (three hundred and fifty miles distant) commodities as bulky as hay and as perishable as blackberries. Along the lines of those quiet country railroads to points two hundred miles distant from New York or Boston a milk-train nightly passes, gathering up from every station its quota of cans of milk for the next morning's supply of those cities. They have a way now of "curing" milk, which, without injuring it, causes it to keep longer, and prevents the cream from rising. A farmer among the hills of Berkshire, who cures his milk by this process, has sent to New York (one hundred and fifty miles off), every night for the last eighteen months, two hundred cans of milk, and has only lost one can by the milk spoiling. For the information of milk consumers, I will here communicate the fact, that the milk which costs us in New York the "war price" of ten cents a quart yields the Yankee farmer only four cents. The strangest thing of all is, that it cannot be brought to our doors for much less than ten cents. Another thing incredible (but true) is, that the Yankee farmer does *not* water the milk, nor even put into each can the "lump of ice to keep it," of which we hear in convivial hours.

Special farming appears to be more remunerative than general agriculture, and is one of the causes of the growing attractiveness of the business. The factories, wherein the milk of a hundred farms is made into cheese or butter, are an unspeakable relief to farmers' wives. Labor-saving machinery is doing wonders for the farming interest, and will do more. The high prices of produce during the last seven years have cleared many thousand farms in New England from encumbrance, and put away in their owners' money-boxes a few United States bonds. In a word, although few honest men will ever find it an easy thing to live, and every one of the legitimate occupations makes large demands of those who exercise them successfully, it may now be said of farming in New England, that it invites, and will sufficiently reward, intelligent labor. The difficulty is the first five years. After that, if you manage well, you may have as much money as is necessary, and work no harder than is becoming. Probably there is now no business in which a little sound sense and extra judicious expenditure yield results so certain, so lasting, so desirable as this of farming.

It seems strange that the mean Yankees should have taken so much trouble as they have to make their homes and villages pleasant to the eye. If the New-Yorker wishes to find a delightful village in which to spend the summer, he has only to go up in a balloon some fine afternoon in June, when the wind is blowing toward the east, and, when the balloon is over New England, let himself gently descend into a field, and make for the nearest collection of houses. He will be almost certain to have reached a pleasant place; but if not, there will be sure to be one a very few miles distant. I have been in New England towns of four or five thousand inhabitants, in which I could not discover by diligent search one squalid house, one untidy fence, one decidedly disagreeable object. They make their very wood-sheds ornamental, and pile the wood in them so evenly that the sawed ends of the sticks make a wall smooth, clean, and compact, pleasing to behold. A frequenter of New England could tell when he had reached that strange land by the wood-piles. Almost everything you see or handle there is a mechanical curiosity, for the Yankees take infinite trouble to invent trouble-saving implements and apparatus. They have most curious and novel hinges, locks, latches, padlocks, keys, curry-combs, pig-troughs, and horse-shoes; and nothing pleases them better than to be the first to have a new and startling invention, such as a front-door key that weighs half an ounce (a pretty little thing of polished steel, fit for the vest pocket, and yet capable of turning a huge lock), or a stove that puts on its own coal, or a gate that opens as the horseman approaches and closes when he has passed through, or a flat-iron that keeps itself hot, or a gas-burner so contrived that the gas lights by being merely "turned on." A genuine Yankee delights to expound such things to the stray New-Yorker, and, in his eagerness, does not mark the impenetrable blank of his guest's countenance as he strives to look as though he understood them. A Yankee establishment, including house, fences, gates, barn, stable, wood-shed, chicken-yard, pig-sty, and tool-box, is a museum of ingenuities, all of which will "work," and all of which were made with a purposed symmetry and elegance.

Some of the older villages have grown exceedingly lovely. A long, wide street, not straight, — O no, *not* straight, — nor violently crooked either, but gently curving as a country road usually does, which sets off to the best advantage the grand old elms lining the street on both sides, and affords many a glimpse of the pretty houses nestling under them, — such is the usual village of New England. Few white fences, few white houses, but almost all that man has made is of a hue to harmonize with the prevailing colors of nature. The pillared edifices of fifty years ago, and the elaborate picket fences, have nearly disappeared, and all is becoming villa-like, neat, subdued, elegant. The width of the street gives room for two wide strips of grass, which beautifully relieve the heavy, dark masses of foliage on each side; and these masses are further relieved by the lawns, the flowers, and the flowering shrubs that surround every house. Sometimes of a morning, when the sun slants across the street, and lights up the grass so that it looks like sheets of emerald, and touches with glory every object, and brings into clear view the distant, pleasing bend of the road, transmuting its very dust into gold, — sometimes, I say, about 7 A. M., in one of these older villages of New England, when the jaded citizen steps out upon the path, and looks up and down the street, the view is such as to melt his heart and haunt him in his softer moments ever after. The scene is at once so peaceful and so brilliant, and its beauty has not been too dearly purchased. It is not one man's ostentation or one class's privilege which has created this enchanting scene; it is not a gorgeous castle, and an exclusive park, with a squalid village near by. *This* loveliness is the result of a sense of the becoming which pervades the community, and which the whole community has indulged. The cost in money is trifling indeed. Looking over the records of a town in Vermont, I happened to fall upon an entry which showed that the town had paid for planting those mighty elms in its public square twenty-five cents each. There are many men in the United States who would count it a rare piece of good luck to be able to buy one of them for twenty thousand dollars, — cash on delivery in good condition.

Of late years there has been a revival of interest in the matter of village decoration in New England. This movement originated in the mind of a public-spirited lady of Stockbridge, Mrs. J. Z. Goodrich, who, in 1853, was chiefly instrumental in forming the famous Laurel Hill Association of that place, since imitated in other towns. The objects of these associations, as expressed in their constitutions, are "to improve and ornament the streets and public grounds by planting and cultivating trees, cleaning, trimming, and repairing the sidewalks, and doing such other acts as shall tend to beautify and improve such streets and grounds." Every person over fourteen who agrees to pay one dollar a year for three years, or who plants and protects one tree under the direction of the executive committee, is a member of the association. Any one may become a life-member by paying ten dollars a year for three years, or twenty-five dollars at one time. To interest the children in the matter, who might otherwise injure the young trees, or tread carelessly on the edges of the paths, all persons under fourteen are admitted members by paying twenty-five cents a year for three years, or "by doing an equivalent amount of work annually for three years, under the direction of the executive committee." This executive committee, who, of course, do all the work of the association, consists of the president, the four vice-presidents, the treasurer, the secretary, and fifteen others, "part of whom shall be ladies." The committee meets once a month, determines what shall be done, at what expense, and under whose supervision. The result is, that the village is properly shaded, the grass on each side of the road is cut at proper times, the paths are trimmed and kept free from weeds, the public ground is improved and beautified, the cemetery is duly cared for, the happiness of every civilized being in the place is increased, and the value of all the village property is enhanced. Once a year the association meets to elect officers, to hear what has been done, how much spent, and what else is needed and desired. Sometimes this annual meeting is held in midsummer out of doors in the public park, and the ladies seize the opportunity to make it a kind of village festival.

Speaking of these associations reminds me of another of the many ways in which the Yankees in their native towns display their meanness. Ever since New England was settled, the inhabitants have had dinned in their ears, two or three times a week, such sentiments as that it is more blessed to give than to receive, that strength is bestowed upon the strong that they may help the weak, and wisdom upon the wise that they may guide the foolish. In fact, the very Constitution of Massachusetts contains an Article upon the encouragement of literature, which, it says, ought to be encouraged for the following reasons: "To countenance and inculcate the principles of humanity and general benevolence, public and private charity, industry and frugality, honesty and punctuality in dealings, sincerity, good-humor, and all social affections and generous sentiments among the people." Hence we can hardly find a town in New England, of any considerable age or wealth, which has not been the recipient of a gift or gifts from one or more of its inhabitants. There is little Stockbridge, among the hills of Berkshire, where the lynx and the otter are still caught, and from which the bear has not been long gone. The village contains but fifty or sixty houses, and the whole town has only a population of about nineteen hundred and fifty; but the following is an imperfect catalogue of the gifts which it has received. First, its remarkably beautiful public ground, containing ten or twelve acres, was a gift to the town from the family known to the whole country by the talents of one of its members, the late Miss Catherine Sedgwick. Upon this fine park the public high school has been built, behind which the ground rises into a rocky and almost precipitous hill, densely covered with wood, affording a capital playground to the boys, and a most agreeable retreat to all the people. Near by is a solid stone structure, the public library building, given to the town by Mr. J. Z. Goodrich. Another native of Stockbridge, Mr. Jackson, had previously had the meanness to start a public library by the gift of two thousand dollars' worth of books, to which other residents had added many valuable volumes; whereupon Mr. Goodrich builds this solid and spacious edifice to contain the books, and to afford a pleasant reading-room for the people in the afternoons, when many of them can spend an hour or two over the papers and magazines. That done, the town took fire, — in town meeting assembled, — and voted four hundred dollars a year for the increase of the library, and the compensation of the young lady who serves as librarian (from 2 to 5 P. M., five days a week). Then President Hopkins, of Williams College, hearing what was going on in his native place, gave to the library an unusually interesting collection of minerals. Other contributions of pictures and books have followed fast; until really the library of little Stockbridge is only inferior to such ancient establishments as that of Newport, which also has grown to its present importance chiefly by gifts and bequests. In Stockbridge, too, there is a very elegant fountain, the marble figures of which, executed in Milan, were presented by a well-known New-Yorker, John H. Gourlie, who has a cottage near it. The town, however, excavated and built the fountain, the water of which comes from mountain springs some miles away. Incredible as it may seem, this ridiculous little village has had the insolence to tap a mountain, and bring excellent spring water into every house that chooses to have it! Another gift is a carved marble drinking-fountain, temporarily placed at the side of the library building. Finally, there is a handsome monument of brown stone, erected, at a cost of two thousand dollars, to the immortal and dear memory of the men of Stockbridge who fell in the war. This was built by general subscription.

The propensity to make presents to the public is so general and so strong in New England, that it requires checking and warning rather than stimulating. In the course of time, when the progress of civilization shall have still further loosened the general clutch upon money, and the man who has the mania for needless accumulation will be generally recognized as a madman, it will probably become necessary to further regulate this matter of public gifts and bequests by law. No man has a right to saddle posterity with a hurtful burden. There is not a man in a million wise and far-seeing enough to give away a million dollars without doing more harm than good. By and by we shall see men competing for the honor and privilege of giving something to the public, and town meetings will be called to consider whether a proffered sum of money will be, upon the whole, and in the long run, a benefit or an injury. There are colleges in New England the efficiency of which would be doubled if the trustees could disregard those conditions of gifts and bequests which frustrate the giver's benevolent intentions.

To a New-Yorker who finds himself for the first time in New England, it is a great disappointment that he can find no Yankees about. In the ridiculous comedy of The American Cousin, the audience is given to understand that Asa Trenchard, the Yankee hero of the play, is a native of Brattleboro', Vermont. A visitor to that delightful town is as likely to find an Asa Trenchard there as he would be to meet a Tony Lumpkin at a dinner-party in Windsor Castle. Brattleboro', forsooth! it would be difficult to discover on earth a village less capable of producing such a preposterous ass. They have a club there for taking the periodicals of Continental Europe, such as the *Revue des Deux Mondes*, the numbers of which circulate from house to house. They have a Shakespeare Club, which assembles on winter evenings to read and converse upon the plays of that poet, each member of the club taking a part. They form other winter clubs to study a language in common under the same teacher. They have an endowed library, for which, no doubt, some liberal soul or souls will provide a building erelong. They have also some vigorous ball clubs and an engine company; but I defy Tom Taylor to discover among them any creature ever so remotely resembling Mr. Trenchard, Salem Scudder, or any of the other stage Yankees. The stage Yankee is gone from the earth. There are no "Yankees" in New England outside of the theatre. Indeed, we may say of the whole of the Northern States, that rusticity in all its forms is disappearing, and everything, as well as everybody, is getting covered with a metropolitan varnish. Go where you will, you cannot get far beyond the meerschaum pipe, white kids, lessons on the piano, and the Atlantic Monthly.

A melancholy feature of village life in New England is the great number of intelligent, refined, and gifted ladies who have no career nor rational expectation of one. A large proportion of the young men leave their native towns at an age when marriage cannot be thought of; they repair to a city, or plunge into the all-absorbing West, and are seen no more, until, perhaps, at fifty-five, their fortunes made, their families grown up, they come back to spend the evening of their days near their childhood's home. Consider, for example, the case of the well-known Field family, and you will see why there are so many old maids in New England. There were six vigorous, ambitious boys of them, sons of a Puritan clergyman, whose doctrine and whose salary were both of the old school. When this fine old bulwark of the faith had given his boys a college education, and assisted them into a profession, what more could he or Berkshire do for them? They must needs adopt Napoleon's tactics, and "scatter to subsist." One, indeed, stayed at home, where he was long a leading lawyer of Western Massachusetts, and represented it in the State senate. Another became a New York merchant, and forced a reluctant world to re-lay the Atlantic cable. Another tried for fame and fortune at the New York bar, and won a superfluity of both. Another distinguished himself as a naval officer. Another emerged to the public view as editor of a leading religious newspaper. Another made his way to a seat on the bench of the Supreme Court of the United States. These able men have had a career in the world, as thousands of other New England lads have had, and are having. But what of the "girls they leave behind them"? Some, it is true, go forth, and make a career; but many seem compelled to remain at home, where they amuse themselves as best they can with German lessons, gardening, fairs, ecclesiastical needle-work, and going out to tea; willing to do any suitable work, but unwilling to deprive of it work-women who must have it. It is easy enough to find villages in New England where there are twenty admirable girls under thirty years of age, and not one marriageable young man.

A precious relief it is to these when the long June days bring at length, after the slow winter and tardy, tedious spring, the first summer visitors, with their huge trunks piled high on the village coach. Not for the new fashions' sake, — O dear, no! There is not a device nor passing whim of fashion which these Yankee girls do not know as soon as it is known in the Fifth Avenue. No city damsel need expect to astonish *them* with her novelties from Paris. Such of the Yankee girls as have been so unfortunate as to catch the clothes mania, now raging in most Christian countries, are walking Harper's Bazars of fashionable knowledge. Very many of them make their own dresses, and trim their own bonnets, but they do it in the most recent and killing manner. The gay summer birds that come to these sweet nooks of New England are welcome for many reasons; they fill the churches, patronize the fairs, enliven the street, and join the tea-parties; but they cannot tell the Yankee girls anything they do not know already, unless it is what Tostée really does, my dear, in *La Grande Duchesse.*

A curious thing about New England is the variety of eccentric characters to be found there. In almost every town there is a farmer or mechanic who has addicted himself to some kind of knowledge very remote from his occupation. Here you will find a shoemaker, in a little shop (which he locks when he goes to dinner or to the post-office, much to the inconvenience of customers), who has attained celebrity as a botanist. In another village there may be a wheelwright who would sell his best coat for a rare shell; and, not far off, a farmer, who is a pretty good geologist, and is forever pecking away at his innocent rocks. Again, you will find a machinist who is enamored of "large-paper" copies of standard works, and rejoices in the possession of rarities in literature which he cannot read. I know an excellent steel-plate engraver, who, besides being a universal critic, is particularly convinced that the entire railroad system of the world is wrong, — ties, rails, driving-wheels, axles, oil-boxes, everything, — and employs his leisure in inventing better devices. Then there are people who have odd schemes of benevolence, such as that of the Massachusetts farmer who went to Palestine to teach the Orientals the true system of agriculture, and was two years in finding out that they would n't learn it. There are morose men and families who neither visit nor are visited; and there is, occasionally, a downright miser, of the ancient type, such as we read of in old magazines and anecdote books. There are men, too, of an extreme eccentricity of opinion. I think there are in Boston about a dozen as complete, immovable, if not malignant Tories, as can be found this side of Constantinople, — men who plume themselves upon hating everything that makes the glory of their age and country. And, speaking of Boston, — solid, sensible Boston, — what other city ever accomplished a feat so eccentric as the production of those twin incongruities, George Francis Train and the Count Johannes?

In matters more serious there is an occasional eccentricity still more marked. So, at least, it is said by those who look deeper than the smiling summer surface of New England. In the religious Report* quoted above I read a startling passage to this effect: "Our purely American communities, that have had a natural growth, are (with an exception soon to be named) religious and church-going communities." That exception, says the Report further on, is where "some form of religious error" — i. e. a creed different from ours — "has prevailed. In some such places there is an obstinate indifference to worship and to religious truth, and even to religious questions in general. In others, a mental indisposition of peculiarly mischievous character substitutes for this indifference *an acrid hostility.* This epidemic — which in some localities has become endemic — is characterized by a general habit of opposition, — a habit, not of eclecticism or of criticism, but of attack and denunciation; not of broad survey and genial correction, but of perverse misconception and invective." In several communities, continues the Report, "the results begin to

* First Report of the [Massachusetts] State Committee on Home Evangelization. Presented to the General Conference [of Congregational Clergymen], September 13, 1866.

appear in a *retrogression towards the paganism of the later empire,* — a virulent hatred of Christianity, an assertion of the sufficiency of philosophy and the uselessness of religion, a contempt for worship and the Lord's Day, and a doubt of immortality."

This is eccentric indeed. It is such eccentricity as the summer visitor seldom has an opportunity of observing; for in the villages which he frequents the entire population on Sunday morning seems to come forth in its excellent Sunday clothes, and gently wind its way to the churches, — much to the discomfort of a city pagan, whom this apparent unanimity leaves to a silent, reproachful solitude. I think the most "acrid" of the pagans of "the later empire," who should witness, from a convenient point, the long lines of well-dressed people strolling churchward on Sunday in a green New England village, all gardens and loveliness, would be compelled to confess (to himself) that this weekly grooming of the whole people, this peaceful assembling, this silent, decorous sitting together for an hour or two, these friendly greetings at the church doors, and the chatty stroll home with neighbors, is rather a good thing than otherwise, and certainly *very* much better than staying at home in the same old clothes, doing the same old work, and being "acrid." If the pagans of the later empire are numerous enough, they should hasten to establish a Sunday gathering, and so get rid of their acridity; for there are but two evils in the world, and one of them is ill-humor.

But how changed is New England religion from the time when Jonathan Edwards made mad the guilty and appalled the free in Northampton and Stockbridge a hundred and twenty years ago! Strange being! Wonderful creed! There was a certain Sunday morning in Northampton, in 1737, when the gallery of the church gave way in consequence of the heaving of the ground in spring. The account which Edwards gives of this event is a most curious study of character, of history, and of mania. He gives, first of all, a careful, exact explanation of what he would have called the "natural causes" of the catastrophe, — showing how the ends of the supporting timbers were drawn out of their sockets by the bulging of the wall. Then he describes the event: "The gallery, in falling, seemed to break and sink first in the middle, so that those who were upon it were thrown together in heaps before the front door. But the whole was so sudden, that many of those who fell knew nothing what it was, at the time, that had befallen them. Others in the congregation thought it had been an amazing clap of thunder. The falling gallery seemed to be broken all to pieces before it got down; so that some who fell with it, as well as those who were under, were buried in the ruins, and were found pressed under heavy loads of timber, and could do nothing to help themselves." But no one was killed, and only one seriously hurt. Why was this? Mr. Edwards answers: "It seems unreasonable to ascribe it to anything else but the care of Providence in disposing the motions of every piece of timber, and the precise place of safety where every one should sit and fall, when none were in any capacity to care for their own preservation." Hence, he continues: "We thought ourselves called on to set apart a day to be spent in the solemn worship of God, to humble ourselves under such a rebuke of God upon us, in time of public service in his house, by so dangerous and surprising an accident; and to praise his name for so wonderful, and as it were miraculous, a preservation."

The stranger who now visits the church belonging to the society of which Jonathan Edwards was the minister finds himself introduced into a spacious and elegant edifice, with all the modern improvements in upholstery and cabinet work. The scene is bright and cheerful. A fine organ, well played, soothes and exalts the mind, and a highly trained quartette discourses beautiful music. If the gallery should break down some Sunday morning, the occupants would not have far to fall, and the church would bring an action against the builder. The sermon, of course, is not such as the acrid pagans of the later empire approve; but it is better than a man can be reasonably expected to produce who has to preach twice a week, and the *first* necessity of whose position is, not to offend the people that pay him.

In these transition times it is hard to be a clergyman in New England; for whether the clergyman advances faster than the people, or the people get ahead of the clergyman, the result is equally distressing to the weaker party. Perhaps there is not a more agonizing situation on earth than that of the clergyman of a modern fastidious church, who, having a sickly wife, six children, and no head for business, has incurred the hideous calamity of knowing too much. If ever we have in America a great fictitious literature, much of the agony of the same will be of that internal and spiritual nature here referred to.

The time was when there was an intimate connection between these town governments and the church, — the established church of New England, — and when all other beliefs and rites were forbidden. Once a man could be lawfully taxed against his will for the support of the Congregational minister, and it was death to say mass. But New England, from its first settlement to the present hour, has always given that sole certain evidence of spiritual life which is afforded by "growth in grace." The essential difference between a wise and a foolish person, between a superior and an inferior community, is, that one learns and the other does not. The Mathers and Edwardses of a former generation are succeeded by the Channings, Beechers, Parkers, Motleys, and Emersons of this; and these, in their turn, will be followed by men equal to the task of carrying on and *organizing* the regeneration which has been so worthily begun. The old restraints and privileges have long ago been abolished, and perfect religious and irreligious freedom prevails. A family can now take a ride on Sunday afternoon, or receive visitors on Sunday evening, without exciting consternation or calling out the constable. In almost every village all the principal sects are represented, and there is usually the utmost possible friendliness between them. At the Congregational church you will generally find the solid aristocracy of the place, — the president of the railroad, the president of the bank, the master of the high school, the employing manufacturers, the old doctor, the rich farmers, the large store-keeper, and the colored man who thinks he waited on General Washington in the Revolutionary War. But, in some towns, the Unitarians have a share of these great men, as well as a good number of the polite people who are sometimes described in New England as "literary." In most villages there may now be found a pretty little box of an Episcopal church, half hidden in foliage, which in summer, during the reign of the summer visitors, is filled to overflowing with the gayest costumes; though in winter, they say, the attendance dwindles to a company which is as small in number as it is fervent in zeal. There is, also, usually a Methodist church, and frequently a Baptist, which have their proportion of adherents. Each of these denominations maintains a vigorous Sunday school, and the friendly rivalry between the schools gives the poorer children many a picture-book, doll, cake, and picnic which they would not otherwise have.

Perfect freedom, I have just said, prevails in religious matters in New England; but this has not long been the case. Some of the elderly people in the elderly towns found it hard to tolerate the building of Catholic churches in their midst, and consequently Catholics occasionally found it difficult to buy ground for the purpose. No one had any lots to sell, or a preposterous price was asked; the true reason being, that the wink had been passed among the land-owners, and an understanding come to that the priest was not to have any land. I am acquainted with a large town in Vermont where these tactics were successful for some years, in spite of the disorderly Sundays in the Irish quarter, which were a weekly argument in favor of the priest's coming. At length, by stratagem, the requisite lots were obtained; and then the Catholics, being put upon their mettle by this inconsiderate opposition, took their revenge by building a twenty-thousand-dollar church of brick instead of a three-thousand-dollar one of wood, as first proposed. Not content with this fell vengeance, they carried their animosity so far as to behave ever after with the strictest propriety on Sundays.

The stranger is surprised to find in small sequestered villages, renowned perhaps in the annals of Puritanism, Catholic churches of good size, with thick walls of handsome and well-cut stone, nearly as white as marble, and surrounded by lawns and shrubbery, not very ill kept. The explanation of the mystery sometimes is, that in these remote villages among the mountains there are human minds all alive to the stir and impulse of the time, to whom the men, the books, the ideas, the aspirations, the dismay, and the despair of the age are more real and familiar than to us who live in distracting cities; and some of these yearning, imaginative souls have listened in their seclusion to the rending cry of Lacordaire in Notre Dame, to Hyacinthe, to Newman, and have been seduced to abandon the hereditary fold, and fly, shivering, to the ancient ark. Hence the Catholic churches are sometimes more costly than they naturally would be, and we find in them a crowded congregation of Irish laborers and their families, and *one* solitary native of ancient name and wealth, who contributed a large part of the building fund. Along the northern border, where many of the laboring class are French, there are a few rather ancient Catholic churches; in some of which the sermon is in French one Sunday and in English the next, and French confessions alternate with English on Saturdays. It were much to be desired that *some* religion had power enough on the frontier to put an end to the petty smuggling that goes on there continually, corrupting the poor man who perpetrates the offence, and the summer visitor who instigates or rewards it.

I think the Catholic bishops must reserve a few wild priests for the remoter country congregations, where there is little chance for proselyting. I witnessed a Catholic service, a summer or two since, in the very heart of New England, which was a chapter of Charles O'Malley come to life, —a bit of old Ireland transferred bodily to the New World. Toward nine o'clock on Sunday morning, the hour appointed for the semi-monthly mass, the people gathered about the gate under the trees, while the ruddy and robust priest stood at the church door, accosting those who entered with a loud heartiness that made every word he uttered audible to the people standing without and to the people kneeling within. He was a jovial and sympathetic soul, who could (and *did*) laugh with the merry and grieve with the sad; but it was evident that laughter came far more natural to him than crying. When he had concluded, at 9.15, a boisterous and most jovial conversation with Mrs. O'Flynn at the door, every word of which was heard by every member of the waiting congregation, he entered the church, and proceeded to the altar, before which he knelt, holding his straw hat in his hand. His prayer ended, he went into a small curtained alcove at the side, where his priestly robes were hanging. Without taking the trouble to let the curtains fall, he took off his coat, in view of the whole assembly, and put on part of his ecclesiastical garments, unassisted by his only acolyte, — a little boy in the usual costume, who stood by. He then went again to the altar, and arranged the various objects for the coming ceremonial; after which he stepped aside and completed the robing, — not even going into the alcove, but standing outside, and reaching in for the different articles. He might have spared the congregation the pain of seeing his struggles to tie his strings behind him; but no; he chose to perform the whole without help and without disguise. When all was ready, he said the mass with perfect propriety, and with unusual manifestations of feeling. But the sermon, if sermon it could be called, was absolutely comic, and much of it was intended to be so. There had been a fair recently for the re-decoration of the altar; and in the first part of his discourse the gratified pastor read a list of the contributors, with comments, in something like the style following: —

"Mrs. McDowd, $ 13.50; and very well done, too, considering they had nothing but cake upon their table, — no, not so much as an apple. John Haggerty, $ 2.70; and indade he 's only a boy, a mere lad, — and a good boy he *is*. Mrs. O'Sullivan, $ 37.98; yes, and $ 27.42 before. Ah! but that was doing well, — that was wonderful, considering what she had to contend with. Mrs. O'Donahue, $ 7.90; and every cent of it got by selling a ten-cent picture. Very well done of you, Mrs. O'Donahue! Peter O'Brien, $ 12.00; good *for* you, Peter, and I thank you in my own name and in the name of the congregation. . . . . Total, $ 489.57. Nearly five hundred dollars! It 's really astonishing! and how much of it, my children" (this he said with a wink and a grin that excited general laughter), — "and how much of it do you think your priest will kape for himself? Not much, I 'm thinking. No indeed. Why should I kape it? What do I want with it? I have enough to eat, drink, and wear, and what more does a priest want? I have no ambition for money, — not I; and you know it well. You know that the whole of this money will be spent upon the altar of God; and we shall spend it with the greatest economy. Not Brussels carpet, of course. That would cost four or five dollars a yard. Good ingrain will do well enough for us at present, and last long enough too; for can't it be turned? You know it can. Twenty years from now, when we are all dead and gone, they'll be turning and turning and turning it, and holding it up to the light, and saying, 'I wonder who laid down this ould carpet!' In all my life, I never saw such an altar as this in a church of this size" (turning to the altar, and surveying it with an indescribably funny attempt to look contemptuous), — "so *mane*, so *very* mane! I tell you, if I had been here when this altar was made, I'd have *wheeled* the man out of church pretty quick." (These last words were accompanied with the appropriate gesture, expressive of taking the delinquent carpenter by the back of the neck, and propelling him thereby down the aisle.) "But what shall I say of those who have given nothing to this fair? Ah! I tell you, when the decorations are all done, and you come here to mass on Sunday mornings, and see God's house and the sanctuary where he dwells all adorned as it should be with the gifts of the faithful, and when you think that you gave not one cent towards it, I tell you you'll blush if there's a blush in you."

After proceeding in this tone for twenty minutes, during which he laughed heartily himself, and made the people laugh outright, he changed to another topic, which he handled in a style well adapted to accomplish the object intended. He said he had heard that some of the "hotel girls" had been swearing and quarrelling a good deal that summer. "Ah," he continued, "I was sorry to hear it! The idea of *ladies* swearing! How wrong, how mean, how contemptible, how nasty, how unchristian! Don't you suppose that the ladies and gentlemen at the hotel have heard how many Protestants are coming into the bosom of the Catholic Church? Don't you suppose they watch you? They know you're Catholics, and don't you suppose they'll be judging of Catholics by *you?* And, besides, who would marry a swearing lady? Tell me *that!* The most abandoned blackguard that walks the streets would n't marry a girl that he had heard swear, for he knows very well that she 'd be a bad mother. If I were a young man, and heard my true love swear, do you think I 'd marry her? *Hey?* do you think I would? By no *manes!* And I wish to God I had spoken about this before; for now the season is almost over, and many of the Protestant people have gone home, and very likely are talking about it now in New York and Boston. You know what they 'll say. They 'll say, 'If that 's the way Catholic ladies behave, you don't catch me turning Catholic.' "

At the conclusion of his discourse he took up the collection himself, saying, as he left each pew, "Thank you," in a strong, hearty tone of voice; and if any one took a little extra trouble to reach over, or put into the box something more than the usual copper coin, he bowed, and said, "I thank you very much, madam, — very much indeed." He was a strange mixture of the father and the ecclesiastic, of the good fellow and the gentleman. In Tipperary, in the Colleen Bawn, in Charles Lever, we are not surprised to find him; but who would have expected to make his acquaintance in a secluded valley of New England, and to discover that he has the largest congregation in the neighborhood? And O how much better is such a priest than one of the howling-dervish description!

So much for life in a New England town; for I have left myself no room to speak of the unequalled efficiency of the Yankee town system in time of war. No despot has ever invented a mode of bringing out "the last man and the last dollar" half so simple, cheap, prompt, and certain as this. As soon as a call for troops is flashed over the wires, the officers of each town can ascertain exactly how many men they have to produce; and they know where the men are, and what the men are, who are most open to an offer. They know what the families of the soldiers require, and those soldiers have an assurance that their families will not suffer in their absence. It was this town system that saved the country in the late war.

Universal liberty may be a dream. Henry Clay's pleasing fancy of a continent of closely allied Republics settling all differences and difficulties by an occasional Congress on the Isthmus of Darien, wherein the honorable giant from Patagonia would join in harmonious debate with the honorable dwarf from Greenland, may never be realized. But if universal liberty is not a dream, if the whole habitable earth is ever to be occupied by educated, dignified, and virtuous beings, it is probable that those beings will arrange themselves in self-governing communities, similar in magnitude, similar in institutions and laws, to a New England town. It is strange that such people as Yankees are said to be, struggling for life in the wilderness against savage man and savage nature, should have hit upon methods which seem scarcely capable of essential improvement.

CONGRESSIONAL PECCADILLOES.

STROLLERS about the Capitol at Washington frequently pause to admire the ingenuity and the studious habits of a certain respectable colored man who serves as door-keeper to an august national court. It is an established principle at Washington that an American citizen visiting the capital of his beloved country shall never be allowed to open a door for himself; and, consequently, wherever there is a door, there must needs be a door-keeper. A being more superfluous than a door-keeper to the room in which this high court is held it would be difficult to imagine. The door has been provided by a grateful nation with a convenient loop or handle of brass, adapted to the meanest capacity, and with a spring which causes it gently to close without the interposition of human hands. It closes, too, upon something soft, so that there is no danger of the deliberations of the court being disturbed by a bang. Most of the persons who enter the room are familiar with all its arrangements; and if their hands should chance to be full of papers, they could easily thrust out one little finger, and, inserting it in the handle, pull the light and unlatched door wide open. Nor does the door-keeper show to a seat the awe-struck visitors who are occasionally attracted to the apartment by curiosity. Within the room other officers, white in color or higher in rank, stand ready to prevent ladies from rushing forward to the bench of the judges or losing themselves among the lawyers within the bar. The sole business of that respectable colored man from 11 A. M. to 3 P. M. is to open a light door which shuts itself. Being a man of resources, he has provided himself with a chair and tied a string to the handle of his door. He goes to his place every morning provided with reading-matter, and there he sits, holding his newspaper or book in one hand, and the end of his string with the other. When any one approaches, he knows it by instinct, and gives the string a mechanical pull, without looking up or being mentally aware that he has performed an official duty.

Behold the typical man in him! He represents a class in Washington. He is one of the small sins which Congress permits and commits.

The sins of this kind which Congress commits are worse than those which it permits. After satisfying the curiosity of the ladies with a view of the Supreme Court, — a work of three minutes, — you naturally ascend to the gallery of the Senate. This is the paradise of door-keepers. I think I counted fourteen doors to this gallery. There are doors which admit only ambassadors, door-keepers' friends, and other privileged persons. There are doors which exclude the public from the Reporters' Gallery, writing-room, and telegraph office. There are many doors which admit ladies, and many more that open into the portions of the gallery used chiefly as a warming-place by unemployed negroes. Each of these doors consists of two leaves that swing together, and are kept shut by the attraction of gravitation. What a field for door-keeping is here! At nearly every leaf of these numerous doors sits or stands a door-keeper, his hand inserted in his brass loop, — one man outside to let in the coming, and another inside to let out the parting guests. From their keeping such a tight clutch upon their handles, I think there must be more door-keepers than there are doors. Every man seems afraid that if he should let go his handle another might get hold of it, and thus rob him of his slight pretext for being on the pay-roll. Half a dozen locks and a hundred latch-keys would deprive of all semblance of pretext the gentlemen who exclude the miscellaneous public from the Ambassadors' Gallery and the Reporters' apartments: and the rest of the door-keeping could be well done by two men. But that would never do in Washington. The pretext for being on the pay-roll is the very thing wanted.

If the visitor is rash enough to hint that two men to each door is rather a lavish expenditure of human force, considering the scarcity of labor on this continent, he is silenced by the question, How could two or three or half a dozen men "clear the galleries"? They could not. Nor could forty, if the auditors were determined to sit fast. But the Speaker's simple order, addressed to people habituated and wholly disposed to obey properly constituted authority, clears them with all requisite despatch. If not, there are thirty-three bored, yawning, inexpressibly idle men about the Capitol, in blue uniform and steeple-crowned hats, who are styled the Capitol police. They have a captain and two lieutenants, to head any onset upon a stubborn public which the Speaker might order, and it would relieve the monotony of their existence to be ordered upon any duty whatever.

Congress has, indeed, furnished itself most liberally with servants. The Senate, which consists of seventy-four members, is served by at least one hundred officers of all grades, from secretary to page. The House, which numbers two hundred and fifty-three members when the States are fully represented, has not less than a hundred and fifty officers, although the investigator does not find so many in the published list. We observe a considerable number of persons employed about the Capitol whose names elude the search of those who pore over the Blue Book of Mr. Disturnell, or the useful and excellent Congressional Directory of Major Ben Perley Poore. If we add to the officers employed about the two chambers the printers and binders who do the work of Congress in the public printing-office, we shall find that Congress has many more servants than members. It may be that most of these are necessary. The Secretary of the Senate may require the assistance of twenty-one clerks. The heating-apparatus of the Capitol may be of such a complicated and tremendous nature that it is as much as fourteen men can do to manage it. Members may read and consult such a prodigious number of books and documents as to need the assistance of more librarians than are employed in the Mercantile Library of New York, which has ten or twelve thousand subscribers, as well as an immense reading-room. Including the librarians of the library proper and those of the sub-libraries and document-rooms of the two houses, there are twenty-four persons in the Capitol supposed to be chiefly employed in ministering to the intellectual wants of members of Congress. All these persons may be indispensable, but they do not seem so to the casual observer. The casual observer receives the impression that the servants of Congress, like those of the government generally, would be improved if two very simple and easy things were done, — the salary of the chiefs doubled, and the number of their assistants reduced one half.

I can show the reader, by relating a little incident which I witnessed in Washington last winter, how it comes to pass that so many more officers get appointed than seem to be necessary. While resting in the office of the public printer, after going over the most admirably complete and efficient printing-office in the country, a well-dressed, polite young man came in, and presented a letter of introduction to the superintendent. Clouds gathered over the face of that functionary as he read it; and he invited the bearer to be seated in a tone which implied that he wished he was in Jericho. I was afterward favored with an explanation of the scene; and that explanation applies to a large number of the names in the Blue Book. A few days before, the superintendent had discharged thirty compositors because he had no work for them. This nice young man, who was one of them, went to one of the senators from his State, stated his case, and asked the senator to procure his reappointment. That senator, not considering the gross impropriety of his interference, but complying with the established custom, wrote a letter to the superintendent, of some length and much urgency, asking him to put his constituent back to the place from which he had been removed. I am afraid that this most improper request was complied with; for the officer to whom it was addressed was a servant of Congress, who might one day want that senator's vote. It is of no consequence whether he complied or not. Every reader acquainted with governments or with human nature knows that nine men out of ten, in that superintendent's place, would have found work, or a pretence of work, for that man. Nor can we so much wonder at the conduct of the senator. He also looks to re-election. He also desires to make friends. This pleasing young man may have an uncle who controls a newspaper or an iron-foundry in the senator's State, and it is convenient, at a critical time, to have the hearty support of a few uncles of that description. The difficulty is, that at Washington there is no rock of security anywhere in the system, against which applications like this can strike and be repulsed. If that superintendent were properly secure in his place, he would have shown the young man to the door, just as any other printer would have done, with the simple remark that he had no work for him.

Some time will probably elapse before the people gain such a triumph over the politicians as to secure permanency of appointment to government officials. Meanwhile members of Congress should disdain to listen to applications like this; especially members whose position has some basis of security.

A stranger to politics and to Washington is astonished to observe how general the feeling is, that a public man is justified in gratifying an impulse of benevolence, or in discharging a private obligation, at the cost of the public. Some time ago, General Grant chanced to be looking out of a window while a salute was firing in his honor, and he saw a man lose one of his legs by the bursting of a cannon. When the man had recovered his health, General Grant was President of the United States. What more natural than that the President should ask Mr. Boutwell to give the unfortunate man, if convenient, a watchman's place in the treasury? He pitied the man, and he had the power to give him effectual relief at the public expense. Most men would have yielded to this impulse of benevolence, as General Grant did, and most men perhaps approved the act. Nevertheless, it is just in this way that the Capitol, the departments, the post-offices, and the custom-houses get clogged with superfluous persons. It is thus that one-legged incompetence pushes from its place two-legged ability. Some one, *who cannot be refused*, asks the appointment, and then one of two things must happen, — either a man must be summarily and unhandsomely, if not inhumanly, thrust from his post, or two men must be set to doing one man's work. Generally, both these things are done. The two men go on for a while, until some new broom sweeps one or both away, to make room for the favorites of another irresistible personage.

An entertaining writer, some weeks ago, favored the public with reminiscences of former administrations, in order to show that the people cordially sustain a President who indulges his personal feelings at the people's cost. He told a story of General Jackson, which might have been true, the incident being entirely characteristic. "General," asked an old friend of the ex-President, at his Tennessee Hermitage, "tell me why you kept yourself and all your friends in trouble, through your first Presidential term, by keeping Mr. Gwinn Marshal of Mississippi?" To this General Jackson replied: "When my mother fled with me and my brother from the oppression of the British, who held possession of North Carolina, we were very, very poor. My brother had a long sickness (occasioned by a wound received from a British officer because he refused to do some menial service), and finally died. In the midst of our distress and poverty, an old Baptist minister called at our log-cabin, and spoke the first kind words my mother heard in her new home; and this good man continued to call, and he finally made our house his lodging-place, and continued to prefer it, when better ones in the neighborhood were at his service. Years rolled on, and this good man died. Well, sir, when the news was brought me that I was elected President, I put up my hands and exclaimed, 'Thank God for that, for it will enable me to give the best office under the government to the son of the old minister who was the friend of my mother, and of me in my youth'; and I kept my promise, and, if it had been necessary, I would have sacrificed my office before he should have been removed."

The feeling was natural and noble. The only question is, whether a man should requite at the expense of his country services done to his mother. The relater of the anecdote appends to it this commentary: "General Jackson was triumphantly re-elected to a second term." It is true; but it was in spite of such errors as this, not in consequence of them. Members of Congress who can remember that mad period of our political history will not justify personal government by the example of General Jackson.

Few of us, perhaps, have an adequate sense of the superior sacredness of public property to private, of public trusts to private. Little things betray our sluggish public conscience. No man, except a thief, would think of taking a sheet of postage-stamps from the desk of a banker or merchant; but, in Washington, it seems to be only men exceptionally honorable who scruple to use, or even to take, franked envelopes, which appear to be lying about everywhere. Still fewer have a proper sense of how much worse it is to steal from all their fellow-citizens than it is to steal from one of them. In everything relating to the government, a citizen of the United States should feel that he is upon his most sacred honor. We are here in double trust. Our difficult and still doubtful experiment is for mankind as well as ourselves. I would not magnify a small sin into a great one; still less would I assume to be more virtuous than others; and yet it seems to me that a citizen of the United States should shrink from accepting a proffered frank, as he would avoid touching only enough pitch to defile the tips of his fingers. I would not blame, but forgive, a Frenchman for cheating his government, which is itself a cheat; but the citizens of free countries defraud and despoil themselves when they do or permit an action which implies that public property is less sacred than private.

A special calamity of the small sins of Congress is, that their results are exceedingly conspicuous, and bring upon Congress an amount of odium or ridicule that ought to be excited only by great transgressions. I have mentioned the superfluous door-keepers and the swarms of officers everywhere to be seen about the two chambers. The amount of money wasted upon these gentlemen is not great; but the waste is obvious and striking. The dullest visitor comprehends that a small party of ladies can gain admittance to a gallery by a light and easy door without the assistance of two able-bodied men. Some of the small sins of Congress entail effects still more glaring, and fix a permanent, unconcealable stain upon the nation itself. Not a stain upon its honor; but such a stain as a lady incurs when her dress comes in contact with a freshly painted railing. We do not want fair Columbia to be thus disfigured. We wish her to be spotless and glorious even in the garments that she wears and in the ornaments that adorn her. We desire her to be tasteful in her splendors.

The reader has probably often asked himself, while wandering about the Capitol, what could possess Congress to throw away the public money upon some of those pictures that disgrace the western continent, and human nature generally, in the Rotunda. He has, perhaps, also, after giving up that conundrum, essayed to conjecture why no member has risen superior to the clamor of economists, and proposed an appropriation of two dollars to whitewash them from the view of mankind. It was bad enough to put them there; but to keep them visible, year after year, and give new commissions to the painters who produced them, are acts almost too abominable to be reckoned among the small sins of the national legislature.

Congress no doubt interpreted correctly the wishes of the people in making the Capitol stately and ornate; and it was an exquisite thought to go on decorating and completing it while the hosts of the Rebellion were intrenched within sight of its rising dome. Every building that belongs to the nation, every object that bears upon its surface the letters "U. S.," should have something in its style and appearance that will convey to the mind of the beholder a feeling of the imperial grandeur of the country's mission and destiny. Those nasty and cheap sub-post-offices in the city of New York, and those conspicuously shabby, rusty, cast-iron lamp-post letter-boxes, are an abomination in my eyes; not merely because they are stupidly inconvenient, but because they are mean in appearance; because I desire that whenever American eyes rest upon an object bearing the stamp of the nation, they should rest upon something which they can contemplate with satisfaction and pride. Hence, it is always a pleasure to get round to the front of the Capitol, and turn away from the shanties, the shops, the sand-heaps, the general dilapidation and shabbiness of the region, and gaze for a while upon the magnificence of that vast range of architecture, with its avalanches of snowy steps, that glorious dome floating lightly over the centre, and the small, brilliant flag above each wing, denoting that Congress is in session. In this brave attempt to express in marble the grandeur and glory of the United States, we see the prophecy of those chaster splendors, that simpler magnificence, which will enchant and exalt our grandchildren when they visit the future and final capital of the country. It was an excellent thing, perhaps, after all, to try our 'prentice hand on Washington, and exhaust all the possibilities of error there.

The interior of the Capitol is chaos, of course. That is unavoidable when a large building is erected over a smaller one. The visitor forgives and is amused at the labyrinthine intricacies in which he is continually lost; and when at last he stands beneath that beautiful dome, which hovers over him like an open balloon of silk illuminated by the sun, he experiences a renewal of the joy which the exterior afforded him. Doubtless, we are running too much to domes; we are putting a dome over every building of much magnitude, — it is such a fruitful source of contracts. But this one justifies itself, and startles the coldest spectator into admiration. It was also a fine conception to place under it in that perfect light a series of large historical paintings. Nor was it necessary that they should be of the highest rank as mere works of art; because it is not certain that there are now living upon earth artists capable of executing paintings of that magnitude in a truly excellent manner. No artist in these times can get the many years of large practice which is necessary for the attainment of the large manner; and, I suppose, the best we can hope for, at present, in pictures of great size, is correct, refined, excellent scene-painting. But some of the paintings in the Rotunda, besides being singularly hideous as pictures, are historical falsehoods, which any school-boy might be able to detect at a glance. That one, for example, which is supposed to have been suggested by De Soto and his men discovering the Mississippi River, — what a curiously ridiculous lie it is, with its display of superb costumes, its well-conditioned horses, and its plump cavaliers as fresh and gay, in their silk and velvet, as if they were careering in the streets of Madrid on a day of festival! What is better known than that these Spaniards reached the banks of the Great River in woful plight after a wearisome march of many months through the wilderness! It is also particularly recorded that De Soto was sparing in expenditure for gay apparel, and that every rag of clothes, except what his followers wore, was burnt after one of their bloody encounters with the Indians. An hour's research in the library of Congress, under the intelligent guidance of the librarian, would have put the painter in possession of all the picturesque details of the real scenes, and given him subjects for several pictures of peculiar interest. A picture could have been composed for that panel which would have such fascinating power as a mere exhibition of truth, that few would have cared to criticise it as a work of art.

But the question recurs, Why are such artists employed? The shameful answer is, Because they lobby for a commission and know how to lobby with effect. It is not an honest ignorance of art and history which has thus disfigured the Capitol; for these paintings are the constant theme of ridicule among members as they are among private citizens. One artist won his commission, it is said, by assiduous flattery of the wives and daughters of members of Congress. While artists of merit were toiling after excellence in distant studios, this wiser man in his generation was enjoying elegant leisure in the drawing-rooms of Washington, where he made sketches in the albums of ladies who could influence votes, or painted their portraits in some Italian or Spanish costume from his portfolio. He is thought to have secured votes by pretending that the excellent but not beautiful wife of a member of Congress reminded him constantly of an exquisite model he once had in Rome, — one of the loveliest creatures in the world. He had, moreover, some little talent in small album-sketches and little fancy portraits in costume. This, doubtless, deceived some members, who did not reflect upon the infinite difference between a grand historical painting and an imitation of the velvet in a cavalier's doublet. If that man's claim to the highest honor which the nation can bestow upon an artist had been openly discussed in committee, his name would never have reached the House at all. It was private lobbying that brought this dishonor upon art, upon Congress, and upon the national taste.

It has been proposed to introduce the rule that no man shall be appointed to office who seeks office. Congress may rely with certainty the most complete upon this, that no artist capable of worthily filling one of the panels of the Rotunda will ever lobby for the commission in the drawing-rooms of Washington. If that artist should ever be wanted, he will have to be looked for and solicited.

The reader has perhaps wondered also why Congress should have selected for the execution of the national statue of Abraham Lincoln a person of no standing or experience as an artist. Miss Vinnie Ream is a young lady of perfect respectability, and, no doubt, highly estimable in her private relations. No one can blame *her* for her good fortune. She has done little more than open her mouth and let the plum fall into it. But what has Congress done? Here was a piece of work to be given out, — the statue of a man as little statuesque as any we can imagine, — which required in the artist a combination of artistic skill and *judgment*, love of the man, and love of truth. The work was to be seen by hundreds who had been familiar with the subject, and by tens of thousands who would take a kind of affectionate interest in the artist's management of its difficulties. The Abraham Lincoln of future generations was to be created. In the selection of the artist a national fame was either to be conferred or enhanced. Congress assigned this work to a girl who had the rudiments of her art still to learn, and who had given no proof of her capacity to acquire those rudiments. She exhibited a model. It was about to be overlooked. She burst into tears. The results to her were, a ten-thousand-dollar commission, a universal celebrity, and two years in Europe, — three immense boons, either of which had been a fit requital for long-tried excellence. And, as if this were not enough, a room was given her in the Capitol itself in which to execute and exhibit her work. Congress bestowed upon this unknown and untried child honors which it has persistently withheld from artists who have conferred upon the country whatever name it has in the world of art, but who hardly know what the word "lobbying" means. Recognition one tenth as distinct and emphatic as this, how it would have cheered the early years of the excellent sculptors of whom the country is proud! Such caprice does not harm *them;* for when Congress confers distinction thus, it parts with its power to confer honor, and sensibly lessens its own.

Five minutes' conversation with Miss Vinnie Ream explains this ridiculous behavior of Congress. She is one of those graceful, animated, bright-eyed, picturesque, undaunted, twinkling little women, who can make men say *Yes* to anything they ask. She also wore a pretty blue, turban-like covering for her hair, which was killing at five paces; and there is that in her manner which puts men in the humor of uttering *badinage*, and at the same time gives them the idea that she is a helpless little body who would cry if she could not have her own way. The visitor to her room in the Capitol had but to stand apart and see the modest audacity of her demeanor, and observe the assured, lively manner in which she held a circle of men in conversation, in order to comprehend why Congress, in its easy, thoughtless good-nature, should have granted to her the most signal honors it ever bestowed upon an artist.

Men are naturally susceptible to the picturesque in woman. It is natural also to feel like caressing and protecting whatever reminds us of tender, graceful childhood. Members had done well to give a private commission to this agreeable young lady by way of encouraging her to attempt acquiring some skill in modelling. But they were false to their trust when they gave her an important public work to execute. Men who are charged by their fellow-citizens with the adornment of national edifices and the bestowal of national honors are much to blame in allowing a blue turban, a pair of speaking eyes, a trim waist, and a fluent tongue to carry off prizes due only to tried merit. Members can form little idea of the dishonor, nay, the contempt, which they bring upon Congress by indulging a whim of this kind. Millions witness the result; only a few individuals see the bright excuse; and of those few only one sex admits that it is any excuse at all.

There is an impression in Washington that a great deal of legislation is influenced by female lobbyists; and the easy success of this young lady gives countenance to the idea. A woman of attractive presence and of a certain audacity of manner, who should be able to live and entertain in handsome style, could no doubt win favor and votes for some measures. Many members come from homely homes, the ladies of which have expended their vivacity and beauty in that American phase of "the struggle for life" which Fanny Fern styles "grappling with Erin." Such members, when they find themselves in a drawing-room next to a lady who expends *her* vivacity in entertaining them, and arrays *her* beauty in all the charms of novel costume and bewitching decoration, are only too apt to surrender to the fascinating influence. But such women cannot be hired to go lobbying. It occasionally happens that a circle interested in a scheme contains one such who will render the service required. Generally speaking, however, the female lobby is small and insignificant. A lady informed me last winter that she had defeated international copyright; and, indeed, she was the Washington agent of the weak opposing influence. But a pebble can stop a six-horse coach when it is going *up* a steep hill, and the horses are tired, the driver indifferent, and the passengers asleep.

Of all the smaller sins of Congress, there are none, perhaps, which excite so much odium as that multitude of petty transgressions covered by the words "Contingent Expenses." The mere running expenses of Congress, including its share of the public printing, amount to about twice the revenue of the government under President Washington. I have tried in vain to get at the total cost of a session of Congress. The mere list of the Contingent Expenses of the House fills a volume of two hundred and twenty pages, and there is no hint anywhere of the sum total. It is certain, however, that a session of Congress costs the country as much as four millions of dollars, including pay, postage, printing, and contingent expenses. "Will the honorable member from Ohio allow me five minutes to make an explanation?" asks an honorable member from Somewhere Else. If that request is granted it costs the people of the United States a little over six hundred dollars. The chaplain's prayer, which usually lasts one minute, consumes one hundred and thirty-eight dollars' worth of time every morning. Calling the Yeas and Nays, an operation of half an hour, comes to over four thousand dollars. Allowing six months for an average session, and twenty days a month as the average number of meetings, Congress costs us something more than thirty-three thousand dollars a day. Who would begrudge his share of this great expense, if it were necessary? It is not necessary. A vigorous man of business, who should have the contract for running Congress, could save enough in the three items of printing, postage, and contingencies to double the salaries of members, give a decent compensation to the justices of the Supreme Court, the judges of the Court of Claims, and heads of departments, and have a handsome surplus for himself. Nothing is so extravagant and undemocratic as to pay such salaries to the judges, cabinet ministers, and members of Congress as to exclude from those high and honorable posts the great body of able men who are neither rich nor reckless. A fraction of the mere waste of Washington would support them all respectably, and render it possible for men of talent who have little property to serve the government.

This book of the Contingent Expenses of the House of Representatives is amusing literature indeed. There is an air of candor about it that edifies the mind. It looks so *very* honest, the publication of such items as "2 mice-traps, 50 cts." "Repairing 3 chairs, $1.50." "Easing drawer, 25 cts." "1 paper of needles, 10 cts." "One long poker, $3.00"; and "2 pounds of putty, 25 cts." It is such a satisfaction to know that the poker which cost so much was long! It is also interesting to note, that to clean and polish that extremely absurd relic of barbarism, the "mace," cost three dollars; and that, during one session of Congress, the people paid for "hauling" more than *ten thousand cart-loads* of documents! There are many items, however, which excite interest of another kind. When we find two hundred "porte-monnaies" charged at prices ranging from $1.20 to $4.25 each, we cannot help feeling that each and every one of those articles is a petty fraud. The United States has not undertaken and is not bound to supply any portion of its servants with porte-monnaies. What a scandal, too, is that annual penknife business! One thousand and ninety-eight penknives, at prices averaging about three dollars each, I find after a few minutes' search charged among the "Contingent Expenses" of the second session of the Fortieth Congress! I could probably make up the amount to two thousand by going through the book, in which the items are apparently published, but are really interred and covered up. There are charges also of "Half dozen Martinique snuff, $ 25.00," "50 lbs. of tobacco, $ 25.00," "2 doz. pocket-scissors, $ 28.00," "2 doz. hair-brushes, $ 48,00," "12 cotton stay-laces, $ 6.00," "5 extra morocco desks, $ 67.00," and endless charges for inkstands, newspapers, and periodicals; stationery by the mountain, of course. I spend my whole time, from January to December, in one unending, unchanging task of spoiling white paper; but I cannot get through more than three reams per annum, which costs about twelve dollars. Knowing how far a little stationery will go, I read of the inconceivable quantities consumed about the Capitol with amazement.

It is to be hoped that none but men in sound health will be sent to Congress, for it costs a great deal to get a member home if he should happen to die in Washington. The following is the bill paid to the Sergeant-at-arms of the House for transporting the body of a deceased member from Washington to Easton in Pennsylvania:—

Hack hire, assistance in care of remains, and arranging for the funeral in the House of Representatives	$ 50.00
18 white silk sashes for officers of House and Senate	254.00
8 black silk sashes for committee of arrangements	96.00
20½ dozen kid gloves	615.00
2 dozen kid gloves	54.00
2 dozen kid gloves	60.00
1 dozen kid gloves	33.00
200 black crape scarfs	300.00
Travel of messenger to New York and return	47.00
Hacks to carry escort and friends to depot	16.00
Fare and expenses of escort and remains from Washington, D. C., to Easton, Pa.	245.00
Hotel bills and hacks at Easton	42.65
Fare and expenses on return to Washington	194.00
Travel of assistant sergeant-at-arms and 2 messengers, Washington to Easton and return, 460 miles each	138.00
	$ 2,144.65

The fee system, it appears, is still employed to compensate some of the officers of Congress. If there is a "call of the House," i. e. a general hunting up of absent members, the Sergeant-at-arms is permitted to charge five dollars and twenty cents for "arresting, bringing before the House, and discharging" each absentee. If a hundred members are absent, which is not unfrequently the case, a call of the House costs the country five hundred and twenty dollars. If witnesses are summoned to testify before a committee, the Sergeant-at-arms charges a fee and mileage for each. Thus every person summoned from New Orleans to testify with regard to the negro massacre cost us three hundred and seventeen dollars, and the cost of merely summoning the witnesses in that affair was $ 2,392. It cost three hundred and seventeen dollars to summon "General Hamlin" to testify before a committee. The object of the committee could no doubt have been accomplished for three cents and a half, — half a cent for stationery and three cents for postage.

Now, if money is to be thrown away in this reckless manner, if the Capitol is to remain the scene of waste and profusion we find it now, then I say the people have a choice with regard to the persons who shall be benefited by it. They do not see any justice or any propriety in Henry Wilson's being compelled to pinch on five thousand dollars a year, while servants of the body to which he belongs retire rich after four years' service. It brings a blush to the cheek of every properly constituted person to think that a justice of the Supreme Court should be compelled to expend his whole salary for two rooms and the board of his family, while a man who gets stationery contracts sets up his carriage and buys pictures. If the government is to be plundered at every point by every hand, it is time the spoils were more fairly divided.

There is only one remedy for this profusion at the Capitol. Congress has honestly attempted to cut off the opportunities for petty larceny. It has attempted it many times, but never with much success. The mileage system, the franking-privilege, the wild and wondrous waste of stationery, the pocketing of French inkstands and costly penholders, the lugging home of half-reams of paper, and all the small stealings of committee-rooms, have been, by turns, the theme of ridicule and the object of legislation. Some leaks have been stopped; but others have been immediately opened, and the same thieves who pilfered under the old law have plundered under the new. We ought to know by this time that a privilege is a thing which is always and everywhere abused. We ought to know that a perquisite is always and everywhere a means of corruption. We ought to know that nearly every one in the world who is compensated by fees gets much too much or much too little, or riots in abundance now, to be starved to-morrow. Let Congressmen simply abolish fees, perquisites, and privileges, and accept in lieu thereof a proper increase to their salaries, — say, double what they now receive. Let members pay their own postage, charge no mileage, subscribe for their own newspapers, buy their own envelopes and writing-paper, and compensate all their officers by salaries.

Nothing short of this will ever answer the purpose. If Congress should permit only so much as a bottle of ink to be furnished to each committee-room, once a week, and charged to Contingent Expenses, a widening crevice would be established through which a torrent of colored fluids would continually pour. Add pens to the ink, and you would see exquisite pen-holders, fitted with the most costly diamond-pointed gold pens, and huge cases of the finest products of Gillott, heaped high in the store-rooms of the Capitol. Complete the list with paper, and you have a thick volume of wonderful items, and run up a stationery bill the mere clippings and extras of which build houses and found estates. The sole remedy is to pay each member a decent compensation, — not less than ten thousand dollars a year, — and allow neither to members nor to committees so much as a sheet of foolscap or a penny pen-holder.

The completion of the Pacific Railroad antiquates the system of mileage, by destroying the necessity for it. Indeed, ever since railroads brought two thirds of Congress within forty-eight hours' ride of Washington, a system of mileage which gives to one member eight dollars for his travelling expenses, to another several hundred dollars, and to another several thousands, has been growing ridiculous. But now that a member from Oregon can get to the capital in eleven days, it is too absurd to pay him fifteen times as much mileage as Henry Clay used to get for his six weeks' horseback ride from Kentucky. Away with Congressional mileage! The honorable member from Oregon will, of course, have to incur a little more expense in getting to Washington than the honorable member from Baltimore; but he will not find this an insupportable burden. He will be pretty sure to have free tickets to most places presented him a few hours after his election, and I am afraid he will be weak enough to accept them, until Congress makes it unlawful for him to do so. More than that, a palace-car will be assigned to his exclusive use, as long as the Pacific Railroads have favors to ask, or retribution to fear, from the body of which he is a member.

The surrender of the franking-privilege, besides being the most popular act which Congress could do, would be also one of the most beneficial to itself. It would operate as a tonic. The flow of Buncombe speech would be checked, millions of infinitesimal frauds would be prevented, and a source of demoralization would be annihilated.

Abolish perquisites, abolish fees, abolish privileges, and double salaries. There would be a little Buncombe opposition from members and editors who set up as champions of economy, but their Buncombe could be triumphantly refuted if Congress *saved* the million and a half additional pay out of the running expenses of the Capitol, the post-office, and the public printing-house.

I believe I express the opinion of all the gentlemen who have held the office of public printer, when I say that half a million dollars per annum is worse than wasted at the public printing-office. Having examined the office, the reports of the superintendent, and several of the more expensive volumes issued, I see clearly enough that if there were such an officer as National Editor, with the usual editorial power to select, cut down, and exclude, he could save the country much more than half a million a year by merely drawing his pencil through useless matter. What havoc he would have made, for example, in the gorgeous quarto (962 pages) in which are preserved the letters, resolutions, and addresses of condolence called forth by Mr. Lincoln's assassination! In that huge and splendid work, which cost us eighteen thousand dollars, there may be ten pages worth saving; and those the National Editor would have forwarded per boy to Newspaper Row, opposite Willard's, at a cost of two car tickets. The saving on that one item would have made the Supreme Bench comfortable for a whole year. In the Agricultural Report for 1867, which fills five hundred and twenty-two "large octavo pages" handsomely illustrated, of which two hundred and twenty-four thousand five hundred copies were given away, at a total expense of a hundred and twenty thousand dollars, what gashes an intelligent National Editor would have made! or rather, would he not have selected the valuable portions and sent copies to each of the agricultural newspapers and periodicals? They would give to matter really valuable all the publicity that could be desired. The Patent-Office Report has annually swollen, until it now makes over two thousand pages, — four large octavos, of which one half the space is occupied by engravings. Of this most expensive work sixty thousand copies are given away. The Reports of the Commissioners to the Paris Exposition of 1867 will fill several profusely illustrated volumes, which will of course be given away profusely. When we read the names of some of the Commissioners, we know very well what a gifted National Editor would do with their contributions.

In the last report of Mr. John Defrees, Congressional printer, a gentleman who knew the precise value of the mountains of books which Congress ordered him to manufacture, we find this interesting paragraph: —

"The Army Register of Volunteers has also been completed in eight volumes. Fifty thousand copies were ordered to be printed, *for sale at cost*, by the joint resolution of June 30, 1864. An edition of five thousand copies of the first four volumes was printed, but finding very little demand for the work, the edition of the residue of the volumes was reduced to one thousand."

For sale at cost! That is the true method, if Congress must manufacture books. Observe how the enormous error of this publication was rebuked and corrected by bringing it to the test of sale at cost. If the people want a book, they will buy it at cost; if they will not buy it at cost, it is proof positive that they do not want it enough to justify an appropriation of their money. It was an amiable idea to preserve the name of every man who fought for his country during the war; but to preserve such a catalogue did not necessitate its publication in eight volumes. Such extravagance keeps alive in the general mind the false, pernicious idea, that the government may properly expend money on principles which would be absurd and ruinous in an individual.

Do members of Congress sell West Point and Annapolis cadetships? I am afraid I must confess that it has been done. Not often; for members are abundantly blessed with nephews, and friends who have nephews, and they are generally besought for those appointments as soon as it is rumored that they intend to run for Congress. Not often; for members generally want all their small change of that nature during the canvass. Not often; for few men of an infinitesimal calibre have yet found their way to Congress. And still I fear that the member who gave a cadetship to the son of a person who presented his wife with a grand piano was in some degree influenced by the circumstance. There are lobbyists who profess to be able to procure cadetships for money, but most of them are strikers. Some members find their election expenses a heavy burden, and I believe that, occasionally, a distinct arrangement has been entered into between a member of the lobby and an anxious father, to this effect: the anxious father agrees to send a check for two thousand dollars to the chairman of the member's committee, as a contribution to the expenses of the election, and the man of the lobby agrees to induce the member to give the anxious father's son a cadetship in one of the national academies. In a very few instances such an arrangement may have been fulfilled. Some members, I fear, regard the duty of making these important appointments in the light of a perquisite, and, as just remarked, the word "perquisite" is generally synonymous with corruption. Congress will perform an act as wise as it will be noble when it relinquishes a privilege that has always been abused, and always must be, by men who have sons, nephews, and election committees.

Before leaving this small branch of a large subject, I must not fail to remark that many of us seem to be unduly alarmed at the corruptions and abuses of the government. The American people are so accustomed to honesty in their dealings with one another, and to a certain frugality of ordinary expenditure, that they start back affrighted from the scene of profusion, and worse than profusion, of government offices. Let us see then how it is with other governments. Let us see if government by the people for the people is less or more profuse, less or more corrupt, than the vaunted governments by a class for a class.

That is a pretty piece of scandal which advocate Mathieu Marais relates in his *Mémoires*, of the dissolute Regent of France and the Abbé de Broglie. The Abbé having warmly commended a certain wine, the Regent said he would like to have some of it, and the Abbé sent him three hundred bottles. The prince insisted on paying for them, and accordingly the priest handed him a bill in proper form, like this: —

His Royal Highness, the Prince Regent Dr.
To the Abbé de Broglie.

60 gallons of wine	400	francs.
300 bottles	60	"
300 corks	15	"
Twine	4	"
Sealing-wax, Spanish	9	"
Baskets	25	"
Carriage	7	"

Total: The Abbey of Mount St. Michael.

The prince paid the bill. The governorship of an abbey, and a handsome income for life of other people's money, was the reward which this man, intrusted with the revenues of church and state, felt to be due to a profligate young ecclesiastic who had given him a moment's amusement. This was in 1721. Fifty years later the young Abbé de Talleyrand won his first preferment, which consisted of two abbeys, by saying a good thing to Madame Dubarry, the king's mistress. He, the most licentious young man in Paris, had sat silent while others amused the mistress with tales of intrigue and gallantry. She asked him at length why he did not favor the company with one of his numberless amorous adventures. "Because," said he, assuming a melancholy tone, "in Paris, at present, it is so much easier to win the favor of ladies than to get preferment in the Church." This small joke made the king laugh, when it was told to him, and it was worth to the youth who uttered it the two abbeys just referred to.

On similar principles the church benefices of every established church on earth have been usually bestowed. That is to say, the appointing power does not usually so much as *think* of appointing the fittest attainable man, but gives or sells benefices, abbeys, bishoprics, archbishoprics, *solely* for its own pleasure and purposes.* If the Archbishop of Canterbury should die to-day, Mr. Gladstone would bestow the vacancy upon that man in England who, in that place, could do most to help him retain and increase his majority in the House of Commons; unless, perchance, the services have already been rendered which give to some person, family, club, or clique, a claim to the appointment. No one could blame him. The system requires it of him. He could not be Prime-Minister, and act on any other principle.

A French gentleman resident in New York related to me the other evening the particulars of a case which he thought showed advantageously for the government of the present usurper. A custom-house officer at a French seaport, after many years of faithful service, was dismissed from his place for accepting two gifts from an importer, of the value of one dollar and thirty cents. Respectable merchants petitioned for his restoration, but the minister replied that he had not the power to restore him; there was no provision in the system of the government for the pardon of such an offence. It simply could not be done. This was supposed

* Since writing this passage, I read the following in an English paper: "The account of the biddings for the next presentation to the rectory and vicarage of Westborough and Dry Donnington, in the county of Lincoln, which was put up to auction at the Mart on Tuesday, certainly offers food for reflection to thoughtful minds. It appears that the living is worth seven hundred and eight pounds per annum. There are two churches to serve, — a mile and a half apart, — service being held alternately at each place, viz. in the morning at one, and in the evening at the other, and *vice versa*. There was, the auctioneer stated, good society; he thought he might add, good hunting, and, allowing one hundred pounds a year to a curate to do the dirty, disagreeable work, such as attending to the sick and dying, there would remain a net profit of about six hundred pounds a year for the rector. The outside sum offered for the privilege of attending to the eternal salvation of the inhabitants of the two parishes in question was four thousand eight hundred pounds. This did not reach the reserve price, and accordingly the living was withdrawn, doubtless to the great disappointment of young divines with 'a call,' but no ready money."

to be extremely virtuous. But, surely, we cannot call that system pure in which the great thieves want so much that they will not and cannot permit the little people to steal at all, — which loads with plunder the men who help steal *all* the revenues of France, and covers with diamonds the women who assist to dazzle and delude the people. At the very time when this poor old man was thrust out into hopeless destitution for a momentary weakness or inadvertence, the woman of one of the head plunderers was selling off some hundreds of thousands of francs' worth of diamonds merely because she had so many jewels that she did not know what to do with them.

In England, too, they are rigid in dealing with petty corruption, — as they ought to be. An instance occurred recently. A navy clerk caused to be conveyed to a timber merchant an intimation that for thirty pounds he would get for him a certain contract to supply timber to one of the navy-yards. Both the clerk and his messenger were tried for conspiracy to obtain money by false pretences, and on being convicted were sentenced to eighteen months' imprisonment at hard labor. This was just. But, on the other hand, there is in this same England an amount and variety of political immorality, particularly among great lords, capitalists, and corporations, which leaves the United States stainlessly pure in comparison. We all know what English elections are. The reason why we all know is, because the corruption at those elections has become an established jest, which the national humorists, such as Hogarth, Dickens, Thackeray, and Bulwer, have found available for their art. Through the works of these great authors we have become perfectly familiar with that corruption, and with the national average of moral feeling which joyfully accepts the bribing and debauching of free citizens as a legitimate source of fun. Englishmen urge foreigners to stay over another steamer on purpose to witness "the humors of an English election," as Spaniards detain their guests for the Sunday bull-fight.

We may also pass lightly over that long period in the history of England when every minister bought an essential portion of his majority by bank-notes put into the hands of members in the House of Commons. "The sums varied," as we learn from Wraxall, "from five hundred to eight hundred pounds a year," which sums were "conveyed" to gentlemen of the House of Commons "in a squeeze of the hand" as they passed the ministerial agent. It was the business of that agent in Lord Chatham's time "to distribute with *art* and *policy*, amongst the members who had no ostensible place, sums of money for their support during the session, besides contracts, lottery-tickets, and other *douceurs*. It is no uncommon circumstance at the end of a session for a gentleman to receive five hundred or a thousand pounds for his *service*."* There has been published a letter from an English minister to Cardinal Henry, who was minister of Louis XV. of France at the beginning of his reign. Here is an edifying extract: "I pension half the Parliament to keep it quiet; but as the king's money is not sufficient, they to whom I give none clamor loudly for a war. It would be expedient for your Eminence to remit me three millions of French livres in order to silence the barkers. Gold is a metal which here corrects all ill qualities in the blood. A pension of two thousand pounds a year will make the most impetuous warrior in Parliament as tame as a lamb."† There is also a letter extant, in which Louis XIV. authorizes his minister to offer the Duke of Marlborough four millions of francs for a peace on certain conditions. With regard to the peace of 1763, against which Lord Chatham so eloquently protested, it is known to have been accomplished by the most lavish expenditure of money and promotion. "The Royal household had been increased beyond all former example. The lords and grooms of the bedchamber were doubled. Pensions were thrown about indiscriminately. Five-and-twenty thousand pounds were issued in one day, in bank-notes of one hundred pounds each. The only stipulation was, *Give us your vote!* .... The city of London refused to address (in favor of peace), although the sum of fourteen thousand pounds was offered to complete the bridge. .... The Lord-Lieutenants had begging-letters sent to them to use their influence; and five hundred pounds, secret service, were added to each letter. The sum of five hundred pounds

* Anecdotes and Speeches of Lord Chatham, Dublin, 1792, Vol. I. 137.
† Memoirs of Pompadour, Vol. I. 57.

was the notorious price of an address. Some addresses cost a much larger sum. The sum was regulated according to the importance and magnitude of the place from which the address was obtained." * We also read, in the memoirs of that time, of men holding offices of which they only drew half the salary, "being *rode* for the other half"; and these individuals, both the riders and the ridden, were not city-clerks and contractors, but men of rank and influence.

But these things occurred a long time ago, — one hundred and six years, — when all the world, except Prussia, was corrupt; and Prussia is an empire to-day because she was not corrupt then. Since that time England has nobly grappled with many a hoary abuse, has made important advances toward free trade and purity of government, and is still pressing onward. And yet we read astounding things of the venality of the present generation of her ruling class. The history of railroads in Great Britain appears to be little more than a history of giant frauds, from the day of honest George Stevenson to that of collapsed Morton Peto. The English biographer of the Stevensons tells us of a great duke who caused the defeat of a railroad bill in Parliament. because the engineer had laid out the line too near one of his Grace's fox covers; of a "party" in a committee of lords offering to withdraw opposition to a projected road for ten thousand pounds; of opposition "got up mainly for the purpose of being bought off"; of railway directors boasting of the number of votes they could "command" in the House of Commons; of parliamentary log-rolling in the "Yankee" style of "You help me roll my log, and I'll help you roll yours"; of a railway bill which it cost the directors eighty-two thousand pounds to get passed; of another, the total cost of passing which was four hundred and thirty-six thousand, two hundred and twenty-three pounds, about *three million dollars* of our present currency; of needy members "conciliated" by being paid five thousand pounds for a strip of land worth five hundred; of members who "systematically sold their parliamentary interest for money considerations"; of an "impoverished nobleman" receiving thirty thousand pounds for a narrow strip of his estate, the whole of which was not worth more than that

* Anecdotes and Speeches of Lord Chatham, Vol. I. 268, 282.

sum, and then selling another corner to another company for a second thirty thousand pounds, thus getting sixty thousand pounds "damages" for what greatly increased the value of his property. "Of course," remarks Mr. J. C. Jeafferson, "it was well understood that the two sums of thirty thousand pounds did not represent the price of the land, but the price of the peer's parliamentary interest."

It seems, too, that many of the petty infamies incident to the infancy of popular government — infamies which we are about to abolish — are in full activity in England. English politicians have not yet discovered the puerility of bribing obscure and utterly uninfluential newspapers by lavish advertising. Advertisements for navy rum were inserted by the last Tory administration in a little weekly paper, circulating a few hundred copies among clergymen of conservative politics. Comic papers of the same politics were subscribed for in considerable numbers for distribution in government asylums. Advertisements were paid for at rates three or four times higher than the regular price. At the time of the last general election, as we learn from the Pall Mall Gazette, "an advertising-agent was instructed by a government department to send advertisements to a certain provincial journal. This journal was so excellent a medium for the purpose that the agent, whose business it is to know these things, was quite unaware of its existence. He had to make inquiries as to whether there was such a newspaper or not. His investigations were successful. It turned out that the influential and widely circulated print had been started a few weeks previously to serve the interest of the Tory candidate for the borough in which it was published. Accordingly, the government advertisements were sent for the support of the paper; and there we have seen them, column after column, week after week."

The same journal informs mankind that this extremely primitive, provincial, and generally useless form of bribery is "rampant" in England, as well as that of giving exclusive news for fulsome laudation. "In short," adds this able newspaper, "it comes to this: it is the custom of ministers in England, as well as in foreign parts, to subsidize the press for their own benefit." But how stupidly they do it! During the recent general election in England, there was a certain "industrious literary compiler," named Townsend, who wrote on the D'Israeli side with great diligence and small effect. He was promised by Mr. D'Israeli, not a petty office in the custom-house for four years, but a post in the mint for life, worth a thousand pounds a year; or, if that should not fall vacant, he was to have the still more lucrative place in the inland revenue held by a brother of the Premier, whose death was daily expected. But before the vacancy occurred, Mr. D'Israeli had lost the power to confer such munificent rewards for services so trifling, and the new ministry, upon the death of Mr. James D'Israeli, had the virtue to abolish the sinecure he had held so long. The disappointment was too much for the unhappy writer, who stabbed himself to the heart; an occurrence which led to the disclosure of the facts. All this is very much in what Englishmen flatter themselves is the American style: only, more so.*

Indeed, they have in England most of the small sins of popular government as well as all of the great ones. I read in the London papers, at the close of a session, that the House of Commons, like the House of Representatives, is idle during the first half of a session; which obliges it to hurry bills through with such velocity at last, that members can hardly catch their titles, but merely ascertain whether an act is favored or opposed by the ministry, and vote accordingly. It appears, also, that ministers cram the public offices with superfluous clerks, and that absurd and fraudulent charges are covered by that convenient word, "contingencies." Dr. Russell was in the Crimea lately, and wrote home to the Times, that "the French and Russian dead have been reverently gathered together, but the English cemetery on Cathcart's Hill is in a shameful

* Here is another anecdote of the last general election in England: "Some time ago a well-educated young Welshman came into possession of a farm left him by his father, and, being a Liberal in politics, he voted at the last election for the Liberal candidate. He was in the habit of churning his butter by water-power, which he obtained from a brook which ran through the land of his neighbor, a powerful conservative landed proprietor, and member of Parliament. To punish the young farmer's audacity in voting according to his principles, the Tory magnate ordered the course of the water to be diverted, so that it might not be used any longer to churn the Radical farmer's butter. This was actually done. The farmer found one day the water turned from his house, and now he has to churn his butter by hand."

state, notwithstanding the thirteen thousand pounds paid by the government for its proper maintenance. The Russian government has done more than could be expected of it, but all the monuments in the cemetery are being chipped to pieces, and no attempt has been made to gather the remains of our fallen soldiers in one spot." There is, also, in England, a "pardon lobby," which can sometimes get a man of rank released from prison before his term has expired; as in the United States a forger of wealthy family can occasionally (though very rarely) procure a similar favor.

Mr. Froude's recent utterance with regard to the prevalence of fraud in England would surely be an exaggeration if applied to the United States. It could not be truly said of the business of America that it is "saturated with fraud." "So deep has it gone," added the historian, "that a strictly honest tradesman can hardly hold his ground against competition. You can no longer trust that any article that you buy is the thing which it pretends to be. We have false weights, false measures, cheating, and shoddy everywhere. Yet the clergy have seen all this grow up in absolute indifference; and the great question which at this moment is agitating the Church of England is the color of the ecclesiastical petticoats." This is not true of the United States, where, as a rule, men of business comprehend well, and act upon their belief, that the sole possible basis of a business permanently great is to give a good dollar's worth for a dollar. Probably Mr. Froude, like Mr. Carlyle, lives very much among his books, and does not possess personal knowledge of anything which cannot be learned in a library. As to the clergy, their existence as a privileged order is in peril; they are engaged in Mr. Darwin's "struggle for life." Clergymen of ability, who have several strings to their bow, do not meddle with the petticoat question.

There is a poem by Mrs. Browning, written before we had emancipated ourselves from slavery, in which she told us that the penalty we paid for consenting to remain under that shameful yoke was that we forfeited the right to glow with indignation, and hurl the sharp rebuke, at atrocious deeds done anywhere on earth. In the presence of our own giant iniquity, we must remain silent when we heard of distant outrage. But the principle to which she gave expression in this fine poem is, perhaps, of universal application. No nation is so pure that it can with propriety point the finger of reproach at another; because, if the sins of one are different from those of the other, it does not follow that they are less. I do firmly believe that the people of the United States are the most honest people in the world; but I do not know that we should be such if it were as hard to live in the United States as it is in the densely peopled and entirely appropriated countries of the Old World. There was no stealing in the California mining-region when every man was making his pile. Considering how much our virtues and our vices are produced by circumstances, it is as ridiculous to boast as it is vulgar to taunt.

Why then parade those examples of the weakness and corruption of other governments? For several reasons. It is comforting to have companions in misfortune, and it is reassuring to know that governments that were once wholly corrupt are now but partially so. The court of Louis XIV. and their servants numbered three thousand persons, and the king carried on his war by the sale of places. There were lieutenant-colonels then in the French army ten years of age, and archbishops under twenty-one. It is not so bad as that in France now; and in England several entire species of corrupt practice have been extirpated. The tendency of governments to become corrupt is powerful and constant, and they can be kept endurably honest only by eternal vigilance. Besides, a year or two since, when the North American Review exposed the government of New York, the English Tories seized the articles with avidity, and caused them to be republished in England, and circulated as "campaign documents." All the Tory organs commented upon them, and drew inferences unfavorable to government by the people for the people; omitting to mention that the corrupt governments of our three largest seaports are sustained by voters whom the Tory system of Europe had kept in brutal ignorance. If New York aldermen steal, it is because Great Britain has been governed by a class. Send us intelligent, educated emigrants, ye supercilious Tories! Send us men trained in the duties of citizenship, and we will soon expel the thieves from city-hall and lobby. We shall do it, as it is; but not as soon as we should like.

After all, we are but serving an apprenticeship in the art of government by the whole people. We have done very well hitherto. Evils have arisen, but they have been grappled with and suppressed. Evils exist, but there is no reason to think that the recuperative energy of the system is near exhaustion. It is only people who do not know much about the period of Washington and John Adams, who think the government was better then than it is now. It is better now, upon the whole, than it was then; and *much* better, considering how difficult a task governments now have. In its worst estate, it was better than the best despotism. Congress, I am sure, will repent of its small sins; and by and by it will so reorganize the public service that the temptation to commit many of them will be removed.

INTERNATIONAL COPYRIGHT.

THERE is an American lady living at Hartford, in Connecticut, whom the United States has permitted to be robbed by foreigners of $ 200,000. Her name is Harriet Beecher Stowe. By no disloyal act has she or her family forfeited their right to the protection of the government of the United States. She pays her taxes, keeps the peace, and earns her livelihood by honest industry; she has reared children for the service of the Commonwealth; she was warm and active for her country when many around her were cold or hostile; — in a word, she is a good citizen.

More than that: she is an illustrious citizen. The United States stands higher to-day in the regard of every civilized being in Christendom because she lives in the United States. She is the only woman yet produced on the continent of America to whom the world assigns equal rank in literature with the great authoresses of Europe. If, in addition to the admirable talents with which she is endowed, she had chanced to possess one more, namely, the excellent gift of plodding, she had been a consummate artist, and had produced immortal works. All else she has, — the seeing eye, the discriminating intelligence, the sympathetic mind, the fluent word, the sure and happy touch; and these gifts enabled her to render her country the precise service which it needed most. Others talked about slavery: she made us *see* it. She showed it to us in its fairest and in its foulest aspect; she revealed its average and ordinary working. There never was a fairer nor a kinder book than "Uncle Tom's Cabin"; for the entire odium of the revelation fell upon the Thing, not upon the unhappy mortals who were born and reared under its shadow. The reader felt that Legree was not less, but far more, the victim of slavery than Uncle Tom, and the effect of the book was to concentrate wrath upon the system which tortured the slave's body and damned the master's soul. Wonderful magic of genius! The hovels and cotton-fields which this authoress scarcely saw she made all the world see, and see more vividly and more truly than the busy world can ever see remote objects with its own unassisted eyes. We are very dull and stupid in what does not immediately concern us, until we are roused and enlightened by such as she. Those whom we call "the intelligent," or "the educated," are merely the one in ten of the human family who by some chance learned to read, and thus came under the influence of the class whom Mrs. Stowe represents.

It is not possible to state the amount of good which this book has done, is doing, and is to do. Mr. Eugene Schuyler, in the preface to the Russian novel which he has recently done the public the service to translate, informs us that the publication of a little book in Russia contributed powerfully to the emancipation of the Russian serfs. The book was merely a collection of sketches, entitled "The Memoirs of a Sportsman"; but it revealed serfdom to the men who had lived in the midst of it all their lives without ever seeing it. Nothing is ever *seen* in this world, till the searching eye of a sympathetic genius falls upon it. This Russian nobleman, Turgenef, noble in every sense, saw serfdom, and showed it to his countrymen. His volume was read by the present Emperor, and *he* saw serfdom; and he has since declared that the reading of that little book was "one of the first incitements to the decree which gave freedom to thirty millions of serfs." All the reading public of Russia read it, and *they* saw serfdom; and thus a public opinion was created, without the support of which not even the absolute Czar of all the Russias would have dared to issue a decree so sweeping and radical.

We cannot say as much for "Uncle Tom's Cabin," because the public opinion of the United States which permitted the emancipation of the slaves was of longer growth, and was the result of a thousand influences. But when we consider that the United States only just escaped dismemberment and dissolution in the late war, and that two great powers of Europe were only prevented from active interference on behalf of the Rebellion by that public opinion which "Uncle Tom's Cabin" had recently revived and intensified, we may at least believe, that, if the whole influence of that work could have been annihilated, the final triumph of the United States might have been deferred, and come only after a series of wars. That book, we may almost say, went into every household in the civilized world which contained one person capable of reading it. And it was not an essay; it was a vivid exhibition; — it was not read from a sense of duty, nor from a desire to get knowledge; it was read with passion; it was devoured; people sat up all night reading it; those who could read read it to those who could not; and hundreds of thousands who would never have read it saw it played upon the stage. Who shall presume to say how many soldiers that book added to the Union army? Who shall estimate its influence in hastening emancipation in Brazil, and in preparing the amiable Cubans for a similar measure? Both in Cuba and Brazil the work has been read with the most passionate interest.

If it is impossible to measure the political effect of this work, we may at least assert that it gave a thrilling pleasure to ten millions of human beings, — an innocent pleasure, too, and one of many hours' duration. We may also say, that, while enjoying that long delight, each of those ten millions was made to see, with more or less clearness, the great truth that man is not fit to be trusted with arbitrary power over his fellow. The person who afforded this great pleasure, and who brought home this fundamental truth to so many minds, was Harriet Beecher Stowe, of Hartford, in the State of Connecticut, where she keeps house, educates her children, has a book at the grocery, and invites her friends to tea. To that American woman every person on earth who read "Uncle Tom's Cabin" incurred a personal obligation. Every individual who became possessed of a copy of the book, and every one who saw the story played in a theatre, was bound, in natural justice, to pay money to her for service rendered, unless she expressly and formally relinquished her right, — which she has never done. What can be clearer than this? Mrs. Stowe, in the exercise of her vocation, the vocation by which she lives, performs a professional service to ten millions of people. The service is great and lasting. The work done is satisfactory to the customer. What can annul the obligation resting upon each to render his portion of an equivalent, except the consent of the authoress "first had and obtained"? If Mrs. Stowe, instead of creating for our delight and instruction a glorious work of fiction, had contracted her fine powers to the point of inventing a nutcracker or a match-safe, a rolling-pin or a needle-threader, every individual purchaser could have been compelled to pay money for the use of her ingenuity, and everybody would have thought it the most natural and proper thing in the world so to do. There are fifty American inventions now in use in Europe from which the inventors derive revenue. *Revenue!* — not a sum of money which, once spent, is gone forever, but that most solid and respectable of material blessings, a sum per annum! Thus we reward those who light our matches. It is otherwise that we compensate those who kindle our souls.

"Uncle Tom's Cabin," like every other novelty in literature, was the late-maturing fruit of generations. Two centuries of wrong had to pass, before the Subject was complete for the Artist's hand, and the Artist herself was a flower of an ancient and gifted family. The Autobiography of Lyman Beecher has made known this remarkable family to the public. We can all see for ourselves how slowly and painfully this beautiful genius was nourished, — what a narrow escape it had from being crushed and extinguished amid the horrors of theology and the poverty of a Connecticut parsonage, — how it was saved, and even nurtured, by that extraordinary old father, that most strange and interesting character of New England, who could come home, after preaching a sermon that appalled the galleries, and play the fiddle and riot with his children till bedtime. A piano found its way into the house, and the old man, whose geniality was of such abounding force that forty years of theology could not lessen it, let his children read Ivanhoe and the other novels of Sir Walter Scott. Partly by chance, partly by stealth, chiefly by the force of her own cravings, this daughter of the Puritans obtained the scanty nutriment which kept her genius from starving. By and by, on the banks of the Ohio, within sight of a slave State, the Subject and the Artist met, and there, from the lips of sore and panting fugitives, she gained, in the course of years, the knowledge which she revealed to mankind in "Uncle Tom's Cabin."

When she had done the work, the United States stood by and saw her deprived of three fourths of her just and legitimate wages, without stirring a finger for her protection. The book sold to the extent of two millions of copies, and the story was played in most of the theatres in which the English language is spoken, and in many French and German theatres. In one theatre in New York it was played eight times a week for twelve months. Considerable fortunes have been gained by its performance, and it is still a source of revenue to actors and managers. We believe that there are at least three persons in the United States, connected with theatres, who have gained more money from "Uncle Tom's Cabin" than Mrs. Stowe. Of all the immense sums which the exhibition of this story upon the stage has produced, the authoress has received nothing. When Dumas or Victor Hugo publishes a novel, the sale of the right to perform it as a play yields him from eighty thousand to one hundred and twenty thousand francs. These authors receive a share of the receipts of the theatre, — the only fair arrangement, — and this share, we believe, is usually one tenth; which is also the usual percentage paid to authors upon the sale of their books. If a French author had written "Uncle Tom's Cabin," he would have enjoyed, — 1. A part of the price of every copy sold in France; 2. A share of the receipts of every theatre in France in which he permitted it to be played; 3. A sum of money for the right of translation into English; 4. A sum of money for the right of translation into German. We believe we are far within the truth when we say, that a literary success achieved by a French author equal to that of "Uncle Tom's Cabin" would have yielded that author half a million dollars in gold; and that, too, in spite of the lamentable fact, that America would have stolen the product of his genius, instead of buying it.

Mrs. Stowe received for "Uncle Tom's Cabin" the usual percentage upon the sale of the American edition; which may have consisted of three hundred thousand copies. This percentage, with some other trifling sums, may have amounted to forty thousand dollars. From the theatre she has received nothing; from foreign countries nothing, or next to nothing. This poor forty thousand dollars — about enough to build a comfortable house in the country, and lay out an acre or two of grounds — was the product of the supreme literary success of all times! A corresponding success in sugar, in stocks, in tobacco, in cotton, in invention, in real estate, would have yielded millions upon millions to the lucky operator. To say that Mrs. Stowe, through our cruel and shameful indifference with regard to the rights of authors, native and foreign, has been kept out of two hundred thousand dollars, honestly hers, is a most moderate and safe statement. This money was due to her as entirely as the sum named upon a bill of exchange is due to the rightful owner of the same. It was for "value received." A permanently attractive book, moreover, would naturally be more than a sum of money; it would be an estate; it would be an income. This wrong, therefore, continues to the present moment, and will go on longer than the life of the authoress. While we are writing this sentence, probably, some German, French, Spanish, Italian, Russian, or English bookseller is dropping into his "till" the price of a copy of "Uncle Tom's Cabin," the whole of which he will keep, instead of sending ten per cent of it to Hartford on the 1st of January next.

We have had another literary success in these years, — Mr. Motley's Histories of the Dutch Republic and of the United Netherlands. As there are fifteen persons in the world who can enjoy fiction to one that will read much of any other kind of literary production, the writers of fiction usually receive some compensation for their labors. Not a fair nor an adequate compensation, but *some*. This compensation will never be fair nor adequate until every man or woman in the whole world who buys a copy of a novel, or sees it played, shall, in so doing, contribute a certain stipulated sum to the author. Nevertheless, the writers of fiction do get a little money, and a few of them are able to live almost as well as a retired grocer. Now and then we hear of an author who gets almost as much money for a novel that enthralls and enchants two or three nations for many months, as a beardless operator in stocks sometimes wins between one and two P. M. It is not so with the heroes of research, like Motley, Buckle, Bancroft, and Carlyle. Upon this point we are ready to make a sweeping assertion, and it is this. No well-executed work, involving original research, can pay expenses, unless the author is protected in his right to the market of the world. This is one of the points to which we particularly wish to call attention. Give us international copyright, and it immediately becomes possible in the United States for a man who is not rich to devote his existence to the production of works of permanent and universal value. Continue to withhold international copyright, and this privilege remains the almost exclusive portion of men of wealth. For, in the United States, there is scarcely any such thing as honest leisure in connection with business or a salaried office.

Now, with regard to Mr. Motley, whose five massive volumes of Dutch History are addressed to the educated class of all nations, — before that author could write the first sentence of his work he must have been familiar with six languages, English, Latin, Dutch, French, German, and Spanish, besides possessing that general knowledge of history, literature, and science which constitutes what is called culture. He must also have spent five laborious years in gaining an intimate knowledge of his subject, in the course of which he must have travelled in more than one country, and expended large sums in the purchase of books and documents, and for copies of manuscripts. Living in the cheap capitals of Continental Europe, and managing his affairs with economy, he may have accomplished his preparatory studies at an expenditure of ten thousand dollars, — two thousand dollars a year. The volumes contain in all about three thousand five hundred large pages. At two pages a day, which would be very rapid work, and probably twice as fast as he did work, he could have executed the five volumes, and got them through the press (a year's hard labor in itself), in seven years. Here are twelve years' labor, and twenty-four thousand dollars' necessary expenditure. Mr. Motley probably expended more than twelve years, and twice twenty-four thousand dollars; but we choose to estimate the work at its necessary cost. Two other items must be also considered: 1. The talents of the author, which, employed in another profession, would have brought large returns in money and honor; 2. The intense and exhausting nature of the labor. The production of a work which demands strict fidelity to truth, as well as excellence in composition, — which obliges the author, first, to know all, and, after that, to impart the essence of his knowledge in an agreeable and striking manner, — is the hardest continuous work ever done by man. It is at times a fierce and passionate joy; it is at times a harrowing anxiety; it is at times a vast despair; but it is always very hard labor. The search after a fact is sometimes as arduous as the chase after a deer, and it may last six weeks, and, after all, there may be no such fact, or it may be valueless. And when all is done, — when the mountain of manuscript lies before the author ready for the press, — he cannot for the life of him tell whether his work is trash or treasure. As poor Charlotte Brontë said, when she had finished Jane Eyre, "I only know that the story has interested *me*." Finally comes the anguish of having the work judged by persons whose only knowledge of the subject is derived from the work itself.

No matter for all that: we are speaking of money. This work, we repeat, cost the author twenty-four thousand dollars to produce. Messrs. Harper sell it at fifteen dollars a copy. The usual allowance to the author is ten per cent of the retail price, and, as a rule, it ought not to be more. Upon works of that magnitude, however, it often is more. Suppose, then, that Mr. Motley receives two dollars for every copy of his work sold by his American publishers. A meritorious work of general interest, i. e. a book not addressed to any class, sect, or profession, that costs fifteen dollars, is considered successful in the United States if it sells three thousand copies. Five thousand is decided success. Seven thousand is brilliant success. Ten thousand copies, sold in the lifetime of the author, is all the success that can be hoped for. Ten thousand copies would yield to the author twenty thousand dollars, which is four thousand dollars less than it cost him.

But Mr. Motley's work is of universal interest. It does

not concern the people of the United States any more than it does the people of England, France, and Germany, nor as much as it does the people of Spain and Holland. Wherever, in the whole world, there is an intelligent, educated human being, there is a person who would like to read and possess Motley's Histories, which relate events of undying interest to all the few in every land who are capable of comprehending their significance. Give this author the market of the world, and he is compensated for his labor. Deny him this right, and it is impossible he should be. England buys a greater number of fifteen-dollar books than the United States, because, in England, rich men are generally educated men, and in the United States the class who most want such books cannot buy them. Our clergy are poor; our students are generally poor; our lawyers and doctors are not rich, as a class; our professors and schoolmasters are generally very poor; our men of business, as a class, read little but the daily paper; and our men of leisure are too few to be of any account. Nor have we yet that universal system of town and village self-sustaining libraries, which will, by and by, abundantly atone for the ignorance and indifference of the rich, and make the best market for books the world has ever seen. England would readily "take" ten thousand copies of a three-guinea book of first-rate merit and universal interest. A French translation of the same would sell five thousand in France, and, probably three thousand more in other Continental countries. A German translation would place it within the reach of nations of readers, and a few hundreds in each of those nations would become possessors of the work. Or, in other words, an International Copyright would multiply the gains of an author like Mr. Motley by three, possibly by four. $20,000 \times 3 = 60,000$.

We are far from thinking that sixty thousand dollars would be a compensation for such work as Mr. Motley has done. We merely say, that the reasonable prospect of even such a partial recompense as that would make it possible for persons not rich to produce in the United States works of universal and permanent value. The question is, Are we prepared to say that such works shall be attempted here only by rich men, or by men like Noah Webster, who lived upon a Spelling-Book while he wrote his Dictionary? Generally, the acquisition of an independent income is the work of a lifetime, and it ought to be. But the production of a masterpiece, involving original research, is also the work of a lifetime. Not one man in a thousand millions can do both. Give us International Copyright, and there are already five publishers in the United States who are able and willing to give an author the equivalent of Gibbon's sixteen hundred pounds a year, or of Noah Webster's Spelling-Book, or Prescott's thousand dollars a month; i. e. maintenance while he is doing that part of his work which requires exclusive devotion to it. Besides, a man intent upon the execution of a great work can contrive, in many ways, to exist — just exist — for ten years, provided he has a reasonable prospect of moderate reward when his task is done. There are fifty men in New England alone who would deem it an honor and a privilege "to invest" in such an enterprise.

Mr. Bancroft's is another case in point. Mr. Buckle remarks, that there is no knowledge until there is a class who have conquered leisure, and that, although most of this class will always employ their leisure in the pursuit of pleasure, yet a few will devote it to the acquisition of knowledge. These few are the flower of their species, — its ornaments and benefactors, — for the flower issues in most precious fruit, which finally nourishes and exalts the whole. We are such idle and pleasure-loving creatures, and civilization places so many alluring delights within the reach of a rich man, that it must ever be accounted a merit in one of this class if he devotes himself to generous toil for the public good. George Bancroft has spent thirty years in such toil. His History of the United States has stood to him in the place of a profession. His house is filled with the most costly material, the spoils of foreign archives and of domestic chests, the pick of auction sales, the hidden treasure of ancient bookstores, and the chance discoveries of dusty garrets. His work has been eminently "successful," and he has received for it about as much as his material cost, and perhaps half a dollar a day for his labor. When the third volume of the work was about to appear, a London publisher offered three hundred pounds for the advance sheets, which were furnished, and the money was paid. The same sum was offered and paid for the advance sheets of the fourth volume. Then the London publisher discovered that "the courtesy of the trade" would suffice for his purpose, and he forbore to pay for that which he could get for nothing. Six hundred pounds, therefore, is all that this American author has received from foreign countries for thirty years' labor. His work has been translated into two or three foreign languages, and it is found in all European libraries of any completeness, whether public or private; but this little sum is all that has come back to *him.* Surely, there cannot be one reader of this volume so insensible to moral distinctions as not to feel that this is wrong. The happy accident of Mr. Bancroft's not needing the money has nothing to do with the right and wrong of the matter. No man is so rich that he does not like to receive money which he has honestly earned; for money honestly earned is honor as well as reward, and it is not for *us,* the benefited party, to withhold his right from a man because he has been generous to us. And the question again occurs, Shall we sit down content with an arrangement which obliges us to wait for works of permanent and universal interest until the accident occurs of a rich man willing and able to execute them? It is not an accident, but a most rare conjunction of accidents. First, the man must be competent; secondly, he must be willing; thirdly, he must be rich. This fortunate combination is so little likely to occur in a new country, that it must be accounted honorable to the United States that in the same generation we have had three such men, — Bancroft, Motley, and Prescott. Is it *such* persons that should be singled out from the mass of their fellow-citizens to be deprived of their honest gains? Besides, riches take to themselves wings. A case has occurred among us of a rich man devoting the flower of his days to the production of excellent works, and then losing his property.

It will be of no avail to adduce the instance of Dr. J. W. Draper. We have had the pleasure of hearing Dr. Draper relate the history of his average day. Up at six. Breakfast at seven. An hour's ride to the city. Busy at the New York University from nine to one. Home in cars to dinner at three. At four P. M. *begins* his day's literary work, and keeps steadily on till eleven. Then, bed. Not one man in many millions could endure such a life, and no man, perhaps, ought to endure it. Dr. Draper happens to possess a most sound and easy-working constitution of body and mind, and he has acquired a knowledge of the laws which relate to its well-being. But, even in his case, it is questionable whether it is well, or even right, to devote so large a part of his existence to labor. It is probable, too, that an International Copyright would, ere this, have released him from the necessity of it, or the temptation to it.

Few of us are aware of the extent to which American works are now reprinted in England. We noticed, the other day, in an English publication, a page of advertisements containing the titles of thirteen volumes announced to be sold at "1*s.*" or "1*s.* 6*d.*" Twelve of the thirteen were American. Among them, we remember, were Mrs. Stowe's "Little Foxes," Dr. Holmes's "Humorous Poems," and Mr. Lowell's "Biglow Papers." The cheap publication stores of Great Britain are heaped with such reprints, the sale of which yields nothing to the authors. We have even seen in England a series of school writing-books, the invention of a Philadelphia writing-master, the English copies of which betrayed no trace of their origin. Nor have we been able, after much inquiry, to hear of one instance in which an English publisher has paid an American author, resident in America, for anything except advance sheets. Mr. Longfellow, whose works are as popular in England as in America, and as salable, has derived, we believe, considerable sums for advance sheets of his works; but, unless we are grossly misinformed, even he receives no percentage upon the annual sale of his works in Great Britain.

And the aggravating circumstance of all this spoliation of the men and women who are the country's ornament and boast is, that it is wholly our fault. We force the European publishers to steal. England is more than willing, France is more than willing, Germany is quite willing, Sweden, Denmark, and Russia are willing, to come at once into an international arrangement which shall render literary property as sacred and as safe in all civilized lands as tobacco and whiskey. All the countries we have named are now obliged to steal it, and do steal it. Who would have expected to find the Essays of Mr. Emerson a topic in the interior of Russia? We find them, however, familiarly alluded to in the Russian novel "Fathers and Sons," recently translated. If authors had their rights, a rill of Russian silver would come trickling into Concord, while a broad and brimming river of it would inundate a certain cottage in Hartford. How many modest and straitened American homes would have new parlor carpets this year, if henceforth, on the first days of January and July, drafts to their address were to be dropped in the mail in every capital of the world which the work done in those homes instructs or cheers! Nor would new carpets be all. Many authors would be instantly delivered from the fatal necessity of over-production, — the vice that threatens literature with annihilation.

There is another aggravating circumstance, — most aggravating. The want of an International Copyright chiefly robs our best and brightest! A dull book protects itself; no foreigner wants it. An honest drudge, who compiles timely works of utility, or works which appease a transient curiosity, and which thousands of "agents" put under the nose of the whole population, can make a fortune by one or two lucky hits. There are respectable gentlemen not far off, who, with pen and scissors, in four months, manufactured pieces of merchandise, labelled "Life of Abraham Lincoln," of which a hundred thousand copies each were sold in half a year, and which yielded the manufacturer fifteen thousand dollars. This sum is probably more than the sum total of Mr. Emerson's receipts from his published works, — the fruit of forty years of study and meditation. It is chiefly our dear Immortals and our best Ephemerals who need this protection from their country's justice. It is our Emersons, our Hawthornes, our Longfellows, our Lowells, our Holmeses, our Bryants, our Curtises, our Beechers, our Mrs. Stowes, our Motleys, our Bancrofts, our Prescotts, whom we permit all the world to plunder. We harmless drudges and book-makers are protected by our own dulness. We are panoplied in our insignificance. The stupidest set of school-books we ever looked into has yielded, for many years, an annual profit of one hundred thousand dollars, and is now enriching its third set of proprietors. No one, therefore, need feel any concern for *us*. But, O honorable members, spare the few who redeem and exalt the country's name, and who keep alive the all but extinguished celestial fire! If American property abroad must be robbed, let cotton and tobacco take a turn, and see how *they* like it. Invite Manchester to come to the Liverpool Docks and help itself. Let there be free smoking in Europe. Summon the merchants of London to a scramble for American bills of exchange. Select for spoliation anything but the country's literature.

The worst remains to be told. It is bad to have your pocket picked; but there is something infinitely worse, — it is to pick a pocket. Who would not rather be stolen from, than steal? Who would not rather be murdered, than be a murderer? Nevertheless, in depriving foreign authors of their rights, it is still ourselves whom we injure most. The great damage to America, and to American literature, from the want of an international copyright law, is not the thousands of dollars per annum which authors lose. This is, in fact, the smallest item that enters into the huge sum total of our loss.

It maims or kills seven tenths of the contemporary literature that must be translated before it is available for publication here. Charles Reade, in that gallant and brilliant little book of his, "The Eighth Commandment," quotes from a letter written in Cologne, in 1851, the following passage: —

"About thirty years ago the first translations from English were brought to the German market. The Waverley Novels were extensively circulated, and read with avidity by all classes. Next came Bulwer, and after him Dickens and other writers. Rival editions of the same works sprang up by the half-dozen; the profits decreased, and the publishers were obliged to cut down the pay of the translators. I know that a translation-monger at Grimm pays about £6 for a three-volume novel.

"These works, got up in a hurry, and printed with bad type on wretched paper, are completely flooding the market; and, as they are much cheaper than original works, they are a serious obstacle to our national literature. Thus much for our share in the miseries of free trade * in translations.

"Now for yours. There are able men in Germany, who, were it made worth their while, could and would put the master works of your novelists and historians into a decent German garb. But under the present system these men are elbowed out of the field."

Change a few names in this passage, and it describes, with considerable exactness, the state of the translation market in the United States. Works, which in France charm the *boudoir* and amuse the whole of the educated class, sink, under the handling of hasty translators and enterprising publishers, into what we call "Yellow-Covered Literature," which is to be found chiefly upon the wharves. Respectable publishers have a well-founded terror of French and German translations; since, after incurring the expense of translation, they have no protection against the publication of another version except "the courtesy of the trade," — a code of laws which has not much force in the regions from which the literature of the Yellow Cover emanates. We are not getting half the good we ought from the contemporary literature of France, Germany, Sweden, Russia, Holland, Italy, and we never shall, until American publishers can acquire property in it by fair purchase, which the law will protect. The business of furnishing the American public with good translations from the French would of itself maintain two or three great publishing houses. There is a mine of wealth there waiting for the removal of the squatters and the recognition of the rightful title-deeds. What would California have been worth to us, or to itself, or to anybody, if its treasures had been *left* to the hurried scratchings over the surface of uncapitalled prospecters? Capital and skill wait until the title is clear. Then they go in, with their ponderous engines, and pound the rocks till the gold glitters all over the heap.

Messrs. Appleton, of New York, have recently ventured to publish good translations and good editions of Madame Mühlbach's historical novels. The name of this lady being

* Upon this expression Mr. Reade justly remarks: "This is a foolish and inapplicable phrase. Free trade is free buying and selling, not free stealing."

new to America, the enterprise was a risk, — a risk of many thousand dollars, — a risk which only a wealthy house would be justified in assuming. The *great* expense of such an undertaking is incurred in making the new name known, in advertising it, in shouting it into the ears of a public deafened with a thousand outcries. An enormous sum of money may easily be spent in this way, when advertising costs from twenty cents to two dollars a line. Suppose the efforts of the publishers are successful, see how beautifully the present system works! The more successful they are, the more perilous their property becomes! It is safe only as long as it is worthless. Just as soon as they have, by the expenditure of unknown thousands, created for the works of this German lady a steady demand, which promises to recompense them, they are open to the inroads of the Knights of the Yellow Cover! See, too, the effects upon the Berlin authoress. Playing such a dangerous and costly game as this, the American publisher dare not, cannot treat with her in the only proper and honorable way, — open a fair bargain, so much for so much. Messrs. Appleton did themselves the honor, the other day, to send her a thousand dollars, gold, which was an act as wise as it was right. We enjoyed an exquisite pleasure in looking upon the lovely document, duly stamped and authenticated, which has ere this given her a claim upon a Berlin banker; and we have also a prodigious happiness in committing the impropriety of making the fact public. Nevertheless, it is not thus that authors should be paid for their own. All we can say of it is, that it is better than nothing to her, and the best a publisher can do under the circumstances.

This business of publishing books is the most difficult one carried on in the world. It demands qualities so seldom found in the same individual, that there has scarcely ever been an eminent and stable publishing house which did not consist of several active and able men. Failure is the rule, success the rare exception. The shores of the business world are strewn thick with the wrecks of ventures in this line that gave every promise of bringing back a large return. It has been proved a task beyond the wisdom of mortals, to decide with any positive degree of certainty whether a heap of blotted manuscript is the most precious or the most worthless of all the productions of human industry. Young publishers think they can tell; old publishers know they cannot. This is so true, that for a publisher to have a knowledge of the commodity in which he deals is generally a point against his success as a publisher; and it will certainly ruin him, unless he has a remarkably sound judgment, or a good, solid, unlearned partner, whose intuitive sense of what the public wants is unbiased by tastes of his own.

It is this terrible uncertainty as to the value of the commodity purchased, which renders publishing a business so difficult, precarious, and unprofitable; and the higher the character of the literature, the greater the difficulty becomes. Publishers who confine themselves chiefly to works of utility and necessity, or to works professional and sectarian, have an easy task to perform compared with that of a publisher who aims to supply the public with pure science and high literature. If any business can claim favorable consideration from those who have in charge the distribution of the public burdens, surely it is this. If in any way its perils can be justly diminished by law, surely that protection ought not to be withheld. We believe it could be shown that the business of publishing what the trade calls "miscellaneous books," i. e. books which depend solely upon their intrinsic interest or merit, yields a smaller return for the capital and talent invested in it than any other. The Harpers have a grand establishment, — one of the wonders of America. Any one going over that assemblage of enormous edifices, and observing the multitude of men and women employed in them, the vast and far-reaching enterprises going forward, — some of which involve a large expenditure for years before any return is possible, — the great numbers of men of ability, learning, and experience who are superintending the various departments, and the amazing quantities of merchandise produced, the mere catalogue of which is a large volume, — any one, we say, observing these things, would naturally conclude, that the proprietors must be in the receipt of Vanderbiltian incomes. The same amount of capital, force, experience, and talent employed in any other branch of business could not fail to put the incomes of the proprietors high up among those which require six figures for their expression. Compare the returns of these monarchs of the "trade" with those of our dry-goods magnates, and our mighty men in cotton, tobacco, and railroads. A dealer in dry-goods in the city of New York has returned as the *income* of a single year a sum half as large as the whole capital invested in the establishment of the Harpers. If the *signal* successes of publishing — successes which are the result of the rarest conjunctions of talent, capital, experience, and opportunity — are represented by incomes of twenty and thirty thousand paper dollars a year, what must be the general condition of the trade? But it is the difficulty of conducting the business at all, not the slenderness of its profits, upon which we now desire the reader to reflect. That difficulty, we repeat, arises from the fact that a publisher buys his pig in a poke. He generally knows not, and cannot know, whether what he buys is worth much, little, or nothing.

But there is one branch of his business which does not present this difficulty, — the reprinting of works previously published in a foreign country. He has the advantage of holding in his hand the precise article which he proposes to reproduce, — a printed volume, which he can read with ease and rapidity; and this is nearly as great an advantage as a manager has who sees a play performed before buying it. He has the still greater advantage of a public verdict upon the book. It has been tried upon a public; and it is a rule almost without exception, that a book which sells largely in one country will not fail in another. Dickens, Thackeray, Reade, Miss Mulock, Anthony Trollope, George Eliot, Dumas, Hugo, George Sand, have in all foreign countries a popularity which bears a certain proportion to that which they enjoy in their own; and even the Chinese novel published some years ago in England was a safe speculation, because it was universally popular in China. The Russian novel before alluded to was a prudent enterprise, because Russia had previously tasted and enjoyed it. Literature of high character is always pervaded with the essence of the nationality which produced it, but it is, for that very reason, the more interesting to other nations.

Don Quixote has more Spain in it than all the histories of Spain; but in the library of the German collector of Cervantes, whose death has been recently announced, there were more than twice as many foreign editions as Spanish. According to the Pall Mall Gazette, there were 400 editions in Spanish, 168 in French, 200 in English, 87 in Portuguese, 96 in Italian, 70 in German, 4 in Russian, 4 in Greek, 8 in Polish, 6 in Danish, 13 in Swedish, and 5 in Latin. Poor Cervantes! How eloquently this list pleads for International Copyright!

It is, then, in the republication of foreign works that our publishers ought to find an element of certainty, which cannot appertain to the publication of original and untried productions. But it is precisely here that chaos reigns. In the issue of native works, there is but a single uncertainty; in the republication of foreign, there are many. No man knows what his rights are; nor whether he has any rights; nor whether there *are* any rights; nor, if he has rights, whether they will be respected. This chaos has taken to itself the pleasant and delusive name of "Courtesy of the Trade." Before the "reign of law" is established in any province of human affairs, we generally see men feeling their way to it, trying to find something else that will answer the purpose, endeavoring to reduce the chaos of conflicting claims to some kind of rule. The publishers of the United States have been doing this for many years, and the result is the unwritten code called the Courtesy of the Trade, — a code defective in itself, with neither judge to expound it, jury to decide upon it, nor sheriff to execute it. This code consisted at first of one rule, — if a publisher issues a foreign work, no other American publisher shall issue it. But it often happened that two or three publishers began or desired to begin the printing of the same book. To meet this and other cases, other laws were added, until at present the code, as laid down by the rigorists, consists of the following rules: —

1. If a publisher issues an edition of a foreign work, he has acquired an exclusive right to it for a period undefined.

2. If a publisher is the first to announce his intention to publish a foreign work, that announcement gives him an exclusive right to publish it.

3. If a publisher has already issued a work of a foreign author, he has acquired thereby an exclusive right to the republication of all subsequent works by the same author.

4. The purchase of advance sheets for publication in a periodical gives a publisher the exclusive right to publish the same in any other form.

5. All and several of these rights may be bought and sold, like any other kind of property.

There is a kind of justice in all these rules. If we could concede that a foreign author *has* no ownership of the coinage of his brain, — if anything but that author's free gift or purchased consent *could* convey that property to another, — if foreign literature *is* the legitimate spoil of America, — then some such code as this would be the only method of preventing the business from degenerating into a game of unmitigated grab. In its present ill-defined and most imperfect state, this system of "courtesy" scarcely mitigates the game at all; and, accordingly, in "the trade," instead of the friendly feeling that would naturally exist among honorable men in the highest branch of business, we find feuds, heart-burnings, and a grievous sense of wrongs unredressed and unredressable. Some houses "announce" everything that is announced on the other side of the Atlantic, so as to have the first choice. Smaller firms, seeing these announcements, dare not undertake any foreign work, even though the great house never decides to publish the book upon which the smaller had fixed its attention. It is only under the reign of law that the rights of the weak have any security. In the most exquisitely organized system of piracy, no man can rely upon the enjoyment of a right which he is not strong enough personally to defend. It is not every house that can crush a rival edition by selling thousands of expensive books at half their cost. Between the giant houses that tower above him, and the yellow-covered gentry that prowl about his feet, an American publisher of only ordinary resources has a game to play which is really too difficult for the limited capacities of man. Who can wonder that most of them lose it?

One effect of this courtesy system is, that many excellent works, which it would be a public benefit to have reprinted here, are not reprinted. Another is, that corrected or improved editions cannot be given to the American reader without bringing down upon the publisher the enmity or the vengeance of a rival. It is not common in Europe for the first editions of important works to be stereotyped; but in America they always are. The European author frequently makes extensive additions and valuable emendations in each successive edition; until, in the course of years, his work is essentially different from, and far superior to, the first essay. *We* cannot have the advantage of the improved version. There is a set of old and worn stereotype plates in the way, the proprietor of which will not sacrifice them, nor permit another publisher to produce the corrected edition, which would as completely destroy their value as though they were melted into type metal. Who can blame him? No one likes to have a valuable property suddenly rendered valueless. "It is not human nature." Mr. Lewes is not justified in so bitterly reproaching Messrs. Appleton for their cold entertainment of his offer to them of the enlarged version of his "History of Philosophy."

"I felt," says Mr. Lewes, "that Messrs. Appleton, of New York, had, in courtesy, a prior claim, on the ground of their having reprinted the previous edition in 1857. Accordingly I wrote to them, through their London agent, stating that I considered they had a claim to the first offer, and stating, further, that the new edition was substantially a new book. [As this is an important element in the present case, allow me to add, that the edition of 1857 was in one volume 8vo, published at sixteen shillings, whereas the new edition is in two volumes 8vo, published at thirty shillings; and the work is so considerably altered and enlarged that a new title has been affixed to it, for the purpose of marking it off from its predecessors.] Questions of courtesy are, however, but ill understood by some people, and by Messrs. Appleton so ill understood that they did not even answer my letter. After waiting more than three months for an answer, I asked a friend to see their London agent on the subject, and thus I learned that Messrs. Appleton — *risum teneatis, amici?* — 'considered they had a right to publish all future editions of my work without payment,' because ten years ago they had given the magnificent sum of twenty-five pounds to secure themselves against rivals for the second edition."

The omission to answer the author's letter, we may assume, was accidental. It is not correct to say that the publishers founded their claim to issue the new edition upon their payment of twenty-five pounds. The real difficulty was, that Messrs. Appleton possessed the plates of the first edition, and could not issue the enlarged edition without, first, destroying a property already existing, and, secondly, creating a new property at an expenditure about four times as great as the sum originally invested. The acceptance of Mr. Lewes's offer would have involved an expenditure of several thousand dollars, at a time when, for a variety of reasons, works of that character could hardly be expected to return the outlay upon them. The exclusive and certain ownership of the work might well justify its republication, even now, when it costs exactly three times as much to manufacture a book in the United States as it did seven years ago. But nothing short of this would warrant a publisher in undertaking it. The real sinners, against whom Mr. Lewes should have launched his sarcasm, are the people of the United States, who permit their instructors, both native and foreign, to be robbed of their property with impunity. Thus we see that a few hundred pounds of metal are likely to bar the entrance among us of a work which demonstrates, in the clearest and most attractive manner, the inutility of all that has hitherto gone by the name of "metaphysics," and which also indicates the method of investigation from which good results are to be rationally hoped for.

It is the grossest injustice to hold American publishers responsible for the system of ill-regulated plunder which they have inherited, and which injures them more immediately and palpably than any other class, excepting alone the class producing the commodity in which they deal. There are no business men more honorable or more generous than the publishers of the United States, and especially honorable and considerate are they toward authors. The relation usually existing between author and publisher in the United States is that of a warm and lasting friendship,—such as that which subsisted for so many years between Irving and Putnam, and which now animates and dignifies the intercourse between the literary men of New England and

Messrs. Ticknor and Fields, and which gathers in the well-known room of the Harpers a host of writers who are attached friends of the "House." The relation, too, is one of a singular mutual trustfulness. The author receives his semiannual account from the publisher with as absolute a faith in its correctness as though he had himself counted the volumes sold; and the publisher consigns the manuscript of the established author to the printer almost without opening it, confident that, whether it succeeds or fails, the author has done his best. We have heard of instances in which a publisher had serious cause of complaint against an author, but never have we known an author to be intentionally wronged by a publisher. We have known a publisher, in the midst of the ruin of his house, to make it one of the first objects of his care to save authors from loss, or make their inevitable losses less. How common, too, it is in the trade for a publisher to go beyond the letter of his bond, and, after publishing five books without profit, to give the author of the successful sixth more than the stipulated price! Let every one speak of the market as he finds it. For our part, after fifteen years of almost daily intercourse with publishers, we have no recollections of them that are not agreeable, and can call to mind no transaction in which they did not show themselves to be men of honor as much as men of business. We have not the least doubt that Mr. Peterson honestly thought he had acquired a right, by fair purchase, to sell the property of Charles Dickens in the United States as long as he should continue in business, and then to dispose of that right to his successor. We are equally confident that Messrs. Harper felt themselves completely justified in endeavoring to crush the Diamond Edition of Thackeray. All this chaos and uncertainty, all these feuds and enmities, have one and the same cause, — the existence in the world of a kind of property which is at once the most precious, the easiest stolen, and the worst protected.

Almost to a man, our publishers are in favor of an International Copyright. We have been able to hear of but one exception, and this is the publisher of but one book, — Webster's Dictionary, — the work of all others now in existence that would profit most from just protection in foreign countries. There is an impression in many circles that the Harpers are opposed to it. We are enabled to state, upon the authority of a member of that great house, that this is not now, and never has been, the case. Messrs. Harper comprehend, as well as we do, that they would gain more from the measure than any other house in the world; because it is the natural effect of law, while it protects the weak, to legitimate and establish the dominion of the strong. International Copyright would benefit every creature connected with publishing, but it would benefit most of all the great and wealthy houses. The Harpers have spent tens of thousands in enforcing the observance of the courtesy of the trade, but they cannot enforce it. It is a work never done and always beginning. It cost them four hundred of our ridiculous dollars for the advance sheets of each number of Mr. Dickens's last novel; and within forty-eight hours of the publication of the Magazine containing it, two other editions were for sale under their noses. The matter for "Harper's Magazine" often costs three or four thousand dollars a number; can any one suppose that the proprietors *like* to see Blackwood and half a dozen other British magazines sold all over the country at a little more than the cost of paper and printing? They like it as little as the proprietors of Blackwood like it. This is a wrong which injures two nations and benefits one printer; and that printer would himself do better if he could obtain exclusive rights by fair purchase. No; Messrs. Harper, we are happy to state, are decidedly in favor of an International Copyright, and so is every other general publishing house in the country of which we have any knowledge.

Consider the case of our venerable and beloved instructor, "The North American Review," conducted with so much diligence, energy, and tact by the present editors. Not a number of it has appeared under their management which has not been a national benefit; and no country more needs such a periodical than the United States, now standing on the threshold of a new career. The time has passed when a review could consist chiefly of the skilfully condensed contents of interesting books, which men could execute in the intervals of professional duty, and think themselves happy in receiving one dollar for a printed page, extracts deducted.

At the present time, a review must initiate as well as criticise, and do something itself as well as comment upon the performances of others. We believe that no number of the North American Review now appears, the matter of which costs as little as a thousand dollars. But it has to compete, not only with the four British Reviews sold here at the price of paper and printing, but with several periodicals made up of selections from the reviews and magazines of Europe. Nor is this all. A public accustomed to buy books and periodicals at a price into which nothing enters but manual labor and visible material is apt to pause and recoil when it is solicited to pay the just value of those commodities. A man who buys a number of the Westminster Review for half a dollar is likely to regard a dollar and a half as an enormous price for a number of the North American, though he gets for his money what cost a thousand dollars before the printer saw it. For forty years or more we have all been buying our books and reviews at thieves' prices, — prices in which everybody was considered except the creators of the value; and the consequence is, that we turn away when a proper price is demanded for a book, and regard ourselves as injured beings. How monstrous for a volume of Emerson to be sold for a dollar! In England and France, when the price is to be fixed upon works of that nature, the mere cost of paper and printing is hardly considered at all. Such trifles are felt, and rightly felt, to have little to do with the question of price. The publisher knows very well that he has to dispose of one of those rare and beautiful products which only a very few thousands of his countrymen will care to possess, or could enjoy if it were thrust upon them. He fixes the price with reference to the facts of the case, — the important facts as well as the trivial, the rights of the author as well as the little bill of the printer, — and that price is half a guinea. The want of an International Copyright, besides lowering and degrading all literature, has demoralized the public by getting it into the habit of paying for books the price of stolen goods. And hence the North American Review, which would naturally be a most valuable property, has never yielded a profit corresponding to its real value. People stand aghast at the invitation to pay six dollars a year for an article, the mere unmanufactured ingredients of which cost a thousand times six dollars.

Good contemporary books cannot be very cheap, unless there is stealing *somewhere*, for a good book is one of the most costly products of nature. Fortunately, they need not be cheap, for it is not necessary to own many of them. As soon as an International Copyright has given tone to the business of writing and publishing books, and has restored the prices of them to the just standard, we shall see a great increase of those facilities for purchasing the opportunity to read a book without buying it, which have placed the whole literature of the world at the command of an English farmer who can spare a guinea or two per annum. It is not necessary, we repeat, to possess many new books; it is only necessary to read them, get the good of them, and give a hearty support to the library from which we take them. The purchase of a book should be a serious and well-considered act, not the hasty cramming of a thin, double-columned pamphlet into a coat-pocket, to be read and cast aside at the bottom of a book-case. It is an abominable extravagance to buy a great and good novel in a perishable form for a few cents; it is good economy to pay a few dollars for one substantially bound, that will amuse and inform generations. A good novel, play, or poem can be reread every five years during a long life. When a book is to be selected out of the mass, to become thenceforth part and parcel of a home, let it be well printed and well bound, and, above all, let it be of an edition to which the author has set the seal of his consent and approbation. No one need fear that the addition of the author's ten per cent to the price of foreign books will make them less accessible to the masses of the people. It will make them more accessible, and it will tend to make them better worth keeping.

When we consider the difficulties which now beset the publication of books in the United States, we cannot but wonder at the liberality of American publishers toward foreign authors, — a liberality which has met no return from publishers in Europe. The first money that Herbert Spencer ever received in his life from his *books* was sent to him in 1861 by the Appletons as his share of the proceeds of his "Essays upon Education"; and every year since he has received upon all his works republished here the percentage usually paid to native authors. This is so interesting a case, and so forcibly illustrates many aspects of our subject, that we will dwell upon it for a moment.

It will occasionally happen that an author is produced in a country who is charged with a special message for another country. There will be something in the cast of his mind, or in the nature of his subject, which renders his writings more immediately or more generally suitable to the people of a land other than his own. We might cite as an example Washington Irving, who, though a sound American patriot, was essentially an English author, and whose earlier works are so English that many English people read them to this day, we are told, who do not suspect that the author was not their countryman. Washington Irving owed his literary career to this fact! His seventeen years' residence abroad enabled him to enjoy part of the advantage which all great authors would derive from an International Copyright, that is to say, he derived revenue from *both* countries. During the first half of his literary career, he drew the chief part of his income from England; during the second half, when his Sketch-Book vein was exhausted, and he was again an American resident, he derived his main support from America. If he had never resided abroad, we never should have had a Washington Irving; if he had not returned home, he would have been sadly pinched in his old age. Alone among the American authors of his day or of any day, he had the market of the world for his works; and he only, of excellent American authors, has received anything like a compensation for his labor. The entire proceeds of his works during his lifetime were $ 205,383, of which about one third came to him from England. His average income, during the fifty years of his authorship, was about four thousand dollars a year. Less than any other of our famous authors he injured his powers by over-production, and it was only the unsteadiness of his income, the occasional failure of his resources, or the dread of a failure, that ever induced him to take up his pen when exhausted nature cried, Forbear! Cooper, on the contrary, who was read and robbed in every country, wrote himself all out, and still wrote on, until his powers were destroyed and his name was a by-word.

A case similar in principle to that of Irving was Audubon, the indefatigable and amiable Audubon. The exceeding costliness of his "Birds of America" protected that work as completely as an International Copyright could; and, but for this, we never could have had it. Audubon enjoyed the market of the world! The price of his wonderful work was a thousand dollars, and, at that period, neither Europe nor America could furnish purchasers enough to warrant him in giving it to the press. But Europe *and* America could! Europe and America *did*, — each continent taking about eighty copies. The excellent Audubon, therefore, was not ruined by his brave endeavor to honor his country and instruct mankind. He ended his days in peace in that well-known villa on the banks of the Hudson, continuing his useful and beautiful labors to the last, and leaving to his sons the means of perfecting what he left incomplete.

But to return to Herbert Spencer, the author of "Social Statics"; or, as we call it, Jeffersonian Democracy, illustrated and applied. Unconnected with the governing classes of his own country, escaping the universities, bred to none of the professions, and inheriting but a slender patrimony, he earned a modest and precarious livelihood by contributing to the periodicals, and wrung from his small leisure the books that England needed, but would not buy. An American citizen, Professor Youmans, felt all their merit, and perceived how adapted they were to the tastes and habits of the American mind, and how skilfully the ideas upon which America is founded were developed in them. He also felt, as we have heard him say, that, next to the production of excellent works, the most useful thing a man can do in his generation is to aid in giving them currency. Aided by other lovers of his favorite author, he was soon in a position to bear part of the heavy expense of stereotyping Mr. Spencer's works; and thus Messrs. Appleton were enabled, not only to publish them, but to afford the author as large a share of the proceeds as though he had been a resident of the United States. Thus Herbert Spencer, by a happy accident, enjoys part of the advantage which would accrue to all his brethren from an International Copyright; and we have the great satisfaction of knowing, when we buy one of his volumes, that we are not defrauding our benefactor.

Charles Scribner habitually pays English authors a part of the profit derived from their republished works. Max Müller, Mr. Trench, and others who figure upon his list, derive revenue from the sale of their works in America. Mr. Scribner considers it both his duty and his interest to acquire all the right to republish which a foreign author can bestow; and he desires to see the day when the law will recognize and secure the most obvious and unquestionable of all rights, the right of an author to the product of his mind.

We trust Messrs. Ticknor and Fields will not regard it as an affront to their delicacy if we allude here to facts which events have already disclosed to the public. This house, on principle, and as an essential part of their system, send to foreign authors a share of the proceeds of their works, and this they have habitually done for twenty-five years. The first American edition of the Poems of Mr. Tennyson, published by them in 1842, consisted of one thousand copies, and it was three years in selling; but upon this edition a fair acknowledgment in money was sent to the poet. Since that time, Mr. Tennyson has received from them a certain equitable portion of the proceeds of all the numerous editions of his works which they have issued. Mr. Fields, with great labor and some expense, collected from periodicals and libraries a complete set of the works of Mr. De Quincey, which the house published in twenty-two volumes, the sale of which was barely remunerative; but the author received, from time to time, a sum proportioned to the number of volumes sold. Mr. Fields has been gathering the "Early and Late Papers" of Mr. Thackeray, one volume of which has been published, to the great satisfaction of the public. Miss Thackeray has already received a considerable sum for the sale of the first edition. Mr. Browning, Mr. Hughes, Mr. Reade, the Country Parson, Mr. Kingsley, Mr. Matthew Arnold, Dr. John Brown, Mr. Mayne Reid, Mr. Dickens, have been dealt with in a similar manner; some of them receiving copyright, and others a sum of money proportioned to the sale or expected sale of their works. Nor has the appearance of rival editions been allowed to diminish the author's share of the profits realized upon the editions published with their consent. Mr. Tennyson counts upon the American part of his income with the same certainty as upon that which he derives from the sale of his works in England, although he cannot secure his Boston publishers the exclusive market of the United States. Comment is needless. Every man who has either a conscience or a talent for business will recognize either the propriety or the wisdom of their conduct. Upon this rock of fair-dealing the eminent and long-sustained prosperity of this house is founded.

Complaints, then, are made of American publishers! We say again, that, after diligent inquiry, we cannot hear of one instance of an English publisher sending money to an American author for anything but advance sheets. Mr. Longfellow is as popular a poet in England as Mr. Tennyson is in America, and he has, consequently, as before remarked, received considerable sums for early sheets, but nothing, we believe, upon the annual sale of his works, nothing from the voluntary and spontaneous justice of his English publishers. We have no right, perhaps, to censure men for not going beyond the requirements of law; but still less can we withhold the tribute of our homage to those who are more just than the law compels, and this tribute is due to several publishers on this side of the Atlantic. But then there remains the great fact against us, that England is willing to-day, and we are not, to throw the protection of international law around this most sacred interest of civilization.

Would that it were in our power to give adequate expression to the mighty debt we owe, as a people, to the living and recent authors of Europe! But who can weigh or estimate the invisible and widely diffused influence of a book? There are sentences in the earlier works of Carlyle which have regenerated American souls. There are chapters in Mill which are reforming the policy of American nations. There are passages in Buckle which give the key to the mysteries of American history. There are lines in Tennyson which have become incorporated into the fabric of our minds, and flash light and beauty upon our daily conversation. There are characters in Dickens which are extinguishing the foibles which they embody, and pages of Thackeray which kill the affectations they depict. What a colossal good to us is Mr. Grote's "History of Greece"! Miss Mulock, George Eliot, Charles Reade, Charlotte Brontë, Kinglake, Matthew Arnold, Charles Kingsley, Ruskin, Macaulay, — how could we spare the least of them? Take from our lives the happiness and the benefit which we have derived from the recent authors of Europe; take from the future the silent, ceaseless working of their spirits, — so antidotal to all that remains in us of colonial, provincial, and superstitious, — and what language could state, ever so inadequately, the loss we and posterity should experience? And let us not lay the mean unction to our souls that money cannot repay such services as these. It can! It can repay it as truly and as fully as sixpence pays for a loaf of bread that saves a shipwrecked hero's life. The baker gets his own; he is satisfied, and holy justice is satisfied. This common phrase, "making money," is a poor, mean way of expressing an august and sacred thing; for the money which fairly comes to us, in the way of our vocation, is, or ought to be, the measure of our worth to the community we serve. It is honor, safety, education, leisure, children's bread, wife's dignity and adornment, pleasant home, society, an independent old age, comfort in dying, and solace to those we leave behind us. Money is the representative of all the substantial good that man can bestow on man. And money justly earned is never withheld without damage to the withholder and to the interest he represents.

We often think of the case of Dion Boucicault, one of the few men now writing the English language who have shown a very great natural aptitude for telling a story in the dramatic form. For thirty years we have been witnessing his plays in the United States. A fair share of the nightly receipts of the theatres in which they were played would have enriched him in the prime of his talent, or, in other words, have delivered him from that temptation to over-production which has wellnigh destroyed his powers. He never received any revenue from us until he came here and turned actor. He gets a little money now by associating with himself an American friend, who writes a few sentences of a play, then brings it to New York and disposes of it to managers as their joint production. But what an exquisite shame it is for us to compel an artist to whom we owe so many delightful hours to resort to an artifice in order to be able to sell the product of his talent! Our injustice, too, damages ourselves even more than it despoils him; for if we had paid him fairly for "London Assurance" and "Old Heads and Young Hearts," if he had found a career in the production of plays, he might not have been lured from his vocation, and might have written twenty good plays, instead of a hundred good, bad, indifferent, and atrocious. We cheat him of our part of the just results of his lifetime's labor, and he flings back at us his anathema in the form of a "Flying Scud." Think of Sheridan Knowles, too, deriving nothing from our theatres, in which his dramas have been worn threadbare by incessant playing! To say that they are trash is not an infinitesimal fraction of an excuse; for it is just as wrong to steal paste as it is to steal diamonds. We liked the trash well enough to appropriate it. Besides, he really had the knack of constructing a telling play, which, it seems, is one of the rarest gifts bestowed upon man, and the one which affords the most intense pleasure to the greatest number of people.

Why, we may ask in passing, did the English stage languish for so many years? It was because the money that should have compensated dramatists enriched actors; because the dramatist that wrote "Black-eyed Susan" was paid five pounds a week, and the actor that played William received four thousand pounds during the first run of the play. In France, where the drama flourishes, it is the actor who gets five pounds a week, and the dramatist who gets the thousands of pounds for the first run; and this just distribution of profits is infinitely the best, in the long run, for *actors*.

There is still an impression prevalent in the world, that there is no connection between good work and good wages in this kind of industry. There was never a greater mistake. A few great men, exceptional in character as in circumstances, blind like Milton, exiled like Dante, prisoners like Bunyan and Cervantes, may have written for solace, or for fame, or from benevolence; but, as a rule, *nothing gets the immortal work from first-rate men but money.* We need only mention Shakespeare, for every one knows that he wrote plays simply and solely as a matter of business, to draw money into the treasury of his theatre. He was author and publisher, actor as well, and thus derived a threefold benefit from his labors. Molière, too, the greatest name in the literature of France, and the second in the dramatic literature of the world, was author, actor, and manager. Play-writing was the career of these great men. It was their business and vocation; and it is only in the way of his business and vocation that we can, as a rule, get from an artist the best and the utmost there is in him. Common honesty demands that a man shall do his best when he works for his own price. His honor and his safety are alike involved. All our courage and all our cowardice, all our pride and all our humility, all our generosity and all our selfishness, all that can incite and all that can scare us to exertion, may enter into the complex motive that is urging us on when we are doing the work by which we earn our right to exist. Nothing is of great and lasting account, — not religion, nor benevolence, nor law, nor science, — until it is so organized that honest and able men can live by it. Then it lures talent, character, ambition, wealth, and force to its support and illustration. The whole history of literature, so far as it is known, shows that literature flourishes when it is fairly rewarded, and declines when it is robbed of its just compensation. Mr. Reade has admirably demonstrated this in his "Eighth Commandment," a little book as full of wit, fact, argument, eloquence, and delicious audacity as any that has lately appeared.

There has been but one country in which literature has ever succeeded in raising itself to the power and dignity of a profession, and it is the only country which has ever enjoyed a considerable part of the market of the world for its literary wares. This is France, which has a kind of International Copyright in its language. Educated Russia reads few books that are not French, and in every country of Christendom it is taken for granted that an educated person reads this language. Wherever in Europe or America or India or Australia many books are sold, some French books are sold. Here in New York, for example, we have had for many years an elegant and well-appointed French bookstore, in which the standard works of French literature are temptingly displayed, and the new works are for sale within three weeks after their publication in Paris. Many of our readers, too, must have noticed the huge masses of French books exhibited in some of the second-hand bookstores of Nassau Street. French books, in fact, form a very considerable part of the daily business of the bookstores in every capital of the world. Nearly one hundred subscribers were obtained in the United States for the *Nouvelle Biographie*, in forty-six volumes, the total cost of which, bound, was more than two hundred dollars. Besides this large and steady sale of their works in every city on earth, French authors enjoy a protection to their rights at home which is most complete, and they address a public accustomed to pay for new books a price, in determining which the author was considered. Mr. Reade informs us that a first-rate dramatic success in Paris is worth to the author six thousand pounds sterling, and that this six thousand pounds is very frequently drawn from the theatre after a larger sum has been obtained for the same work in the form of a novel.

What is the effect? Literature in France, as we have said, is one of the liberal professions. Literary men are an important and honorable order in the state. The press teems with works of real value and great cost. The three hundred French dramatists supply the theatres of Christendom with plays so excellent, that not even the cheat of "adaptation" can wholly conceal their merit. Great novels, great histories, great essays and treatises, important contributions to science, illustrated works of the highest excellence, compilations of the first utility, marvellous dictionaries and statistical works, appear with a frequency which nothing but a universal market could sustain. In whatever direction public curiosity is aroused, prompt and intelligent efforts are made to gratify it. Nothing more surprises an American inquirer than the excellent manner in which this mere task-work, these "booksellers' jobs," as we term them, are executed in Paris. That *Nouvelle Biographie* of which we have spoken is so faithfully done, and is so free from any perverseness or narrowness of nationality, that it would be a good enterprise in any of the reading countries to publish a translation of it just as it stands. French literature follows the general law, that, as the volume of business increases, the quality of the work done improves. The last French work which the pursuit of our vocation led us to read was one upon the Mistresses of Louis XV., by Edmond and Jules de Goncourt. We need not say how such a subject as this would be treated by the cheated hirelings of the Yellow Cover. This work, on the contrary, is an intelligent historical study of a period when mistresses governed France, and the passages in the work which touch upon the adulterous tie which gave fair France over to these vampires are managed with a delicacy the most perfect. The present hope of France is in her literature. Her literary men are fast educating that interesting and virtuous people to the point when they will be able to regain their freedom and keep it safe from nocturnal conspirators. They would have done it ere now, but for the woful fact that only half of their countrymen can read, and are thus the helpless victims of a perjured Dutchman and his priests.

What the general knowledge of the French language has done for French literature, all of that, and more than that, an International Copyright law would do for the literature of Great Britain and the United States. Here are four great and growing empires, Great Britain, the United States, the Dominion of Canada, and the states of Australia, in which the same language is spoken and similar tastes prevail. In all these nations there is a spirit abroad which will never rest content until the whole population are readers, and those readers will be counted by hundreds of millions. Already they are so numerous, that one first-rate literary success, one book excellent enough to be of universal interest, would give the author leisure for life, if his rights were completely protected by international law. What a field for honorable exertion is this! And how can these empires fail to grow into unity when the cultivated intelligence of them all shall be nourished from the same sources, and bow in homage to the same commanding minds? Wanting this protection, the literature of both countries languishes. The blight of over-production falls upon immature genius, masterpieces are followed by labored and spiritless repetitions, and men that have it in them to inform and move mankind grind out task-work for daily bread. One man, one masterpiece, that is the general law. Not one eminent literary artist of either country can be named who has not injured his powers and jeoparded his fame by over-production. We do not address a polite note to Elias Howe, and ask him how much he would charge for a "series" of inventions equal in importance to the sewing-machine. We merely enable him to demand a dollar every time that *one* conception is used. Imagine Job applied to for a "series" of Books of Job. Not less absurd is it to compel an author to try and write two Sketch-Books, two David Copperfields, two Uncle Toms, two Jane Eyres, or two books like "The Newcomes." When once a great writer has given such complete expression of his experience as was given in each of those works, a long time must elapse before his mind fills again to a natural overflow. But, alas! only a very short time elapses before his purse empties.

It was the intention of the founders of this Republic to give complete protection to intellectual property, and this intention is clearly expressed in the Constitution. Justified by the authority given in that instrument, Congress has passed patent laws which have called into exercise an amount of triumphant ingenuity that is one of the great wonders of the modern world; but under the copyright laws, enacted with the same good intentions, our infant literature pines and dwindles. The reason is plain. For a labor-saving invention, the United States, which abounds in everything but labor, is field enough, and the inventor is rewarded; while a great book cannot be remunerative unless it enjoys the market of the whole civilized world. The readers of excellent books are few in every country on earth. The readers of any one excellent book are usually very few indeed; and the purchasers are still fewer. In a world that is supposed to contain a thousand millions of people, it is spoken of as a marvel that two millions of them bought the most popular book ever published, — one purchaser to every five hundred inhabitants.

We say, then, to those members of Congress who go to Washington to do something besides make Presidents, that time has developed a new necessity, not indeed contemplated by the framers of the Constitution, yet covered by the Constitution; and it now devolves upon them to carry out the evident intention of their just and wise predecessors, which was, to secure to genius, learning, and talent the certain ownership of their productions. We want an international system which shall protect a kind of property which cannot be brought to market without exposing it to plunder, — property in a book being simply the right to multiply copies of it. We want this property secured, for a sufficient period, to the creator of the value, so that no property in a book can be acquired anywhere on earth unless by the gift or consent of the author thereof. There are men in Congress who feel all the magnitude and sacredness of the debt which they owe, and which their country owes, to the authors and artists of the time. We believe such members are more numerous now than they ever were before, — much more numerous. It is they who must take the leading part in bringing about this great measure of justice and good policy; and, as usual in such cases, some one man must adopt it as his special vocation, and never rest till he has conferred on mankind this immeasurable boon.

OUR ROMAN CATHOLIC BRETHREN.

ONE thing can be said of our Roman Catholic brethren, and especially of our Roman Catholic sisters, without exciting controversy, — they begin early in the morning. St. Stephen's, the largest Catholic church in New York, which will hold five thousand persons and seat four thousand, was filled to overflowing every morning of last November at five o'clock. That, however, was an extraordinary occasion. The first mass, as housekeepers are well aware, usually takes place at six o'clock, summer and winter; and it was this that I attended on Sunday morning, December 8, 1867, one of the coldest mornings of that remarkably cold month.

It is not so easy a matter to wake at a certain hour before the dawn of day. One half, perhaps, of all the inhabitants of the earth, and two thirds of the grown people of the United States, get up in the winter months before daylight; and yet a person unaccustomed to the feat will be utterly at a loss how to set about it. At five o'clock of a December morning it is as dark as it ever is. The most reckless milkman has not then begun his matutinal whoop, and the noise of the bakers' carts is not heard in the streets. And if there should be a family in the middle of the block who keep chickens, there is no dependence to be placed upon the crowing of the cocks; for they crow at all odd, irrational times both of night and day. Neither in the heavens above nor in the yards beneath, neither in the house nor in the street, is there any sign or sound by which a wakeful expectant can distinguish five o'clock from four, or three, or one. It is true, madam, as you remark, that there *is* such a thing as an alarm-clock. But who ever has one when it is wanted? People who get up at five every morning can do without; and those who get up at five once in five years, even if by any chance they should possess an alarm-clock, forget in the five years of disuse how the little fury is set so as to hold in all night and burst forth in frenzy at the moment required. This was my case. The alarm went off admirably an hour too late, and woke up the wrong person. It was only a most vociferous crowing of the cocks just now reviled as unreliable that caused me to suspect that possibly it might be time for me to strike a light and see how the alarm-clock was getting on. Our Roman Catholic brethren, in some way or ways unknown, habitually overcome this difficulty; for fifty thousand of them, in New York alone, are frequently at church and on their knees before there are any audible or visible indications of the coming day.

It was a very cold and brilliant morning, — stars glittering, moon resplendent, pavement icy, roofs snowy, wind north-northwest, and, of course, cutting right into the faces of people bound up the Third Avenue. An empty car went rattling over the frozen-in rails with an astonishing noise, the conductor trotting alongside, and the miserable driver beating his breast with one hand and pounding the floor with one foot. The highly ornamental policeman on the first corner was singing to keep himself warm; but, seeing a solitary wayfarer in a cloak scudding along on the ice, he conceived a suspicion of that untimely seeker after knowledge; he paused in his song; he stooped and eyed him closely, evidently unable to settle upon a rational explanation of his presence; and only resumed his song when the suspected person was five houses off. There was scarcely any one astir to keep an adventurer in countenance, and I began to think it was all a delusion about the six-o'clock mass. At ten minutes to six, when I stood in front of the spacious St. Stephen's Church in Twenty-Eighth Street, there seemed to be no one going in; and, the vestibule being unlighted, I was confirmed in the impression that early mass did not take place on such cold mornings. To be quite sure of the fact, however, I did just go up the steps and push at the door. It yielded to pressure, and its opening disclosed a vast interior, dimly lighted at the altar end, where knelt or sat, scattered about one or two in a pew, about a hundred women and ten men, all well muffled up in hoods, shawls, and overcoats, and breathing visibly. There was just light enough to see the new blue ceiling and its silver stars; but the sexton was busy lighting the gas, and got on with his work about as fast as the church filled. That church extends through the block, and has two fronts. As six o'clock approached, female figures in increasing numbers crept silently in by several doors, all making the usual courtesy, and all kneeling as soon as they reached a pew. At last the lower part of the church was pretty well filled, and there were some people in the galleries; in all, about one thousand women and about one hundred men. Nearly all the women were servant-girls, and all of them were dressed properly and abundantly for such a morning. There was not a squalid or miserable-looking person present. Most of the men appeared to be grooms and coachmen. Among these occupants of the kitchen, the nursery, and the stable there were a few persons from the parlor, evidently of the class whom Voltaire speaks of with so much wrath and contempt as *dévots et dévotes*. There were two or three men near me who might or might not have been ecclesiastics or theological students; upon the pale and luminous face of each was most legibly written, This man prays continually, and enjoys it.

There is a difference between Catholics and Protestants in this matter of praying. When a Protestant prays in public, he is apt to hide his face, and bend low in an awkward, uncomfortable attitude; and, when he would pray in private, he retires into some secret place, where, if any one should catch him at it, he would blush like a guilty thing. It is not so with our Roman Catholic brethren. They kneel, it is true, but the body above the knees is bolt upright, and the face is never hidden; and, as if this were not enough, they make certain movements of the hand which distinctly announce their purpose to every beholder. The same freedom and boldness are observable in Catholic children when they say their nightly prayers. Your little Protestant buries its face in the bed, and whispers its prayer to the counterpane; but our small Catholic brethren and sisters kneel upright, make the sign of the cross, and are not in the least ashamed or disturbed if any one sees them. Another thing strikes a Protestant spectator of Catholic worship, — the whole congregation, without exception, observe the etiquette of the occasion. When kneeling is in order, all kneel; when it is the etiquette to stand, all stand; when the prayer-book says bow, every head is low. These two peculiarities are cause and effect. A Protestant child often has some reason to doubt whether saying its prayers is, after all, "the thing," since it is aware that some of its most valued friends and relations do not say theirs. But among Catholics there is not the distinction (so familiar to us) between those who "belong to the church" and those who do not; still less the distinction (nearly as familiar in some communities) between believers and unbelievers. From the hour of baptism every Catholic is a member of the church, and he is expected to behave as such. This is evidently one reason for that open, matter-of-course manner in which all the requirements of their religion are fulfilled. No one is ashamed of doing what is done by every one in the world whom he respects, and what he has himself been in the habit of doing from the time of his earliest recollection. A Catholic appears to be no more ashamed of saying his prayers than he is of eating his dinner, and he appears to think one quite as natural an action as the other.

On this cold morning the priest was not as punctual as the people. The congregation continued to increase till ten minutes past six; after which no sound was heard but the coughing of the chilled worshippers. It was not till seventeen minutes past six that the priest entered, accompanied by two slender, graceful boys, clad in long red robes, and walked to his place, and knelt before the altar. All present, except one poor heathen in the middle aisle, shuffled to their knees with a pleasant noise, and remained kneeling for some time. The silence was complete, and I waited to hear it broken by the sound of the priest's voice. But not a sound came from his lips. He rose, he knelt, he ascended the steps of the altar, he came down again, he turned his back to the people, he turned his face to them, he changed from one side of the altar to the other, he made various gestures with his hands, — but he uttered not an audible word. The two graceful lads in crimson garb moved about him, and performed the usual services, and the people sat, stood, knelt, bowed, and crossed themselves in accordance with the ritual. But still not a word was spoken. At the usual time the collection was taken, to which few gave more than a cent, but to which *every one* gave a cent. A little later, the priest uttered the only words that were audible during the whole service. Standing on the left side of the altar, he said, in an agreeable, educated voice: "The Society of the Holy Rosary will meet this afternoon after vespers. Prayers are requested for the repose of the souls of —"; then followed the names of three persons. The service was continued, and the silence was only broken again by the gong-like bell, which announced by a single stroke the most solemn acts of the mass, and which, toward the close of the service, summoned those to the altar who wished to commune. During the intense stillness which usually followed the sound of the bell, a low, eager whisper of prayer could occasionally be heard, and the whole assembly was lost in devotion. About twenty women and five men knelt round the altar to receive the communion. Soon after this had been administered some of the women began to hurry away, as if fearing the family at home might be ready for breakfast before breakfast would be ready for them. At ten minutes to seven the priest put on his black cap, and withdrew; and soon the congregation was in full retreat. But by this time another congregation was assembling for the seven-o'clock mass; the people were pouring in at every door, and hurrying along all the adjacent streets towards the church. Seven o'clock being a much more convenient time than six, the church is usually filled at that hour; as it is, also, at the nine-o'clock mass. At half past ten the grand mass of the day occurs, and no one who is in the habit of passing a Catholic church on Sunday mornings at that hour needs to be informed that the kneeling suppliants who cannot get in would make a tolerable congregation of themselves.

What an economy is this! The parish of St. Stephen's contains a Catholic population of twenty-five thousand, of whom twenty thousand, perhaps, are old enough and well enough to go to church. As the church will seat four thousand persons, all this multitude can hear mass every

Sunday morning. As many as usually desire it can attend the vespers in the afternoon. The church, too, in the intervals of service, and during the week, stands hospitably open, and is usually fulfilling in some way the end of its erection. How different with our churches! There is St. George's, for example, the twin steeples of which are visible to the home-returning son of Gotham as soon as the Sound steamer has brought him past Blackwell's Island. In that stately edifice half a million dollars have been invested, and it is in use only four hours a week. No more; for the smaller occasional meetings are held in another building, — a chapel in the rear. Half a million dollars is a large sum of money, even in Wall Street, where it figures merely as part of the working capital of the country; but think what a sum it is when viewed as a portion of the small, sacred treasure set apart for the higher purposes of human nature! And yet the building which has cost so much money stands there a dead and empty thing, except for four hours on Sunday! Our Roman Catholic brethren manage these things better. When *they* have invested half a million in a building, they put that building to a use which justifies and returns the expenditure. Even their grand cathedrals are good investments; since, besides being always open, always in use, always cheering and comforting their people, they are splendid illustrations of their religion to every passer-by, to every reader of books, and to every collector of engravings. Such edifices as St. Peter's, the cathedrals of Milan and of Cologne, do actually cheer and exalt the solitary priest toiling on the outskirts of civilization. Lonely as he is, insignificant, perhaps despised and shunned, he feels that he has a property in those grandeurs, and that an indissoluble tie connects him with the system which created them, and which will one day erect a gorgeous temple upon the site of the shanty in which now he celebrates the rites of his church in the presence of a few railroad laborers.

While these successive multitudes have been gathering and dispersing, something has been going on in the basement of St. Stephen's, — a long, low room, extending from street to street, and fitted up for a children's chapel and Sunday-school room. The Protestant reader, it is safe to say, has never attended a Catholic Sunday school, but he shall now have the pleasure of doing so. It ought to be a pleasure only to see two or three thousand children gathered together; but there is a particular reason why a Protestant should be pleased at a Catholic Sunday school. Imitation is the sincerest homage. The notion of the Sunday school is one of several which our Roman Catholic brethren have borrowed from us. This church, hoary and wrinkled with age, does not disdain to learn from the young and bustling churches to which it has given all they have. The Catholic Church, however, claims a share in the invention, since for many ages it has employed boys in the celebration of its worship, and has given those boys a certain training to enable them to fulfil their vocation. Still, the Sunday school, as now constituted, is essentially of Protestant origin. Indeed, the energetic and truly catholic superintendent of St. Stephen's school, Mr. Thomas E. S. Dwyer, informed me, that, before beginning this school, he visited all the noted Sunday schools in New York, Protestant, Catholic, and Jewish, and endeavored to get from each whatever he found in it suitable to his purpose.

The basement of St. Stephen's, being three hundred feet long, fifty or sixty feet wide, and only about *ten* feet high, looks more like a section of an underground railroad than a room. It is so very low that, although abundantly provided with windows on both sides, it is necessary always to light many jets of gas. In the ceiling is fixed part of the heating apparatus of the church, — a circumstance that does not tend to the purification of the atmosphere. At one end of this exceedingly long room is a small, plain altar, with the usual candles and other appurtenances; and on one side of the room, about midway, is a large cabinet organ, with an enclosure about it for the choir of children who chant the responses and psalms of the mass. On the walls between each window are the showy pictures usually found in Catholic institutions. At nine o'clock, when I took my seat in one of the pews of this long, low apartment, children with the reddest cheeks and the warmest comforters were thundering in, and diffusing themselves over the floor, — the girls taking one side of the room and the boys the other. When Mr. Dwyer began this school a few years ago, only two hundred children attended, — a mere handful in a Catholic parish, — but every teacher bound himself to visit each of his pupils once a month, and so endeavor to interest the people in the school. The effect was magical. Children came pouring in, until now the average attendance is two thousand, and there have been in the school at one session three thousand three hundred and forty.

The noise continued to increase till ten minutes past nine, when nearly every pew was filled, and the side extensions following the cruciform plan of the church were also crowded with the younger children seated upon benches, each bench having a teacher at one end. Meanwhile, the candles of the altar had been lighted, the choir had assembled, and the organ had been opened. A bell tinkles. A priest is at the altar, attended by two boys, who had come in unobserved amid the confusion. The bell rings again. Every child gets upon its knees, and every adult also, except the lonely heathen before mentioned. It was a truly affecting spectacle, — the rows of little boys, with a tall teacher at the head of each row, all kneeling in the candid, upright manner in which our Roman Catholic brethren always do kneel. There was still, however, a great noise of boys coming in and kneeling, and it was some minutes before there was any general approach to silence.

This mass, like the early one in the church, was performed without the priest's uttering one audible word. The responses and the psalm-like portions of the mass were sung by the choir, which consisted of one man, one woman, and about twenty children, who sang very well, and very appropriate music. But in that low, crowded, noisy room the music had as much effect as if performed in a tunnel, or at the bottom of a large, deep well. Thus, as the priest said nothing, and the choir could not be understood, the children were thrown, as it were, upon their own resources; and those resources, it must be owned, were insufficient. Many of the boys followed the service in their little prayer-books, and most of them refrained from conversation. There were always some, however, who kept up a sly whispering in the ears of their neighbors, and the countenances of a very large number were expressive of — nothing.

But what strains are these? Old Hundred introduced into the mass! Slightly altered, it is true, but unmistakably Old Hundred. And again: the children of the choir break into one of our most joyful tunes, which is sung in every Protestant church, on an average, once every Sunday the year round. Later in the mass the choir sang one of the regular Sunday-school airs, such as Mr. Root of Chicago composes, — similar in character to "If at first you don't succeed, try, try again." To think of Catholic children presuming to express their joyful emotions by the aid of Protestant music! Congress, perhaps, will be petitioned next winter for an Inter-Denominational Copyright Law.

The supreme moment of the mass, announced by the ringing of the bell, is at the elevation of the host. Now, for the first time during the service, there was silence in the room; and every head was bowed, while the priest said inaudibly, in Latin: "Accept, O Holy Father, almighty, eternal God, this immaculate Host, which I, thy unworthy servant, offer unto thee, my living and true God, for my innumerable sins, offences, and negligences, and for all here present; as also for all faithful Christians, both living and dead, that it may be profitable for my own and for their salvation unto life eternal. Amen." Soon after this solemnity, ten or fifteen children, from nine to eleven years of age, went to the altar and communed. All this army of children, except a very few under seven years of age, have been confirmed, and consequently are communicants. Many hundreds of them had been recently confirmed, — clad in white garments, adorned with flowers, accompanied by parents and friends, and surrounded by whatever is most expressive of joy and hope. In this easy and pleasant way our Roman Catholic brethren "join the church." As we have already observed, there is not, among Catholics, anything of that distinction between those who "belong to the church" and those who do not, which is so painful, and, as some of us think, so deeply demoralizing, a circumstance of American life. There are good Catholics and bad Catholics, devout Catholics and neglectful Catholics; but all are Catholics; all are members of the church; all can at any moment resume neglected obligations without taking the public into their confidence. The attitude and condition of each soul is a secret known only to itself and to one other. Hence there is no such thing as a roll of members in a Catholic parish, and there are no formalities attending the transfer of a member to another parish. The poor emigrant is at home in the first church he comes to, and every priest is his father. This is one of the most important differences between our Roman Catholic brethren and ourselves; and it is one which gives them a most telling advantage in this country among educated persons who love virtue and loathe the profession of it.

This Sunday-school mass lasted thirty-five minutes, at the end of which the priest put on his black cap and retired. A curtain was then drawn across the altar, which exempted all from the obligation of bending the knee on passing it. A furious uproar arose when the mass ended, caused by the gathering of the classes around the teachers and getting ready for the next exercise, which was catechism. For about half an hour the whole body of children were engaged in saying their lesson, and in hearing the comments of the teachers upon it; and as there were two thousand of them the noise was great. Nevertheless, there was very little intentional disorder, although the air was so agonizingly impure as to enhance tenfold the difficulty of keeping order, and of keeping in order. Windows were opened, but it was of no use; the air never can be even tolerable in that basement when there are five hundred persons in it. After the catechism the superintendent mounted a platform in the midst of his flock, and reduced them to silence by the sound of his bell. Then he crossed himself, and said, "In the name of the Father, the Son, and the Holy Ghost. Amen," while all the children rose to their feet. He then said, "The Gospel for the day is," — and read it to the children, all standing. He next said, "Kneel"; and all knelt on both knees, with the body upright. He said a very short prayer (five or six short sentences), which the children repeated after him. The school was then dismissed.

Usually, however, they spend the last fifteen minutes in singing a few simple songs, set to easy, lively music. Dr. Cummings, who was the late pastor of this church, and was venerated in it, composed a Sunday-school hymn-book in the last years of his life. The reader, perhaps, may be curious to know what kind of hymns our Roman Catholic brethren teach their children to sing. Well, cut out of this book one tenth of its contents, in which the saints are invoked and a few Catholic peculiarities are referred to, and it would be found suitable to any Protestant Sunday school. There is, for example, a "Song of the Union," which might very properly be sung in Faneuil Hall on the Fourth of July:—

"Ere Peace and Freedom, hand in hand,
Went forth to bless this happy land,
And make it their abode,
It was the footstool of a throne;
But now no sceptre here is known,
No King is feared but God.

"Americans uprose in might,
And triumphed in th' unequal fight,
For Union made them strong:—
Union! the magic battle-cry,
That hurled the tyrant from on high,
And crushed his hireling throng!

"That word since then hath shone on high
In starry letters to the sky,—
It is our country's name!
What impious hand shall rashly dare
Down from its lofty peak to tear
The banner of her fame?"

The same strain of patriotism is continued in the three other stanzas. There are many hymns such as the following, called "A Child's Hymn to his Guardian Angel," which hovers over the line that divides poetry and superstition:—

"How kind it is of you to come,
Bright angel, from your starry home,
And watch by night and watch by day
Beside a sinful child of clay!
How good and pure I ought to be,
Who always live so near to thee.
Beneath thine eyes the whole day round,
Where'er I tread is holy ground.

"And if I had my wish I would,
Dear angel mine! be always good;
This minute I would rather die
Than say bad words or tell a lie.
I always feel disposed this way,
Whene'er I kneel me down to pray;
But I forget when church is o'er,
And am as naughty as before.

. . . .

"But I would love to fear the Lord,
And shun each sinful deed and word,
Not do the sin, then feel the force
Of bitter shame and keen remorse.
I wish to think of God and thee
Whenever pretty things I see,
Till every flower that gems the sod
Shall make me think of thee and God."

Interspersed among such simple and innocent songs as this there are a few which Protestants disapprove : —

"O Mary! Mother Mary!
We place our trust in thee;
Our faith shall never vary,
Though weak the flesh may be.
Too oft, with steps unwary,
From duty we have bent:
O Mary! Mother Mary!
Thou teach us to repent."

But, on the other hand, there are no appeals to base terror, no horrid pictures of future hopeless torment. The only thing in the book that even calls to mind the fearful threats of eternal vengeance with which all children used to be terrified, degraded, and corrupted is a hopeful and sympathetic little hymn entitled "Purgatory" : —

"When gentle showers
Cool the parched beds,
Languishing flowers
Lift up their heads.
Christ's precious merits,
Like gentle rain,
Soothe the good spirits
In their great pain.

"To the dim region,
Where dear ones mourn,
Love and religion
Bid us oft turn.
Prayer hath the power
To give them peace,
Speeding the hour
Of their release."

Such are the exercises of a Catholic Sunday school : mass, thirty-five minutes ; catechism, about the same time ; singing, fifteen minutes ; the Gospel of the day read ; a prayer of five lines ; to which is occasionally added a short address by the pastor. The following summary of the Annual Report of this school for 1867 will interest some readers. The word "Mission," which occurs in it, signifies "revival," or "protracted meeting," concerning which something further may be said:—

Number of children on Register	2,346
Average attendance of children	1,607
Average number of children late	97
Number of teachers on Register	230
Average attendance of teachers	176
Average number of teachers late	9
Number of classes in Sunday school	210
Increase in the number of children on Register over 1866	762
Increase in the average attendance of children over 1866	427
Increase in the number of teachers on Register over 1866	62
Increase in the average attendance of teachers over 1866	31
Increase in the number of classes over 1866	54
Number of children at Festival, Jan. 13, 1867	3,000
Number of children at Festival, Oct. 27, 1867	3,434
Number of children to confession during Mission	2,900
Number of children who received communion during Mission	1,660
Number of children confirmed during Mission	1,530
Total number of visits to children during the year	4,973
Increase in the number of visits to children over 1866	436

THOS. E. S. DWYER, *Sup't.*

JOHN J. WELDON, }
FRANCIS A. REILLY, } *Secretaries.*

It is a beautiful thought to gather the children of a community, for a short time, — an hour and a half, no more, — on Sunday morning, in some very inviting and perfectly salubrious place, where they shall enjoy themselves in singing songs and hymns, and hear something cheering and beneficial, and to join in any other exercises which the affectionate ingenuity of their elders may be able to devise. It is a lovely idea, and one which civilization, having once possessed, can never again let go. So far, the idea has been carried out imperfectly; and it will perhaps never be made the most of until the churches all give up the attempt to expound the universe, and settle down to their final grand vocation, — that of inculcating virtue, instructing ignorance, and cheering human life. This Sunday school of our Roman Catholic brethren will doubtless improve when its zealous and amiable teachers have better facilities and a better school-room. It has already an excellent feature: this one session of an hour and a half is, at once, church and Sunday school; and nothing more is required of the children during all the rest of the day. There is no afternoon school, and the children are not expected nor advised to hear a second mass. Our Roman Catholic brethren never compel young children, over-schooled during the week, to attend Sunday school from nine to half past ten; to remain in church, understanding nothing of what is said and done there, until past twelve; and then, after dinner, to endure both school and church again, happy if they escape them in the evening. Of all the contrivances for making children sicken at the thought of everything high and serious this is the masterpiece. Fortunately, it is now scarcely known, except in a few very remote and benighted places. The time is near at hand, when the great joy of the week to the children of the United States will be the hour and a half of the Sunday school. Often, when hearing Mr. Dickens read, the thought occurred to us: What a splendid exercise some such reading as this for a Sunday school! Among a dozen teachers, surely there would always be one with a little natural aptitude for reading and personating, who would consent to go into training for a year or two, and then give all the children, every Sunday, half an hour of rapture, and an endless benefit, by reading something suitable.

Protestants who visit Catholic institutions for the first time, and converse with those who have charge of them, are surprised to find how little good Catholics differ from other good people. These teachers of the St. Stephen's Sunday school, for example, their *tone*, manner, feeling, cast of countenance, remind you continually of Protestant persons engaged in the same calling. They are as candid and open as the day. They are as truly and entirely convinced of the truth of their religion as any Protestant ever was of his, and their habitual feeling towards Protestants is — compassion. They think their religion is altogether sweet and engaging, full of comfort and hope; and they yearn to see all the world partaking of its joys and consolations. Just as we in our ignorance pity them, so do they in their ignorance pity us. The habitual feeling of good Catholics, with regard to their church and the rest of the world, was well and truly expressed by the late pastor of St. Stephen's, Dr. Cummings: —

"World of Grace! mysterious Temple!
Holy, Apostolic, One!
Never changing, ever blessing
Every age and every zone;
Church, sweet Mother! may all nations
Know thee, love thee as of yore:
May thy children learn to prize thee,
Daily, hourly, more and more."

Ignorant Catholics, of course, like ignorant Protestants, sometimes despise or hate those who differ from them on subjects which are far beyond all human comprehension. But the general feeling of our Roman Catholic brethren towards us is a tender and warm desire that we should immediately abandon our gloomy and abortive religion, and come back to the true fold, where all is cheerfulness, certainty, and love, — especially, *certainty!* There is nothing they pity us so much for as the doubt and uncertainty in which they suppose many of us are living concerning fundamental articles of faith. A Catholic cannot doubt; for the instant he doubts he ceases to be a Catholic. His church is "infallible"; hence his doctrine must be right. His priest is the director of his soul; he has but to obey his direction. Thus a good Catholic has intellectual satisfaction and peace of conscience both within his reach; and he truly pities those who grope in mental darkness, and carry the burden of their sins, without the possibility of ever being *quite* sure they are forgiven. The priest says: "I absolve thee"; but it is on certain conditions named, with which a person can comply, and with which he can *know* he has complied.

There is an impression among Protestants that the Catholic priests are not believers in their own creed; but that, being convinced of the necessity which exists in unformed minds of believing something absurd and fictitious, they recognize that necessity, and have organized superstition without sharing it. We sometimes hear Protestants parodying the ancient remark concerning the Roman augurs, and wondering whether two priests can ever look one another in the face without laughing. That there are Catholic statesmen and monarchs who take this view of the religion they profess is probable enough. Voltaire himself admitted, when his house had been robbed, that hell was an excellent thing to frighten thieves with, and he consigned to it the particular thieves in question most heartily. His friend, Frederick of Prussia, who was as thoroughgoing an unbeliever as himself, was in the habit of laughing at Voltaire's zeal against the faith of Christendom; and used to tell him, that, even if he could succeed in destroying that faith, which he could not, every ignorant mind would immediately attach itself to falsehoods still more extravagant and pernicious. At that day, too, there were not wanting in France abbés and bishops who passed their lives in deriding the church from which they derived their subsistence. But even then and there the vast majority of the working clergy were perfectly sincere and very laborious pastors, and gave the hungry peasant the greater part of the little comfort he enjoyed.

No candid person can associate much with the Catholic priests of the United States without becoming aware of the entireness and strength of their faith in the doctrines they teach, — without being convinced of their fidelity to the vows they have taken. Why remain priests if they have ceased to believe? It is not the life a false man would choose in *this* country. What with the early masses, the great number of services, the daily and nightly calls to the bedside of the dying, the labor and anxiety of hearing confessions, the deprivation of domestic enjoyments, the poverty (the Archbishop of New York has but four thousand dollars a year and his house), and what with the social stigma which in some communities the very name of Catholic carries with it, — there are few vocations in which a fervent believer would find more joy, and in which a hypocrite would suffer so much weariness and disgust. In one sickly time, two years ago, an assistant priest of a populous New York parish was summoned sixty-five times in eight days to administer the communion to dying persons, and forty-five of those times were between sunset and sunrise. The salary of an assistant priest, in these dear times, is four hundred dollars a year, a room, and a portion of the fees he receives for marriages, baptisms, and masses for the dead, — the whole being a bare subsistence, averaging about eight hundred dollars a year. The pastor of a church receives six hundred dollars a year, a house, and a portion of the fees just mentioned. In a few very extensive city parishes the priest may get a little more money than he really needs; but the great majority receive just enough for the three necessities, — food, clothes, and charity.

The manner in which our Roman Catholic brethren select and train their priests insures at least sincerity. It is a training which, in favorable cases, develops every noble trait of human nature except one, — the sceptical, question-asking faculty, to which all improvement, all progress, is due. Some of the sweetest, purest, and loveliest human beings on this earth are Roman Catholic priests. I have had the pleasure, once in my life, of conversing with an absolute gentleman: one in whom all the little vanities, all the little greedinesses, all the paltry fuss, worry, affectation, haste, and anxiety springing from imperfectly disciplined self-love, — *all* had been consumed; and the whole man was kind, serene, urbane, and utterly sincere. This perfect gentleman was a Roman Catholic bishop, who had spent thirty years of his life in the woods near Lake Superior, trying (and failing, as he frankly owned) to convert rascally Chippeways into tolerable human beings. "I make pretty good Christians of some of them," said he; "but *men?* No: it is impossible." But while I so highly rate this exquisite human being, I must remember that his task in life had been far easier than ours. The two grand difficulties of human life he never encountered, — the difficulty of earning his subsistence, and the difficulty of rearing a family. "Thirteen year of temper in a palace," says Doctor Marigold, "would try the worst of you; but thirteen year of temper in a cart would try the best of you." The Catholic priest *ought* to be far gentler and sweeter than other men, since he has neither a cart to drive nor a temper to live with. It is also much easier to live in a grand, lofty, contemplative way, in the forest, than in New York or Chicago. A Catholic priest, indeed, would be much to blame if he failed to attain a high degree of serenity, moral refinement, and paternal dignity.

The training of priests is severe and long. They come to the altar to be ordained, with faces pallid and wasted by long fasting and late watching. Years before, when they were little boys in the Sunday school, they were noted for their docility, and their interest in all that related to the

Church. The pastor marked them, observed them. As soon as they were old enough, they aspired to serve the priest at the altar; and this ambition was at length, after due trial and preparation, gratified, to the great delight and pride of parents and relations. A Protestant can hardly imagine the joy of Catholic parents at seeing their son ministering to the priest at the altar. Besides being a conspicuous reward for his good behavior, and a kind of guaranty of his future good conduct, it is also something done toward his eternal salvation. Our Roman Catholic brethren, abounding in faith as they are, scoff at the idea of being "justified by faith alone," and feel themselves bound "to work out their salvation." The zealous lad, impelled partly by this motive, but chiefly by natural love of the self-denying and devoted, soon belongs to the select band of altar boys, who glory in assisting at the earliest mass, and in masses performed at midnight. The pastor converses with the parents, and if they consent, but cannot afford the expense of educating the boy for the priesthood, ways are found of aiding him through the preliminary studies. Those studies, — what are they? Latin, Greek, theology, and whatever else cultivates the imagination and assists faith, without giving play to that best something in the best human minds which will not take things for granted, — which inquires, doubts, denies, reasons, and presses on to better ways of thinking. That most powerful instinct, too, which urges the young man, like the spring bird, to seek his mate, has to be extinguished or controlled; and to this end fasting, watching, and other painful mortifications are enjoined, increasing in intensity as the time draws near for the final and irrevocable act of renunciation. With pinched cheeks and sunken eyes, and souls on fire, the young men kneel to receive ordination, while all good Catholics who look upon the scene are filled with a feeling that would be compassion if it were not triumphant joy. "We believe," says a convert, who witnessed the ceremony lately, "there were few dry eyes in that basement chapel when the long ceremony came to its close, when the last words of benediction had been given to the newly consecrated priests by the uplifted hands of the bishop; and cold and selfish must have been the heart which did not linger to send up a fervent petition that God would give perseverance to those youthful and self-devoted laborers in his vineyard. But never shall we forget the zeal and eagerness with which the first mass of each new priest was attended, or how the crowd, men, women, children, pressed forward at its close to receive the benediction from those innocent and now sanctified palms. So precious is this first blessing from a newly ordained priest, that old priests and even bishops come eagerly forward, and bow their heads under the freshly anointed hands."

Sincere! The sincerest believers in the world are our Roman Catholic brethren. Faith, like every other faculty or habit, grows strong by exercise. Every time a Catholic attends mass, he is required to perform the most tremendous act of faith ever attempted by the human mind since its creation. Whatever may be weak or wanting in Catholics, they abound in faith.

Our Roman Catholic brethren are acquiring so great an estate in the United States, and acquiring it so rapidly, that it becomes a matter of public concern how they get it, what they do with it, and, especially, what they *will* do with it by and by, when it shall have become the largest property held in the country by or for an organization. Other organizations usually live from hand to mouth; but, somehow, the Catholics always contrive to have a little money ahead, to invest for the future. The Catholic Church, seven tenths of whose members are exempt from the income tax because their income is under a thousand dollars a year, is a capitalist, and has the advantage over other organizations which a man has over his fellows who, besides earning his livelihood, has a thousand dollars to operate with. There are spots in the Western country, over which the prairie winds now sweep without obstruction, that will one day be the sites of great cities. Our Roman Catholic brethren mark those spots, and construct maps upon which, not existing towns alone are indicated, but probable towns also. A professor of one of our Western colleges saw, two years ago at Rome, a better map of the country west of the Mississippi than he ever saw at home; upon which the line of the Pacific Railroad was traced, and every spot was dotted where a settlement would naturally gather, and a conjecture recorded as to its probable importance. Five hundred dollars judiciously invested in certain localities now will buy land which, in fifty years, or in twenty, may be worth one hundred millions. Thirty-seven years ago the best thousand acres of the site of Chicago could have been bought for a dollar and a quarter an acre; and there is one man now in Chicago who owns a lot worth twenty thousand dollars which he bought of the government for fifteen cents and five eighths. Now, there are in the Roman Catholic Church men whose business it is to turn such facts to the advantage of the church, and there is also a systematic provision of money for them to expend for the purpose.

Look at our island of Manhattan! Sixty-seven years ago there were but one or two small Catholic churches upon it. It was not until 1808 that there was such a personage as a Roman Catholic bishop of New York. Run over the diocese now, and what do we find? Churches, 88; chapels attached to institutions, 29; colleges and theological seminaries, 4; academies and select schools, 23; parochial schools, one to nearly every church; charitable asylums and hospitals, 11; religious communities of men, 6; of women, 10. But this enumeration, as every New-Yorker knows, conveys no idea of the facts. Everything which our Roman Catholic brethren buy or build is bought or built with two objects in view, — duration and growth. Hence massive structures, and plenty of land! Wherever on this island, or on the lovely waters near it, you observe a spot upon which nature and circumstances have assembled every charm and every advantage, there the foresight and enterprise of this wonderful organization have placed, or are placing, something enormous and solid with a cross over it. The marble cathedral which is to contain ten thousand persons is going up on the precise spot on the Fifth Avenue which will be the very best for the purpose as long as the city stands. Yet, when that site was selected, several years ago, in the rocky wilds beyond the cattle-market, no one would have felt its value except a John Jacob Astor or a Roman Catholic Archbishop. This marvellous church so possesses itself of its members, that Catholic priests are as wise and acute and pushing for the church as the consummate man of business is for his own estate. Our excellent and zealous friends, the Paulist Fathers, when they planted themselves on the Ninth Avenue opposite Weehawken, bought a whole block; and thus, for less money than one house-lot will be worth in five years, secured room enough for the expansion of their community and its operations for ten centuries! And there is the Convent of the Sacred Heart, in the upper part of the island, — the old Lorillard country-seat; and the great establishments of the Sisters of Charity on the Hudson, where Edwin Forrest built his toy-castle, — were ever sites better chosen? Mark, too, the extent of the grounds, the solidity of the buildings, and the forethought and good sense which have presided over all the arrangements.

All these things cost money, though bought and built with most admirable economy. Fifty million dollars' worth of land and buildings the church probably owns in the diocese of New York; one half of which, perhaps, it acquired by buying land when land was cheap, and keeping it till it has become dear. Protestants will not fail to note the wisdom of this, and to reflect upon the weakness and distracted inefficiency of *our* mode of doing business. But the question remains: How was the other half of this great estate accumulated in half a century by an organization drawing its revenues chiefly from mechanics, small storekeepers, laborers, and servant-girls? Why, in the simplest way possible, and without laying a heavy burden on any one. The glory of the Catholic Church, as we all know, is, that it is the church of the poor; and in this fact consists its strength, as well as its glory.

The unit of the Catholic Church is the parish. A certain number of parishes constitute the diocese, and a certain number of dioceses form an arch-diocese; but the beginning of everything is the parish. Just as a company of troops is at once a whole and a part, small in itself, but imaging in its organization the whole army, independent and yet subordinate, such is a parish to the Church Universal. It so happened that a new parish was organizing in the city of New York, while this article was forming out of chaos; and I read from the front windows, stuck upon a lamp-post (in violation of an ordinance), a handbill which explains how it is done: —

"NOTICE TO CATHOLICS.

"A NEW PARISH.

"The Most Reverend Archbishop McCloskey has appointed the undersigned to take charge of a new parish, which will extend from the east side of Fourth Avenue to the East River, and from the north side of Eighteenth Street to the south side of Twenty-Fourth Street.

DEMILT HALL,

Northwest corner of Second Avenue and Twenty-Ninth Street, will be opened on and after Sunday, Jan. 5th, 1868, for divine service.

"On Sundays, at Eight o'clock.

"High Mass, Nine o'clock.

"On Holy Days of Obligation, Mass at Seven and at Nine.

"On other days, Mass at Seven.

"Sunday school will meet at the Hall on Sundays at Eight o'clock, A. M., and will continue one hour after Mass.

"At the Eight-o'clock Mass on Sundays, and at the Nine-o'clock Mass on Holy Days, a portion of the Hall will be reserved for children.

"Confessions will be heard every Saturday, commencing at Four o'clock, P. M.

"R. L. BURTSELL, D. D., *Pastor.*

"CHRISTMAS DAY, 1867."

Observe now the simplicity and efficiency of the system. St. Stephen's parish, containing twenty-five thousand Catholic souls, had become too populous to be adequately served by one church; and therefore this slice (a mile long and a quarter of a mile wide, containing, perhaps, ten thousand Catholics) is cut off from it to form a new parish. The archbishop looks about among his clergy for a priest fitted by nature and circumstances to organize a parish and provide for it suitable buildings. The priest selected feels himself honored by the appointment; it is promotion to him; it is reward and stimulus. He comes to his new field unshackled, except by the general laws and usages of the Church. The same Church which tries and tests with such unrelenting severity the candidates for the priesthood trusts her priests with great freedom, great power, great responsibility, while supplying them with the most powerful motives to exertion. She supplies both kinds of motives, the noble and the commonplace. This priest has a church to build, schools to form, a parish to create. He has no wife: the Church is his spouse. He has no child: the Church is his HEIR! Professional pride, *esprit du corps*, human ambition, and all the other ordinary motives to exertion, conspire in this man with benevolence and religion: since he firmly and entirely believes that the Roman Catholic Church is the sweetest, holiest, sublimest thing known to man, — his best consolation here, and his surest passport to happiness yonder.

In union there is strength; and yet when a thing is to be done, one man must do it. Our Roman Catholic brethren contrive to work at once, with the power of a union of two hundred millions of members, and with the efficient force which only an individual can wield. This priest of the unformed parish is as independent as the captain of a frigate on his own quarter-deck, who must ever keep an eye on the signals of the admiral's ship, but who when the signal says *Go in*, lays his ship alongside, and carries on the action in his own way, subject only to the rules of the service. This priest, too, is not required to waste his force and the best of his time in writing brilliant sermons for the entertainment of a cloyed, fastidious congregation. His is healthier, manlier work. He has to do, at times, with contractors, masons, carpenters, architects. He is out of doors a good deal, watching the progress of buildings, upon the erection of which his heart is set, and the completion of which will gratify his pride as well as his benevolence, besides entitling him to consideration elsewhere. Seeing what a healthy and full life these Catholic priests lead, I no longer wonder to find them so round, contented, cheerful, and merry.

Our priest, as we see in the handbill, hires a hall, and begins. The enterprise is self-sustaining from the first day. His three masses on Sunday, his daily mass, his vesper services, his pew-rents, his fees, bring in money enough for all expenses, and a surplus for the church which is to be erected. At every mass there is a collection. A building committee is formed; subscription-books are opened; fairs are held. In three years, come to this new parish, and you shall see: 1. A large and handsome church; 2. A good parsonage, next door to it; 3. A five or six story building adjoining for a parochial school, with two thousand children in it under the instruction of the Sisters of Charity and the Christian Brothers. This is no exaggeration; for I am only stating here what has actually occurred in the next parish, — that of the Immaculate Conception, in East Fourteenth Street. Seven years ago, when Dr. Morrogh was appointed pastor of this parish, there was neither church, parsonage, nor school. He now has an excellent church, which he is about to enlarge, a sufficient parsonage, and an exceedingly spacious and handsome school-house, wherein, by the time these lines are read, he will have twenty-five hundred children. It is true that Dr. Morrogh possesses unusual executive ability; but, on the other hand, his church is in the heart of one of the tenement-house regions, and he probably has not a hundred men in his parish who ever have a hundred dollars all at once. Probably he can boast — and a proud boast it is for a Christian minister — that nine tenths of his flock are laboring men and domestic servants. And it is these poor people who have solaced themselves by paying for these buildings, which cannot have cost less than two hundred thousand dollars. Nor has it been a heavy burden to any one but the pastor. "Many a night I have lain awake," said he, "wondering where the money was to come from to go on with." But for the people of the parish it was easy enough. Are there not fifteen thousand of them? If each contributes ten cents a week, does it not come to seventy-eight thousand dollars a year?

The regular revenues of a Catholic church in a city are numerous and large. Here is the Church of St. Stephen's, for example; let us endeavor to estimate its income: —

Six-o'clock mass on Sunday morning	$10.00
Seven-o'clock mass " "	25.00
Nine-o'clock " " "	25.00
Sunday-school collection	10.00
High mass at half past ten	40.00
Vespers	20.00
Six week-day masses, in all	25.00
Total weekly income :	$155.00

This is equal to $8,060 for a year. Add to this the rent of 600 pews, at an average of $75 each, and we have an annual revenue of $53,060. The pew-rent, I believe, averages more than this; although the pews stand open to every comer, except at high mass and vespers.

Such is the income. The expenses are not great: —

Pastor's salary	$600
Three assistant priests, in all	1,200
Sexton, not more than	1,000
Organist, probably	1,000
Choir, about	4,000
Fire and gas, possibly	1,000
Total expenses	$8,800

This leaves an excess of income over expenditure of $42,260. This excess, except a small annual tax for the archbishop and the general interests of the diocese, is all expended in the parish. Upon most of these new city churches there is a debt which has to be provided for. If the parish is old enough to be out of debt, you may be sure it needs a new or an enlarged church, for which a fund is forming. If its church is sufficient, and the parsonage adequate, then you may expect to see the pastor directing the construction of a parochial school-house, large enough to draw off from the over-crowded public schools of the neighborhood the two thousand too many children on their rolls. Or, perhaps, there is connected with the church a religious community whose operations are expensive. Thus, by the unstimulated, quiet operation of the system, all our cities will be covered with costly Catholic structures, which will constantly increase in splendor and number. In some New England villages, and in several New England towns, the Catholic Church is already much the most solid, spacious, and ornate ecclesiastical edifice in the place. It must be so; for the poor, besides being more generous than the rich, are hundreds of times more numerous, and their pennies flow in a continuous stream. Nor do they confine their gifts to copper coin. "An Irish housemaid," says a paragraph just afloat, "has given a stained-glass window to the Catholic Church at Concord, New Hampshire." Nothing more credible. Two servant-girls, in this very house where I am now writing, educated their brother for the priesthood, — keeping on year after year, spending nothing for their personal gratification, literally nothing, but sustaining him respectably, until one ecstatic day they went off in their Sunday clothes, their two faces radiant with joy, to see him ordained. Having accomplished this work, they next saved the sum requisite ($ 250 each) for their honorable admission into a laborious religious order, in which they now are. And yet the self-indulgent Parlor has the insolence to think itself morally superior to the self-denying Kitchen. The Recording Angel, if there is such a book-keeper, has something to enter to the credit of the Kitchen much oftener, probably, than he has to that of the apartments above it.

But we are talking of the financial system of the church. The archbishop, as before observed, draws a small sum annually from each parish; he also derives something from the revenues of the cathedral; and he controls the large fund arising from the sale of lots in the Catholic cemeteries, — all of which are the property of the diocese. Our Roman Catholic brethren decidedly prefer to be buried in cemeteries of their own. No strict Catholic will bury a member of his family in Greenwood or Mount Auburn, for he does not feel that God Almighty's ground is quite good enough for his bones to moulder in until a bishop has said a few words over it. We must pardon him this harmless foible, in consideration of our own similar weaknesses. The fact remains, however, that the income of the cemeteries adds something considerable to the central fund of the diocese, which is applied to objects of diocesan importance. We may illustrate the working of this part of the system by showing how the new cathedral in the city of New York was started, how it has been continued, and how it is to be carried on to completion. This edifice will probably cost two millions of dollars. It would cost ten millions if it were to be built by the city government.

When Archbishop Hughes made up his mind, about ten years ago, that the time had come for beginning a cathedral that would be worthy of the chief city of the Union, the debt upon the old cathedral had not been extinguished, the cemetery fund was almost consumed in enlarging and improving the cemeteries themselves, and the archbishop was dependent for his mere maintenance upon the product of the tax upon the parishes. No matter; the time had come for beginning; and every New-Yorker now sees how perfectly the commencement of the enterprise was timed. But there was no money. If it had been a Protestant enterprise, this fact would have presented a slight impediment. It is only our Roman Catholic brethren who can undertake two-million-dollar cathedrals without having any money. The archbishop caused a circular letter to be written, announcing his design, and requesting the person addressed to contribute toward it one thousand dollars. A copy of this letter, signed by the archbishop, was sent to every Catholic in the diocese known to be rich enough to afford himself the luxury of giving away a thousand dollars. A similar letter, also signed by the archbishop, was addressed to every Catholic who could be supposed capable of giving five hundred dollars; and another letter to many who could be rationally expected to give two hundred and fifty dollars; each of whom was invited to confer upon himself the pleasure and advantage of giving the sum mentioned in the epistle addressed to him. Such requests are never made without due consideration, and they are seldom refused. Nor is the church too particular as to *whose* money it shall accept. I have before me a Catholic subscription paper, on which may be read: —

Charles O'Conor	$250.00
John Morrissey	500.00

All is fish that comes to the church's net. By this expedient the archbishop raised three hundred thousand dollars, — enough to buy the land, lay the foundation, and carry up the walls a few feet. About the time the war broke out the money was gone, and it was highly convenient to stop. The orphans and the widows of the war were a heavy charge upon all the city parishes. The ordinary collections at Christmas and Easter (sacred to the orphan in all Catholic churches) were utterly insufficient, and the people were called upon for further aid, which of course they gave most liberally. It was obviously not a time to be building marble cathedrals for posterity, and so the walls were carefully boarded over. The war being ended, the new archbishop issued a requisition, calling upon each pastor of a parish for a contribution to the cathedral fund, and allowing him a certain time in which to collect it. Work upon the building has been resumed, and will probably go on until it is completed; for the old cathedral is out of debt, and the cemetery fund is now productive.

The archbishop, be it observed, is the almost absolute ruler of the priests of his province. He places them, removes them, suspends them, according to his own good will and pleasure, subject to the laws and usages of the church. There is no appeal against his decisions, except to Rome; and this resource is seldom within the compass of a priest. Rome is far away, and a priest appealing against the judgment of his superior must have a very good case or a very good friend, in order to obtain a favorable judgment. But, on the other hand, a dignitary of the church is severely and long tested before promotion, and he is practically elected by the very men whom he is afterwards to govern. Soon after the death of an archbishop, the higher clergy of the province assemble to express their preferences with regard to his successor. They send three names to Rome. Opposite the first name is written, *Dignus,* worthy. Opposite the second, *Dignior,* worthier. Opposite the third name is written, *Dignissimus,* most worthy. The office is almost invariably assigned to the person whom his brethren thus indicate as their choice. The instances are rare in which an American prelate has abused his power over the clergy, and I believe no priest has yet applied to Rome for the redress of a grievance.

Among our Roman Catholic brethren the instinct of organizing and co-operating is wonderfully developed. I have before me a list, not complete, of the Catholic orders, which contains the names of two hundred and fifty-one varieties, each of which is an expression and a permanent gratification of the desire of some benevolent soul. One example: Two hundred and fifty years ago, a French priest, named Vincent de Paul, was requested by a lady of his flock to call the attention of the congregation to the case of a destitute family lying sick a mile from the town. He did so, and with such effect that the poor people were supplied with food in profusion, so that much of it was spoiled before they could consume it. This priest, being one of those men whom every event instructs, was led to reflect upon the need there was in every large town of having the benign impulses regulated, and the gifts of the benevolent husbanded, so that none of them should be wasted, and the supply should never be exhausted. The result of his meditations we behold in the order of the Sisters of Charity, which all the world approves, and will ever approve. But this was not all the good arising from Father Vincent's reflections. To-day nearly every Catholic parish in large towns, in Europe, Asia, Africa, America, and Australia, has within it a society called a "Conference of St. Vincent de Paul," the object of which is the systematic and judicious relief of the poor of the parish. These societies form one vast system of charity; each conference reporting to a diocesan centre, each diocese reporting to a national centre, and each nation to the Head Centre of the organization,— a cardinal residing at Paris. From him again, as the blood pulses back from the heart to the extremities, a quarterly report is sent to every corner of Christendom, which reaches every individual member of each conference. Any reader curious to know the practical working of the system can gratify his desire by expending ten cents at any Catholic bookstore, where he can buy the "Rules of the Society of St. Vincent de Paul."

Then there is the "Propaganda," or, as we should term it, the missionary system. This, too, is an organization which embraces the whole world, and to the funds of which tens of millions of Catholics contribute. Each member of the organization gives one cent a week toward the extension of the domain of the Church. In every ten members there is one person who is authorized to receive the weekly coppers, and pay the dime over to an individual who is the centre of ten tens. By the time the money reaches *his* hands it has become a dollar, and he hands the dollar to one who receives for ten of these ten tens. We have now rolled up the sum to ten dollars, which is paid to the head of ten of the hundred tens; and so it goes on swelling until it reaches the chief of the propaganda, another cardinal, who lives at Lyons. He, in turn, sends to the societies a report of the grand result, which, by a system of handing from one ten to another, is made to reach every giver of a weekly cent. Thus is the money raised which sustains the Church beyond the bounds of Christendom, and buys the sites of churches where as yet there is no human habitation.

There is no end to the charities of our Roman Catholic brethren and sisters, and all that they do in this way is done with the efficiency and power of a disciplined organization. An admirable case in point is that of a community in Paris, which consists of an equal number of blind and seeing sisters. In each cell there is one of each; and it is part of the occupation of the sister who can see to aid, wait upon, and read to the sister who is blind. It does the heart good merely to know that such a sweet device as this has ever been conceived. There is a little book published in Paris (and we ought to have such in our cities) which contains a catalogue and brief account of all the charitable organizations there, — *Manuel des Œuvres et Institutions de Charité. Publié par Ordre de M*[gr.] *l'Archevêque*, &c. It contains a description of one hundred and ninety-two benevolent societies and systems. Any one would be puzzled to think of a malady, misfortune, deprivation, or peril for which there does not exist in Catholic Paris some organized remedy, mitigation, or prevention. The mere enumeration would exhaust all my remaining space, and I can only mention a few. There are societies for aiding mothers before, during, and after confinement; some of which give in-door, others out-door aid; some bearing the whole charge, others part; some aiding mothers themselves to form a fund against the time, and others insuring the required aid, whenever needed, in return for the payment of a small sum periodically. There are societies for the preservation and assistance of every conceivable description of needy children, — lost children, abandoned children, neglected children, destitute children, bad children, blind, deaf and dumb, and crippled children; children subject to fits, convalescent children, children whose mothers have to go out to work, children who want to be apprenticed and cannot pay the required premium, children who have no one to teach them their catechism; orphan children in asylums, orphan children living with relatives, orphan children in places, orphan children adopted, Polish orphans, Jewish orphans. Besides special hospitals for almost every kind of curable and incurable maladies, there are asylums for every description of disabled persons, — the blind, the deaf and dumb, the crippled, the aged, the imbecile, the incompetent of all kinds and degrees. And this vast system of charity is carried on by our Roman Catholic brethren and sisters, and most of the work is done by persons dedicated for life to the service of the afflicted, and trained to discharge their vocation in the best manner.

It is interesting to observe how each part of the Catholic system, besides promoting the general object, works in special harmony with special aims. Example: it is the wish, it is the fixed intention, of our Roman Catholic brethren to have a free school in every parish in the United States sufficient for the accommodation of all the Catholic children resident in the parish. In the diocese of New York there are sixty-one of these parochial schools, in which about twenty-five thousand pupils are taught, greatly to the relief of the cruelly crowded public schools. The religious instruction given in these schools consists of a lesson in the catechism, the saying of a few short Catholic prayers, the reading of the Gospel for the day, and an occasional exhortation; the whole occupying, on an average, twenty minutes a day. But it is not for the sake of the direct religious instruction that the pastors are so desirous of having parochial schools. There are several orders in the church which are devoted to the work of instruction, — the Christian Brothers, some of the Sisters of Charity, the Ladies of the Sacred Heart, and many more. It is from these orders that the teachers of the parochial schools are drawn; and it is the *Catholicizing* effect upon the minds of the children, of these still, self-contained, cheerful persons that the pastors chiefly value. There is a marvellous economy, too, in the system; for these pious sisters and devoted brothers only require the necessaries of life. Dr. Morrogh pays into the treasury of the Sisters of Charity two hundred dollars per annum for each sister employed in his school! The sisters live at the house of their order in Fifteenth Street, and go forth every morning to the schools to spend a laborious day in instructing ignorance, returning at noon and at night to their religious home. It will cost Dr. Morrogh about eight thousand dollars to sustain his school, possibly ten thousand. It would cost the city of New York eighteen thousand dollars. It happened to be a snowy day on which I visited this school, and no one went home to dinner. But when dinner-time came, an apparatus containing a hot dinner for the sisters was brought round to them from their home near by, and they all sat down together in a nice little room to enjoy it, with the musical accompaniment of twelve hundred romping girls.

Surely there is something admirable and imitable in all this.

Of course there is shadow to be put into the picture. This amazing organization, or system of organizations, is the accumulated practical wisdom of many thousand years; but it is the work of imperfect human beings, and partakes of their imperfection. "There is a provision in nature," says Goethe, "to prevent trees from growing up into the sky." Else, Commodore Vanderbilt would own all the railroads, and we should all turn Catholics immediately. Every Protestant knows, or thinks he knows, precisely what the defect is which prevents this interesting tree from growing up into the sky, and spreading its branches over the whole earth. I think I know. I think it is because there is not a sufficient provision in it for adapting its doctrine to the advancing mind of the race.

Our Roman Catholic brethren, for example, firmly believe that miracles are daily wrought among them. They inform me, that the most noted miracle yet performed in the United States occurred in the city of Washington on the 10th of March, 1824. Bishop England, of Charleston, who ranked very high in the estimation of his brethren, investigated this miracle, published an account of it, and appended to his narrative the affidavits of thirty-seven persons, all of whom testified to the miraculous nature of the event. Mrs. Ann Mattingly, widow, aged thirty-four, residing with her brother, the Mayor of Washington, had been afflicted for six years with a hard and painful tumor in the lower part of the left breast, which four of the leading physicians of the city pronounced incurable, and for which they prescribed only palliative applications and medicines. She suffered all that a woman could suffer and live, — vomitings of blood, intense chills, pain almost insupportable, a most distressing cough, until she was reduced to a skeleton, and lay at death's door. From long lying in bed, her shoulders and back were ulcerated to such a degree that it was torture to her to have her linen changed or to move in bed. In the fifth year of her illness the tidings began to be spread abroad in America of the wonderful cures wrought in Europe through the prayers of a certain Prince Hohenlohe, a venerated priest of the Catholic Church; and some of the friends of the afflicted lady besought her to make known her sufferings to this holy man, and beg his intercession in her behalf. The pastor of her church, with the consent of the Archbishop of Baltimore, wrote to the princely priest, — as many others did in all parts of the world, — asking his prayers for this lady's recovery. The priest ascertained, however, that the Prince Hohenlohe had already made known his intentions with regard to all sick persons out of Europe who desired his prayers. He would pray for such on the tenth day of every month at nine o'clock in the morning, and he called upon all who wished to enjoy the benefit of his intercession to fulfil certain conditions. They must have faith in the efficacy of prayers; they must repent anew and deeply of their sins; they must form an immovable purpose to lead an exemplary life; they must perform a Novena, or nine days' devotion, in honor of the Holy Name of Jesus; they must confess, do penance, and receive the sacrament; and, finally, on the appointed day, the tenth of any month, at nine A. M., they must unite in prayers with the prince, far away on the other side of the ocean.

With all these conditions Mrs. Ann Mattingly complied. The priest of her church, two hundred of her friends and fellow-Catholics, as well as some other sick persons, shared in the Novena, and the archbishop of the province "graciously promised to join in prayer with them on the appointed day, 10th of March instant." The Novena was begun on the first day of March, 1824, so that it might end on the tenth. As there is a difference of six hours between the time at Washington and at the place in Germany where the prince lived, the priest appointed the hour of three in the morning for the last solemn act of supplication, and so notified all the families and persons concerned. At nine in the evening before, Mrs. Mattingly, who apparently had not many hours to live, confessed, and received absolution. At two in the morning, the priest who was in special charge of the Novena said mass in the church, and carried thence the sacrament to the afflicted lady's room, where he arrived about half past two. She was then so low and so incessantly tormented by a cough, that the priest was apprehensive she would die before she had communed. The sacrament, however, was administered, and it cost the lady a painful effort of six minutes to swallow it. The solemn ceremony being ended, the priest wrapped up the sacred vessels and implements, gave the usual blessing to the kneeling family (five in number, all of whom swear to these and the following statements), and was making his last adoration of the Host before leaving, when he heard a deep sigh issuing from the direction of the bed. He turned, and behold, — a miracle! Mrs. Mattingly sat up, stretched her arms forward, clasped her hands, and said, in a clear though weak voice, "Lord Jesus, what have I done to deserve so great a favor?" Sobs and shrieks burst from the persons present. The priest rose from his knees, and hastened to the bedside. She raised his hand. "Ghostly father," she cried, "what can I do to acknowledge such a blessing?" "Glory be to God!" he exclaimed; "we may say so. O, what a day for us!" On being asked to tell what she felt, she said, "Not the least pain left."

She went on to say, that, being overcome by her sufferings, and in expectation of immediate death, she had said to herself, "Lord Jesus, thy will be done!" and at that instant she was completely relieved from all her pains. "I wish to get up," she cried, joyfully, "and give thanks to God on my knees"; and so she did, and remained kneeling for fifteen minutes without fatigue. She walked; she dressed herself; she came down to breakfast; she ate heartily, and remained up all day, receiving the visits of friends and strangers, who came in crowds to see her. Every trace of the tumor was gone! *The ulcers upon her back had vanished, and left no scar;* and, what was strangest of all, the matter which those ulcers had discharged had all disappeared, both from the bed-clothes and from her own night-dress!! Upon this last point Bishop England is emphatic. "I am perfectly convinced," he says, "that, were I disposed to collect the testimony relating thereto, it would appear to the satisfaction of every unbiassed, impartial, and judicious reader, unquestionable, that as miraculous a change took place in the state of the clothing of the bed and of the body as there did in the state of the body itself."

This assertion of the Bishop is safe, because upon such subjects *no* reader is unbiassed, *no* reader is impartial.

This narrative illustrates a very important difference between our Roman Catholic brethren and ourselves. A good Catholic, no matter what his rank or culture, believes in such things without an effort. It was not necessary for the faith of Catholics that Bishop England should gather such a mass of testimony. Three good witnesses would have sufficed quite as well as three dozen. But no amount or quality of testimony could convince a Protestant mind that Mrs. Mattingly's tumor was cured miraculously, and her linen miraculously cleansed. For my part, if the President and Vice-President, if the whole Cabinet, both houses of Congress, and the judges of the Supreme Court, had all sworn that they saw this thing done, and I myself had seen it, — nay, if the tumor had been on my own body, and had seemed to myself to be suddenly healed, — still I should think it more probable that all those witnesses, including myself, were mistaken, than that such a miracle had been performed. Such is the incredulity of a modernized mind, especially if that modernized mind has occasionally served on a jury, and so learned the value of human testimony.

How different with Catholics! "Why!" says Father Hecker, "we do not worship a dead God! Where is the improbability? No one doubts God's ability to heal his faithful servants; why should we find it so hard to believe that he does so? Protestants usually admit that miracles were once performed, and they still use language in their prayers which implies an expectation of miraculous aid. We Catholics have a living practical *faith* in Providence, which you Protestants think you have, and have not. And where is your authority for saying that, during a certain period of the world's history, miracles were wrought, but that there came a moment when they ceased to be wrought? Why is it rational to believe in a miracle which occurred Anno Domini 32, but wholly irrational to believe in one wrought Anno Domini 1868?"

These are not the precise words of the Superior of the Paulists, but such are some of his ideas. I did not, do not, cannot answer his questions. My office is merely that of reporter. I have yet to relate the special measures now on foot for the conversion of us all, and the grounds upon which our Roman Catholic brethren rest their confident expectation of being in another generation or two the dominant church of the United States.

Are we all going to be Roman Catholics, then, about the year 1945?

So we are assured by some of our more sanguine Roman Catholic brethren. And, really, the ancient church, not in this young country only, but in Europe too, and especially in France, Germany, and England, appears to be renewing its youth, and pressing forward most vigorously to occupy and reoccupy. It is regaining its audacity. It is beginning again to take the initiative. It hits back once more. It even succeeds in turning the laugh against us sometimes, which is a great point gained. It has taken the church eighty years to recover from the mockery of one man, and it is now using his terrible weapon against its own enemies. Few better burlesques have ever been written than the one recently published in England, and republished in New York, entitled "The Comedy of Convocation in the English Church," in which the one great excellence of that church is ridiculed in the most delicious manner. The point of superiority of the Church of England over some others is, or was, that it allowed a wide latitude of opinion, and did not set up to be an infallible teacher. This is the point ridiculed; but the novelty of the burlesque is, that it is so exquisitely and good-naturedly done. *The new blood is beginning to tell.* There is one extractible passage of this masterpiece of fun, which may serve to illustrate the new spirit of which I speak. "Archdeacon Jolly," one of the speakers at the imaginary convocation, explains the operation of a new society, which, he said, was called "The Society for considering the best Means of keeping alive the Corruptions of Popery in the Interests of Gospel Truth."

"It was, of course," the jolly Archdeacon continued, "a strictly secret organization; but he had been favored, he knew not why, with a copy of the prospectus, and as he had no intention of becoming a member, he would communicate it to the house. It appeared from this document, and could be confirmed from other sources, that a deputation was sent last year to Rome to obtain a private interview with the Pope, in order to entreat his Holiness *not* to reform a single Popish corruption. A handsome present was intrusted to the deputation, and a liberal contribution to the Peter's Pence Fund. The motives set forth in the preamble of the address presented to his Holiness were, in substance, of the following nature: They urged that a very large body of most respectable clergymen, who had no personal ill-will toward the present occupant of the Holy See, had maintained themselves and their families in comfort for many years exclusively by the abuse of popery; and, if popery were taken away, they could not but contemplate the probable results with uneasiness and alarm. Moreover, many eminent members of the profession had gained a reputation for evangelical wit, learning, and piety, as well as high dignities in the Church of England, by setting forth in their sermons, and at public meetings, with all their harrowing details, the astounding abominations of the Church of Rome. The petitioners implored his Holiness not to be indifferent to the position of these gentlemen. Many of their number had privately requested the deputation to plead their cause with the amiable and benevolent Pius IX. Thus the great and good Dr. M'Nickel represented respectfully that he had filled his church, and let all his pews, during three-and-twenty years, by elegantly slandering priests and nuns, and powerfully illustrating Romish superstitions. A clergyman of noble birth had attained to the honors of the episcopate by handling alternately the same subjects, and a particularly pleasing doctrine of the Millennium, and had thus been enabled to confer a valuable living on his daughter's husband, who otherwise could not have hoped to obtain one. An eminent canon of an old Roman Catholic abbey owed his distinguished position, which he hoped to be allowed to retain, to the fact of his having proved so clearly that the Pope was Antichrist; and earnestly entreated his Holiness to do nothing to forfeit that character. A well-known doctor of Anglican divinity was on the point of quitting the country in despair of gaining a livelihood, when the idea of preaching against popery was suggested to him, and he had now reason to rejoice that he had abandoned the foolish scheme of emigration. .... Finally, a young clergyman, who had not hitherto much distinguished himself, having often but vainly solicited a member of his congregation to favor his evangelical attachment, at length hit upon a new expedient, and preached so ravishing a discourse on the matrimonial prohibitions of the Romish Church, and drew so appalling a picture of the domestic infelicities of the Romish priesthood, that on the following Monday morning the young lady made him an offer of her hand and fortune."

Nothing could be better for its purpose than this, and the whole pamphlet of one hundred and thirty-eight pages is executed quite as well. The surprising feature of the performance is, that the author never lapses for a single instant into ill-temper, — such is the strength of his talent, and the entireness of his faith. In conversing with Catholic priests, I have been repeatedly struck with the same imperturbable good-humor, the same *absolute* confidence in the impregnability of their position.

Another fruit of the church's recovered audacity lies before me, in the Abbé Maynard's new "Life of Voltaire," called forth, apparently, by the great stir in France resulting from the proposal to erect a national monument to Voltaire in Paris. "You are a humbug," said Voltaire to the Church, in ninety-seven volumes duodecimo. "You 're another," replies Abbé Maynard, in two volumes octavo.

This indefatigable Abbé has gone over the thousand volumes or so which contain the yet unwritten story of Voltaire's life, and has gathered from them every incident and every sentence the cold relation or quotation of which would make against his subject. The result is, that his work is, at once, the truest and the falsest upon Voltaire ever written; most of the facts which he chooses to give are stated with a certain exactness, but most of that in Voltaire's career which made it worth while to relate those facts at all is not mentioned. It is evident, nevertheless, that the Abbé is as honest as he is patient; he merely cannot *see* anything in Voltaire except his poor, human foibles. His work is chiefly interesting as another evidence that our Roman Catholic brethren are becoming militant again, and do not mean to be hit without striking out from the shoulder at their assailant.

By a curious chance, it happened that the same steamer which brought these two thick volumes from France brought also *Le Vrai Voltaire*, of M. Pompery, also published in 1867, in which two things are asserted of the great master of mockery: 1. That he was the most extraordinary of men; and, 2. That he was *the consummate Christian of all times!* Both of these works came to me in the same brown-paper parcel. Both were published in the same Paris, in the same year; both were written by Frenchmen for Frenchmen. Such a creature is man when he shuts up in party that mind of his which was meant to range free over the whole! Of these two works, that of the Abbé is by far the most able and thorough; and he does not fail to urge home to the Paris of this moment that the virtuous people of France are still those who go to mass and confess their sins. Ah! *that* is the difficult argument to answer! As the authoritative expounder of the universe, the mission of the church may, indeed, be nearly accomplished; but as an organization for the inculcation of virtue, the best part of its career is only just now beginning.

Persons who are so unfortunate as to be obliged to travel much in the public vehicles and vessels of the city of New York frequently have religious tracts offered them by a fellow-sufferer, who draws a bundle of them from his pocket, and hands them around. It has, perhaps, occurred to others besides myself, what a powerful means of doing good this might be if the tracts were written in just the right way, on just the right subjects, by truly enlightened and sympathetic men; and perhaps others have wondered, besides myself, that such an obvious and easy way of spreading abroad good knowledge, good principles, and good feeling should be so long neglected by persons capable of using it with effect. I hope yet to see our omnibuses littered with tracts written by such persons as Mr. Emerson, Dr. Holmes, Mr. Lowell, Mr. Norton, Mr. Curtis, Dr. Bellows, Horace Greeley, Dr. Chapin, Mr. Mayo, Mr. Higginson, Mrs. Stowe, Gail Hamilton, Mr. Beecher, Goldwin Smith, Charles Dickens, and all the other good fellows of either sex who love their species, and have a wise or friendly word to say to them. It will only be necessary for them to write a great deal better than they ever did before.

Our Roman Catholic brethren have at length awoke to the power of the four-paged tract, and they are using it with increasing frequency and skill. This movement mitigates the horrors of city travel; for the Catholic tracts, besides containing much information little known to us Protestants, are written in a lively strain, often in the form of dialogue. It is not a bad thing, about half-way down town, to have politely put into your hands a sprightly little piece, upon "What my Uncle said about the Pope."

"One day, in the Central Park, we sat down on a nice shady seat, and Uncle George took out a newspaper to read. As his eye glanced down the columns he suddenly gave a grunt, and hit the ground very sharply with his cane.

"'Got the gout, Uncle?' said I.

"'No, my dear, it's nothing but the old Pope again.'

"'Who is he, Uncle?' I inquired.

"'I am sorry to say he's a bad man, my dear,' replied Uncle George, looking at me over his spectacles, 'and always was.'

"'Why don't the police take him up, then, and try him?' I asked.

"'Because there are so many people who believe him to be a good man,' answered my uncle; 'and as for *trying* him, Fred, there's been plenty of that, if you only understood it; but the oftener he is brought into court, the fewer witnesses you can get to appear against him, and he always manages to come off "not guilty."'

"'How many people believe he is a good man, Uncle?' I inquired. 'A dozen now, I should n't wonder?'

"'A dozen!' exclaimed the old gentleman; 'see here'; and he commenced drawing figures on the gravelled walk with his cane. 'There,' said he, pointing to the sum he had marked on the ground, 'what do you make of that?'

"'There 's a 2,' said I, 'and a naught, and an 8, and six more naughts. Why, Uncle, that 's *two hundred and eight millions!*'

"'That 's about it, my dear.'"

It is much more amusing to read such a sprightly performance as this than to sit opposite six pairs of eyes, occupied only in the embarrassing task of not "catching" any of them. Useful knowledge, too, is acquired. It is agreeable to know the exact figures about anything. There is a tract upon "Article II. of the Popular Creed," which is, "All men cannot believe alike." There is also one upon Article I. of the same creed: "It is a matter of no importance what a man believes, if he be only sincere." There is another entitled "What shall I do to be saved?" This is a dialogue, and the main question is thus answered:—

"*Earnest Inquirer.* Will you be kind enough to tell me what practical answer is given in the Catholic Church to Catholics themselves who ask the question, 'What shall I do to be saved?'

"*Catholic.* A Catholic is usually baptized in infancy, and is thereby invested with all the privileges of a Christian. As he grows older, he is taught the principles of his religion. If he lives up to them, and obeys God's commandments, he is always the friend of God, and does not need to ask the question at all, just as a native-born citizen who has never forfeited his citizenship needs not to inquire how he shall become a citizen. But if he turns away from God by sin, then .... the short practical answer to his question is, Prepare yourself, and come and make an humble and contrite confession of your sins."

Most of the thirty tracts already issued are evidently designed to be read by Protestants, and aim to give correct statements of certain Catholic doctrines which Catholics claim are habitually misstated by Protestants. In the publication of these and other cheap works a Catholic Publication Society has been formed, precisely similar in design to the "Methodist Book Concern." In short, our Roman Catholic brethren are adopting, one after another, all our Protestant plans and expedients; they are turning our own artillery against us. As usual with them, it is one man who is working this new and most effective idea; but, as usual with them also, this one man is working by, with, and through an *organization* which multiplies his force one hundred times, and constitutes him a person of national importance. Readers who take note of the really important things transpiring around them will know at once that the individual referred to is Father Hecker, Superior of the Community of the Paulists, in New York, editor of the "Catholic World," and director of the Catholic Publication Society. It is he who is putting American machinery into the ancient ark, and getting ready to run her by steam. Here, for once, is a happy man, — happy in his faith and in his work, — *sure* that in spreading abroad a knowledge of the true Catholic doctrine he is doing the best thing possible for his native land. A tall, healthy-looking, robust, handsome, cheerful gentleman of forty-five, endowed with a particular talent for winning confidence and regard, which talent has been improved by many years of active exercise. It is a particular pleasure to meet with any one, at such a time as this, whose work perfectly satisfies his conscience, his benevolence, and his pride, and who is doing that work in the most favorable circumstances, and with the best co-operation. Imagine a benevolent physician in a populous hospital, who has in his office the medicine which he is *perfectly certain* will cure or mitigate every case, provided only he can get it taken, and who is surrounded with a corps of able and zealous assistants to aid him in persuading the patients to take it!

This excellent and gifted man is a native of the city of New York, where his two brothers are well known as controlling the business of supplying the city with every description of flour and meal; their establishment being among the most extensive of the kind in the world. The father of these three boys was a Presbyterian, the mother a Methodist; but neither of them was a severe or exacting sectarian, and the boys were allowed the usual free range among all the churches of the town. It was an affectionate, entirely virtuous, and estimable family, of German origin, with a decided bias among the younger members toward spiritual inquiries and subjects. The three boys, in particular, had the true German fondness for one another, and, in due time, went into business together, — that very business which has since grown to such wonderful proportions. They began, however, as bakers and dealers in flour in a small way; all three, I believe, working at the kneading-trough and at the oven's fiery mouth. Their business prospered; it soon became evident that a great success was within their reach, to attain which they had nothing to do but go on in the way they were going. But this assurance of success having been reached, one of the brothers ceased to find the business interesting. He was young, vigorous, athletic, full of life and cheerfulness, and he said to himself: "A man requires but a few cents a day (this was nearly thirty years ago) for his sustenance; why take all this trouble to get those few cents? Is there nothing better or other for a man to do in his short life than earn his living? Must I expend my whole revenue of strength in merely getting the very trifling supplies needed to keep the bodily machine going? — must I really?" Revolving such thoughts in his anxious mind, he continued faithfully to knead the dough and draw the loaves. Always an eager reader, he now became a student. He used to be up at four in the morning studying Kant and the other metaphysicians; and, as kneading does not engross the mind, he nailed his algebra to the wall before his trough, that he might use the unemployed portion of his intellect while at his work. But, whatever he studied, the questions ever present with him were, What is man? whence came he? why is he here? whither is he going? what does it become him to do? — questions which no creature worthy of the name of man ever escaped, or ceased to ask, until he had either found answers, or ascertained them to be unanswerable.

In quest of light upon these problems, he went the round of the sects, attending the services, reading the books, and conversing with the leaders of each. What he longed for was a life of self-renunciation,—a life wholly devoted to worthy objects external to himself. He used to ask Protestants, how he, I. T. Hecker, baker, of the city of New York, could fulfil such injunctions as, "Sell *all* and follow me," and, "Forsake father and mother for my sake." They answered that these were figurative expressions, or, if not figurative, yet not applicable to the case of a young gentleman of good business prospects, residing on the populous island of Manhattan in the nineteenth century. "It was going too far; it was mere youthful enthusiasm; it was not suited to the nineteenth century; there was no occasion for anything of that kind in modern times." These remarks silenced him for a while, but did not satisfy him; he was still seeking his religion, and with a deeper longing than before. He resolved to make it the business of his whole existence, if necessary, to find the solution of his difficulty. "It is a necessity," he said to himself, "to find a religion coinciding with the dictates of reason, and commensurate with the wants of our whole nature, or else to wait for its revelation. If I find no such religion, and God deigns not to reveal it, then on my tomb shall be written: 'Here lies one who asked with sincerity for truth, and it was not given. He knocked earnestly at the door of truth, and it was not opened. He sought faithfully after truth, and he found nothing.'" He now avoided female society, because he was determined, until the great question was settled, to keep his destiny in his own hands, and not complicate the difficulty by blending with his own the fate of another. He withdrew from business also; gave up those brilliant prospects opening before the house of Hecker Brothers, and set out on a journey in search of wisdom. The world has but one way of judging a case of this nature: "Poor Hecker is crazy"; and perhaps the world is not wholly in the wrong.

Every reader has heard of Brook Farm in Massachusetts, where Hawthorne, Ripley, C. A. Dana, G. W. Curtis, and many other young philosophers, took up their abode twenty-five or thirty years ago, and sought to realize in their daily life all that this young New-Yorker was meditating. They, too, had indulged the fond delusion of increasing the happiness by lessening the difficulties of life, and of arranging their lives upon a better system than the natural order. To Brook Farm the youthful seeker after wisdom directed his steps, and cast in his lot with the noble band. It naturally fell to his share to make the bread for the household, which he did on the true Hecker principle. No one found at Brook Farm what he sought there. After nine months' residence Mr. Hecker left that unpeaceful abode no wiser than he came, and went off with Thoreau to one of that philosopher's extremely inexpensive places of residence. They experimented together upon the necessary cost of maintaining human life, and upon this point they actually arrived at a result. They discovered that they could live well enough upon nine cents a day each, — an island of certainty in a sea of doubt, but not large enough for a dwelling-place for two souls. Thoreau found it sufficient for himself for a while, and wrote a highly entertaining book relating his residence thereon.

Meanwhile, the brothers and friends of Mr. Hecker were pressing him to return and resume his place in the ever-expanding business. After much reflection, it occurred to him that a man having many other men in his employment might perhaps find a sphere for all his nobler aims in promoting *their* welfare. He may have been reading Carlyle's fantastical Toryism in Past and Present, where this particular kind of impertinence is highly extolled. However that may be, he consented, about the time of his coming of age, to return to the ordinary life of men, and to take his proper place in the business, on two conditions: 1. That the three brothers should possess all things in common, have no separate purse; and, 2. That he should have control of all the men employed. His brothers gladly consenting, he returned. He now tried in all ways known to him to benefit the workmen. He fitted up a nice room, and stored it well with books, periodicals, and games, in which he invited them to pass their leisure hours. He endeavored to give them good advice, as well as to comfort and encourage them. But it would not do. The attempt to teach others only brought home the more painfully to his mind how sorely he needed instruction himself. He was trying to feed other men, while himself was starving. Groping in the dark, blind, blind, blind, he was presuming to guide the steps of his fellows. If he asserted something respecting their duty, and they questioned it, he knew of no infallible standard to which he could appeal. He could not tell them what man's duty really was, for he knew not why man was placed here, nor what placed him, nor whither he was bound, nor whether he was bound anywhither. He did not quite like to confess this to the men he was trying to help; but if they pressed him close, he stammered and hesitated, and, if they pressed him closer, he was dumb. He persevered, however, for a year. Then he gave it up, and resumed his studies and wanderings. He was fully determined not to expend the whole of his energies, and most of his time, in earning that ridiculous sum of nine cents a day needed for keeping the bodily apparatus going. And as for guiding the men engaged in helping him get those nine cents, it would be time for him to teach them when he himself had found out something.

Fourierism came up about this time. Mr. Brisbane, a young man of fortune, returned from Europe full of the dreams and theories of Fourier, which he proceeded to expound to the public in the young Tribune; and highly creditable it was, both to the man and to the newspaper, to do and risk so much in the discussion of such a subject. To err in the service of man is nobler than to be wise for one's self. Mr. Hecker became acquainted with Mr. Brisbane, discussed Fourierism with him, and, without being able yet to point out the fatal defect in the system, felt that it would not work.

Up to this period — about the twenty-second year of his age — he had never so much as thought of looking into the Roman Catholic doctrine or practice. It had not crossed his mind that there *could* be anything worth considering in a creed only known to him as the one held by Irish laborers and servants, whom he had seen kneeling before the church doors on Sunday mornings. He was led to think of the Catholic Church through one of its fiercest enemies. About twenty-five years ago there was a preacher in New York named Brownlow or Brownlee, who conceived the brilliant and original scheme of gaining distinction in his profession by calling his Roman Catholic brethren hard names, and holding them up to the execration of mankind. New York was a very provincial place then, and there was still a considerable number of persons living there who could be taken in by charlatanry of that nature. So Brownlow, D. D., flourished for a while. He denounced the Catholic Church most fluently in the old Chatham Street chapel, and by and by set up a weekly paper called "The Downfall of Babylon," in which he continued the work. In this amusing periodical he inserted a good many extracts from Catholic works, from the decisions of councils held in the Middle Ages, and, especially, from those of the more recent Council of Trent. I can myself remember an interesting list of "anathemas" in "The Downfall of Babylon," which led me to expend a small sum at a book-stall, in the days of my youth, in the purchase of the volume containing the complete catalogue of the same, as pronounced by the council just named. It is really remarkable how uniformly denunciation and persecution help their objects. Almost any Catholic priest you meet can name "converts" who were made such by people of the Brownlow species, and by such events as the Philadelphia riots of 1844, in which one or two Catholic churches were burned. Such things excite *inquiry*, and when once a person has reached the point of suspecting that Catholic priests are not the designing and insidious monsters which the Brownlows say they are, a reaction is apt to set in, which is often strong enough to carry him into the ancient fold.

No one will be made a Catholic by reading such discourses as that which now has the honor to engage the reader's attention, although it is written in a spirit of sincere respect for the most venerable and the most indispensable of existing institutions. If you wish to make converts, you must adopt the Scarlet Woman style, and set on a mob to burn churches.

Mr. Hecker was an occasional hearer of the infuriate Brownlow, and an occasional reader of his "Downfall." He read with particular interest, and with nascent approval, some of the decisions of the Council of Trent, especially the one that repudiates Luther's doctrine called "justification by faith alone," which had long appeared to him questionable, if not absurd and injurious. It seemed to him, or began to do so, that it was more congenial to human nature, and more reasonable, for man to work out his salvation, and to be able to merit something of his Creator. Even so recently as twenty-five years ago, many people still attached importance to these theological niceties, which now few unprofessional persons regard or know anything about. So long as all are agreed that good works are to be done, — as many of them as possible, — and bad works are to be left undone, — the modernized mind cares little for the precise theological process by which these duties are established. It was also pleasing to this young Protestant to know, that the Catholic Church, as a church, had uniformly opposed the doctrines named after Calvin, who burned his brother at the stake because that brother indulged in some vagaries of opinion upon subjects about which no man's opinion has any value, since it cannot be founded upon knowledge.

But it was not these things that made this young inquirer after truth a Roman Catholic. The great conversions are not effected through the understanding. What he wanted was, to *devote* himself to something high and good; and he soon discovered that the strength of the Catholic Church lies in the very fact that it furnishes opportunities for every kind and every degree of self-sacrifice. Those dreams of "selling all that he had," of "forsaking father and mother, brother and sister," of dedicating his entire existence to noble labors, which his Protestant friends had pitied, derided, and disapproved, he found that the Catholic Church recognized, understood, welcomed, blessed, and employed. If a compassionate girl had a genius for nursing the sick; if a gifted woman felt herself impelled to instruct the ignorant; if a man had within him an undeveloped power to rouse the torpid consciences of vicious men; if another thought he could serve his fellows best by a life of contemplation; if another would go to the ends of the earth to civilize the savage; if an heiress aspired to a nobler fate than such a marriage as an heiress usually incurs; if a man of fortune desired to employ himself and his wealth in noble uses; yes, and if a poor, deceived woman, placed in relations to the world inextricably false, longed to atone for the error of an hour by a lifetime of devotion, and to consecrate her very contrition to the service of her kind, — this ancient Church, he was assured, opened her bosom to all and each of these, and gave them the opportunity they craved. It was *this* that won the heart of the anxious wanderer, tired by his six years of perplexity and unrest. He was living with Thoreau in Massachusetts, in their usual abstemious manner, when the grand decision was made, and to Thoreau it was first communicated. The convert was then twenty-three years of age; and, now that he is forty-seven, he still looks back to that moment as the most fortunate of his life; for he has found in the service of the Church the complete realization of his early dreams.

He soon felt what our Roman Catholic brethren call a "vocation" to the priesthood, which was recognized as genuine, and he went to a convent in Germany to complete his preparation for the office. After his ordination he returned to his native land, and joined one of the numerous orders which play into and co-operate with the general work of the Church.

I have alluded to the fact that last November the largest Catholic church in New York was filled to repletion every morning at five o'clock. There was a "mission" then going on in that church. We Protestants should call it a "revival," or a "protracted meeting." Whatever our Roman Catholic brethren do, as I have before observed, they do by means of an organization; and that organization is made, by discipline and subordination, to work with the singleness of aim and the efficient force of one man. These Catholic revivals, or "missions," are conducted by orders of priests, specially endowed, trained, and organized for the purpose. Men gifted with a particular talent for holding attentive large congregations, and for recalling attention to neglected obligations, find their place and work in such orders as these. At the appointed time, the priests of the church in which a mission is to be held are reinforced by a delegation from one of these orders, and the great work of reviving religious feeling begins. The first mass is celebrated at five in the morning, for the convenience of the mighty host of laboring men and women; and a moving sermon is preached to them before the kitchen fires are lighted, before the hodman's breakfast is ready. This first vast audience is dismissed about a quarter past six, and at seven another assembles; at nine, another; and, in some cases, yet another at half past ten. In the afternoon confessions are heard, and every confessional is occupied; for there are relays of priests for every part of the work. In the afternoon, too, classes of Protestants sometimes meet for the purpose of receiving special instruction in the faith and practice of the Church from one of the priests who, being himself a convert, is better able than his brethren to anticipate and answer their inquiries. In the evening, still the work goes on until ten; vespers, confessions, exhortations, fill up the evening hours, and fan the rising flame. The conscience-stricken Catholic is not tortured with doubts either as to what he ought to do or as to whether he has done it. The injunction of the Church is perfectly simple: If you are truly sorry for your sins, and mean to forsake them, confess to a priest, comply with his direction, joyfully accept absolution, and keep your resolve to lead a new life. As the "mission" continues, the feeling spreads and deepens, the confessionals are more and more beset, until all but the hopeless reprobates of the parish are partakers of the influence. The mission may last ten days, two weeks, or a month, according to the size and circumstances of the parish; and when it is over the mission priests retire to their own abode, to refresh themselves by rest, study, and contemplation for another mission in a remote part of the diocese. Thus no one is fatigued, no one need lapse into formality and coldness.

It was in one of these orders that Father Hecker first exercised his vocation in his native land, and he labored in it in various parts of the country. But this mission work brought him into contact chiefly with Catholics, and he felt a particular yearning to bring into the fold of the Ancient Church such persons as he had known at Brook Farm, and in the intellectual circles of Massachusetts and New York, who, he felt, could alone attain peace in the Catholic Church, and only there find a way of bringing their high moral feeling to bear upon masses of their countrymen. He remembered, also, how completely and how long he had misunderstood the Church, and that, but for the accident of his falling in with the absurd "Downfall of Babylon," he might have lived and died in ignorance of its true character. He felt that there was need of a special organization for spreading abroad in the United States correct information respecting Catholic doctrine and practice. Convinced, too, that the day was near at hand when his Church was to be dominant in the United States, he desired to do something toward aiding Catholics themselves to rise to the height of their "vocation," so that they might use in the noblest way the power which was about to fall into their hands. He had a conviction, and still has it, that there is something peculiarly congenial to Republican America in the stately decorums of his Church, — its gentle doctrine, its severe exactions, its brotherly equalities, and in the grand assemblage of all the fine arts in the Supreme Act, in which man pays homage to the divinity by exhibiting his own. In church, he remembered, Protestants say, "*Man is totally depraved.*" At the political meeting the same Protestants assert, "*Man is capable of self-government.*" There is no such contradiction, he maintains, in the Catholic mind. What the Catholic believes as a Catholic he can also believe as a citizen. "It is only since I have been a Catholic," says Father Hecker, "that I have been a consistent and intelligent citizen of a republic."

A new order then, he believed, was called for in the New World, and the scheme was approved by his ecclesiastical superiors. When our Roman Catholic brethren have resolved upon a project of this nature, they proceed to execute it in the most sensible and business-like manner. If the world is to be moved, the first requisite is to get a fulcrum for the lever; for there is no use in having a lever unless there is a fulcrum on which to rest it. When a new order is to be founded, the first thing is to secure a small piece of the earth's surface, which it can possess in fee simple, upon which its home and working-place can be permanently built. Now, observe how all the parts of this astonishing organization work together! Father Hecker, provided with the due authorization, goes forth to raise the money needed to make the first payment upon a piece of ground. His previous missionary labors had brought him into favorable relations with a great number of parishes, and those labors he continued while begging the money for the new enterprise. From Quebec to New Orleans he went, rousing Catholics to confess and forsake their sins, *and* asking contributions to his scheme.

It is surprising what a talent our Roman Catholic brethren have for raising money. The Superior of the Dominican Community, which is now building a convent in New York, raised in the city alone, in two weeks, forty thousand dollars toward paying for the edifice. "One man's money is as good as another's," appears to be a familiar principle with our Roman Catholic brethren; and, accordingly, some of our New York city office-holders are frequently called upon to disgorge a trifling portion of their booty, — a check for five hundred dollars, or some small matter of that kind. It has been discovered, also, that *candidates* for city offices have a tenderness for the orphan, a pride in the new cathedral, an interest in the publication of Catholic works, and a desire for the conversion of heretics, which causes them to adorn many subscription-papers with their signatures. What an advantage over *us* our Roman Catholic brethren have in being able to tax sinners for the suppression of sin, and to use stolen money in inculcating honesty! We poor Protestants never think of asking a gambler, a city politician, or a thief to subscribe money for the promulgation of principles which, if universally accepted, would ruin his trade. *We* place nearly the whole burden of sustaining virtue upon the virtuous!

Father Hecker raised the requisite sum, and reported himself and it to the Archbishop of New York. Immediately his special enterprise was made to co-operate with the general work of the diocese in such a way that each should aid the other directly, powerfully, constantly, and forever. On the outskirts of the city, between the ground now occupied by the Central Park and the Hudson River, a region then dotted with shanties and enlivened by goats, the Archbishop laid out a new parish, and appointed Father Hecker pastor of it; who forthwith bought the best block of ground in the neighborhood for the site of the church and for the home of the new community. All gathers round a church — parochial school, parsonage, convent, college, seminary — in the Catholic world; this alliance, therefore, was nothing new, but in strict accordance with the system. Thus, a movement designed to convert Mr. Emerson and his friends, and the educated people of America, was made, *first of all*, to minister to the spiritual wants of the poorest and most ignorant people living in the Northern States.

It is *this* exquisite feature of the system, — this care for the very poorest and forlornest of human kind, — this caring for them *first*, just as we help children first at the table because they are the hungriest and least patient, — this sweet blending of the two extremes of human nature in the same project, — it is *this* that melts the heart and gives pause to the mind. If it were possible for me to be a Catholic, — which I think it is not, — it is this that would bring me to it. If, in this city of New York, there is any such thing as realized, working Christianity, it may be seen in one of its poor, densely peopled Catholic parishes, where all is dreary, dismal desolation, excepting alone in the sacred enclosure around the church, where a bright interior cheers the leisure hours; where pictures, music, and stately ceremonial exalt the poor above their lot; and where a friend and father can ever be found. And observe: these blessings are not doled out to them as charity; these poor people have the privilege of paying for them and sustaining them. The church is their own; the spacious and elegant school-house is their own; the priest is supported and the whole expense of every part of the parish system is borne by them. And nothing else in the parish works well or economically but the church. The landlord gives them bad lodgings for high rents; the city officials leave mountains of filth before their doors; the water will not flow in the upper stories; the grocery store is on so small a scale that its profits must be exorbitant. All in their lot, all in their surroundings, is mean, nasty, inefficient, forbidding, — except their church.

Ten years have passed. Upon the ground bought by Father Hecker we now see a large and handsome church, adorned with pictures much superior to those usually found in Catholic churches here. The fashionable quarter of the city has been drawing nearer to it, so that now the congregation is composed of those who live in brown-stone houses, as well as of those who assist in building them; and the service is performed with an elegance and finish seldom seen in the United States. Adjoining the church is a spacious and commodious house for the Fathers and students belonging to the new community, who are called Paulists. The community now consists of six priests, twelve students, and four servants, — all but one or two of whom are "converts," i. e. Catholics who were once Protestants. The special work of this community is, to bring the steam printing-press to bear upon the spread of the Catholic religion in the United States. The matter published by the Catholic Publication Society, the new tracts, the articles of the monthly magazine called "The Catholic World," and the smaller volumes designed for Sunday-school libraries, are chiefly written or edited by the Paulist Fathers. Every Catholic church has connected with it several voluntary societies; such as the Altar Society, of ladies, who take care of the decoration and purification of the altar; the Conference of St. Vincent de Paul, for the relief of the poor; the Society of the Holy Rosary, for simultaneous devotion; the Society of the Holy Infancy, for the promotion of missions in heathen lands; the Father Mathew Society, for mutual protection against the poor man's worst enemy; the Sunday-school Society, of teachers, — all these Societies are so many organizations, ready-made, for the distribution of the tracts and volumes prepared by the Paulist Fathers in their pleasant retreat near the Hudson River.

This community, in one important particular, differs from other Catholic orders, — it exacts no special vows of its members. Father Hecker is an American, a patriotic American, an American who believes in American principles, — in short, he is what we used to call a good Jeffersonian Democrat. Being that in politics, he desires to be it also in religion; for he is of opinion that a proposition which is true at the polls cannot be false before the altar. Jefferson says, All men are equals. True, says this American priest, because they are all brothers. Jefferson says, Man is capable of self-government. True, adds Father Hecker, for man is made in the image of his Creator. This Paulist Community, therefore, is conducted on American principles: "the door opens both ways"; no man remains a moment longer than he chooses; and every inmate is as free in all his works and ways as a son is in the well-ordered house of a wise father.

What a powerful engine is this! Suppose the six ablest

and highest Americans were living thus, freed from all worldly cares, in an agreeable, secluded abode, yet near the centre of things, with twelve zealous, gifted young men to help and cheer them, a thousand organizations in the country to aid in distributing their writings, and in every town a spacious edifice and an eager audience to hang upon their lips. What could they *not* effect in a lifetime of well-directed work? Father Hecker lives so remote from the worldly anxieties, that he did not know the amount of his own salary until I told him. That is not in his department. He has nothing to think of but his work.

Father Hecker and his colleagues propose to convert us by convincing our reason. There is nothing which they deny with so much emphasis and vehemence as the common assertion, that the Roman Catholic Church demands of man the submission or abdication of his reason. Father Hecker, in his spirited and eloquent little book entitled "The Aspirations of Nature," is particularly strong upon this point. "Man has no right to surrender his judgment," he tells us. "Endowed with free-will, man has no right to yield up his liberty. Reason and free-will constitute man a responsible being, and he has no right to abdicate his independence. Judgment, Liberty, Independence, these are divine and inalienable gifts; and man cannot renounce them if he would." Again he says: "Religion is a question between God and the soul. No human authority, therefore, has any right to enter its sacred sphere. *Every man was made by his Creator to do his own thinking.*" And again: "There is no degradation so abject as the submission of the eternal interests of the soul to the private authority or dictation of any man, or body of men, whatever may be their titles." And again: "Reasonable religious belief does not supplant Reason, nor diminish its exercise, but presupposes its activity, extends its boundaries, elevates and ennobles it by applying its powers to the highest order of truth." And once more: "There are several primary, independent, and authoritative sources of truth. Among others, and *the first*, is Reason." These passages are in curious contrast to the wild denunciations of human Reason in which Luther indulges, and which Father Hecker quotes only to condemn: "Reason, you are a silly blind fool"; "Reason is the Devil's bride, a pretty strumpet," etc.

Our Paulist friends, too, are the furthest possible from being alarmed at the discoveries of science; for they do not insist on the literal infallibility of the books composing the Bible. They would not feel that either the Church or the public morals was in danger if a bishop on the other side of the globe should catch Moses tripping in his arithmetic. With them, it is the CHURCH that is infallible, i. e. the collected, deliberately uttered moral sense of mankind, enlightened by the Author of it, and which is therefore for individuals the supreme, unerring conscience. Galileo would be in no danger nowadays if his discoveries should appear to cast a reflection upon the statement that Joshua commanded the sun and moon to stand still, and they obeyed him. "The geologist," observes Father Hecker in one of his most eloquent passages, "may dig deep down into the bowels of the earth till he reaches the intensest heats; the naturalist may decompose matter, examine with the microscope what escapes our unaided observation, and unveil to our astonished gaze the secrets of nature; the astronomer may multiply his lenses till his ken reaches the empyrean heights of heaven; the historian may consult the annals of nations, and unriddle the hieroglyphics of the monuments of bygone ages; the moralist may expose the most delicate folds of the human heart, and probe it to its very core; the philosopher may, with his critical faculty, observe and define the laws which govern man's sovereign reason, — and Catholicity is not alarmed! Catholicity invokes, encourages, solicits your boldest efforts; for at the end of all your earnest researches you will find that the fruit of your labors confirms her teachings, and that your genuine discoveries add new gems to the crown of truth which encircles her heaven-inspired brow."

How interesting to observe the noble heart endowing with its own nobleness whatever it loves! How resistless the influence of this large and free America, which transfigures all things and persons into a likeness to itself!

The question now recurs: Will the Paulist Fathers succeed in their darling object of bringing over a majority of the people of the United States to the ancient faith? I can state some of the grounds of their own unbounded confidence in the coming supremacy of their church. First, its past progress has been startlingly rapid. In the year 1800 there were in the United States one Roman Catholic bishop, fifty-three priests, and about 90,000 members. There are now seven archbishops, forty bishops, three mitred abbots, about 3,100 priests, sixty-five Catholic colleges, fifty-six convents of men, one hundred and eighty-nine convents of women, and (according to Catholic calculation) 4,800,000 Catholic population. In other words, in 1800 the Catholics were something like one seventieth of the whole population of the United States; they are now about one sixth! They have also increased faster than the general population of the country. Thus between 1840 and 1850 the general increase was thirty-six per cent; the Catholic increase, one hundred and twenty-five per cent. Judging from the past, our Roman Catholic brethren conclude that in the year 1900 they will form one third of the population of the country, and perhaps a majority in the controlling cities and States of it. The property of the Church increases at a rate still more rapid; since, in addition to the new purchases, the Church shares largely in the constant increase in the value of real estate. The only class of laborers in the country who always earn much more money than they need are domestic female servants; and they spend most of their surplus either in direct contributions to the Church, or in bringing across the ocean new members. As a rule, a female servant can appropriate one half of her wages to these objects if she chooses. How many of them choose to do so is known to housekeepers, and, still better, to bankers who sell small drafts on Ireland and Germany.

Then, again (as Father Hecker fails not to notice in his recent contribution to the *Revue Générale* of Brussels, upon *La Situation Religieuse des États Unis*), our Roman Catholic brethren claim to be better propagators than we can boast of being. It is obvious, they say, that Catholic families are more numerous than Protestant. This august and holy mystery of generation the ancient Church invests with sacramental dignity, and makes the marriage tie indissoluble. Father Hecker is wrong in attaching importance to the hateful thing called free-love, and to the kindred abomination that took to itself the name of Bohemianism. Nothing ever excited a deeper or a more general loathing among Protestants than these things did. They had but few adherents, and were of no account. Mormonism, also, which he mentions in this connection, is an exceptional and transient triumph of one vigorous Saxon who was resolved to have a harem without taking the trouble of turning Turk. But the great number of divorces, the very frequent revolt of parents against the sublime duties of their lot, the murder of unborn offspring, the dying out of the old New England families, their ancient farms occupied by healthier Europeans, mostly Catholics, — these things, Father Hecker thinks, prove "the complete impotence of Protestantism to impose and make respected the rein which public morality demands," and announce the coming supremacy of a Church powerful enough to guard the issues of life. Now, the best man is he who can rear the best child; the best woman is she who can rear the best child. The whole virtue of the race — physical, moral, mental — comes into play in this most sweet, most arduous, most pleasing, most difficult of all the work done by mortals in this world. If, therefore, it is true that Catholics do this work so much better than Protestants, the case is closed; we must all turn Catholics, or make up our minds to see the race continue to dwindle. This is, of course, too vast and awful a subject to be treated here. I will venture merely to express the conviction, that the first people to discover and successfully practise the art of rearing children in the new conditions of modern life will be persons who will seek for the requisite knowledge where alone it is to be found, — in science. These will communicate it to others, and then, perhaps, the various churches will adopt, hallow, and impart it.

Our Roman Catholic brethren dwell much upon the enormous expense of the Protestant system, as well as upon its signal inefficiency. Upon this point we may profitably consider what they say. Take the case of any of our vigorous country towns in the Northern States, and what do we find there? Generally, *six* churches struggling to maintain themselves; *six* clergymen, all in the false position of having to instruct people upon whom their children's bread depends; *six* clergymen's families, in the equally false position of being nominally at the head of society upon a thousand dollars a year and a donation-party; *six* organizations attempting, with anxious feebleness, to do the work of one. And no Catholic can discern any great difference between them. He cannot see, for example, why the Methodists and the Episcopalians would not both gain enormously by *re*-uniting. One would gain the power and vitality of numbers, the other would gain in decorum and dignity. The Episcopal Church would no longer rest under the blighting stigma of being the rich people's church, and the Methodists would be restrained from the spiritual riot of the camp-meeting. Then there are the Unitarians and the Jews, why should not they come together with the same mutual advantage? The Jews would only have to give up one or two usages, the relics of a barbarous age; the Unitarians would merely be required to make their sermons shorter and simpler, and adopt part of an ancient ritual. The Calvinistic sects, too, why should they keep apart? It looks to a reflective Catholic priest as though one grain of common sense would suffice to reduce the churches in all our villages one half in the next six months.

Our Roman Catholic brethren count upon important accessions through their convent schools, conducted by Sisters of Charity and by other orders, male and female. These schools are numerous, important, and increasing; and I think that one fourth, perhaps one third, of all the pupils in them are children of Protestant parents. Few persons are competent to judge of an institution who have never been inmates of it, because nothing is easier than to deceive completely all but the acutest visitors. Still, these Catholic schools have some advantages over most of ours, which catch the eye and captivate the imagination. We are apt to undervalue decorum, etiquette, manner, demeanor, and all the minor details of discipline and subordination. We are apt to forget that children were not included in the first sentence of the Declaration of Independence. We trust them too much in some particulars, and too little in others. The teachers of Protestant private schools have seldom any vantage-ground of rank of a nature to aid them in securing respect and obedience. The principal is often an anxious and dependent man; often he is grossly ignorant and vulgar; while the subordinate teachers are poor and overworked, and without the means of gaining a proper ascendency over their pupils. Many of them, in these commercial cities, where nothing is sincerely honored except the bank account, come out of garrets every morning, to teach boys and girls who live in mock-palaces, and who have no conception of anything higher or more desirable than to live in a mock-palace. Have not I myself seen the insolent unlicked cubs of the Fifth Avenue and streets adjacent making the lives of gentlemen of learning and eminent worth bitter to them by their riotous contempt of authority and decency, and no teacher connected with the school in a position which justified his felling the young savages to the floor? Have I not seen the principal of a boarding-school running an annual "revival" as a good business operation, and forbidding the poor dyspeptics under his charge to receive the visits of their parents on Sunday afternoons?

Certainly, these convent schools, which are now so popular, are free from some of the objections and difficulties that lessen the usefulness of many of our fashionable private academies. Among the "traditions" of the Catholic Church, there is one to the effect that children are children, and have a right to be kept from doing themselves irreparable harm, — peaceably if they can, forcibly if they must. The teachers of the convent schools — all the resident teachers — are sufficiently independent of the good-will of the pupils, without being too much so for their own good. The convent possesses property, guards and maintains its inmates in their own home, and yet in a great degree it depends upon the income derived from the school. The garb of the nun, of the Christian Brother, of the Sister of Charity, as well as the serenity and dignity of their demeanor, hold impudence in check, and teach the young victims of successful speculation that there *are* distinctions other than those indicated by marble fronts and rosewood stairs. There is a certain civilizing influence, too, which comes of compelling the minute observance of the etiquette of each apartment and each situation.

I was present once when the young ladies attending the

principal convent school upon the island of Manhattan entered their chapel, on Sunday afternoon, to see four or five of their number, who had become "converts" at the convent, baptized. It was a truly exquisite scene. No manager of a theatre ever arranged anything more effective for the stage; and yet it was well adapted at once to impress the minds and tame the bodies of the three hundred romping girls who took part in it. Perhaps in no other way can I better show the reader what our Roman Catholic brethren and sisters are doing to attract the children of wealthy Protestants into their schools, than by briefly describing what I saw on that pleasant Sunday afternoon in May.

On the summit of a gentle slope, surrounded by trees and shrubbery, in a part of the island where the ancient, renowned loveliness of Manhattan has not been obliterated, and commanding a view of the Hudson, the Harlem, and the Sound, — the Palisades bounding the view on the west, the arches of the High Bridge visible in the north, the Sound stretching away to the northeast, and the city of New York spreading over all the southern half of the island, — stands the group of solid, but not uninviting, structures which form the establishment, chief among them the chapel. On this warm spring day all the doors stood open; and it was evident, as soon as we alighted under the covered entrance, that something joyful was going forward. The parlors were full of happy parents, conversing with happy daughters, and a joyous hum pervaded all the rooms. The chapel is spacious, elegant, and very lofty; and it is adorned with the usual large altar-piece, as well as with many smaller pictures. Nearly the whole space upon the floor is covered with plain black-walnut pews, without doors or cushions. These are for the young ladies; visitors sit near the entrance, in pews raised a little from the floor; the nuns have raised seats along the sides of the chapel, — each sister having a little pew to herself, and sitting with her face to the altar. At the appointed moment the pupils began to enter in procession, by the middle aisle, two by two, walking almost as slowly as it is possible to walk, — just moving, no more, and doing so in absolute stillness. Not an audible tread; not a whisper; not an eye upraised. All were dressed alike in pink summer dresses, with a white veil over their heads. They seemed to be softly floating in, and winding round into the black-walnut seats, like the tinted clouds of sunset. First came the little girls, who, upon reaching the middle aisle, bent one knee to the ground, and then glided slowly to the slow, soft music of the organ all down the aisle to the altar, where they divided, — one line moving to the right, the other to the left, and so curled round into the first pews, which they entered at the end nearest the wall. Thus the pleasing pageant was *prolonged.* As the procession continued, its interest both changed and increased, because the little girls were followed by larger, until we had the pleasure of looking upon young ladies in the bright lustre of their maturing charms. In every particular, this procession was arranged just as a Kemble or a Wallack would have arranged it. The same devices were employed, both to prolong and increase the pleasure of the spectator, which are employed upon a well-conducted stage. Especially were the most impressive objects of all reserved for the last. Finally came the young ladies who were about to be baptized, all clad in white dresses, and covered with a long white veil, *each of them resting an arm upon the shoulder of a sister attired in black,* — the venerable Superior of the Convent being one. Nothing was ever seen more picturesque or more affecting, nor anything more legitimate and proper. When all the pupils were standing in their pews, and the candidates for baptism had placed themselves before the altar, a sister who was in one of the side niches made a slight, scarcely audible click with a small instrument concealed in her hand. Instantly the whole pink cloud of girls softly knelt, and remained kneeling till another click was heard, when they nestled back to their seats. The black line of kneeling nuns along the sides of the chapel, the parterre of young loveliness on the floor, the altar blazing with lighted candles, made up a spectacle as pleasing as it was impressive. At the conclusion of the service the girls glided out in the same silence and slowness; and the newly baptized closed the train, leaning, as before, upon the shoulders of the sisters.

Ten minutes after, the whole three hundred pupils, except those who rejoined their parents in the parlors, were on the full romp in their large sitting-room, running, shouting, in unrestrained hilarity! No Sunday gloom! No goody, nauseous books! No forced seriousness of demeanor!

The arrangements of the school seemed excellent. The best school-room I ever saw in a private school, the loftiest, airiest, most spacious and elegant, is the one belonging to this establishment. In one wing of the building are thirty music-rooms, so constructed that a girl may be practising in every one of them without disturbing or being disturbed. The sleeping-rooms are a happy compromise between the injurious privacy of a separate apartment and the injurious publicity of a common room; and the means of ventilation appeared to be sufficient. Despite these excellent features and arrangements, the school may be a very bad one; the minds of the pupils may neither be profitably exercised nor suitably fed; yet every reader can see how such schools as this are calculated to captivate parents and allure children. Probably seven of their Protestant pupils out of ten become Catholics sooner or later.

Conversions to the Catholic faith, it seems, have been more numerous since the war than before. During the "mission" recently held at St. Stephen's, in New York, the number of converts was eighty. This is nothing to boast of, considering the extent of the parish and the duration of the "mission"; nor, indeed, have converts ever yet come in with any great rapidity. It is the quality of the converts, not their numbers, of which we hear so much; the expected rush has not yet begun. I am informed that a few educated persons in most city parishes are inquiring, with more or less earnestness, into the Catholic faith, and I am further assured that these inquiries generally end in conversion. Among the most frequent causes assigned by inquirers for dissatisfaction with their hereditary belief are the following: The difficulty of believing in the literal infallibility of the whole Bible; the gloom of the Sabbatarian Sunday; the ban placed by many sectarians upon innocent pleasures, such as dancing and the drama, which tends to drive young people into guilty pleasures; the frenzies of the camp-meeting, more revolting, in some parts of the country, than the howlings and whirlings of the

Dervishes of Turkey; the painful uncertainty which many persons feel, all their lives, whether their souls are "saved" or not; the dulness and barrenness of the public service, in which a duty is assigned to *every* clergyman which only one in a thousand can discharge, namely, the production of two powerful and entertaining sermons every seven days. The effect of the war in multiplying conversions is explained thus: The Catholic Church alone escaped division; since the Catholic Church alone kept itself always and entirely aloof from the political questions involved. The spectacle of this unity in the midst of such contention and severance has proved captivating, I am told, to several educated minds. I have been assured by a distinguished Protestant general, who served in important commands during the whole war, that the only chaplains who, *as a class*, were of much utility in the field were Roman Catholic chaplains; which he attributes to the fact, that they alone were accountable to ecclesiastical superiors. It may be that the exploits of some of our Protestant chaplains in the way of "living on the country" contrasted with the strict observance, by Catholic chaplains, both of military and ecclesiastical rule, had some effect upon observant Protestant minds.

Such are some of the reasons assigned for the unbounded confidence with which our Roman Catholic brethren count upon being the final and eternal Church of the United States. These reasons the reader is competent to estimate.

For fifteen centuries the Christian Church has undertaken to perform for all the inhabitants of Christendom two offices having no necessary connection, and therefore capable of being separated. One of these offices I have styled, in a previous page, expounding the universe; or, in other words, assuming to declare with authority what people must think concerning the origin of things, the destiny of man, the nature of the Supreme Being, and the general government of the world. During the past three centuries or more a conviction has been gaining ground, that no man or body of men is competent to do this. On such subjects it is now agreed among the intelligent part of mankind, that one man's theory or conjecture, however interesting or consolatory it may be, cannot be binding on any other man. It is now agreed, among those whose thoughts finally become the thoughts of mankind, that on such subjects as these *there can be no such thing as a guilty opinion.* This part, therefore, of the Church's service to Christendom is now nearly accomplished. It will be quite accomplished when the greater part of the inhabitants of Christian countries are made partakers of modern knowledge. During former ages, the Church did a kind and needed service, perhaps, in concealing from man his own ignorance. He now knows his ignorance; he also knows the only method which can ever exist of lessening it; and he knows, consequently, that in this matter priests cannot aid him.

But the other duty of the Church remains, — that of inculcating virtue, assisting regeneration, guiding, cheering, ennobling human life. This remains. This will never be needless as long as man is weak, virtue difficult, and vice alluring. Human reason is not equal to the task of forming an adequate theory of the universe; but it is equal to the task of discovering how men ought to feel, and how men ought to act. No body of men can ever have the right to say what we ought to think concerning the "Unknowable"; but any man, by a life of fidelity and charity, can acquire absolute certainty respecting the duties we owe to ourselves and one another.

The churches will be slow to assent to these truths, — familiar as they are to men of the world; but the indifference of the public to everything "doctrinal," and its eager interest in everything "practical," will continue to have its effect. Do we not see the Pope, who began his reign by establishing a new doctrine, end it by regulating the dress of women? Do we not see a grand council of bishops rising superior to theological subtleties, to consider the pernicious consequences of keeping up balls after midnight? Have we not seen the leading Calvinistic clergyman of New York soaring above all Calvin's gloomy crudities, and addressing himself to the nobler, higher, and more difficult work of throwing light upon the duties of employers to employed? Poor work he made of it; but everything must be pardoned in a beginner. It is easy to make a passable sermon upon points of "doctrine"; but the moment you tackle such subjects as *that,* you have arrived at the hill Difficulty, and must prepare for a tough climb.

All history, all political economy, all morals, are involved in that servant-girl question.

In every community are produced a few persons who are endowed with a special aptitude for discerning what is right and becoming. The problem is, By what means shall these be discovered, trained, and afforded an opportunity to act upon the general conscience? For many centuries this was done by the Roman Catholic Church, and done, too, with a considerable degree of efficiency. It employed women in this vocation as well as men, children as well as the mature. It was, so to speak, a complete moral and religious apparatus. If the same office is still to be performed for mankind, I think the organization that performs it will have to study deeply and long the Roman Catholic Church, and borrow from it nearly every leading device of its system, especially these three, — celibacy, consecration for life, and special orders for special work.

Celibacy was a most masterly device; its inventor should be trebly canonized; it is the great secret of the efficiency of the Roman Catholic Church. An idea of such power and value will never be lost. I do not doubt that, in the future as in the past, men and women who fall in love with their species will often find it best to remain unmarried, since the proper rearing of a family is itself a career, and demands most of a life. Political economy has taken up this subject. The remarks upon it of Mr. John Stuart Mill * should be attentively considered by humane persons. "Little improvement," he says, "can be expected in morality until the producing of large families" (in densely peopled countries) "is regarded with the same feelings as drunkenness or any other physical excess. But while the aristocracy and clergy are foremost to set the example of this kind of incontinence, what can be expected from the poor?" In Mr. Mill's system, celibacy and married continence play a part of the first importance.

Destruction has gone far enough. The time is at hand when we can begin to think of reconstruction.

"Faith," says Sainte-Beuve, "has disappeared. Science, let people say what they please, has destroyed it. It is absolutely impossible for vigorous, sensible minds, conver-

* Principles of Political Economy, Vol. I. p. 458, American edition.

sant with history, armed with criticism, studious of the natural sciences, any longer to believe in old stories and old Bibles. In this crisis there is only one thing to do in order to avoid languishing and stagnating in a decline, namely, to move rapidly and to march firmly on toward an order of reasonable, probable, corrected ideas, which beget conviction instead of belief, and which, while leaving to the vestiges of neighboring creeds all liberty and security, prepare in all new and robust minds a support for the future."

This may apply to a few individuals in a few countries. If it were true of all men of all countries, not the less would it be difficult to live purely, honorably, and wisely; not the less would it be necessary for each child to begin at the rudiments and acquire the art of living, almost as though it were the first creature whom temptation ever allured; not the less would self-control be painful and long to learn. Who does not need help in this great matter of proper and happy living?

Suppose, then, that all the churches are about silently and insensibly to abandon the attempt to regulate opinion. Suppose the word "orthodoxy" abolished. Instantly the long quarrel between the Heart and the Head of Christendom ceases; Sainte-Beuve takes a Sunday-school class; Mr. Emerson writes tracts. All that is efficient in the Catholic system will be preserved, and all that is good in the Protestant will be joined to it; and no one will care to inquire in 1945, whether it is this all-conquering America which has become Catholicized, or the ancient Church which has become Americanized. Whatever there is of good and suitable in this Church, whatever there is of good and suitable in the universe, America will assuredly appropriate.

HOW CONGRESS WASTES ITS TIME.

ONE of the oddities of human nature is its patient endurance of obvious, easily remedied inconveniences. No man ever spoke, and no man ever listened to a speech, in the Representatives' Hall at Washington, without being painfully aware of its unsuitableness to the purpose for which it was intended. It was intended to afford accommodation for three hundred gentlemen while they debated public questions and conversed on public business. Almost all debate in a modern parliamentary body naturally takes the tone of conversation, because nearly every topic that arises is some question of detail the principle of which is not disputed. It is only on rare occasions that the voice of a speaker endowed with reason would naturally rise above the conversational tone. The main business of Congress is to determine how much money shall be raised, how it shall be raised, and for what objects it shall be spent. The stricter States-rights men of the early time used to say, that, when Congress had made the annual appropriations, only one duty remained, which was to adjourn and go home. This was an extreme statement. It is, I think, a most important part of the duty of Congressmen to converse together, in the presence of the whole people in reporters' gallery assembled, on subjects of national concern; but even on a field-day of general debate, when principles are up for discussion, it is still calm, enlightened, dignified conversation that is most desirable. Members are well aware of this. Flights of oratory generally excite derisive smiles upon the floor of the House, and no man is much regarded by his fellow-members who is addicted to that species of composition.

But neither conversation nor calm debate is possible in

the Representatives' Chamber. It is large enough for a mass-meeting. The members are spread over a wide expanse of floor, each seated at a desk covered and filled with documents and papers, and they see themselves surrounded by vast galleries rising, row above row, to the ceiling. When a man begins to speak, though he may be the least oratorical of mortals, he is soon forced into an oratorical condition of mind by the physical difficulty of making himself heard. Compelled to exert his lungs violently, he endeavors to assist and relieve the muscles of his chest and throat by gesticulation, and this brings the color to his cheeks and contributes to work up the whole man into the oratorical frenzy that puts a stop to all useful, elucidating operation of the brain. Often, very often, have I seen a member of the House, superior by nature, age, and education to the clap-trap of harangue, rise in his place, full-charged with weighty matter on a subject utterly unsuited to oratory, and attempt to address the House in the temperate, serene manner which is alone proper when intelligent minds are sought to be convinced. At once he becomes conscious that no one can hear him beyond the fifth desk. His voice is lost in space. He raises it; but he cannot make the honorable member hear to whose argument he is replying. He calls upon the Speaker to come to his rescue, and Mr. Speaker uses his hammer with promptitude and vigor. The low roar of conversation, the rustle of paper, the loud clapping for the pages, subside for a moment, and the member resumes. But even during that instant of comparative silence, he is scarcely heard, — he is *not* heard unless he "orates," — and, a moment after, his voice is drowned again in the multitudinous sea of noise. Still he will not give up the attempt, and he finishes with the wildest pump-handle oratory of the stump. It is not his fault. He is no fool. He would not naturally discuss army estimates in the style of Patrick Henry rousing his countrymen to arms. If he does so, it is because nature has so limited the reach and compass of the human voice, that he cannot make himself heard unless he roars; and no man can keep on roaring long without other parts of the body joining his lungs in the tumult.

This is really a matter of first-rate importance; for,

whatever else man is or has, we are sure he possesses an animal nature, and hence is subject to physical conditions that are inexorable. If we could assemble in that enormous room the sages, statesmen, and orators of all the ages, we should not get from them much profitable debate. The hall is good enough; only it wants taking in. There is no need of such extensive accommodation for the chance visitors to the Capitol; since the whole people, as just remarked, as well as a respectable representation from foreign countries, are present in the gallery of the reporters. Three or four hundred gallery seats would answer better than the present thousand.

We ought not to be ashamed to learn something of the details of parliamentary management from a people who have had a Parliament for eight centuries. When the city of Washington was laid out, — 1790 to 1800, — the people of the United States had caught from the enthusiastic Republicans of France a certain infatuation for the ancient Romans; and hence the building for the accommodation of Congress was styled the Capitol; and, in furnishing the chambers for the Senate and House, the seats were arranged in semicircles, after the manner of the Roman senate-house. There was such a relish then for everything Roman, that it is rather surprising honorable members were not required to appear in their places wearing Roman togas. Nothing seems to have been copied from the British Parliament, except that object which Oliver Cromwell saw before him when he dissolved Parliament, one April day in 1653, and bade a soldier near him take away that fool's bauble, — the mace. But perhaps there are one or two other features of the British House of Commons that might have been considered. Never would the House of Commons have formed a Fox, a Sheridan, a Canning, a Peel, a Palmerston, or a Gladstone, if those masters of parliamentary conversation had been obliged to speak in such an apartment as our present Representatives' Hall. I have been in the House of Commons when important debates occurred, and every leading speaker on both sides did his best, but no man put forth any great physical exertion. Sir Robert Peel rarely, Palmerston never, departed from the easy manner and unforced tone of conversation. A great debate was only the more or less animated talk of able, experienced, well-informed gentlemen; and it retained this tone chiefly because the auditors were so close around the speakers that conversation could be heard. No desks obstructed and filled up the floor, tempting members to write. No heaps of pamphlets and newspapers rose before them, luring them to read. *All reading and writing had been done before the House met*, and nothing remained but to talk it over. Ministerial and opposition members sat on long benches, facing one another, with a mere alley between them; and the strangers' gallery was a cockloft up near the ceiling, which would hold, when crammed, a hundred and twenty people.

The reader has perhaps not forgotten the astonishment that seized him when first he caught sight of the tumultuous scene afforded by the House of Representatives in session. I suppose we are all so used to it now, that we have ceased to see in it anything extraordinary. A deliberative body, indeed! From the gallery we look down upon semicircles of desks, at which members are writing, reading, and gossiping, apparently inattentive to what is going on. Outside of the outer semicircle is a crowd of men standing in groups talking together. The sofas that line the walls are usually occupied by men engaged in conversation; and in the lobbies beyond there is a dense crowd of talkers, who contribute their share to the volume of noise. Inside the inner row of desks, between the members and the Speaker's lofty throne of marble, the business of the House is brought to a focus. There, at a long row of marble desks, sit the shorthand reporters, who prepare for the "Globe" the official verbatim report of the proceedings. Above and behind them, at another row of marble desks, sit the clerks who keep an official record of whatever is done. Above and behind these, in his marble pulpit, with his mace at his right hand, his compass-like clock and excellent ivory hammer before him, behold the Speaker, most attentive of members, and the only one among them all who is expected to know at every instant the business before the House. On the marble steps connecting these three platforms are the pages, the circulating-medium of the House, who spring at the clapping of a member's hands to execute his will. From the midst of the great chaos of members, members' desks, boots, and litter of documents, a Voice is heard, — the voice of one who is supposed to be addressing the House. Not a member listens, perhaps, nor pretends to listen; not even the Speaker, who may be at the moment conversing with a stranger just presented to him, or may be signing documents. He knows that the Voice has seventeen minutes and three quarters longer to run, and his sole duty with regard to that Voice is, to bring down his well-made hammer with a good rap on the desk when its time is up. The only attentive persons are the shorthand reporters; but as they merely sit and write, without ever looking up, the absurd spectacle is often presented, of a distinguished gentleman delivering a most animated harangue to a great crowd of people, not one of whom appears to be regarding him. His right hand quivers in the air. He cries aloud. His body sways about like a tall pine in a torturing gale. "Yes, Mr. Speaker, I repeat the assertion"; — but Mr. Speaker is giving audience to three of his constituents, who stand, hat in hand, on the steps of his throne. "I appeal to gentlemen on the other side of the House"; — but no: neither the gentlemen on the other side of the House, nor his own intimate friends near by, pay him the poor compliment of laying down their newspapers or looking up from the letters they are writing.

Why these desks? why this general absorption of members in writing, reading, and conferring? Why the frequent necessity of hunting up members in their committee-rooms? It is because Congress meets four hours too soon! It meets at 12 M. instead of 4 P. M. It meets long before the daily work of members is done, before the morning's news is stale, before the relish of the mind for excitement is sated, before the mood has come for interchange of ideas, for converse with other minds.

Every one knows that the hard labor of Congress is done in committee-rooms and in the private offices of members; but, I presume, few persons are aware of the great amount and variety of duty which now devolves upon members who are capable of industry and public spirit. There are idle members, of course; for in Congress, as everywhere else, it is the willing and generous mind that bears the burden and pulls the load. It is with members of Congress as with editors, — most of their labor consists in considering and quietly rejecting what the public never hears anything about. Beau Brummell *wore* but one neck-tie, but his servant carried down stairs half a dozen failures. A magazine contains twenty articles; but, in order to get that twenty, the editor may have had to examine four hundred. During the session, Washington being the centre of interest to forty millions of people, it is the common receptacle of the infinite variety of schemes, dreams, ideas, vagaries, notions, publications, which the year generates. When a citizen of the United States conceives an idea or plans an enterprise, one of the things he is likely to do is to write a pamphlet about it, and either send a copy to each member of Congress, or hire a small boy to place a copy upon each member's desk just before twelve o'clock. The international-copyrightists, I remember, took that enlightened course, fondly believing that no member who called himself a human being could read such moving arguments without being impatient to vote for the measure proposed. But when I began to look into Washington affairs, I discovered that hundreds of other people were continually employing the same too obvious tactics. Pamphlets come raining down upon members in a pitiless storm. On going into the office of a member one morning, when he had been absent twenty-four hours, I had the curiosity to glance at the mail which had accumulated in that short time. It consisted of one hundred and eight packages, — about one third letters, and two thirds newspapers and pamphlets. I think a member whose name is familiar to the country will usually receive, in the course of a long session, a good cart-load of printed matter designed expressly to influence legislation.

More vigorous schemers, or rather schemers with longer purses, soon discover that pamphlets are rather a drug in Washington, and send delegations or agents to "push" their projects by personal interviews. Nearly all these enterprises are either in themselves absurd, or else they are beyond the range of legislation; but members have to bestow attention enough upon them to ascertain their nature and claims. At least, many members do this, and by doing it effect a great deal of unrecorded good. Many a member of Congress does a fair day's work for his country outside of the chamber in which he sits and the committee-rooms in which he labors. Many members, too, have extensive affairs of their own, — factories or banks to direct, causes to plead in the national courts, articles to write for their newspapers.

Let them get all this work and all committee work done before the Houses meet, and then come together at four o'clock in the afternoon, in snug convenient rooms without desks, and talk things over in the hearing of mankind. This would obviate the necessity for the two sessions which give the Sergeant-at-arms so much lucrative employment, and party-going members such annoyance. I think, too, it would discourage and finally abolish the pernicious custom of reading speeches, as well as that kindred falsehood of getting speeches printed in the "Globe" which have never been delivered at all. A distinguished senator remarked in conversation last winter, that when he came to Congress, fifteen years ago, not more than one speech in five was written out and read, but that now four in five are. I have known a member, who had an important speech prepared, seriously consider whether he should deliver it in the House of Representatives, or offer it as a contribution to the "Atlantic Monthly." He concluded, after deliberation, to deliver the speech to the House, because he could reach the country quicker in that way; and he accordingly roared it, in the usual manner, from printed slips, few members regarding him. The next morning, the speech was printed in every important daily newspaper within fifteen hundred miles of Washington.

Among the great purposes of a national parliament are these two: first, to train men for practical statesmanship; and, secondly, to exhibit them to the country, so that, when men of ability are wanted, they can be found without anxious search and perilous trial. The people of free countries can form little idea of the embarrassment which a patriotic despot suffers when he must have an able, commanding man for the public service, and there is no tried and tested body of public men from which to choose. The present Emperor of Russia, at more than one critical time, I have been assured, has experienced this difficulty: the whole vast empire with its teeming millions lies before him subject to his will; but it is dumb. Russia has no voice. Her able men have no arena. No man is celebrated, except as heir to an ancient name, or commandant of an important post. No class of men have had the opportunity to stand up before their countrymen, year after year, and show what they are, what they know, what they can bear, what they can do, and what they can refrain from doing, in keen, honorable, courteous encounter with their peers. One lamentable consequence is, that when an emperor, rising superior to the traditions of his order, strikes into a new and a nobler path, and looks about him for new men to carry out the new ideas, he has no knowledge to act upon. France has been muzzled for nearly twenty years. The time is at hand when the muzzle will fall off; but the controlling men who should have been formed and celebrated by twenty years of public life in a parliament are unformed and unknown. The people will want leaders; but leaders that can be trusted are not extemporized.

This congressional essay-writing threatens to reduce us to the same condition. The composition of an essay, in the quiet solitude of a library, is a useful and honorable exertion of the human mind; but it is a thing essentially different from taking part in public debate, and does not afford the kind of training which a public man needs. It does not give him nerve, self-command, and the habit of deference to the judgment of other minds. It does not give him practice in the art of convincing others. We cannot get in a library that intimate knowledge of human vanities, timidities, prejudices, ignorance, and habits, which shut the mind to unaccustomed truth, and turn the best-intentioned men into instruments of evil. The triumphant refutation of an opponent in a composition calmly written in the absence of that opponent, — how easy it is, compared with meeting him face to face, and so refuting him in the hearing of an empire, that, if *he* be not convinced, tens of thousands of other men are! Essay-writing does not knock the conceit out of a man like open debate; nor yet does it fortify that just self-confidence which enables one to hold his own against eloquent error and witty invective, and sit unmoved amidst the applause and laughter that frequently follow them. It does really unfit a person for grappling with the homely, every-day difficulties of government. It tends to lessen that unnamed something in human beings which gives ascendency over others, and it diminishes a man's power to decide promptly at a time when his decision is to take visible effect. Nor does a written essay give any trustworthy indication of its author's character or force. A false, barren, unfeeling soul has been an "absolute monarch of words," capable of giving most powerful expression to emotions which it never felt, and to thoughts imbibed from better and greater men.

The substitution of written essays, read from printed slips, for extemporized debate, deprives the public, therefore, of one of the means of knowing and weighing the men from whom the leading persons of the government would naturally be taken; and it deprives members of Congress of part of the training which public men peculiarly need. It is to be hoped that when the House of Representatives moves into a smaller room, and Congress meets at four in the afternoon, the reading of speeches will be coughed down, and that Congress will resume its place as one of the national *parliaments* of the world.

If the reader has ever been so unfortunate as to be personally interested in a measure before Congress, he has doubtless been exasperated by observing that, while Congress has much more to do than it can do, it wastes much more than half its time. The waste of time, in the last days of a short session, with the appropriation bills still to be acted upon, and a crowd of expectants in the lobbies waiting for their bills to "come up," is sometimes excessive, absurd, and, to parties concerned, almost maddening. I shall long remember a certain day in the House of Representatives, when I chanced to sit next to a gentleman whose whole fortune and entire future career, as he thought, depended upon the action of the House concerning a bill which was expected to come up in the course of the afternoon. He was a stranger to me, but I gathered from his conversation with his friends, who clustered around him on the floor before the session began, that he had been a waiter upon Congress for two years. *Now*, he thought, the decisive hour had come: that day, he believed, would send him home made or marred for life. Sitting so near him as I did, I could not help regarding the proceedings of the House that day with his eyes and his feelings.

Punctually at twelve, the rap of the Speaker's ivory hammer was heard above the din of conversation, the rustle of papers, and the noise of the ushers admonishing strangers to withdraw. A chaplain entered, who took his stand at the Clerk's desk, just below the Speaker, and began the usual prayer. I had the curiosity to ascertain the exact number of persons who appeared to attend to this exercise. The number was three : first, the Speaker, who stood in a graceful attitude, with clasped hands and bowed head, as though he felt the necessity of representing the House in a duty which it did not choose itself to perform; second, one member, who also stood; third, one spectator in the gallery. Scarcely any members were yet in their seats, and the hall exhibited a scene of faded morocco chair-backs, with a fringe of people in the distance walking, standing, conversing; the prayer being an extempore one, the chaplain grew warm, became unconscious of the lapse of time, and prolonged his prayer unusually. Never was there a religious service that seemed more ill-timed or more ill-placed than that which opens the daily sessions of the House of Representatives. There is a time for all things; but members evidently think that the time to pray is *not* then nor there. The prayer can have no effect in calming members' minds, opening them to conviction, or preparing them for the duties of the occasion, because members' minds are absorbed, at the time, in hurrying the work of their committee-rooms to a conclusion. We might as well open the Gold-Room with prayer, or the daily sessions of the stock-brokers. Mr. Daniel Drew would probably assume an attitude of profound devotion, but other gentlemen would do what many members of Congress do, — *avoid going in until the prayer is finished.* In fixing times and places for devotional acts, we are now advanced far enough, I trust, to use our sense of the becoming and the suitable, and to obey its dictates. Members should certainly come in and "behave," or else abolish the chaplain.

My Expectant did not fret under the prolongation of the prayer. He had made up his mind to that apparently. Nor was he moved when a member rose and asked to have a totally unimportant error corrected in yesterday's "Globe." After this was done began a scene that wasted an hour and a half, and disgraced, not this House alone, but the country and its institutions. Two witnesses, who had refused to answer the questions of an investigating-committee, and had afterwards thought better of it, and given the information sought, were to be discharged from the custody of the Sergeant-at-arms. The prisoners were of the lowest grade of New York politician. One of them, a good-humored, dissolute ruffian of twenty-three, was so precocious in depravity that he had already been an alderman, and had afterwards been concerned in the congenial business of distributing forged naturalization-papers. I became acquainted with this fellow-citizen during his detention in the lobby, and he informed me, as I contemplated the diamond pin in his shirt, that he would have come on to Washington that winter, not as a prisoner, but as a member of Congress, if he had been old enough. This was a flight of the imagination. The despots of the Democratic party in the city of New York take excellent care that the really desirable things at their disposal fall to the men who can pay for them. They give the wretches whose votes they employ showers of Roman candles about election time, but they do not pave their streets, nor remove their heaps of garbage. They have no objections to a poor devil's picking up a diamond pin or so as alderman or councilman; but when it comes to member of Congress — O dear, no! they rarely take such things even for themselves.

These prisoners being residents of New York, there was an opportunity for a few members to make a little home capital by publicly taking their part. One after another the city members, in the view of the whole House and the crowded galleries, went up to the ex-alderman, as he stood in front of the Speaker, shook hands with him, smiled upon him, and exchanged jocular observations with him. A chair was brought for his convenience, and while his case was under consideration, he held a levee in the aisle, sitting; while the Sergeant-at-arms, representing the authority of the House, stood behind him. Mr. James Brooks paid him his respects, nodding benignantly. Mr. Fernando Wood bowed with courtly grace, and uttered friendly words. Mr.

Robinson (ah! Richelieu, you deserve better company!) was merry with him. A member moved that one of the prisoners be "discharged from custody." "Why not say *honorably* discharged?" asked a Democratic brother; which, of course, led to the expected wrangle. But the main effort was to get the ex-alderman clear without his paying the costs of his arrest and transportation to Washington, — seventy-five dollars. Now mark the purposed waste of time. It was moved that the prisoner be discharged on paying the costs of his arrest. A Democratic member moved to amend by striking out the words, "on paying the costs of arrest," alleging that the witness was a poor man, and could not procure so large a sum. The diamond pin glittered at this remark. I think, too, that the officer who had had charge of the prisoner the night before must have smiled; for the young alderman had not been abstemious, and he had broken one of the commandments in an expensive manner. The question was put. A few scattered *ayes* responded; and these were followed by such a simultaneous and emphatic roar of NOES as ought to have settled the question. A Democratic member demanded the yeas and nays; and, as it was doubtful whether this demand would be sustained, he called for tellers on the question whether the yeas and nays should be taken or not. Monstrous robbery of precious time! First, two members take their stand in front of the Speaker, and the whole House, first the yeas and then the nays pass between them, — a curious scene of huddle and confusion. The tellers reporting that the demand is sustained, the ayes and noes are ordered; which, with the time already consumed, wastes three quarters of an hour. The amendment, as every one knew it would be, was voted down.

Nothing had yet been done in the case. An amendment had been offered and rejected, — no more. The main question now recurred: Shall the prisoner be discharged on paying the costs? The sense of the House was known to every creature; but the few Democrats from New York, not regarding the convenience and dignity of the House, but thinking only of the Sixth Ward and the possible effect of their conduct there, must needs repeat this costly farce. Again they forced members to file between tellers; again they condemned two thousand persons to endure the tedium of the roll-call; again they compelled anxious expectants to chafe and fret for three quarters of an hour. It was past two o'clock before this trifling matter was disposed of. The House was then in no mood for private business, and this unhappy man was kept in suspense till another day.

He received his quietus, however, before the session ended. I saw him, a few days after, come into a committee-room, followed by two or three members, who, I suppose, had been pleading his cause. His face was very red, and it betrayed in every lineament that the vote of the House had crushed his hopes. If any dramatist would like to know how a man comports himself under such a stroke, I will state that this gentleman did not thrust either of his hands into his hair, nor throw himself into a chair and bury his face in his hands, nor do any other of those acts which gentlemen in such circumstances do upon the stage. He walked hastily to the faucet, filled a glass with water, and drank it very fast. Then he filled another glass, and drank that very fast. He then said to the members present, who expressed sympathy with his disappointment, "Gentlemen, you did the best you could for me." Next, he put on his overcoat, took up his hat, went out into the lobby, and so vanished from history.

It was not this unfortunate suitor alone, nor the class whom he represented, that suffered keenly upon the occasion before mentioned. Committees were anxious to report; members were watching for an opportunity to introduce matters of great pith and moment; foreign agents were waiting for the House to act upon the affairs which they had in charge; an important revision of the internal-revenue system, upon which a committee had expended months of labor, was pending, and was finally lost for want of the time thus wantonly wasted. Surely it is within the compass of human ingenuity to devise a method of preventing a handful of members from frustrating the wishes of a majority? Three fourths of the House desired to go on with the business of the day; and, of the remaining fourth, only half a dozen really cared to conciliate the class represented by the prisoner. Why not take the yeas and nays by a machine similar to the hotel indicator? From the remotest corner of the largest hotel, a traveller sends the number of his room to the office by a pull of the bell-rope. The inventor of that machine could doubtless arrange a system of wires and words by which the vote of the House could be taken, and even permanently recorded, by a click of a key on each member's desk. In an instant every name might be exhibited in bold characters, — the ayes on the Speaker's right, and the noes on his left, — legible to the whole House; or the ayes and noes might be printed on prepared lists. Until such a contrivance is completed, the Speaker might be empowered to put a stop to such obvious filibustering as that just described. There has never yet, I believe, been a Speaker of the House of Representatives who might not have been safely intrusted with much addition to his power. "All power is abused," says Niebuhr; "and yet some one must have it." Such Speakers as Henry Clay, General Banks, Mr. Colfax, and Mr. Blaine would not be likely to abuse power so abominably as the minority of the House do whenever they fancy they can please sweet Buncombe thereby.

A good deal of precious time is consumed by Congress in misgoverning the District of Columbia, or in doing just enough to prevent the people of the District from governing themselves. Who invented the District of Columbia? Why a District of Columbia? It is a joke in Washington, that, for sixty-five years, Congress voted fifteen hundred dollars every session for the salary of "the keeper of the crypt," because no member had the moral courage to confess his ignorance of the meaning of the word. The jokers say that many members thought it was some mysterious object, like the mace, without which Congress would not be Congress. Certain it is that the money was voted without question every year, until in 1868 the item caught the eye of General Butler, and he asked members of the Committee on Appropriations what it meant. No one being able to tell him, he went down forthwith into the crypt of the Capitol in search of its "keeper." No such officer was known in those subterranean regions. After a prolonged inquiry, he discovered that soon after the death of General Washington, when it was expected that his remains would be deposited in the crypt under the dome, Congress created the office in question, for the better protection of the sacred vault. Mrs. Washington refusing her consent, the crypt remained vacant; but the office was not abolished, and the appropriation passed unchallenged until General Butler made his inquiry, when it was stricken out. Is not our District of Columbia a similar case? The District is instilled into the tender mind of infancy, and we have all taken it for granted. But what need is there of depriving a portion of the American people of part of their rights, or of compelling them to travel across a continent to vote? Why use an apparatus so costly, complicated, and cumbersome as the Congress of the United States to get a little paving done in Pennsylvania Avenue, or some soup given out to a few hundred hungry negroes? Do California and Oregon send members across the continent to attend to the lamp-posts of a country town? Are honorable gentlemen to travel all the way from the extremity of Florida or the farthest confines of Texas to order some new boards to be nailed down on the Long Bridge?

Unable to answer such questions as these, or get them answered, I thought that possibly there might be some military advantage arising from the system, which would serve as an offset to its manifest inconveniences. But the jurisdiction of Congress did not prevent officers of a hostile army from walking into the White House one very warm day in the summer of 1814, and eating Mrs. Madison's excellent dinner, while the soldiers under their command were ravaging the town and burning the Capitol. Nor was it the authority of Congress that kept the Confederate Army on the other side of the Potomac after the battle of Bull Run. No harm appears to have come from giving back to Virginia the forty square miles which she contributed to the original hundred; and I cannot think of any evil or any inconvenience that would result if Congress were to restore to Maryland her sixty, and pay taxes on the property of the United States, like any other guardian or trustee.

This is a matter of much importance, because there seems to be some danger of the government's repeating the stupendous folly of creating a Federal City. No less distinguished a person than General Sherman appears to take it for granted that there is some necessity for the government to be sovereign in a little principality around the public edifices. "In my opinion," he lately wrote, "if the capital is changed from Washington to the West, a new place will be chosen on the Mississippi River, several hundred miles above St. Louis. . . . . I have interests in St. Louis, and if allowed to vote on this question, I would vote against surrendering St. Louis city and county, with its vast commercial and manufacturing interests, to the exclusive jurisdiction of a Congress that would make these interests subordinate to the mere political uses of a Federal capital. Nor would any National Congress make the capital where it had not exclusive and absolute jurisdiction for its own protection and that of the *employés* of the government. Therefore, if the capital be moved at all, it must go to a place willing to surrender its former character and become a second Washington City."

This is an appalling prospect for posterity, — a *second* Washington City! I could wish that General Sherman had given some reasons for his assumption; for while the good resulting from the jurisdiction of Congress is not apparent, the evils are manifest. The arriving stranger, who usually has the pain of riding a mile or two in Pennsylvania Avenue, naturally asks why that celebrated street is so ill paved, so dusty, so ill lighted. It is one of the widest streets in the world; and as it runs two miles without a bend and without a hill, the winds rushing along it from the distant gap in the mountains raise clouds of dust that are wonderful to behold and terrible to encounter. At other times the street is so muddy that people call a carriage to take them across. In the evening the whole city is dim, dismal, and dangerous from the short supply of gas. Ladies who intend to give a party endeavor to select an evening when there will be no evening session; because when the Capitol is lighted the gas-works are so overtasked that every drawing-room in the city is dull. The dilapidation of the bridges, the neglected appearance of the public squares, the general shabbiness and sprawling incompleteness of the town, strike every one who comes from the trim and vigorous cities of the North. In things of more importance there is equal inefficiency. Since the war closed, Washington has been a poverty-stricken place. The war gathered there several thousands of poor people, who became instantly helpless and miserable when the army was withdrawn, with its train of sutlers, storekeepers, embalmers, and miscellaneous hangers-on. In one of the last weeks of the last session, I remember the business of the nation was brought to a stand while a member coaxed and begged a small appropriation from Congress to keep several hundreds of colored people from starving. I myself saw the soup-houses surrounded by ragged, shivering wretches, with their pails and kettles, soon after ten in the morning, although the soup was not distributed until twelve. Washington, being peopled chiefly by under-paid clerks and their worse paid chiefs, the charity of the city was even more overtasked than its gas-works; and there seemed no way in which those poor people could be saved from starvation, except by a gift of public money, — national money, — the property of Maine, Oregon, Florida, California, and the other States. The absurdity of the act was undeniable; but when human beings are seen to be in the agonies of starvation, constitutional scruples generally give way. Congress might just as properly have voted thirty thousand dollars to relieve the suffering poor of San Francisco. The accidental proximity of those perishing people gave them no claim upon the national treasury which the poor of other cities did not possess.

The stranger, I repeat, observing these and many other evidences of inefficient government, naturally asks an explanation. The explanation is, that the unhappy city has two governments, namely, Congress, and its own Mayor and Aldermen, — one very rich and close, the other very poor and heavily burdened with expense. Between these two powers there is a chronic ill-feeling, similar to that which might exist between a rich uncle and a married nephew with a large family and many wants, — both living in the same house. The old man is under the impression that he makes his nephew a munificent allowance, to which he adds Christmas and other gifts on what *he* considers a liberal scale. His numerous other heirs and dependants share this opinion. They even reproach him for his lavish benefactions. They go so far as to say that he ought not to have paid that last heavy plumbing bill for letting the water into the house. The young man, on the other hand, so far from being grateful for his uncle's generosity, is always grumbling at his parsimony; and every time an unusual expense has to be incurred, there is a struggle and a wrangle between them as to which shall pay it. "Pay it out of your income," says Uncle Sam. "No, my dear sir: this is a permanent addition to your estate," replies the nephew. "You require me," he continues, "for your own convenience and advantage, to reside in this huge, rambling, expensive mansion, far away from towns and markets; and I am thus compelled to live on a scale which is out of all proportion to my slender means. It is but fair that you should help me out." The old gentleman assents to the principle; but he never can be brought to come down as handsomely as the young nephew feels he ought. Hence the feud between the two.

This state of things is injurious to both; but to the city government it is demoralization and paralysis. After many years of silent and of vocal strife, there has come about a kind of "understanding" that Congress is to "take care" of Pennsylvania Avenue, and the city government is to do all the rest. But the real object of strife appears to be which government shall most completely neglect the duty assigned it; and each excuses its neglect by pointing to the inefficiency of the other. The remedy appears simple and feasible. Let Congress restore to Maryland her sixty square miles, and pay taxes on the national property. By this inexpensive expedient, Congress would get rid of the troublesome task of misgoverning a small principality, and the city government would be put upon its good behavior, and supplied with adequate means and motive.

The question of the removal of the capital is scarcely ripe even for serious consideration, since we cannot know for ten years or more what effects will be produced by the Pacific railroads, built and to be built; nor whether the country is to extend northward, southward, in both directions, or in neither. If Canada is to "come in," then Mr. Seward may be right in his conjecture that the final capital of the United States will be somewhere near the city of St. Paul. If

Cuba is to be ours, if the other large islands of the West Indies are to follow, if we are to dig the Darien Canal, and the United States is to compete with Great Britain for the commerce of the world, then the future capital may properly be an Atlantic seaport, New York perhaps. If we are to take upon ourselves the grievous burden of Mexico, and extend our empire along the Pacific coast, then some central city yet to be created may be the predestined spot. If none of these things is to happen, the beautiful and commodious city of St. Louis presents almost every advantage that can be desired. Many years must probably elapse before any of these *ifs* are out of the way. In the mean time no reason appears why Congress should not gladly permit the people residing in the District of Columbia to take care of their own municipal affairs. There would then be one committee the less, one lobby the less, one whole class of ill-defined and undefinable claims the less. It would not require ten years of lobbying, under that system, to get Pennsylvania Avenue paved; nor would Congress have to spend precious time in providing soup for the poor.

But the greatest time-consumer of all is the frequently settled but always reopening controversy respecting the right of Congress to appropriate money for "internal improvements." We are at sea again on this subject. It will not remain settled. The stranger in the Capitol, who looks over the heaps of pamphlets and documents lying about on members' desks and on committee-room tables, discovers that a large number of able and worthy people are under the impression that Congress may be reasonably asked to undertake anything, provided it is a desirable work, and will cost more money than parties interested find it convenient to raise, — *anything*, from a Darien Canal to the draining of a silver mine, from the construction of a whole system of railroads to the making of an experimental balloon. There are those who want Congress to buy all the telegraphic lines, and others who think that all the railroads should be public property. The strict-constructionists are reduced to a feeble cohort, and yet Congress adheres to the tradition of their doctrines, and is fain to employ devices and subterfuges to cover up its departures therefrom. But no one knows how far Congress will go, and this uncertainty lures

10

to the capital many an expensive lobby, who wear out their hearts in waiting, and who waste at Washington the money and the energy that might have started their enterprise.

While waiting one day in the room of a Washington correspondent, I noticed upon the table a large, square, gilt-edged, handsomely bound volume, resembling in appearance the illustrated annuals which appear on the booksellers' counters during the month of December. Upon taking it up, I observed upon the cover a picture, in gold, of a miner gracefully swinging a pickaxe, with golden letters above and below him informing me that the work was upon the "Sutro Tunnel, Nevada." I opened the volume. Upon one of the fly-leaves I had the pleasure of reading a letter, in fac-simile, signed Adolf Sutro, which showed that Mr. Sutro was an elegant penman and wrote in the French manner, — one sentence to a paragraph, — thus: —

"We have a vast mining interest: we also have a large national debt.

"The development of the former will secure the early payment of the latter.

"The annexed book contains much information on the subject.

"A few hours devoted to its perusal will prove useful, interesting, and instructive."

Having read this neat epistle, I turned over a leaf or two, and discovered an engraving of "Virginia City, N. T.," and opposite to the same the title-page, of which the following is a copy: "The Mineral Resources of the United States, and the Importance and Necessity of Inaugurating a Rational System of Mining, with Special Reference to the Comstock Lode and the Sutro Tunnel in Nevada. By Adolf Sutro. Baltimore: John Murphy & Co. 1868." The work consisted of two hundred and thirty-two large pages, of which both the paper and the printing were of the most expensive kind. The substance of Mr. Sutro's message can be given in a few sentences: 1. The Comstock Lode in Nevada, the most productive series of silver mines in the world, having yielded seventy-five million dollars' worth of silver in six years, has now been dug so deep that it costs nearly as much to pump out the water as the mines yield. 2. Mr. Sutro wants Congress to tap the mountain by means of a tunnel, — the Sutro Tunnel, — so that the water will all run out at the bottom, far below the silver, leaving the mines dry. 3. If that is not done, the mines cannot be worked much longer at a profit. 4. Capitalists will not undertake the tunnel, because they are not *sure* there is silver enough in the lode to pay for it. 5. Mr. Sutro is perfectly sure there is. 6. There are many similar lodes in Nevada. 7. Therefore it is "the duty and interest of the government to aid in the construction of one tunnel as an index work," to show that there *is* silver enough in such lodes to pay for such tunnels.

This is the milk in that magnificent cocoanut. The idea is ingenious and plausible. I should like to see it tried. But who needs to be told that, under the Constitution of the United States, as formerly interpreted, Congress has no more right to advance money — or, as the polite phrase now is, "lend the credit of the government" — for such an object as this, than it has to build a new kind of steamboat for the Fulton Ferry Company, because the company is not certain it will answer? The inventor *is* certain. He gets a great album printed, and goes to Washington to lobby for the money. Now, to produce a thousand copies of such a work as this costs ten thousand dollars; and it *indicates* a lobby that may have cost twenty thousand or fifty thousand more. What a waste is this! And there are fifty lobbies every winter, in Washington, pushing for objects as obviously beyond the constitutional power of Congress as the Sutro Tunnel. These lobbies not only cost a great deal of money, but they demoralize, in some degree, almost every person who has anything to do with them. Nearly all of them fail, as a matter of course; but not until they have tempted, warped, perverted, corrupted, men who, but for such projects, would leave Washington as innocent as they came to it.

Take this scene for example. A Washington correspondent, sauntering towards the Capitol, is joined by the chief of one of these lobbies, to whom he has been casually introduced. There are about sixty correspondents usually residing in Washington during the winter, of whom fifty-five are honorable and industrious; having no object but to serve faithfully the newspapers to which they are attached;

and generally no source of income but the salary which they draw from those newspapers, — from thirty to a hundred dollars a week. The other five are vulgar, unscrupulous, and rich. They belong to insignificant papers, and sell their paragraphs to inexperienced men who come to Washington to get things "through," and desire the aid of the press. Lobbyists who understand their business seldom approach correspondents with illegitimate propositions, because they know that the representatives of influential newspapers cannot sell their columns, and would disdain to attempt doing so. The corrupt five, who prey generally upon the inexperienced, occasionally get lucrative jobs from men who ought to be ashamed to employ them. They make it a point to cultivate a certain kind of intimacy with members, — a billiard-room intimacy, a champagne-supper intimacy. They like to be seen on the floor of the House of Representatives, and may go so far as to slap a senatorial carpet-bagger on the back. It is part of their game to walk down Pennsylvania Avenue arm-in-arm with a member of Congress, and to get the *entrée* of as many members' apartments as possible. Some members who know and despise them are yet in some degree afraid of them; for any man who can get access to a newspaper can do harm and give pain. To the publicity of the press there are as many avenues in the country as there are newspapers to exchange with; and any paper, even the most remote and least important, is competent to *start* a falsehood which the great thunderers of the press may copy, and which no denial can ever quite eradicate from the public mind. These jovial fellows, who treat green members to champagne, and ask them to vote for dubious measures, are also the chief calumniators of Congress. It is *they* who have caused so many timid and credulous people to think that the Congress of the United States is a corrupt body. They revenge themselves for their failure to carry improper measures by slandering the honest men whose votes defeated them. They thrive on the preposterous schemes to which a loose interpretation of the Constitution has given birth.

But my friend who was strolling toward the Capitol was not one of the scurvy five, but of the honorable fifty-five; and, strange to relate, the lobby chief who escorted and took him aside was a master of his art. But the scheme which he represented was in imminent peril, and it was deemed essential that the leading papers of the West should, at least, not oppose it. It was thought better that the papers should even leave the subject unmentioned. It were needless to give in detail the interview. The substance of what our lobbyist had to propose to this young journalist was this: "Take this roll of greenbacks, and don't send a word over the wires about our measure." From the appearance of the roll, it was supposed to contain about as much money as the correspondent would earn in the whole of a short session of Congress. What a temptation to a young married man and father! — a quarter's salary for merely *not* writing a short paragraph, which, in any case, he need not have written, and might not have thought of writing. He was not tempted, however; but only blushed, and turned away with the remark that he was sorry the tempter thought so meanly of him. It is illegitimate schemes, such as ought never to get as far as Washington, that are usually sought to be advanced by such tactics as these.

Either by a new article of the Constitution, such as President Jefferson proposed sixty-five years ago, or by a clearly defined interpretation of existing articles, the people should be notified anew that Congress is not authorized to expend the public money, or "lend the public credit," for any but strictly national objects, — objects necessary to the defence and protection of the whole people, and such as the State governments and private individuals cannot do for themselves. Any one who has been in Washington during the last few winters, and kept his eyes open, must have felt that this was a most pressing need of the time. It is sorrowful to see so much effort and so much money wasted in urging Congress to do what it cannot do without the grossest violation of the great charter that created it.

I feel all the difficulty of laying down a rule that will stand the test of strong temptation. The difficulty is shown by our failures hitherto; for this question of the power of Congress to do desirable works has been an "issue" in Presidential contests, and the theme of a hundred debates in both Houses. President Washington, influenced perhaps by his English-minded Secretary of the Treasury,

Hamilton, evidently thought that Congress could do almost anything which the British Parliament could do; and we see him urging Congress to realize Hamilton's dream of a great National University. John Adams shared this opinion. When Mr. Jefferson came into power, in 1801, on a strict-constructionist issue, Republicans thought the thing was settled. But no: there occurred an opportunity to buy Louisiana, and that opportunity seemed transient. Napoleon wanted money desperately, and had sense enough to understand the uselessness of Louisiana to France. Jefferson yielded. He bought Louisiana, and *then* asked Congress to frame an amendment to the Constitution that would cover the act. I never could see the necessity for an amendment for that case; for it certainly belonged to "the common defence" for the United States to own its own back door. Then came that perplexing surplus of 1805, when Mr. Jefferson asked Congress to take the whole subject of internal improvements into consideration, and frame an article of the Constitution which would be a clear guide for all future legislation. It was not done. The war of 1812 betrayed the weakness of the country in some essential particulars, and broke down the strict-construction theory, while confirming in power the party of strict-constructionists. Madison revived the project of a National University, *without* asking for a new article; and the old Federalist ideas gained such ground, that, when John Quincy Adams came into power, in 1825, Congress was asked to do more than Hamilton had so much as proposed in Cabinet-meeting. Jackson, impelled by his puerile hatred of Henry Clay, re-established the strict-construction principle; but it would not remain re-established. In 1843, Congress gave Professor Morse twenty thousand dollars with which to try his immortal experiment with the telegraph. Congress had no right to do this; but the splendor of the result dazzled every mind and silenced all reproach. Then came Mr. Douglas's device by which a Democratic Congress was enabled to set up a railroad company with capital from the sale of the public lands, and leave to the railroad company all the profit upon the investment. Finally was achieved the masterpiece of evasion called "lending the public credit."

I never could see the necessity of any device to justify Congress in constructing *one* Pacific Railroad outright; because it was a cheap and necessary measure of "common defence." That railroad defends the frontiers against the Indians better than mounted regiments, and defends the Pacific States better than costly fleets. But the most strained reading of the Constitution cannot make it authorize the building of a railroad beginning and ending in the same State, nor justify the voting of public money to make scientific experiments. Probably there are now in Washington at least fifty lobbies (or will be erelong) working for schemes suggested by those two violations of trust, to the sore tribulation of members of Congress, and to the grievous loss of persons interested.

The time is favorable for an attempt to settle this question, because it does not now enter into the conflict of parties. Perhaps the Congress of an empire like this *ought* to have power to aid in such a work as the Darien Canal. Perhaps the mere magnitude of the undertaking makes it exceptional, makes it necessarily national. It *may* properly belong to an imperial parliament to aid scientific experiments which are too costly for individuals to undertake. Perhaps a national Congress is incompletely endowed unless it *can* reward services that cannot otherwise be rewarded, — such a service, for example, as that rendered by the discoverers of the pain-suspending power of ether. If so, let the power be frankly granted, but carefully defined. If not, let the fact be known. There should be an end of evasions, devices, and tricks for doing what the Constitution does not authorize. A tolerably well-informed citizen of the United States should be able to ascertain with certainty, before going to Washington and publishing a gorgeous album, whether his enterprise is one which Congress has or has not the constitutional right to assist.

THE CLOTHES MANIA.

THAT Alpine hat which broke out upon us with so much violence, and which, I am told, has not yet spent its force in the interior States, is a good illustration of the way in which a fashion originates, "takes," spreads, rages, declines, dies away in the distance, and is lost to view, until it pleases our sovereign lords, the fashion-makers, to spring it upon mankind again. The son of a New York hatter, late in the year 1867, while making the tour of Europe, found himself at Naples, where he noticed a pretty green hat that was much in vogue, called the Alpine hat. It was steeple-crowned, with wide brim, and a broad black ribbon round the crown which was further decorated by a feather. It differed from the familiar Tyrolese hat, which we often see at the opera upon the heads of picturesque banditti, chiefly in having the brim turned up instead of down, and in having a deep, regular dent or cleft in the top of the crown, such as all soft hats have when they are first unpacked. The young hatter, though on pleasure bent, had a mind attentive to business, and he sent one of these hats home to his father, who placed it in his store for the amusement of his customers. It was as though he had said, "See what things those absurd foreigners wear! Yes, sir, they actually wear that kind of thing in Naples; out of doors, and in broad daylight! Just fancy a man wearing a green hat, with a feather in it, in the streets!"

For three months or more this hat, so pretty at Naples, so ridiculous in New York, was exhibited in the hat-store in Broadway without exciting in the breast of any man a desire to possess it. The realistic drama was then in fashion. Managers advertised their new effects as patented; dramatists sought the twofold protection of the Patent

Office and the copyright law, and would not permit the hero of another man's play to incur any but an original peril. The hats worn upon the stage being thus as real as the real water of the stage fountain and the real donkey of the stage cart, this romantic hat was not in request for the drama. Indeed, it remains unsold at the present moment, and may still be inspected by the curious. But one day it occurred to the philosophic mind of the hatter who owned it, that, apart from its green color and its feather, the fundamental ideas of this hat were good, and were also in harmony with the tastes of the American people. He thought he saw in it a taking compromise between the orthodox respectability of the stiff and glossy cylinder, and the too careless lowering loaferism of soft felt. He thought he could Americanize the Naples hat in such a way as to combine the safety of the stove-pipe with the grace that is latent in the slouch. Then he said, "Make me a dozen hats of that pattern, but black and without a feather." In due time, the hats were placed in the store for sale. The hit they made was immediate and most decided. Every one who saw them was delighted with them, and they were all sold in a few hours. It is a long time since hatters have offered the public so pleasing a union of the becoming, the comfortable, and the convenient. And about this time arrived in New York the gallant band of English cricketers, wearing hats somewhat similar; and these gentlemen, performing daily in the presence of a great multitude, gave an impetus to the fashion. In a short time, the originator was selling a hundred Alpine hats a day, and all the other hatters were in full cry after them. In a few weeks, one half the better dressed men in New York were happy in the consciousness of having their heads more becomingly covered than they ever were before; and the other half secretly craved the same happiness, but were prevented from indulging their desire by the noble dread of wearing a hat that "everybody" wore.

In this little story of the Alpine hat is contained, as I have said, all the principles that control the rise, spread, and extinction of fashions. But in order to present the subject properly, we must go back of the Alpine hat, and see by what steps we arrived at the state of mind and taste which caused so many of us to adopt it so eagerly. And this is a subject which goes down to the depths of human nature. As the topmost leaves of the tallest tree draw their nourishment from the far distant and unseen root, and take their form, color, and texture from the tree's constitution and circumstances; as there is a natural necessity that the leaves of the willow shall be long and the leaves of the holly shall shine; so the feathers in ladies' bonnets and the shape of men's hats, and all the seeming caprices of fashion, are controlled by law, originate in the nature of things, and are influenced by the controlling events of history. I do not know why walking-sticks are seldom carried at present in our streets, where, three years ago, it was common to carry them; but if any one had a month in which to find out, he could find out; and very likely his investigation would carry him up among the great events and men of the age. He might have to write to Count Bismarck about it; the national debt may have something to do with it. The shade of care that comes over the countenances of a community when times are hard, and which our faces have worn for the last three years, since our burden began to settle down heavily upon us (the flush-money of the war being all spent, and the fictitious prosperity of war having been succeeded by its proper reaction), may explain it; for a walking-stick is the natural accompaniment of a mind at ease. It is when we go forth to stroll among the girls in the Fifth Avenue on a fine afternoon, that we take a cane with us; not when we are going down town to collect or borrow money. But I leave this interesting branch of the subject to future investigators, and return to my hats, merely reporting, for the information of those investigators, that, during the whole of the year 1868, the walking-stick trade was exceedingly dull, and that in 1864 and 1865 it was very brisk indeed.

Among the pictures in the gallery of the New York Historical Society, there is one representing the interior of the Park Theatre, on an evening in 1822, during the performance of the elder Matthews. Every face in the audience is a portrait, the object of the artist being to assemble upon one canvas portraits of all the leading persons then moving in the society and business of New York. Often as I go into this interesting gallery, I never fail to take a look, in passing, at the round-faced, burly fathers of the present kings of commerce and finance. What a contrast, their amplitude of countenance and form, their good-humored torpidity of intellect, their consummate, solid respectability, with the sharper-featured, more slender, slightly intellectualized "operators" of the present time; connoisseurs in tandems, pictures, books, operas! As the persons in that distinguished audience are in full dress, the picture serves as an historical fashion-plate. The greater number of those stout gentlemen wear the most voluminous white neckcloths, which seem to have been wound round and round their necks, completely filling up the space between the coat and the countenance. Others have on those high stiff stocks which many of us remember, — things of buckram covered with black silk, satin, or velvet, fastened behind with a buckle that was not always invisible. From out the depths of the stocks, stiff and sharp-cornered collars thrust themselves toward heaven. The coat-collars of these solid gentlemen are several inches high, and only less stiff than a pine board. A few of the spectators, who are standing at the back of the pit, have their hats on, and those hats are immense; they are structures, regularly built, bell-crowned, and covered with the beaver skins which Mr. Astor brought from the far-distant haunts of his trappers. Most of the ladies wear bonnets, which also are vast, wide-spreading, and lofty, apparently of construction scarcely less massive than the beavers of their husbands.

Stiff and cumbrous as the clothes in this picture seem to us, they are light and easy compared with the cocked hats, the padded coats, stiffened with buckram, the wigs, the overflowing ruffles, the knee-breeches and great buckles, from which victorious democracy, in Jefferson's early day, delivered the fathers of these fathers who sit so solemnly enjoying Charles Matthews the elder. Old men used to be about New York who remembered when the young dandies of the Democratic party, in 1801, — the year of Mr. Jefferson's inauguration, — first dared to show themselves in Broadway without wig or pigtail. It was thought to be an innovation scarcely decent for a young man to go about the streets exhibiting his own hair; and many men surrendered the pigtail only with life. When Mr. Jefferson discarded his short breeches, silk stockings, and silver-buckled shoes, and concealed his well-formed legs in pantaloons, the Federalists were prone to regard it as the trick of a demagogue to secure the favor of the mob. A *gentleman* in trousers and short hair! But what better could be expected of a Democrat and an atheist?

After the revolutionary ferment, which in Europe ended in defeat under Napoleon, and here in peaceful victory under Jefferson, there was a reaction toward the opinions which are called conservative, and this reaction expressed itself in stiffness and uniformity of dress. People forty years of age can remember the high stock, the cruel shirt-collar, the ruthless coat-collar, the prodigious bonnet, and the general setness and severity of costume which prevailed among us, before Channing, Dickens, Carlyle, Emerson, Beecher, and the New York Tribune had begun the emancipation of the American understanding from the tight-fitting armor of opinions in which it was once confined. The primness and stiffness of the ladies who used to walk past the Astor House when it was the one grand hotel of the city, and when the fashionable walk was between the Battery and St. Paul's Church, can only be realized by those who remember their leg-of-mutton sleeves bulged out with buckram, and their lace handkerchiefs carried in their hands before them in a ludicrously precise and uniform way. The dress of the men was only less formal, cumbrous, and unyielding. Over all hung heavily the large black beaver hat; which maintained its supremacy so long because it harmonized with the stiffness and angularity of the rest of the attire.

It required three great historical events merely to circumscribe the dominion of the stove-pipe hat. First, the Mexican War revealed to a large number of American citizens the unsuspected truth, that the head of man could be covered becomingly without resorting to the stiff beaver. A good many officers and soldiers brought home from Mexico the wide-brimmed, steeple-crowned, flexible hat worn by Spaniards and Spanish creoles; but the large and sweeping picturesqueness of that tropical production was felt to be incongruous with the square-shouldered, tight-fitting garments worn by the busy and punctual men of American cities. Few had the courage to face a staring population, and most of those spacious hats were hung on pegs as mementos of warlike adventure. Then occurred the discovery of gold in California, and the wonderful rush across the Plains, around Cape Horn, and over the Isthmus, which compelled thousands of people to discard from their attire everything that was not pliable. The Mexican soft hat, modified to suit the American taste, became part of the uniform of the gold-seeking multitude, and was frequently seen in the streets of the Atlantic cities. But neither the war with Mexico, nor the discovery of California gold, nor both these important events together, sufficed to make the soft hat fashionable. Something more was needed. Europe had to be convulsed, and half a dozen ancient thrones shaken, before the scene became possible which gave a rival to the stiff cylinder.

The Mexican War began in 1846. Captain Sutter's men discovered the glittering particles of gold in the California mill race, in 1848. On a certain day in December, 1851 (the soft-hat manufacture being then in full activity), the most picturesque human figure which recent America has had the pleasure of beholding flashed upon two hundred thousand of us as we stood packed in Broadway, between the Battery and Union Square, — two miles and two thirds of excited people, every creature of whom desired in his secret soul to be a pleasing object of contemplation to his friends and the public. We saw the hero of the hour but for half a minute each, as he passed, standing in his barouche, his pale and handsome face set off so strikingly by that graceful hat, with the large black feather wound about it. What a beautiful object he was! The mere beauty of the man and his costume was such as to excite in every susceptible beholder a thrill of delight. I can see him now, the splendid Magyar, the magnificent, marvellous, histrionic Kossuth!

It was done! The stove-pipe had a rival; the feather, of course, was a thing to which we could not lift our souls. It has pleased Heaven so to constitute these northern climes, and the races inhabiting them, that a male of our species, who wears a feather in his hat of his own free will, must be either more or less than man. We could not attain to the feather; but the KOSSUTH HAT, adapted to the American taste, immediately appeared, and from that day to this the stiff cylinder has never been able to reign over us with its former absolute sway.

An unpopular article of attire is the hat stigmatized as the stove-pipe. It is generally reviled as the acme of inconvenience and ugliness. It binds the head, and reddens the skin; it is heavy, large, inflexible, expensive, easily injured, difficult to restore, and very much in the way on a journey, in a crowd, or at a public meeting. No one pretends to admire or defend it. And yet there is something in the breast of the respectable citizen which prompts him, upon the whole, to prefer it; and, consequently, that hat, to this hour, is worn by about one half of the men in cities and large towns. There is, besides, a tendency in men, after indulging in soft infidelities for a while, to return to this unyielding head-covering. If between the sublime and the ridiculous there is a whole step, there is only a finger's breadth between the becoming and the absurd; and a staid citizen, when he ventures upon a soft hat, is not *quite* sure on which side of that dividing finger he is. But the stiff hat is a fixed quantity; he feels safe in it; and he is content not to be picturesque so long as he is sure not to be ridiculous. In itself, the hard hat is unpleasing and irrational, but it harmonizes with the angularity and stiffness which solid men still affect in the rest of their attire. Hence in Boston and Philadelphia, it is more frequently seen than in New York. The time has been in those two cities when the credit of a young man would have suffered if he had walked to his business in any other kind of hat than one of that polished and unyielding description which was once associated in the public mind with punctuality in meeting pecuniary obligations. If his hat was flexible, what guaranty had the public for the rigidity of his principles?

The Alpine hat took half our heads by storm, because it held out to us the alluring prospect of being *safely* picturesque. The dent in the crown was regular; the brim was somewhat broad, but it was not allowed to flap about of its own free will; and that wide black ribbon round the crown gave richness and dignity to the whole. In truth, the soft hat was arranged in its most becoming form, and then *fixed* in that form by block and stiffening. Such was its success in reconciling discordant conditions, that I saw the president of one bank and the cashier of another going down town wearing the Alpine hat, at a time when it was in high favor with the easy-going gentlemen of the press. Every one must feel that this savors of the millennium; the Alpine hat, indeed, expresses clearly the spiritual condition of the age, that half-fledged freedom of the soul, that longing to be free, without quite daring to launch away from the native twig, which is characteristic of so many at present.

In most of our large libraries there are collections of costume-books sufficient to show how immediately a change of opinion reveals itself in costume; and many modern historians have recorded the fact. Henri Martin, in his History of France, frequently pauses to note the connection between changes of spiritual condition and changes in the general style of dress. "In order to judge of a community," he says in one place (Martin, XII. 124), "it almost suffices to see its costume, that faithful interpreter of the bodily habits, which reflects always those of the spirit." Handling masses of illustrated works, and living near galleries of old pictures, he observed that both the morals and the minds of his countrymen have been faithfully reflected in the clothes they preferred. Under Francis I., French fashions were elegant and voluptuous; at the immoral court of Henry III., they were extravagant and monstrous; in the time of Henry IV., they had a military cast; under glorious Richelieu, the costumes assumed "a nobleness, a severe and picturesque amplitude, a style at once graceful and distinguished, never equalled in modern Europe." Fashions in that age, as in every age, originated in the country where there was most money and most leisure to spend upon dress, which then was Holland. Venice once gave the law to fashionable Europe, then Spain, then Holland, then France. While Louis XIV. was a gay and gorgeous personage, the costumes of his court were gay and gorgeous, but when he had been scared into a kind of repentance, and settled down with Madame de Maintenon into the steady-going married man, and no one could hope for royal favor who did not attend mass once a day, costumes became heavy, ugly, awkward, a monstrous blending of the courtly and the puritanic. Then, when the Regent brought pleasure into fashion once more, instantly the cumbrous extravagances of the old court were abandoned, and dress became simpler, costlier, and more elegant. As the Revolution approached, democratic ideas were fashionable in chateaus and grand drawing-rooms. All costume and all decoration became simpler and less expensive. English modes were introduced, the splendid carriages with panels painted by artists of repute, and heavy with elaborate decoration, all disappeared, and Paris was sombre with chariots, dark-colored and devoid of ornamentation, in the London style. Later, meanness and shabbiness of attire were the height of the mode in Paris, where republicans of ancient lineage and renown strove to express in this way their newly felt brotherhood to the less fortunate of mankind. Under Napoleon, all fashions for men had something in them of a military character, Napoleon reserving to himself the striking simplicity of a field uniform.

We have all observed, I suppose, what Mr. Herbert Spencer mentions in one of his essays, that the character of a political meeting can be inferred from the dress of those who attend it. "At a chartist demonstration," he tells us, "a lecture on socialism, or a *soirée* of the friends of Italy, there will be seen many among the audience, and a still larger ratio among the speakers, who get themselves up in a style more or less unusual. . . . . Bare necks, shirt-collars à la Byron, wonderfully shaggy great-coats, numerous oddities in form and color, destroy the monotony usual in crowds. . . . . And when the gathering breaks up, the varieties of head-gear, the number of caps, and the abundance of felt hats, suffice to prove that were the world at large like-minded, the black cylinders which tyrannize over us would soon be deposed." These remarks apply as well to New York as to London. They perfectly describe the motley assemblies which used to crowd the old Tabernacle in Broadway, when Theodore Parker lectured to all that was most advanced and enlightened, as well as to much that was eccentric and affected, in the city. On the other hand, how uniform and precise the dress of the men who issue in dark clouds about 12.15 on Sundays, from churches where all endeavor to think alike, and engage an able man, at great expense, to assist them in so doing! In those Theodore Parker days, members of the press sported various peculiarities of costume; especially men connected with the journal supposed to be most at variance with public opinion. Since that time, extremes of opinion have drawn nearer together, and we now observe that the public-spirited and exemplary workingmen of the New York press, Bohemians of the new school, only discard so much of the conventional in costume and demeanor as is inconvenient and irrational. Compared with people of twenty years ago, we are all radicals, and our clothes show it. The eccentrics of the old Tabernacle platform have generally chosen to conform to the fashions of a public with which they are no longer much at variance; and the public, less trammelled than formerly by orthodoxies in politics and theology, dress more easily, comfortably, and variously.

Certainly, men do. If any one thinks ladies do not, I would like to show him a set of fashion-plates of 1820 to 1830, now lying before me. *Paniers*, do you say? Paniers first came in, I believe, about six months after the marriage of Louis XV., which occurred in 1725. They have been in fashion several times since, but they have never been so light, so modest, so harmless, so little worn, and so generally ridiculed as now. We can at least boast that they are not now regarded as an affair of state, disturbing the peace of courts, and calling for the interference of a prime minister. That gossiping Paris lawyer, Barbier, in his diary for 1728, has a curious passage relating to the paniers then worn at the French court, a passage which may console some readers whom the sight of a panier causes to despair of the human race.

"One would not believe," says Barbier, "that the Cardinal [Fleury, prime minister] has been embarrassed with regard to the paniers which women wear under their petticoats to render them large and spreading. They are of such a size, that when the ladies sit down, the whalebones are pushed out and make such an astonishing spread that they have been obliged to have arm-chairs made on purpose. Only three women can get into a box at the theatre without crowding. The fashion has gone to such an extravagance, as extreme fashions always do, that when the princesses are seated on each side of the queen, their petticoats, which rise as they seat themselves, hide the queen's petticoat. That seemed improper, but it was difficult to devise a remedy. By dint of pondering (*à force de rêver*) the Cardinal has decided that there shall always be an empty chair on each side of the queen, which will prevent the inconvenience; and the pretext is, that those two chairs are reserved for Mesdames de France, her daughters" (twins, two years old).

Thus the wise old priest, who governed France for so many years, arranged this great affair. It soon appeared, however, that the princesses did not like *their* petticoats concealed by the paniers of adjacent duchesses, and the Cardinal was obliged to grant them a vacant stool on each side. This offended the duchesses, who desired the same privilege. But Cardinal Fleury, like Dickens's immortal London barber, had to draw the line *somewhere*, and he drew it so as to exclude the duchesses, which led to a bitter war of pamphlets and epigrams, in the course of which one pamphlet was publicly burned by the executioner (Barbier, II. 37 and 41). Much as we may regret to see young loveliness disfiguring itself with these things in the Fifth Avenue, we can find comfort in the reflection that Mr. Seward has not been obliged to interfere, nor has the public hangman earned the smallest fee in consequence of the revived fashion.

Fashion is a necessity of human nature; because, while we all desire to be pleasingly attired, not one in ten thousand of us is able to invent any article of dress or decoration that shall be truly becoming. Nothing is more universal than the wish to be well-looking; and the feeling is so strong that a person had almost better not be born at all than be born two feet too tall or too short, or with any other very marked personal peculiarity that cannot be concealed. Byron's morbidness with regard to his lameness was not an unusual case. Turn loose, in a large school of rough boys or girls, a child who has a squint eye, or a humpback, or a red patch on its face, or who is extremely fat or lean, or tall or short, or whose clothes are very different from those worn by the rest, or who has some unconquerable peculiarity of speech or manner, and that child will suffer an acute misery of which no one can form an idea who has never experienced it. Nor is this a peculiarity of childhood. What would induce a respectable citizen of Boston to walk down Washington Street in top-boots, or wearing a hat of 1830? Where is the woman strong-minded enough to calmly endure the stony stare of an omnibus full of female critics who have spied out something awry or antique in her costume? It is a tremendous ordeal. We are so constituted that we like to be like one another; and so general is this desire, that one of the signs of madness is an inclination to oddity in personal adornment. It is hard for us to believe in the soundness of a person's judgment who turns his collar down when every one else turns it up, or who lets his hair grow very long when the rest of mankind have theirs cropped. It is only in these advanced days and in these two or three most advanced nations, that there is any real liberty of choice whether we shall go bearded or shorn, and whether we shall take evening sustenance in a coat with a tail behind, or in one with a tail all around it. Indeed, there are circles even in metropolitan London, Paris, and New York, where a person, otherwise unexceptionable, would be grossly undervalued if he should presume to present himself in any other than the regulation coat.

Many suppose that it is only the circles dependent upon Paris for their personal decoration which are subject to these rigors. Not so. Nothing delivers from the tyranny of fashion but real elevation and independence of character; and, accordingly, the most abject slaves of fashion are to be found among the barbarous races and classes. Mr. Oscanyan tells us, that in the harems of the East, where Paris fashions are unknown, the changes in the shape of the ladies' dresses, and in the mode of adorning their persons, are as frequent as with us; and, although those changes are often so trifling that a foreigner would not notice them, a lady who cannot follow the new mode is as miserable as a New York servant-girl would have been a year or two ago without a hoop-skirt. We read in Marco Polo that it was so with the ladies of the harem countries, six hundred years ago. "A peculiar fashion of dress," he records of one of those countries, "prevails among the women of the superior class, who wear below their waists, in the manner of drawers, a kind of garment in the making of which they employ, according to their means, a hundred, eighty, or sixty ells of fine cotton cloth; which also they gather or plait, in order to increase the apparent size of their hips; those being accounted the most handsome who are most bulky in that part." Paniers again! And when the captains who sailed under Prince Henry the Navigator, first landed upon the Western coast of Africa, years before Columbus commanded a ship, they discovered that the unclad beauties of Guinea were devoured by the same passion to be in the mode. "That woman among them," writes an old translator of the valiant and talkative Cadamosto, "who has the largest breasts, has the glory of being considered the most handsome. For this purpose, each female, ambitious of this prerogative, when they attain their seventeenth or eighteenth year submit themselves to the operation of having their breasts tied around with strings, and so closely drawn that they almost sever them from the body, and by means of daily efforts of stretching and dilation, give them at length such an extension as to hang down to the navel. No greater bliss can arrive to their sex than success in this attempt."*

And a traveller of to-day tells us that he carried with him a bountiful supply of the prettiest and costliest colored beads into the interior of Africa, hoping thereby to conciliate a powerful tribe and purchase their good offices; but when he arrived among them, he found, to his dismay, that the fashion in beads had changed, and that his were not in vogue. Colored beads were out, white beads were in. Not a negro of them, nor a negress, would look at his beautiful assortment of brilliant-hued beads, the choicest product of Birmingham; but the rage was for a certain kind of very cheap and common white beads, which the traders had introduced. Give me a week in the Astor Library, and I will furnish an octavo volume of facts like these, showing that the desire to be in the mode is universal, and that this desire is strongest in the weakest of our species.

The root of it all is, the deep and poignant shame which

* Narrative of First Voyage of Cadamosto to Coast of Africa, 1455.

we experience from physical defects, — a feeling most necessary and salutary. Every man wishes to be of the proper number of inches round the chest, and every woman wishes to be beautiful in form and feature. There is not a fashion now prevalent in the world, and probably never has been one, which did not originate in the desire on the part of some one to display a physical excellence, or conceal a physical defect. Nature abhors bodily insufficiency. For five years past, men have stood aghast at the fantastic tricks which ladies have played before high Heaven with their own and other people's hair, as well as with that of horses and other innocent creatures. This wondrous hair system, which has prevailed throughout Christendom, all originated in the fact that the hair of a certain conspicuous woman became, by incessant dressings, very thin. Those shoes, too, which have the heel near the middle of the foot, and destroy the harmony of every movement, owe their currency to a foolish and groundless superstition, that a small foot is a sign of superior lineage. Some lady whose position required her to wear fine clothes in the gaze of many of her fellow-mortals had a large foot, which her obliging shoemaker strove to diminish by putting the heel an inch or two nearer the toe than it ought to have been. The trick seemed to answer the purpose, and from that time every lady in six nations, not exceptionally firm and sensible, has gone rocking on a pivot. Constantly, for the last three hundred years, ladies have been preached at for wearing their dresses too low; but such is the passion of human beings for displaying physical excellence, that just as often as the conspicuous lady of the age is well formed the fashion returns, and women indulge their desire to appear as lovely as nature made them.

In every community of which we have any knowledge, there is that one conspicuous person or class whom the rest admire, envy, and imitate. But this elect few, who alone have much time or means to expend upon the decoration of the body, are ever striving to be as *distinguished* in appearance as they suppose themselves to be in reality; and thus there is always going on a game of cross-purposes between the few and the many. The young men of New York who give their whole mind, such as it is, to the adornment and display of their persons, were glad enough to wear Alpine hats while only their own circle had them; but the moment those hats began to be generally worn, the dandies gave theirs away, and fell back upon styles which had some little peculiarity. The Astrakhan cap, high, and without a visor, gave solace to some, and caused the lobby of the French Opera to assume an Alaskian aspect, as though the Russians on their way home had stopped a few nights in New York to see the new piece. If the dandies succeed in adopting a kind of hat that pleases the public, more and more of the Alpines are laid aside, until they finally disappear beyond the Alleghanies, and spread themselves over the Valley of the Mississippi. Thus it is with all fashions. They are invented by taste or suggested by accident; they are adopted by the few who live but to dress; they are taken up by the public who have only time to ask what is worn; they are then abandoned by the ornamental class, and successively by the classes who are uneasy if they do not resemble them; and, at last, they are only seen on the persons of the multitude, who buy clothes with the intention of wearing them out, and who execute that intention.

Several causes have conspired of late years to stimulate our natural and commendable love of personal decoration, until most of us expend too much money upon it, and many are possessed by a kind of mania for changing and multiplying their garments, and for having them made of materials needlessly expensive.

Eighteen years ago, the President of the Republic of France betrayed the country which had trusted him, stole its liberties in the night, laid robber hands upon its treasury, dishonored its noblest citizens by carting them to jail in prison vans, murdered in cold blood several hundreds of innocent men and women in the streets of Paris, and transported hundreds more to a hot unhealthy region of the tropics. This was the Andersonville of usurpation. It transcended all that had ever been done in that kind, — joining to the extreme of dastardly meanness the extreme of audacious cruelty, and being totally devoid of palliation or excuse, except that invented by the head liar of the gang who perpetrated it. The man in whose name the deed was done appears to have furnished nothing but the lies; the audacity, and what little courage was shown, being supplied by others. Mr. Kinglake's chapter upon this usurpation (Invasion of the Crimea, Vol. I. Ch. XIV.) strikingly confirmed by some American narratives to which that author had not access, exhausts the subject, and avenges the human race, which is deeply injured whenever man's faith in man is lessened by the deliberate betrayal of a solemnly accepted trust. Mr. Kinglake, I say, has avenged our outraged race; for which, I trust, we are all duly grateful to him. Nothing remains but for France to bring the perfidious wretch to trial for the special wrong done to *her*, and execute upon him the penalty to which he may be condemned.

As usual in such cases, a woman was found willing to share the bed and booty of the successful robber. She was young, beautiful, well formed, and of just such a mind as to submit joyfully to spend half the day in trying on articles of wearing apparel, and the other half in displaying them to a concourse of people. It became, too, and remains an important part of her duty to amuse, dazzle, and debase the women of France, by wearing a rapid succession of the most gorgeous, novel, bewildering costumes, the mere description of which has developed a branch of literature, employs many able writers, and mainly supports fifty periodicals. Here is a vain, beautiful woman, living in the gaze of nations, who has the plunder of a rich kingdom with which to buy her clothes, and the taste of a continent to devise them for her; for to Paris the *élite* of all tailors, dress-makers, milliners, and hair-dressers go from every capital in Europe. Whatever there is in France of truly noble and patriotic — and there are as many noble and patriotic persons in France as in any country — avoids the vicinity of this woman; while around her naturally gather the thoughtless and the interested. The women in this circle imitate her as closely as women can whose husbands have not stolen the treasures of a nation; all except one, it is said, and she is the real queen of fashion.

Both these leading women have certain physical defects which they wish to conceal, as well as certain unusual charms, of which they intend the most shall be made. One is beautiful and tall. The other is ugly and short, but graceful, vivacious, and interesting. The hair of one of them growing scanty behind, all women felt the necessity of carrying a pound of horsehair under their own, and swelled out in the region of the back hair to an extent that now seems incredible. If the parting of the hair widens, and begins to resemble baldness, then frizzing comes in, which covers up the deficiency. A few gray hairs bring powder into fashion. Other insufficiencies send paniers on their way round the world. For these women, and especially the one who figures in the centre of the group, occupy that conspicuous place to which for two centuries past more female eyes have been admiringly directed than to any other; and there reside near them a band of writers who live by chronicling every new device of decoration that appears upon their persons. So able, liberal, and sensible a journal as the Pall Mall Gazette finds it necessary to station an industrious member of its staff within sight of these people, for the sole purpose of telling the best women in England what clothes the worst women in France wear. I should suppose, from looking over the periodicals which publish fashion news, that there must be in Paris as many as a hundred writers who derive the whole or part of their income from describing the dresses worn in the ancient palaces temporarily occupied by the usurper and his dependants; and many of these writers do their work so well, that their letters are a most potent stimulator of the passion for dress which is so easily kindled in the minds of the ignorant and immature.

This poor woman, who is the immediate cause of the mischief, is, we are told, an anxious and unhappy being, as well she may be. She struggles to conciliate. A forced, fixed smile is ever upon her face, when that face is seen by others. In her growing anxiety, she naturally redoubles her efforts to dazzle and beguile the people in whose sight she dwells, and on whose money she dresses. When the Hour comes, I hope she will be mercifully judged, for she has already expiated the venial sin of yielding to a temptation which only a very superior woman — one really honest and thorough-bred — could have resisted. It is probable that she now regards the wearing of those tremendous costumes merely as her contribution towards housekeeping; as though she said to her husband, "*You* keep down the men by muzzling the press and flattering the army, and I 'll fool the women by wearing the most stunning costumes that ever struck envy to the female heart."

Then the marriage laws of France, and the universal custom of demanding a dowry with a wife, have necessitated other arrangements than marriage between the sexes; have called into existence a large class of women who are well named the *demi-monde*, — a something between respectable married women and those who are wholly out of the pale of respectability. I presume this class is not more numerous in proportion to the rest of the population now than they were when the loyal Barbier, indignant at the epigrams launched at Louis XV. when he established his first mistress at court, exclaimed: "Every one else keeps a mistress; why should n't the king have one?" The demi-monde may not be proportionally more numerous than in the year 1735, but they have, as a class, a hundred times more money to spend. Empty head, vacant time, full purse, — these are the main constituents of the people subject to the clothes mania. Since the discovery of gold in California in 1848, I suppose more people have undergone a complete change of circumstances than ever before in so short a space of time. From that heavily laden marquis in England, who toils at the management of an estate yielding an income of three thousand pounds sterling a day, to the rag-pickers of the streets, we all have more money to spend than we used to have; and one of the things we are surest to do, when we have some superfluous cash, is to go to Paris and buy pleasure with it, — pleasure being a chief product of that capital. Of course, there must be a prodigious number of semi and wholly unfortunate women there who have heaps of gold, and nothing to do but to copy or burlesque the showy women of the Tuileries.

Heavens! What a carnival of folly they are holding, — those women of the palace and of the demi-monde! That is, if we may believe our assiduous friends, the reporters of fashions. The most curious and amusing feature of it is, the great number of things that are now regulated by fashion. I read in one fashion-letter that American young ladies were greatly in vogue in Paris until last year; but during the present season it has not been *fashionable* to have them at balls and parties, because it has been discovered that, under elegant and most costly costumes, some of them concealed an ignorance surpassing that of a servant-girl. I read in another of these epistles, that such is the rage for light hair, that ladies whose hair is not of the fashionable hue tie it up into the smallest possible space, and wholly cover it with light curls, frizzles, and powder. Another informs us that the costumes of the Conspicuous Woman of France, which are sometimes changed four times a day, and the most expensive of which are never worn more than twice, vary in *sentiment* with the occasion; so that when she attends a council of ministers, so called, she wears a dress of "a grave, reflecting tone, on which hues of steel-gray meet rays of studious brown, the *ensemble* being burnished armor." Two years ago, we are further assured, it was fashionable to be seen making caps and dresses for some poor woman's baby; but babies are past, and now no lady of fashion does anything with needles less elegant than "Venetian *guipure* or netting," whatever that may be. Mourning dresses and mourning customs, it seems, also vary, and we are favored with minute descriptions of the styles worn at Père-la-Chaise on the day when custom enjoins that graves shall be visited. Coffins, we are told, are *again* covered with black cloth "puffed like upholstery."

Indeed, if the reader will take the trouble to look over a few of the fashion-letters from Paris, he will discover that fashion now prescribes not only every article of dress and personal decoration, but that there is scarcely anything which it does not regulate. In the course of a week or two I have gathered paragraphs telling me what cards I must use for every occasion on which cards can be supposed to come into play; how I must be buried, if I wish to have the thing done as it should be; what styles of tombstone are now in fashion; what color my horses would have to be, if I had any; whether the wheels and the body of my carriage must contrast or match; what medicines, and school of medicine, and practitioners of medicine, it is fashionable to employ, as well as what diseases are now in vogue. I am notified, also, that in England, at present, the fashionable *religion* is Ritualism. Strangest of all, I am seriously assured by the *Moniteur de la Mode* itself, that it is now the height of fashion, not to follow the fashion, but to go to the studio of your *artiste* in clothes, and demand of her a creation, — a costume wholly original. "There is no woman of fashion who does not ask *des confections faites exclusivement pour elle.* As soon as a thing has been seen, she wishes it no longer." This calls to mind the advice which the author of Pelham gave to the London dandy of thirty years ago, which was, that if he saw his most favorite, most costly, most stunning waistcoat copied by another man, he should instantly give his own away to his valet. No other course was open to a man of true *ton.*

The solemnity with which these things are stated is sometimes extremely ludicrous. The force of the comic can no further go than in a paragraph printed last winter in a New York paper, which notified the public that a family was in affliction from a cause both novel and distressing. An elegant bridal veil of "real point lace" had been ordered in Paris for a young lady who was to be married the next day. It had not arrived, and "the family of the bride were very much *concerned,* fearing that white *tulle* would have to be substituted." Carlyle should have had this for "Sartor Resartus." "Concerned" is good.

The truth is, that the two conspicuous persons in France are in a position which is both false and precarious. Being essentially histrionic persons, they employ histrionic arts, one of which is, rapid and frequent changes of costume. One of these people plays emperor, and the other plays empress; and they have set all the fools in Christendom dressing for parts. "A remarkable toilet," says a fashion-letter, "is a hunting-robe, to be worn by a belle, who looks on while the hunters mount in their saddles, but does not follow them."

The cost of all this is beyond arithmetic to compute. Never before were the treasures of a frugal and laborious people, such as the French are, wasted so wantonly. No mistress of Louis XIV., no titled harlot of the Regency, not Pompadour, not Dubarry, ever squandered the money of the French with such reckless profusion as the woman now occupying the apartments in which they dwelt. "The cream of novelty," says a letter from Paris, "is a garland so contrived that, as the heat of the dancing-room becomes greater, the petals composing this garland open gradually, then fall into the hair, disclosing a diamond or a ruby in each." Another: "A new fashion is, to have buttons and jewelry of the same shade as the ribbon sashes; thus a maize taffeta is worn with amethyst, and coral jewelry with coral-colored ribbons." Another: "The ladies at Compiègne dress four times a day, and vie with one another in magnificence." "The Empress's toilets are all ravishing. On Sunday, at mass, she wore a blue satin trained dress, trimmed with Russian sable, with a polonaise of the same, likewise trimmed with sable, and a bonnet of iris velvet with aigrette." This was a simple church dress. One of the evening costumes was "an apricot silk, puffed all round the bottom with apricot tulle; flounces worked with silver, fuchsia pattern, and trimmed with Venetian fringe of white silk. Over this an immense train of white satin, softened by apricot tulle, worked with silver fuchsias and fringe round the borders."

In this style do women of a certain mind dress when they have the plunder of a great kingdom at command. The Princess Metternich, when she came to spend a few days at Compiègne, felt it necessary to bring with her twenty-six trunks full of clothes; and we read of a French bride who had sixty thousand francs' worth of handkerchiefs as one item of her outfit. In a word, the surplus money which ought to be educating France is at present chiefly wasted in disfiguring a few thousand Frenchwomen.

The time was when the ladies who led society in France had other claims to the homage of men than the clothes they wore. The time *was*, do I say? The time *is*. The women who dress with this shameless disregard of morality and taste are, in no proper sense, leaders of the society of the country upon which they have fastened. They are not the successors of those amiable, intelligent ladies to whom Martin refers, when he says: "The ancients created conversation between men. Conversation between the two sexes, the true and complete conversation, was born in

France; and this is not one of the least of our titles to the esteem of mankind, little as we think of it now, when we have departed so far from our former elegance of manners" (Martin, XII. 424). Nor are these dull, ignorant people worthy to be ranked with the Frenchwomen of whom Sydney Smith wrote: "There used to be in Paris, under the ancient *régime*, a few women of brilliant talents, who violated all the common duties of life, and gave very pleasant little suppers." There can be no pleasant little suppers with persons dressed in the manner just described. No conversation is possible with a woman who has five hundred thousand francs' worth of satin, lace, and jewels on her mind. These women are in fact purely histrionic persons, actresses, with whom a few words may be exchanged as they stand dressed to "go on"; but their minds are so preoccupied with their parts, their audience, and their trains, that conversation is out of the question. Happily, the play will end erelong, and then they will slink out of the stage door and go home, carrying their toggery with them.

It is sometimes spoken of as a shame to the ladies of America, England, and Christendom generally, that they should have stooped to imitate the women temporarily conspicuous in betrayed and plundered France. Perhaps, many centuries hence, mankind will have advanced so far in moral feeling and genuine civilization, that a wrong done to any portion of the race will be keenly felt by every other portion, and a face unjustly slapped in Australia will make cheeks tingle in Greenland. At present, however, this is not the case, and most of us bear the sorrows of others with fortitude. Ladies do not generally read the newspapers; do not as yet consciously share in the public life of the race; do not even generally *know* how the person whose garments they copy got her insatiable little hand into the treasury of saving, industrious France; do not see the transparent artifices by which the French are amused and flattered, while they are held down and plundered; do not recognize in the bewildering costumes of the Conspicuous Woman a means of corrupting one sex and enslaving the other.

Ladies do not think of politics when they go to Stewart's to buy a new dress, and are much less concerned to know what is fashionable in France than what is "going to be worn" by the influential ladies of their own circle. Each country has its professional fashion-makers, who adapt French patterns to that country's climate, circumstances, and taste, and it is with these that ladies have to do. Not one lady in a million, who has ceased to part her hair, or who hides the symmetry of her form in a panier, sees any connection between those acts and the politics of Europe. Let us not presume to censure the fairer part of creation. A woman with a full purse and an empty head *must* dress, or do worse; and, being totally unable to devise costumes herself, she *must* follow the fashions invented by people who have less money and more brains than herself.

These fashion-makers have become in some capitals, especially in New York, a numerous and very capable class; and they, too, have been powerful stimulators of the clothes mania. I may say, indeed, that a sort of conspiracy exists between the makers and the originators of clothes, the grand object of which is to compel people to buy new garments before their old ones are worn out. I say *compel*, not merely tempt them to do so by the invention of new and pleasing styles (though that, too, is done), but *force* young and susceptible people to cast aside garments not half worn out, by making them prematurely old-fashioned.

I can best explain how this is done by recurring to an article already mentioned, the stove-pipe hat, which, being still worn by about one half the men in the United States, is what is styled "a leading article." The great question which the chief hatters of this nation revolve in their ingenious minds is this: How can we make men dissatisfied with the hats they have, and fly to others which they see the dandies wear? As many changes can be made in a hat as can be rung on those abominable "nine bells" of the arithmetics. A hat has a crown and a brim. That crown can be high, low, straight, steeple, or bell-shaped; and that brim can be narrow, wide, curling, straight, turned down or turned up. The whole structure can be large or it can be small. Of all the shapes which this kind of hat can assume, the one most popular, the one hardest to change, is the very one which happens to be most in vogue at this writing (February, 1869), namely, a moderate-sized bell, with a rather wide, curling brim. No shape is becoming to so many persons as this; and hence, though the straight crowns and steeple crowns seldom run more than two years, the bell, once well established, can seldom be made to seem absurd in less than seven years. Now, the trick of the hatters, as of all other fashion-makers, male and female, is this: first, to push or develop the reigning fashion, as rapidly as possible, to an extreme which savors of the ridiculous; and then, as rapidly as possible, to recede from that extreme to an opposite one. At present the tendency is to make hats larger, more bell-like, and with a brim of more pronounced curl. But the impulse in that direction is nearly exhausted, and the newest hats begin to look absurdly large, too bellish, and curling. The moment is at hand when a movement, more or less violent, will take place in the opposite direction. If the hatters dared, they would dart at once to a minute and natty steeple crown; but the public, in that case, would shy, and keep on wearing the bells. The next extreme, whatever it may be, will not be reached under two years, and it will be approached by such numerous and gradual changes, that most of our hats will be considerably worn before we begin to be ashamed of them. Our tyrants will beware of going too fast with us; for, after all, we can be masters if we will. We have to be deluded with the name and forms of freedom, while many of us are in reality the unresisting slaves of five men who keep Broadway hat-stores.

The recent tight trousers illustrate the same device. They grew tighter, and tighter, and tighter, until it was perilous to go abroad, and many of our young fellows looked like Master Shallow in his young days, when, as Falstaff informs us, he resembled "a forked radish, with a head fantastically carved upon it with a knife." The moment a ridiculous extreme of tightness had been well established, our lords, the tailors, kindly shook out a reef, and relieved us. But the tight trousers, which they had compelled us to buy, hang on their pegs unworn, or adorn the store fronts of Chatham Street. Among the ladies, the present rage is to load every article of visible attire with ornament. "We know," says the editress of our chief fashion-paper, "of a costume lately made, on which eighteen women spent two days in making the trimming." If the *modistes* are true to their principles, they will push this fashion of excessive ornamentation until it becomes utterly monstrous; and *then*, when every wardrobe is bursting with absurdity, they will turn as short a corner as they dare, and rush to an opposite extreme of simplicity. The object of all these tailors and dress-makers is, to make us loathe our clothes while they are still as good as new. But they could not work their will upon us without the co-operation of the small class in all our cities who live only to dress, and whose one cry is, "Give us something new to wear." These *start* a fashion and give it a chance to "take." And as fortune is ever apt to favor the brave, it sometimes happens that accident aids the bold innovator who suddenly cuts off our coat tails, or takes in our trousers until we cannot pick up a lady's handkerchief. All garments look well upon a fine form; and there *are* legs which are more admirable the more distinctly they are revealed. Let but a perfectly formed man of some note wear tights and a bob-tail a few times in the view of the public, and every dandy is impatient until he has converted himself into a forked radish.

And yet our fashion-makers, though they have stimulated the clothes mania, are probably the very persons who will do most to cure it. Such, at least, was my impression the other day, after going over the largest fashion-making establishment in the world. America, which is destined to try all the experiments and solve all the problems, seems to have it in charge also to teach the Northern races how to dress. When an American takes hold of a thing, he is pretty sure to give it plenty of air. He is the great Advertiser. He instinctively aims at the million, knowing well that there is little else in America but million, and knowing also that he who draws permanent tribute from the million must devise something truly serviceable. We have in New York four establishments whose sole or chief business is to invent fashions, sell fashion-plates, paper patterns, and printed directions for cutting garments. The one which I visited employs sixty persons, and is about to occupy the whole of a large building, of which the rent is fifteen thousand dollars a year. The stranger is shown into one "studio," where a "corps of artists," men, sit assiduous, drawing upon stone the fashion prints for men's clothes, to which the chief tailors of the city have contributed each one suit. There I saw the coats, waistcoats, trousers, hats, neckties, and boots which were to be in fashion five months later; for, as the fashion-plate is sent to subscribers in February, it has to be drawn some weeks before; and the ingenious authors of it have to project their minds into the future, and infer what men can be made to buy in June, from what they fancy in December. Sometimes they hit it, sometimes they miss; the public may jump at a new device, or let it alone; for, after all, the public can be led only by being led in the way in which it is inclined to go. He is the great fashion-maker who knows best how to interpret the unconscious tendency of the public taste.

In another room of this building is another "corps of artists," women, who contrive new fashions for the ladies, sold in the form of paper patterns, with directions for cutting attached. Now the great hits achieved in this "studio," the patterns which sell most and longest, are such as combine with elegance the greatest number of utilities. The *staple* patterns are those which can be made easily, look well in cheap material, and harmonize with many other garments. I was expected to be surprised at the information (but I was not), that the person in New York who has shown the greatest fertility in inventing these universal and lasting patterns is "a girl from the woods of Maine," who never saw fashionable costume till she was a grown woman, and now earns sixteen hundred dollars a year by the inventive talent which she was accidently discovered to possess. This establishment publishes an illustrated catalogue, which contains pictures and descriptions of more than a thousand garments of ladies and children's wear, patterns of any of which, with full directions for cutting, are sold for a few cents. There appears to be a great economy of brains and labor here, — three men and four women inventing the clothes for a great part of a populous country. These "artists" are becoming independent of Paris. They take all the Paris fashion-periodicals, read the fashion-letters from that city, adopt any device that seems to them suitable to America; but they never think of introducing a fashion merely *because* it has found favor with the temporary occupants of French palaces, or the demi-wives of the transient millionnaires of the Paris Bourse.

It is a curious thing, too, that the magazines and weekly papers published by or for the fashion-makers are as a class remarkable for good sense and healthy feeling. If they fill the souls of some ladies with visions of costume impossible to a slender purse, they have excellent editorials showing how wrong it is to sacrifice the substantial interests of a family to the false decoration of one or two members of it. They give alluring pictures of babies' lace dresses, — $ 150 to $ 400 at Stewart's, — but they tell mothers that it is highly ridiculous to provide such costly bibs for the absorption of sour milk. One of these papers — and it is a paper of most excellent tone, full of capital advice and just satire — has a circulation of sixty thousand copies, and it is, therefore, compelled to give its chief attention to the promulgation of really useful patterns. It follows the law which is converting the fashion-manufactories from stimulators into correctors of mania. The universal and prompt dissemination of every new device makes it impossible for any woman to gain *distinction* by novel changes of attire; and we already see, at grand parties, that a few ladies of entirely assured position avoid in their dress everything that savors of the startling, and usually forbear the use of those very costly fabrics which they alone *can* wear without starving or stinting more important interests. Such ladies, of course, never exhibit anything conspicuous or costly in the street, and some of them even go to an extreme in the disregard of appearances out of doors. Of late, a few have gone further, and denied themselves the pleasure — to them alone an innocent pleasure — of wearing satin, velvet, and much lace.

Goethe says that folly can seldom be cured by denying to it all indulgence, and recommends that, in some cases, it should be nauseated by "intoxicating draughts." In this way, also, the fashion-papers may be of service, aided as they are by the fearful excesses in which some of the clothes maniacs indulge. There were "receptions" given last winter in New York, which were, in the most literal meaning of the word, *nothing* but exhibitions of wearing-apparel. No lady had any other object than to display her own costume, and to scrutinize that of others; nor when she afterwards discoursed of the entertainment, had she anything to communicate except descriptions of dresses such as we read in letters from Paris. Indeed, the mere magnitude of the dresses was such in January and February, that every lady had as much on her mind in making her way about, as the pilot of one of those magnificent Bristol steamboats has on his, when, at 5.15 P. M., the stately craft moves majestically among the numberless ferry-boats and sailing vessels of the East River. A moment's inattention, and smash! the cabin is stove in. One glance at a friend who may be two or three dresses off, and rip! away go the gathers. In time, let us hope, such experiences as these may prove to be the nauseating draughts which Goethe recommends.

Men's dress is now nearly perfect. It is cheap, durable, convenient, various; and it may be elegant and becoming in a high degree. By devoting to the subject thirty minutes per annum, — fifteen in May and fifteen in September, — a man may provide himself with all the clothes which can contribute either to the comfort or the adornment of his person. A dress suit will last through ten seasons of pretty frequent parties, and still be presentable; nor does it need any great firmness or good sense to enable a man to smile at the devices of tailors and fashion-makers, and stick to his clothes till they are worn out. As a rule, men in the United States do not dress well enough. A million of us ought to dress every evening for dinner, who do not, merely because we are not civilized enough. Our dirty streets and crammed public vehicles discourage dressing, and we indulge the delusion that we have not time or strength to dress after the labor of the day is done, though many mechanics do it who work ten hours a day, and travel an hour and a half besides.

With ladies, it is otherwise. Many of them have entirely run to clothes, as cucumbers run to seed. Men begin to maintain the Mahometan doctrine, that women have no souls. In former times, it was only the few thousand ladies connected with courts and aristocracies, who were subject to this kind of mania. But, at present, few women wholly escape it. In remote villages you will see foolish virgins in three or four different costumes on the same Sunday, and in cities you will find the wives of plain, laborious men squandering more money on a child's dress than would maintain three sons in college.

We have all become so used to witnessing this entire devotion to dress, that when, by chance, we observe indications of intellectual or unimpaired physical life in a lady who has grown up under present influences, we are startled.

Twice in my life I have fallen in love at first sight. The first time was in a bookstore in Boston, in the street named after the Father of his country. I was fresh from New York, where my afternoon walk is usually up the Fifth Avenue, a street in which the Mahometan doctrine just mentioned does not always seem so very irrational. This first love of mine was a girl of about seventeen, with a lovely bloom on her cheeks, and she wore a dress of blue something (not silk) with white spots in it. It was when I found out what that sweet girl had come to the store to buy that I gave way to the weakness alluded to above. She was lovely in herself, but, great heavens! she was there buying a GAZETTEER! Here was a young lady, aged seventeen, who took interest enough in the world she inhabited to desire a catalogue of its contents! Amazing! Long she hesitated, anxious to choose the best. Shall it be Lippincott? Shall it be Harper? She made up her mind at last, paid for the book, and completed her conquest by carrying it home herself. I never saw her more; I know not her name; but I love her still, and often have a distracting vision of her when I see "those others" in the Avenue.

The other time was on the long piazza of a seaside hotel, also in New England. *She* was a married lady, a mother, and a writer of verse and prose. It had been her singular good fortune to be reared on that rockbound coast in such a way that her growth was never checked by excessive school, nor her freedom of movement hampered by irrational dress, or by false ideas of propriety. Her father being a landlord, a fisherman, a lighthouse keeper, and a man of sense and information, she had plenty of boats, rocks, fishing-tackle, and suggestive conversation; and so grew up absolutely free from every one of the pernicious restraints of a defective civilization. At the same time her mind was duly nourished with honest knowledge, and kept totally free from all the contracting superstitions. I never spoke to her. I should not know her face to-day, if I saw it. But what instantaneously captivated my affections was the wondrous beauty of her *step!* Just to watch the glorious harmony, the perfect *concert,* of her movements, — was rapture. It is *this* darling of my memory in her coarse blue Dio Lewis boat-dress, that I think of when I see those gorgeous ladies carrying down the steps of a fashionable house an immense armful of clothes which they have been exhibiting at a reception.

LOG-ROLLING AT WASHINGTON.

THERE is a tradition in Washington that the lobby arose while General Jackson was waging war against the last United States Bank, from 1830 to 1836. But lobbying is as ancient as governing. It is also as legitimate and necessary, since the governing power is in need of the special knowledge which it is the proper office of a lobby to supply. It is only when the governing power is weak or corrupt or too transient, that there is danger of the lobby laying aside its modest office of supplying information, and assuming the mastery. As weak kings are governed by favorites and mistresses, so ill-constituted parliaments are governed by lobbies.

And, speaking of weak kings and their lobby of favorites, it was interesting to observe in Washington, during the administration of Andrew Johnson, how the vices of the old courts reappeared with the circumstances that produced them. A recent writer gives a short description of the rapacious lobby that surrounded the Scotchman called James I., king of England, every word of which applies with exactness to the state of things in Washington during the two years ending March 4, 1869: "In addition to the officials whose pay was nearly nominal, the king was surrounded by a crowd of hungry courtiers whose pay was nothing at all. To them flocked day by day all who had any favor to beg, and who hoped that a little money judiciously expended would smooth the way before them. Some of the applicants, no doubt, were honest men, who merely wanted to get a chance of doing honest work. But there were not a few whose only object was to enrich themselves in some discreditable way, and who were ready to share the booty with those who would lend them a helping hand in their roguery."*

Every well-informed resident of Washington will recognize the literal truth of the description. Like king, like lobby. Johnson was probably not a corrupt man, in the lowest sense of the word. His refusal of the carriage and horses offered to him by his admirers may not have been the mere buncombe it was supposed to be; and he probably went home to Tennessee carrying with him only the savings of his salary, and the contempt of the universe. And yet he could hardly have been ignorant that prostitutes of one sex sold his pardons, and prostitutes of another sex sold his offices. James I. of England, who also had his pardon lobby and his "appointment lobby," was aware, probably, that his favorites sold him every day, and was perhaps not unwilling to enrich them in so economical a manner. There are people whose self-love is such that they can associate happily only with their worshippers, having always to be on their good behavior with equals, which is irksome. These flatterers of Johnson were a relief to him after consorting with gentlemen, and he freely paid them for their gossip and adulation with the goods intrusted to his administration. Around such men as James I. and Andrew Johnson — infirm of purpose and yet pigheadedly obstinate, ignorant but unteachable, bashful and vain, transplanted from a lower to a higher civilization — a corrupt and vulgar lobby naturally gathers; for there will always be an affinity, if not a resemblance, between the lobby and the power which it influences. When Cromwell was Protector, great Milton wrote the foreign despatches, — the alliance being natural between real power and special knowledge. Character raised the unlettered Washington to a genuine equality with the men around him, who knew so much more than he. Fancy *him* chatting familiarly on a sofa of the Presidential mansion with a woman of the street, or giving valuable appointments at the solicitation of a purchased renegade!

The founder of our Congressional lobby was Alexander Hamilton; and his great achievement as a log-roller was a perfect specimen of the art, both in its modes and its results.

* Gardiner's Prince Charles and the Spanish Marriage.

There was, it is true, a resolute and acrimonious lobby at the time of "*the* Congress," — the body that governed the thirteen States during the Revolutionary War; the Lee lobby, for example, that nearly succeeded in getting Franklin recalled from France, and would have done it but for the superior lobbying of the French minister. But, under the present Constitution, Hamilton was the great original lobbyist; and, as they still employ some of his methods of administration in the Treasury Department, so the Washington lobby still uses his tactics in carrying bills through Congress.

There were two distracting bills before Congress in the spring of 1790; one proposing that the general government should assume the debts (twenty-one millions of dollars in all) incurred by the several States during the Revolutionary War; the other a bill for removing the capital from New York to Philadelphia, where it should remain ten years, and then be transferred to the shores of the Potomac. Neither of these bills could command a majority of both Houses. The creation of a city in the wilderness, far from every source of the supplies needful for a government, when commodious cities like New York, Philadelphia, and Baltimore, abounding in every requisite, already existed, seemed to the disinterested portion of Congress just as absurd as it does to us; and the measure, on its merits, never could have been passed. The opposition to it, however, though decided enough, was mild and trifling compared with the abhorrence and disgust excited by the Assumption Bill. It is not easy for a student of the present day to account for the singular violence of this opposition to a measure which seems to us reasonable, natural, and just.

Except the Missouri Compromise struggle, this contest was, as Mr. Jefferson remarks, the "most bitter and angry ever known in Congress before or since the union of the States." Why? It was not the magnitude of the sum involved, although twenty-one millions in 1790 was as great an addition to the public burden as two hundred millions would be now. Nor were the debts of the two sections far from being equal. If Massachusetts owed four millions, so did South Carolina. New Hampshire and Georgia each owed three hundred thousand. Rhode Island and Delaware, New Jersey and Maryland, had each the same debt. Nothing was proposed but the cancellation of the State bonds and the issue of United States bonds in their stead; and this, because the debts had been incurred for the common cause.

The rancor of the Southern opposition arose partly from their State pride and their dread of centralization, but chiefly, as it seems, from their rustic, provincial detestation of what they called stock-jobbing. To the country gentlemen it seemed undeniable, that a man who bought a soldier's claim in 1789 at its market value, and sold it in 1790 at its market value, and thus gained two hundred dollars, had cheated a scarred veteran of the Revolution out of a portion of his nobly earned "pittance" by "insidious arts." There were wild stories afloat of the fortunes made by New York speculators who had contrived to get early information of Hamilton's funding policy. It was said that, as soon as the passage of the Funding Bill became pretty certain, three swift pilot-boats had slipped out of harbor, winged for distant ports, to buy up the depreciated claims. "Couriers and relay-horses by land," says Jefferson, "and swift-sailing pilot-boats by sea, were flying in all directions." Members fully believed this, and doubtless the lobby was not inattentive to its interest on this occasion, and *did* turn its knowledge to account. Cruel wrong, no doubt, was done to war-worn patriots and lonely widows, ignorant of what was passing in New York; and country members did themselves honor by their eloquent disgust at such heartless spoliation. It was this feeling that caused the loss, by a small majority, of the Assumption Bill, which the Southern members regarded only as a device to supply the Wall Street of that day with twenty-one millions of additional material upon which to exercise its "insidious arts."

But, in the course of the long and most keenly contested debate on the bill, the commercial members, too, had become heated; so that, when the bill was rejected, the feeling of the House was such that it was impossible to go on with the public business. The House abruptly adjourned. It met the next day, and again adjourned without attempting to transact business. Congress met every morning for several days, Mr. Jefferson records, only to adjourn immediately, "the parties being too much out of temper to do business together," and some of the members threatening a "secession and dissolution."

Hamilton, Secretary of the Treasury, upon whose report the defeated bill had been founded, and of whose system the assumption was an important part, was distressed and alarmed. But the resource of the lobby remained. In the nick of time he met in the street Mr. Jefferson, recently returned from France, and then Secretary of State. To him the anxious financier depicted the terms of the situation, "walking him backwards and forwards before the President's door for half an hour," and calling upon him as his colleague and the friend of General Washington to rally to the support of the administration, and save at once it, the measure, and the Union. As the bill had been lost by a very small majority, General Hamilton thought it probable that "an appeal" from so influential a Virginian "to the judgment and discretion of some of his friends might effect a change in the vote," and set the machine of government going again. "Come and dine with me to-morrow," said Mr. Jefferson, "and I will ask a friend or two to meet you, and we will talk it over."

Fatal dinner! How often, amid the dust and desolate vastness of Washington, its hopeless shabbiness, dulness, and dearness, have I wished that the soup that day had disagreed with these gentlemen, and they had been obliged to go home before the removal of the cloth had introduced the business of the occasion! But it did not. The dinner put the guests into a compliant humor. The city of Washington was destined to exist, first, as the capital of the country, and, after that, as a marble quarry for posterity, having the peculiarity of furnishing the marble ready cut. The discussion took place, and the company soon agreed that, whatever might be thought of assumption, disunion was worse, and that, therefore, the defeated bill must be reconsidered. But to effect this, some members must change their votes, must vote for a measure which they *hated*. This was a difficulty. The log was hard to roll, — "pill," Mr. Jefferson styles it. "It was observed," he says, "that this pill would be peculiarly bitter to the

Southern States, and that some concomitant measure should be adopted to sweeten it a little to them. There had before been propositions to fix the seat of government either at Philadelphia or at Georgetown on the Potomac; and it was thought that by giving it to Philadelphia for ten years, and to Georgetown permanently afterwards, this might, as an anodyne, calm in some degree the ferment which might be excited by the other measure alone; so two of the Potomac members (White and Lee, but the former with a revulsion of stomach almost convulsive) agreed to change their votes; and Hamilton undertook to carry the other point."

Thus log-rolling began; or, as Mr. Jefferson would have named it, *pill-swallowing.* Thus originated the art of making honest and patriotic men vote for measures of which they violently disapproved. It is surprising that the art should have been carried so far toward perfection in the first specimen, which, the lobby will observe, contained many of the important elements: two measures, neither of which could pass, each favored and each opposed by the same interests; a compromise effected by social influence; the precise terms arranged at a dinner; and, finally, *mischief the result,* lasting, far-reaching, and irreparable. The evils resulting from assumption refuse to become apparent to a modern inquirer, although the democrats of the early day held the measure in execration, and continued to denounce it as long as they lived. But the evils which have flowed from "the concomitant measure" are evident enough, without reckoning the expense of providing a marble quarry of that singular character for posterity.

It is not surprising that a system begun by party leaders so distinguished should have been continued in a body every member of which comes to Washington in the double capacity of national representative and local claim-agent. Every member has charge of some local or private interest, on which he alone is fully informed, and which cannot become the subject of a general debate. One wants a lighthouse on a rock which may wreck a fishing-smack in the course of ages. Another wishes his local harbor improved. Another desires increased protection on the fabric which his constituents manufacture. Very many are anxious for subsidies for branch railroads. Some are charged with the business of getting one more superfluous arsenal or navy-yard established. Most members feel a particular interest in some eminently reasonable claims upon the justice of Congress, which they are desirous to carry both for selfish and unselfish reasons. In many instances the private interest which a member has in charge is vital to him; for it sent him to Congress, keeps him there. Every member, therefore, has votes to exchange for votes; and it sometimes seems as if all legislation at Washington had degenerated into log-rolling. On almost any day in the latter half of a session a spectator may see specimens of all the three varieties of log-rolling, which are these: 1. Help me to roll my log, and I 'll help you to roll yours. 2. If you don't help me to roll my log, I won't help you to roll yours. 3. If you hinder the rolling of my log, yours shall never budge.

It may be that one of the logs ought to roll, and the other ought not. In that case, a member of Congress is subjected to the kind of temptation to which men not exceptionally strong in character or position may be expected to yield. And it is in this way that the astounding votes of respectable members may usually be explained, — their votes for public as well as for private objects. It needs little reflection to understand what an advantage, under the log-rolling system, an unscrupulous, pushing member has over one of really superior powers who is troubled with modesty and conscience, and who has to legislate in a hall where calm debate is useless because inaudible. It is also easy to see how an unscrupulous administration can go into the lobby, and get votes for national measures by compelling its adherents to vote for private or local ones.

As a rule, the more objectionable a measure the more numerous its lobby. Gentlemen of the press in Washington, who contemplate life from the reporters' gallery, say that the moral quality of a measure can usually be inferred from the buzz and stir that are to be observed about the Capitol when it is expected to come up. A revision of the tariff, for example, crowds the hotels and committee-rooms; but there is no lobby for international copyright. One man in Philadelphia, and one woman in Washington, sufficed to kill international copyright the winter before last; but President, Cabinet, Commissioner Wells, the Democrats, the Free-Trade League, the Evening Post, Charles Sumner, and the universe generally, proved unequal to the task of defeating the bill increasing the duty upon copper. Copper had a lobby.

For nearly thirty years after the invention of log-rolling over Mr. Jefferson's wine (he was a connoisseur in wine, and had imported some kinds from France that were new to his guests on this occasion), the log-rolling lobby generally exerted their powers upon objects which possessed a public character. The lobby, such as we see it now, came in with the protective system in 1816. The book of the tariff, that curiosity of literature, with all its pleasing contents from absinthe to zinc, is a monument to the zeal, skill, audacity, and perseverance of the log-rolling lobby. It used to be said, when the tariff was undergoing its quadrennial revision, that Congress consisted of three houses, — Senate, House, and Tariff Lobby. Even if the principle of protection were sound, our tariff is open to the fatal objection that the greater number of its provisions were arranged to suit private interests, not to promote the public good. Calico has had its lobby; and so have copper, iron, salt, wool, and every fabric made by man. It is the public that is not represented in the lobby when the tariff is undergoing manipulation. The public has been represented only by that small number of members of Congress who are not identified with a private interest, and who have made a particular study of the laws of trade. In no legislature on earth have such members ever been a majority; and we must consequently look to the very lobby that created our tariff system for the influence that will gradually destroy it. Before many years have passed, we shall see the manufacturers of the United States clamoring for free trade; and then the lobby will change sides. American manufacturers will not always be content with a system that excludes them from the markets of the world, and which is a confession and proclamation of inferiority. It is possible, too, that, before the end of the present century, the art of self-government may have made such progress as to admit of the public being represented in Congress by a powerful and brilliant minority.

Meanwhile, some of the exploits of the tariff lobby are highly amusing; that is, they are amusing to the boys who throw the stones, and to the spectators that line the shore, but the pelted frogs do not find them laughable. A young firm, which has invested its all in a manufactory, is not amused to discover that the alteration of a line in the tariff list has killed enterprise and made property valueless. In the disinterested spectator, however, some of the incidents related in Mr. Commissioner Wells's report may excite a smile; particularly since the Protectionists in the House proclaimed that report unanswerable by attempting to rob its author of his pittance of a salary. The report being thus admitted to be correct by its opponents, its anecdotes have an additional value. "In carrying out the idea of protection," remarks Mr. Wells, "Congress has assumed that whatever is for the advantage of a private interest must be for the advantage of the public interest also." "The result has been," he continues, "a tariff based upon small issues, rather than upon any great national principle"; and this tariff, while it acts as a bad stimulant to some enterprises, is torpidity and death to others.

Amusing case in point. In 1864 American spool-thread makers discovered that some of their English rivals were evading the duty by sending over fine thread in skeins and hanks instead of winding it on spools as usual. A spool-thread lobby appeared in Washington, the result of which was that the tariff was amended with an eye single to the interests of American spool-thread manufacturers. A duty was placed upon unwound fine thread, that was equivalent to prohibition. All was joyous in the circles interested, until, on enforcing the new rates of duty, two disagreeable facts came to light. One was, that very fine unwound thread is an essential article in some branches of manufacture; the other was, that the article could not be procured on the continent of America. Here was a coil. Another lobby went to Washington, on behalf of the manufacturers of suspenders, gaiters, lastings, coburgs, and other similar products, many of whom absolutely could not continue business if the new duties were collected. One establishment did actually close; others were suspended; others ran at a loss for a while; and much unwound thread, ordered before the spool-thread lobby had performed its work, was sent back to Europe. When the new lobby arrived in Washington, Congress had adjourned, and nothing could save the embarrassed industries but an *interpretation* of the tariff that would admit unwound thread at lower rates for the purposes to which it is essential. The Secretary of the Treasury took the responsibility of sanctioning a violation of the law. He decided that fine thread designed for sewing must pay the new rate, but fine thread to be used in certain manufactures should come in on the old. "By this decision only," says Mr. Wells, "several branches of American industry, involving probably more of capital and labor than was represented by the article which it was originally intended to protect, were saved from absolute destruction." This was extremely comic; *except* to the few hundred families whose means of living were suddenly threatened or suspended, without warning, and without act of their own.

The performances of the salt lobby are equally striking. One of them would make a subject for a poem. "In the Gulf of California," Mr. Wells informs us, "there is an island — Carmen — where salt of remarkable purity is deposited by natural agencies in inexhaustible quantities. The situation and condition of this island are such that it would seem as if it were intended to be the natural and cheap source of supply of salt for the whole Pacific coast of our country; and yet, by the agency of men, and in the name of protection, this free gift of God and this great source of national wealth has been rendered practically of no account, inasmuch as the royalty exacted by the Mexican government, the United States tariff added, and the expenses of collecting and transportation, in the aggregate amount so nearly to the price of salt obtained from other sources in San Francisco, as almost completely to eat up all profits, and thus close in a great degree the only market to which it can be taken. The result of all this is, that capital and labor, in a section of country where capital and labor are of all things most in demand, are withdrawn from other employments and diverted to doing that which Nature herself has already done much more perfectly, namely, making salt from sea-water in the bay of San Francisco, at a cost of from seven to ten dollars per ton." Mr. Bungay, who sang with so much spirit the completion of the Pacific Railroad, could surely do well with this glorious triumph of the salt lobby.

To these two anecdotes borrowed from Mr. Wells I will add one of my own, which is so variously representative, that the relation of it gives the whole history of American manufactures and their lobby, past, present, and future.

Bunting, the material of the star-spangled banner, is the subject of the tale. Until within these few years no bunting was made in the United States. The "flaunting lie" of the years preceding the war, the "rag" of secession, and the innumerable flags that streamed over ship, fort, and army, on the part of the United States, were made in England, as were also the flags of our previous wars. But five years ago, some knowing Yankees in Lowell (induced by an act of Congress that promised a contract for a year's supply of army and navy to whosoever should first produce an article of bunting equal to the best English) mastered the peculiar difficulties attending this branch of manufacture, and won the prize. Before the year ended the war had closed. The demand for bunting was diminished by three fourths, and the English bunting could still be sold in New York cheaper than the American could be produced at Lowell. Need I say that, in these circumstances, a bunting lobby asked an increase of duty upon the foreign fabric? The duty was promptly fixed at the modest rate of twenty cents per square yard, plus thirty-five per cent of the value; which was in strict accordance with the system as by lobby established. The result has been that a hundred and twenty persons have been drawn from other occupations in a State where enterprise languishes and life is imbittered by the scarcity of labor, and set at work making bunting. But among these hundred and twenty persons there are several of great ingenuity, who contemplate nothing which they do not desire to improve. Hence, two capital and several minor improvements in the article produced, as well as better and cheaper modes of producing it. These Lowell Yankees print the stars and stripes, instead of sewing them on, and give you a flag without a stitch in it, lighter, more elegant, and more durable than those formerly in use.

Now, with a universal, international system of patent-right and copyright, and a tolerable approximation to freedom of trade, — i. e. with decent "protection" to the NATURAL RIGHTS OF MAN, — these Yankees could give the whole world the immediate benefit of their inventions, while reaping a munificent reward for themselves. But under the system of protection to whatever private interest can command a lobby, their operations are limited to the narrow field of one country. The very protection which stimulated the business limits it by making the product too dear to compete with the foreign article in other countries. Give the Lowell men a fair chance, and they will supply half the world with flags; just as the Steinways, Chickerings, Webers, Knabes, and others would sell American pianos in every capital in Europe, if there were not from two to six duties or taxes on every leading article that enters into the composition of a musical instrument. But the tariff lobby, which got us into this scrape, must get us out of it. The Natural Rights of Man will never send an expensive lobby to Washington, though they may come at last to be powerfully represented within the bar. But the time is probably not very distant when bunting, calico, ships,* wool, cloth, silver, pianos, iron, steel, copper, and coal will roll their several lobbies into one grand overwhelmning lobby, and demand that those great interests be allowed as fair a chance in the markets of the world as the same interests in other countries. The system of confining protection to whatever branches of business can afford a lobby or a member, is perhaps nearer its downfall than many suppose.

But this very system indicates the incorruptibleness of Congress, and the impotence of money to carry measures against the current. Mr. Greeley informs us that there is a British lobby in Washington,† and I learned last winter

* Mr. D. McKay, the noted shipbuilder of Boston, estimates the duties upon the articles required for a ship of one thousand tons at $ 8,665.33 in gold. Messrs. Steinway reckon the duties and taxes upon a grand piano at $ 180 in currency.

† "Many, whose duties or pleasure called them to Washington at intervals from fifteen to twenty-five years ago, will recollect a small, bright, active, witty person known as George Dwight, who was quartered in that city throughout each session of Congress. Of his private life I know nothing; but his large and fine parlor at one of the great hotels was open to a wide circle, and he there dispensed a generous though by no means indis-

that there was a French lobby also; and if the Senate goes on rejecting and neglecting treaties according to its pleasure, we shall doubtless have soon a lobby of all nations, since it is with the Senate that foreign powers must henceforth negotiate. When we consider the immense capital represented by the French and English lobbies, and the enormous advantage which slight changes in the tariff list would give foreign manufactures, and when we also bear in mind that American enterprises are usually in their infancy at the time when they seek protection, we may safely infer that it is not mere length of purse that enables a lobby to carry its point. In truth, there is a general impression in Congress and in the country, that compliance with the American manufacturers' lobby is "protection to American industry." The railroad subsidy system would also have been impossible, if Congress and the country had not been impatient for the construction of the great roads to which it has been applied.

Probably there has never been such a persistent exertion of log-rolling energy as when President Buchanan was trying to force slavery upon Kansas by means of the Lecompton Bill, and a powerful india-rubber interest was lobbying for the extension of the Chaffee patent. These were the two logs. The Lecompton lobby was directed by Cornelius Wendell, who had been clearing a hundred thousand dollars a year from the public printing, whose bank account ran up to "nine hundred and twenty-nine thousand dollars in two years," and who had behind him the entire administration, with all its resources of men, money, and influence. The head of the Chaffee-patent lobby was that most indomitable of all the india-rubber men, — Horace H. Day, owner of the Chaffee patent, a man capable of spending seventy thousand dollars upon an election. Both of these lobbies spent

criminate hospitality. Observing that he was evidently neither very rich nor a man likely to waste his substance in reckless prodigality, I at length asked a mutual acquaintance, 'How does Dwight support all this?' and was answered: 'Very easily; he is the agent here of the British woollen interest [manufacturers and exporters], well salaried to watch the legislation of Congress and look after the welfare of his employers.' Several others subsequently confirmed this statement, and told me that he furnished statistics, estimates, etc., for the Secretary of the Treasury (R. J. Walker), and had thus exercised a powerful influence in shaping the tariff of 1846." — HORACE GREELEY, N. Y. Tribune, 1869.

money, both before and after the junction, as freely as it is ever spent for such purposes. Wendell had his check-book always ready, and Day kept a band of lobbyists in pay for two sessions. Newspapers were bought, subsidized, and established, for the purpose of denouncing members of Congress who would not come in to the support of Lecompton; and the friends of such members were systematically turned out of custom-houses, post-offices, and navy-yards. Contingent interests in Chaffee were given to correspondents,—one to the correspondent of the leading religious newspaper of the time; and Mr. Day even took the precaution of assigning a contingent interest to a female "medium," in exchange for the advice which "she got from the other world to aid the Chaffee patent." He had a list of Chaffee members in his pocket, which he would show to Wendell when they met; and Wendell, a much more experienced lobbyist than himself, would warn him that, in Washington, promising support to a measure was a very different thing from voting for it. Among other expedients, the President attempted to bribe the editor of a Philadelphia newspaper, offering him the Liverpool consulship and ten thousand dollars in money.* But all would not suffice. When the bills came to the test of a vote in the House, both failed, a large number of Chaffee members not voting at all, and Lecompton failing in strict accordance with the known political circumstances. Kansas was free, and all the india-rubber men were at liberty to macerate their crude material with the aid of Mr. Chaffee's masterly invention.

The testimony on this subject fills many hundred pages, but not a word was elicited showing corruption in a member of Congress. Several lobbyists swore that they knew of no member whom they would dare approach with money; and the general tone of the evidence leads the reader to the same conclusion.

A lobby occasionally attempts to carry a point by sur-

* From the testimony taken before the Covode Committee, June 12, 1860:—

Wendell. "I carried $10,000 for the purpose of giving it to Colonel Forney, in the event of his accepting the place abroad for some three weeks."

Chairman. "By whose authority or instructions?"

Wendell. "Well, sir, it might be said to be by the President's."

prise. I witnessed a scene of the kind last winter in the House of Representatives, which shows how extremely cautious members should be not to act upon the information given by an interested lobby before they have heard the lobby of the other side. The most honest man in the world will go wrong if he neglects this precaution. Indeed, it may be necessary by and by for Congress to adopt the rule contemplated by the legislature of Massachusetts, compelling lobbyists to present their cases before the proper committee, and making it unlawful for a member to converse privately with an interested person on legislative business.

But to my scene. One afternoon in February last, while the House in Committee of the Whole was working its slow and toilsome way down, item after item, through the Army Appropriation Bill, under the leadership of the alert and vigorous Mr. Blaine, now the Speaker of the House, a clause of the bill was about to pass without debate, when Mr. Fernando Wood, of New York, rose and offered the following curious amendment: "But no part of the sum [appropriated] shall be paid to Alexander Dunbar for his alleged discovery of the mode of treatment of horses' feet." There had been no mention of the said Dunbar in the clause, nor of his mode of treating horses' feet, nor of any other system of treatment; and the very name of the man was evidently unknown to the House. Mr. Wood proceeded to explain that the Secretary of War, General Schofield, had made a contract (authorized by act of Congress) with Alexander Dunbar, by which the latter was to receive twenty-five thousand dollars for imparting his system of horseshoeing and hoof-treatment to the veterinary surgeons and cavalry blacksmiths of the army. "And I am advised," continued the member from New York, "by those who are judges of that subject, that the man is totally ignorant, that he knows nothing about the diseases of horses' feet, and that he rather perpetrates injury upon the poor animals than produces any benefit to them."

Fernando Wood, in his air and demeanor, is one of the most dignified and impressive members of the House. He attends carefully to his dress; and, as to his "deportment," Mr. Turveydrop would contemplate him with approval.

For such a personage to rise in his place, and, in a measured, serene manner, discourse thus upon a subject of which no man on the floor knew anything whatever, could not fail to produce some effect. Mr. Blaine could only say, that he had never heard the name of Alexander Dunbar before; but that he thought the amendment cast a severe reflection upon the Secretary of War. Mr. Wood insisting, the amendment was finally amended so as to make the exclusion apply to the whole Appropriation Bill, and thus cut off the unknown Dunbar entirely; and in this form, I believe, it passed the Committee of the Whole, and was prepared for submission to the House; at least, Mr. Wood agreed to withdraw his amendment in order to amend it in the way described.

It did so happen that there was a person sitting in a commodious corner of the reporters' gallery, who, though a stranger to Mr. Dunbar, and singularly ignorant of horses, yet knew all about the Dunbar system and its discoverer. That person, strange to relate, was myself; and, if it had not been a little out of order, I should have shouted a few words of explanation over the vast expanse below. Rising superior to this temptation, and thus avoiding the attention of the Sergeant-at-arms, I constituted myself a Dunbar lobby, and imparted to as many members as possible some of the facts which I am now about to communicate to the reader. Some years since, the mysterious Alexander Dunbar, an honest, observant farmer and contractor, of Canada, was driving a lame horse on a hilly road. He noticed that the horse was lamest when going down hill, but not lame at all going up hill. Having observed this peculiarity for several miles, he began to speculate upon the cause; and, by carefully examining the action of the horse's feet, he discovered it. The blacksmith had pared the hoof on the wrong principle, — cutting it close where it ought to have been left thick, and leaving it unpared where nature constantly produces a redundancy. He tried his hand at remedying the mistake. He cut boldly at the parts that were in excess, and the lameness was cured! A few judicious cuts with a sharp knife, and a shoe adapted to the natural growth of the hoof, — this is all there is of the Dunbar system, which was elaborated by the mystical

Alexander after some years of observation and experiment, suggested by this incident. He found that many cases of lameness of years' standing could be cured radically and almost instantly by simply paring the hoof aright and altering the shoe.

We have in New York an enthusiast on the structure of the horse, — Mr. Robert Bonner, whose stable contains six of the fastest trotting-horses in the world. He was led to study the anatomy of the horse by endeavoring to get at the reason why some horses can trot in 2 : 20 farther than an ordinary nag can in five minutes. He was curious to know just where the trotting talent lies; and this led to other inquiries. Hearing by chance of Mr. Dunbar's discovery, he investigated it most thoroughly, and came to the conclusion that the Dunbar system was founded in the eternal nature of things. I suppose that, during the last three years, Mr. Bonner has, with his own hands, pared the hoofs of fifty horses on the Dunbar plan, and thereby cured a dozen cases of lameness supposed to be incurable. In his great desire to test the discovery, he has travelled a hundred miles sometimes for the sole purpose of having a lame horse shod in the Dunbar style, very frequently paring the hoofs himself. Recently the discoverer has been among us, and his system, after having been adopted in several of the largest stables in the United States, was introduced into the army. But, as usual, his success was damage to other men; particularly to the proprietors of a patent horseshoe, which Mr. Dunbar was compelled to say was *not* made in accordance with the eternal nature of things. Hence, a patent-horseshoe lobby! Hence, Mr. Fernando Wood's strange amendment! Mr. Dunbar's friends, however, rallied in time to enlighten the House, and no harm was done; but the occurrence shows how a member of Congress may be misled, unless he makes it a principle and a point of honor never to act upon an *ex parte* statement.

On this point the late investigating committee of the Massachusetts legislature offers some excellent remarks. It seems that the strikers of the Boston lobby have made such an outcry with regard to the alleged corruption of the legislature during the last year or two, that a committee was appointed to find out how much fire there was beneath all this smoke. They report, as might have been expected, that there is no fire at all, — not a smouldering ember, not a spark. After my investigations at Washington, I am fully prepared to believe this, and I do entirely believe it. They add, that a lobby has no legitimate place except in a committee-room, where both sides can be heard and testimony recorded.* It were much to be desired, that the lobby at Washington were as insignificant and impotent as the lobby at Boston. The *hired* lobby is. The fellows who lay themselves alongside of green new-comers, and pretend to have "a twist" on this member, and an unbounded influence over that, and give out that they correspond with seven papers, all daily, are about as influential in one place as they are in the other. This is not the kind of lobby from which danger is to be feared. The lobby that carries its measures has exceedingly little to do with such.

The lobby which is to be feared is that which sends members to Congress, which has millions of acres and dollars at command, and is engaged in schemes dear to the pride and important to the interests of the nation. It is to be regretted that Mr. Jefferson's advice was not acted upon, to amend the Constitution so as to empower Congress to do everything for the country, in the way of internal im-

* The following is an extract from this interesting report, much of which is as true of Washington as it is of Boston: "The committee are satisfied that the influence of the lobby (so called) is greatly overestimated. A certain number of persons, known as lobby members, receive very considerable sums of money from corporations and other parties having business before the legislature. In the opinion of the committee, this influence is not legitimate in matters of legislation. Committees are provided by the legislature, to whom all matters are referred and before whom all matters are legitimately heard. Whoever desires to present testimony or statements can do so before these committees, and this testimony legitimately reaches both branches of the legislature through these several committees. The parties referred to as lobby-men are not lawyers, and have no legitimate professional calling at the Capitol, but are supposed to have more or less influence in private talks and conversations by partial presentation of matters to individual members. The committee believe money expended in the employment of these men is wasted by the parties who expend it, and that the influence of such expenditure has a tendency to demoralize legislation and create suspicions of integrity of members where suspicion should never rest. The committee, in all their examinations, have had no reason to suppose that any member either of this or any previous legislature has been influenced by any improper or dishonorable motives."

provements, which no State or combination of States, or company of individuals, could be reasonably expected to accomplish. The idea of the system established in 1787 was, that the general government should do whatever the interests or the honor of the whole country required to be done, and which the separate States could not do for themselves. The time is not distant, perhaps, when we shall deplore that Congress did not regard a railroad across the continent as a "post-road," or as a measure essential to the "common defence" of sections so widely separated, and build the road outright with the public money. We might thus have saved a tract of land nearly as large as France, and kept out of the Capitol a lobby that may in time become formidable indeed. The directors of the Pacific Railroad can already, if they choose, enrich a member of Congress, or a hundred members, by merely investing a trifling sum of money for them in the sites of future Chicagos. It is no joke to have half a dozen men in the lobby, wielding such an engine and directing such an estate.

The subsidy system originated in the acute mind of the late Stephen A. Douglas of Illinois, and the first railroad aided by a grant of land was the Illinois Central, in 1850. Mr. Douglas, Senator though he was, was the chief of the Illinois Central lobby, and his management of the bill was the most ingenious, audacious, complicated piece of log-rolling that has ever been placed on record. It was his boast, too, that this "pioneer bill," as he styled it, "went through without a dollar, pure, uncorrupt." Without a dollar, — yes; pure and uncorrupt, — no.

His first exploit was to get rid of Mr. Holbrooke, who, as far back as 1835, had conceived the project of connecting Chicago and Cairo by a railroad, and to whom had been granted a charter for its construction by the Illinois legislature. On the strength of this charter, and in the fullest confidence that the road would one day be built, Holbrooke had invested his whole fortune in Cairo lots, lands, and projects. Here was Holbrooke's weakness and Douglas's opportunity; for these two able and not over-scrupulous men had become antagonists on this railroad scheme, and it was a question which of the two should confer the boon on the State. Holbrooke wanted the millions, and Douglas the glory, that would result from success. After years of manœuvring at home, where Holbrooke had the advantage, the scene of strife was transferred to Washington, where Douglas was then all-powerful. Douglas had already applied for a grant of land in aid of the road; but Holbrooke had procured the passage of an act through the legislature (or, as Douglas charged, had a clause fraudulently inserted in an act), conveying to *his* company whatever lands Congress might grant. Upon this, the Little Giant introduced a new bill, terminating the road at a different point on the Ohio, and thus reducing Cairo to its original condition of utter worthlessness.

This brought the redoubtable Holbrooke to his knees. "*Spare my Cairo!*" was his imploring cry. "With pleasure," replied the Senator, "provided you surrender your charters and leave Illinois Central to me." Holbrooke surrendered the charters, and Douglas brought in his bill granting alternate sections of land along the line of the projected road.

Such was his preliminary performance. His next step was less difficult, but more striking. The Senators and Members from Alabama and Georgia were opposed to the bill, on the old ground that grants of land for such a purpose — internal improvement of a single State — were unconstitutional. As a Democrat, Mr. Douglas should have respected, should have shared, this scruple. Perhaps he did, but he overcame it; and he addressed himself to the task of overcoming theirs in a manner that was business-like at least. While visiting his children's plantation in Mississippi, he found it convenient to go to Mobile, where he at once inquired the way to the office of the Mobile Railroad, recently suspended for want of money. He was lucky enough to catch the president and directors at the office, just as they had concluded the business which had called them together. The champion of Jeffersonian and Jacksonian Democracy did not stop to argue the constitutional question with these gentlemen, but proposed to them a game of log-rolling. He offered to tack to his bill a clause giving *their* suspended road a grant of lands, provided the Senators and Representatives of Alabama and Mississippi would vote for the bill. The president and directors, rejoicing in this unlooked-for prospect of relief, instantly gave their assent, disposing of the votes of their absent Senators and Members as though they owned them. But, no, said the cool-headed Senator from Illinois; your Senators and Members have already voted against my bill, and it is necessary for your legislatures to instruct them to vote for it. This presented no difficulty to that knot of railroad directors, and the compact was concluded on the spot; one director saying, that if Senator Foote did not vote for the grant he should never be re-elected to the Senate. Cautioning them all to keep secret *his* connection with the affair, Douglas took his leave, and went straight to Washington, "being afraid to be seen in those parts."

In due time the legislative instructions reached Washington, as per agreement. Mr. Douglas then had occasion to exert his histrionic talents. Senator King of Alabama, and Davis of Mississippi, who had been most decided in their opposition to the bill, "cursed their legislatures," and could scarcely believe their eyes. In their perplexity, they consulted Douglas, and asked his aid in drawing the clause which was to include the Mobile Road in the grant. With all the dignity of a man who felt himself aggrieved, Mr. Douglas declined their offered support, saying that he felt sure of being able to carry his bill without their aid; but feigned to be softened at length, and agreed, as a favor to *them*, to admit the clause which they desired. The solemn farce was maintained to the end. The Southern Senators, as Douglas anticipated, were in no haste to comply with disagreeable instructions, and, consequently, when he sent them word one day that he was about to call up his Illinois Central Bill, they came hurrying to the chamber, with no amendment ready, and begged him to draw one for them. He had had an amendment carefully drawn by one of the best lawyers in Congress, which he handed to Mr. King of Alabama, and immediately moved to proceed with the bill. Mr. King then rose, in his usual dignified manner, and asked the Senator from Illinois to accept an amendment. The Senator from Illinois was obliging enough to do so. The Senators from Alabama and Mississippi all voted for the bill, and it passed the Senate with the additional clause.

This was an essential point gained; but the decisive battle was to be fought in the House of Representatives. And here Mr. Douglas performed feats of log-rolling which, I think, have never been equalled in any legislative body. The log-rolling art, begun in 1790 by Hamilton and Jefferson, made marvellous progress in the short space of sixty years.

When the bill stood at the head of the Speaker's list, and Douglas could count in the House a majority of fifteen "pledged" to support it, Mr. Harris of Illinois moved to proceed with the business on the Speaker's table. This called up the bill, and roused the dormant opposition. By the adroit management of that opposition, a test motion was precipitated upon the House, which left the bill in a minority of one; and this, notwithstanding weeks of previous log-rolling, and the fifteen pledged majority. "*We had gained votes*," says Mr. Douglas, "*by lending our support to many local measures*." But, at the important moment, you see, some of the "pledged" votes were not forthcoming, which is often the case in Washington. Let Mr. Douglas relate what followed: —

"I was standing in the lobby, paying eager attention, and would have given the world to be at Harris's side, but was too far off to get there in time; and it was all in an instant, and the next moment a motion would have been made, which would have brought on a decided vote, and have defeated the bill. Harris, quick as thought, pale and white as a sheet, jumped to his feet, and moved that the House go into Committee of the Whole on the slavery question. There were fifty members ready with speeches on this subject, and the motion was carried. Harris came to me in the lobby, and asked me if he had made the right motion. I said, 'Yes,' and asked him if he knew what was the effect of his motion. He replied it placed the bill at the foot of the calendar. I asked him how long it would be before it came up again. He said, 'It would not come up this session; it was impossible; there were ninety-seven bills ahead of it.'" *

But the Little Giant would not give it up. For many days and "nights" he racked his brain for an expedient.

* A Brief Treatise on Constitutional and Party Questions, by J. Madison Cutts, p. 196.

It occurred to his mathematical mind, at last, that the same tactics applied to the ninety-seven bills would place *them* also, one after the other, at the bottom of the calendar, and his own bill, finally, at the top. The plan was adopted. Ninety-seven times Mr. Harris, or else some member not supposed to have any particular interest in the Illinois Bill, moved to clear the Speaker's table; ninety-seven times a certain other member moved to go into Committee of the Whole on the slavery question; ninety-seven times this always welcome motion was carried. Sometimes these tactics would be employed twice in the same day, and send two bills tumbling to the bottom of the ladder. And the Illinois Bill constantly gained friends by the process; for was not Harris, who had it in charge, continually moving to call up bills in alliance with it? The odium all fell upon the member who continually frustrated Harris's benevolent intentions. "All praised *us*," says Mr. Douglas; "said we were acting nobly in supporting them. We replied, 'Yes, having defeated our bill, we thought we would be generous, and assist you.' All cursed Mr. ——. Some asked me if I had not influence enough to prevent his motion. I replied he was an ardent antagonist, *and that I had nothing to do with him*, to the truth of which they assented." That member was, indeed, a political opponent of Mr. Douglas, but he was a personal friend, and was acting in this matter in pursuance of an express agreement with the Senator from Illinois. The Illinois Bill gradually worked its way to the top of the list once more, when it was passed by a majority of three. It cost Douglas two years of hard work, in and out of Congress, to accomplish this result.

I have dwelt upon this masterpiece, because it includes almost every known device and trick of the log-rolling art. The ease with which the legislatures of Illinois, Alabama, and Mississippi were handled by a few railroad chiefs; the manner in which a lobbyist with a mathematical head converted the just rules of the House of Representatives into an engine of injustice; the unblushing audacity with which an honorable Senator, and candidate for the Presidency, could first lie, and then boast that he had lied; — these are among the points that should excite reflection. But neither those three legislatures nor Congress could have been wielded in this manner by one man, if there had not been in those bodies, and in many of the people whom they represented, an impatient desire to have the works executed in aid of which a principality was granted. The three interested States were, of course, well pleased to have railroads completed which for fifteen years they had in vain been trying to execute for themselves; and the rest of the country was absorbed in the great public questions of the time. This feat was performed in the very heat and tempest of the slavery debates of 1850.

Presidents and directors are the lords of the world at present. There have always been rich men; but in former times great capital was dead or torpid, — invested in vast landed estates, — and the revenue spent in luxury and ostentation. But the steam-engine has generated a new kind of capitalists, — men of brain, ambition, and industry, wielding millions of *active* capital, and controlling thousands of human beings, — men capable of everything except the tranquil enjoyment of life, and who rest only when they lie down to rest forever. These are the children of the steam-engine, which compels everything to be done on the great scale, — manufacturing, travelling, and finally agriculture, — and has called into being a class of men capable of directing immense enterprises and of wielding enormous sums. In England these men generally get into the small circle of the ruling class, marry into ruling families, get themselves elected to Parliament, govern the British empire, as we may say, legitimately; and hence, their power is not absolute, but limited. In the United States they have usually found it more convenient to govern in the lobby, and their power threatens to become unlimited, through their easy control of law-making bodies. If, just now, they are turning their thoughts toward getting within the bar, and some have found their way thither, it is that they may operate the more effectually as log-rolling lobbyists.

It is startling to hear these people talk of legislatures, and their *complete* subserviency. My eye was caught the other day by this passage in an affidavit of Mr. Daniel Drew of New York: "We" (directors of the Erie Railroad) "went over to New Jersey; we stayed over there some weeks; *we got a law passed by the New Jersey Legislature* to enable us to transact the business of the company over there, so that we might not be plagued by the courts of New York," *alias* Fisk, Jr. The off-hand, matter-of-course manner in which the fact is mentioned would be remarkable, if we were not so familiar with the state of things at Trenton. Probably it cost Mr. Drew little more than the writing of a letter, to get the law passed. Usually, however, legislatures are managed by log-rolling, or, as Mr. Washburne of Illinois styles it, ring legislation, — "combinations of different and distinct interests for the purpose of forcing legislation upon subjects grouped together, when not one of them could stand separately," — a system, he observes, which is "becoming the curse of the country." *

Mr. Washburne declined to state whether anything of this kind is done in Congress, because it would not have been "in order." But there is another gentleman in the House of Representatives, of similar name, General C. C. Washburn of Wisconsin, who, in the most nonchalant way, in the course of the same debate, let the cat out of the bag. "Every intelligent member of Congress knows," said he, "that any company representing a capital of one hundred millions of dollars can defeat any legislation that ever may be sought here in the interest of the public." Many years had passed since a sentence had so impressed and puzzled me as this; and, after brooding over it for eleven months, I went to Washington purposely to see what it meant. There is something in the phraseology of it which causes it to lay violent hold of the mind. "Every *intelligent* member!" Greenhorns may think that Congress is the supreme power in this land; but intelligent members know that the lobby can defeat *any* legislation that can *ever* be sought in Washington in the interest of the public. It is a truly tremendous statement, and, for one, I think it is much too

* "I say it with shame," added Mr. Washburne, "it has prevailed in my own State, Illinois. It was by this 'ring legislation' that our last legislature got through that series of acts, the new State House, the Agricultural College, the Southern Penitentiary, and perhaps some others, which, if not promptly repealed, will entail millions and millions of public debt on our people, already groaning under a load of taxation almost too grievous to be borne. It is this 'ring legislation' that threatens particularly to fasten upon the people of our State the new State House, one of the most monstrous schemes ever thrust through a legislative body, and which has met with almost universal execration from all parties." — *Speech on the Pacific Railroad, March* 10, 1868.

sweeping. It may, at length, become true; but up to this time, potent as the lobby is, and skilled as it is in log-rolling, it has won signal triumphs in Washington only when it has been supported by a strong and wide-spread feeling out of doors. The Pacific Railroad, for example, — was ever a public work so vehemently desired as that? Congress made a hard bargain for the country in subsidizing the road so lavishly; but, at the time the bargain was made, it did not seem so unreasonable, and the public was in a mood to submit to any conditions, provided the road were hurried forward.

The millionnaires in the lobby, however, are most powerful in Washington, and their power seems likely to increase with their rapidly augmenting wealth.

Think of the mere amount of money which a man, or a small number of men, can now control. "I can check for fifteen millions," is the boast of a person who but yesterday drove a pedler's wagon. Two or three men, styled The Erie Railway Company, receive fifteen millions of dollars a year from that road, employ twelve thousand men, lease hundreds of miles of other and connecting railroads, own twenty steamboats on the Great Lakes, control lines of steamboats on Long Island Sound, expend twenty-five millions a year, run a New York court, keep a judge, and can have what they wish at Albany, even to being endowed with absolute power over all this property for five years. One gentleman, past the time of life when our forefathers used to retire from business, deliberately selected as the amusement of his old age (he really regards it in that light) the getting control of all the railroads connecting New York with the Western country. He began the pastime by buying one road a hundred and sixty miles long outright, with his own money; for this gentleman can check for much more than fifteen millions. Old as he is, he may live long enough to accomplish his purpose; and he certainly would, if he were fifty years of age instead of seventy-five. Another able, untiring man has a dry-goods store in New York which contains precisely the space of two hundred dry-goods stores of average size, and does about the amount of business that two hundred average stores would do, and does it at less than half the average expense. Two great houses, the Capulets and Montagues of Rhode Island, are said (falsely, no doubt, but with some show of truth) to divide that pleasant, busy, thriving little State between them; and New Jersey does really appear to have abdicated her political being in favor of Camden and Amboy.

We must bear in mind also that this massing tendency is a law of nature, which the steam-engine has only stimulated and aggravated. In every pond the strong-coarse devour the weak-fine. The savage pickerel grows great by gobbling up myriads of gentle perch and tender trout. In every age the same problem presents itself in a changed form, How the weak-fine are to keep the strong-coarse a little within bounds. In one age the pickerel is the feudal system; again, it is a priestly hierarchy; or it is both these in alliance. At another time it is Philip II., or Louis XIV., or Napoleon Bonaparte. In England, at present, it is what that intelligent English newspaper, the Pall Mall Gazette, calls the "Inevitable Landlord." This paper, a few weeks ago, had a noticeable article upon the all-devouring British pickerel, in the course of which it said: "Almost every economical improvement which can be suggested, every saving in cost of production, every relief from inconvenient encumbrances, every measure designed for the improvement of the condition of the toiling classes of society, ends by putting more money into the pockets of that order which certainly does not suffer from the lack of it. Let science apply her novel resources to the cultivation of the land, and up goes the rent. Let sanitary improvements in towns be carried out at great cost to the public in general, the final benefit (in a pecuniary sense) is reaped by the house-owner. Let railways and telegraphs bring the most distant parts of the productive area of our soil into immediate competition with those previously more available, and the territorial proprietors of the regions thus rendered more accessible, after a short time, make their bargains with the tenant according to the raised value of the land."

This is merely the present English form of the universal difficulty, which form we have not yet reached, and may never reach. *We* have to contemplate the time, not distant, when all our towns will be Lowells, all industry a mill, all land model farms ploughed by steam, and all the resources of the country wielded by presidents and boards. With us it is the inevitable DIRECTOR who looms up, formidable and menacing.

It is to be observed, also, of these check-drawing magnates, that they have learned, of late years, how much better it pays to unite, and prey upon the public, than it does to fight, and prey upon one another. They will fight long enough to ascertain whether one *can* devour another; but when they have discovered that this cannot be conveniently done, then they are apt to unite, and rush hungry upon mankind. I have quoted a few words, above, from an affidavit of Mr. Daniel Drew, founder of a theological seminary. The same affidavit concludes with the following passage: "Gould and Fisk have recently been engaged in locking up money; they told me so; they wanted me to join them in locking up money, and I did to the extent of one million dollars, and refused to lock up any more; I had originally agreed to lock up four million dollars, but when money became very tight I deemed it prudent to decline to go any farther, and unlocked my million. The object of locking up is to make money scarce. They had money enough of the Erie Railway Company to lock up to make money scarce and affect the stock market, — to make stocks fall, because people could n't get the money to carry them; they sent, I have understood, three millions to Canada, to a bank there."

The reader will never know what he lost by skipping those columns upon columns of affidavits in small type, which darkened the New York newspapers in the early part of 1869, — affidavits shot at one another by directors contending for the control of the Erie Railway. The publishers of the newspapers were right in refusing to insert the affidavits, except as advertisements at so much a line, because no one could rationally be expected to read them. But those who did read them were amused and edified. An attentive reader could see both games played, that of combining to plunder, and that of fighting to devour. The victors succeeded, at length, in getting the unhappy Founder of a Theological Seminary in a position that would have excited pity in any but a director's breast. He came to one of them on a Sunday morning, and simply begged for mercy, but begged in vain. He would not be denied. He pleaded till one o'clock on Monday morning, without producing any effect upon his fellow pickerel, who had him in that terrible Erie corner. Since the world was created, never before did a founder of a theological seminary pass such a Sunday.

Many recent instances in which corporations have first contended for each other's destruction, and then united for the purpose of having the public at their mercy, are familiar to us all, and need not be mentioned. Corporations omnipotent within their range result from these unions; corporations which pay their legal advisers much more money per annum for an occasional hour a day than the public pays its highest servants for exhausting toil the year round. These corporations, huge and powerful as they now are, are capable of uniting again in the lobby at Washington for purposes common to several of them; and we have the opinion of a veteran member of Congress, that they will never exert themselves in that lobby without accomplishing their object.

When this state of things is contemplated, people sometimes reassure themselves by saying that the press is left, to represent, and contend for, the public. But is it? Who is the controlling man of most of our great newspapers, — the editor or the stockholder? If any one is in doubt on this point, he has only to ask the co-operation of some of the leading newspapers in urging a reform which will involve the risk of pecuniary loss. In many cases, he will find that it is the stockholding mind which *decides* questions of that nature. The editor would attack a flagrant abomination; but the man controlling a majority of the stock calls his attention to the fact that the flagrant abomination advertises two or three columns a day, and the flagrant abomination is either not attacked at all, or it is flattered by the kind of attack that advertises it most effectively. The editor is generally man enough to look to the future, and comprehend the policy of forming journalists to fill the places by and by of the present leaders of the press. He would stimulate and reward young ambition, — exulting to compensate able and valiant service liberally; but the stockholder thinks naturally of his *next* dividend, and puts the office upon an allowance. Flourishing as the press is, as a mere business, it is for the moment in a condition of arrested development. The young journalist climbs to a certain height; but when he has done his apprenticeship, and has fitted himself for something of command, he finds that he has attained all that the press now has to bestow upon mere talent and skill. It is only money that can advance him another step. The stockholder blocks the way. The editor is dethroned. The stockholder reigns.

This is no one's fault. It is, after all, only a stage in the march of the press, where, for a brief period it halts, to perfect new arrangements. Like every other institution and interest of civilized man, the press has to adjust itself to the steam-engine, which first enabled, and now compels, it to be immense, and thus necessitates the stockholder. When the mere presses, that a daily newspaper in a large city must have, cost a hundred thousand dollars, and the telegrams average five hundred dollars a day, there must be more money invested in a daily paper than an intellectualized man ever possesses except by an accident. The irruption of the moneyed stockholder into the press presents peculiar inconveniences only because newspapers are, in some degree, an intellectual product, — not a mere commodity or manufacture, like screws or flour. An editor is naturally the servant of the public, not the servant of a few men who have raised money enough to buy shares in a newspaper.

The stockholder cannot be expected at once to perceive these truths, and it is his vocation and duty to look to the dividends. He seems, at present, rather disposed to regard the writers for the press very much as managers of theatres used to regard dramatists, — such managers as the one who gave Douglas Jerrold five pounds a week, and made twenty thousand pounds by one of his plays. These men arrested the development of the English stage for sixty years, as the stockholder now arrests the development of the daily press. But, doubtless, a way will be devised by which journalists, pure and simple, without submitting to the nuisance of making money, will be restored to a just share of the power, honor, and safety now enjoyed and abused by the stockholder. Either this will be, or the press will decline and degenerate.

Congress and journalism, then, are in the same boat. Directors and stockholders threaten the independence of both. In the lobby they employ their talents in log-rolling; and when they want important service from the press, they can buy shares. Any newspaper in the country, except perhaps two, could be bought outright for two millions of dollars; and what are two millions to men who control fifteen hundred miles of railroad and a "greenback mill," and have it in their power to shoot into Wall Street new stock by the wagon-load? Congress is not corrupt; the press is not corrupt. Both are threatened with paralysis; but neither will be paralyzed. Every age has its difficulty. This is ours, and we shall overcome it.

OUR ISRAELITISH BRETHREN.

DID the reader ever try to compute what it has cost our Israelitish brethren to keep two Sundays a week, and four sets of holidays a year? Besides their own religious and national festivals, they have been compelled, generally under ruinous penalties, to abstain from business on those of the countries in which they have dwelt. Thus in Catholic countries, for several centuries, they were obliged to be idle: 1. Fifty-two Sundays; 2. Thirty holidays of obligation; 3. Fifty-two Saturdays or Sabbaths; 4. An average of twelve other holidays of their own: total, one hundred and forty-six days per annum, or about two days in every five! In Protestant countries, the usual number of idle days, including their fifty-two Saturdays and twelve festivals and fasts, has been one hundred and ten, or about two days in every six. In other words, the Jews in Catholic countries have been obliged, by law and conscience, to abstain from business nearly three days a week, and in Protestant countries a little more than two. Of late years, since Catholics have become much less strict in the observance of Sundays and holidays, the Jews suffer more inconvenience in Protestant than in Catholic lands. The rigor of the Scotch and the Puritan Sunday is especially grievous to them, even to the present hour; while in Paris, Hamburg, and Vienna Sunday is, in some branches of business, the best day of the week.

This fact of the double set of holidays would alone have sufficed to exclude them from agriculture. A ripe harvest will not wait from Friday till Monday for any of our scruples; and two good planting days lost in a late, wet spring would often make the difference between a crop and no crop. Fancy a market-gardener in strawberry time, or a florist in May, obliged to cease work half an hour before sunset Friday afternoon, and unable to offer anything for sale till Monday morning! Even the thirty Catholic holidays of obligation placed the farmers of Catholic countries under a disadvantage that was obvious to all who lived near the line dividing a Catholic from a Protestant country. Voltaire, who lived for thirty years close to the frontier of France, within two miles of Protestant Geneva, dwells upon this in many a passage of exquisite satire. Readers remember the scene in which the priest rushes from the tap-room, "red with wrath and wine," to rebuke the yeoman who had "the insolence and impiety" to plough his field on a Saint's day, "instead of going to the tavern and drinking like the rest of the parish. The poor gentleman was ruined: he left the country with his family and servants, went to a foreign land, turned Lutheran, and his lands remained uncultivated for many years." If thirty extra holidays were a serious injury to French farmers, it will not be questioned that ninety-four made agriculture an impossible pursuit to Israelites.

Except where Jews lived together in large numbers, as in Poland and some parts of Germany, the same fatality of their lot sufficed to exclude them from most workshops, counting-rooms, and stores. Who could take an apprentice with the understanding that he was to be always absent on Saturdays? Who, a clerk, on the condition of not having him on the busiest day of the week? Even here, in these free cities of America, where Jewish merchants and bankers are often obliged to employ Christian clerks, they labor under the disadvantage of having to pay salaries for three hundred and nine days' work per annum, while only getting two hundred and fifty-seven days' attendance. In short, if the reader will take the trouble to trace all the consequences of the conscientious adherence of our Israelitish brethren to their holy days, he will discover that during many centuries of their dispersion among Christian nations, that adherence would have been enough of itself to confine their able men to the trade in money and jewels, and their ordinary men to petty traffic and hard bargaining. Money at interest keeps no holy day. Like the trees of the Scotch laird in the novel, it grows while the owner sleeps. It earns revenue both while the lender prays in the synagogue and while the borrower worships in the cathedral. On Good Friday as on the Day of Atonement, through merry Christmas and joyous Purim, on the days of Passover, the fourth of July, the fifth of November, still it yields its increase. Hence strong Israelites usually deal in money; and as to the rank and file, we must allow, if we would be just, that the trader who has to keep his shutters closed two or three days a week must, as a general thing, carry on business at small expense, and make the most of every transaction.

But if, a thousand years ago, the Jews had reached that point of development which would have enabled them with a good conscience to give up their seventh-day Sabbath, and rest only on ours, it would not have availed to give them a choice of occupations. In the night of superstition, no Jew could own or hold land on endurable conditions in any country of Christendom. Nor could he belong to any guild of mechanics; and hence he could not be himself a mechanic, nor apprentice his son to a mechanic. He could not lawfully hire a Christian servant in some countries. He could not enter a university or a preparatory school in any country; and so the liberal professions were closed to him. He could not be an artist, even if any Christian prince would have bought pictures of him, because, in the black ages, there were only two kinds of pictures that yielded much revenue or renown, — New Testament scenes, and indecent pictures from the Greek and Roman poets. The former a Jew could not paint; the latter he would not, for the Jews have preserved, through all vicissitudes, a certain chastity of mind and taste, which makes such subjects abhorrent to them. A good Jew knows better than most men the unutterable preciousness of an unprurient soul and an uncontaminated body; for there is nothing which his religion inculcates so sedulously and in so many ways. At the present hour they are probably the chastest seven millions of people under the sun.

The tory Carlyle, with the baser instinct of his party, — which is, to grovel before the strong and trample on the weak, — makes this exclusion of the Jews from all the more honorable and expanding pursuits the occasion of a most bitter taunt. The celestial powers, he says, when a people have become hopelessly debased, sometimes toss them in utter contempt a great bag of money, as if to say, "Take *that!* Be *that* your portion!" How cruelly unjust is this! The Encyclopædia Britannica, an invaluable work, but uniformly narrow and reactionary on religious subjects, while admitting that, in the dark ages, Jews had no choice but to be money-lenders, while allowing that they had no means either of revenge or self-defence, except in extorting usurious interest from their plundering oppressors, stamps with reprobation their "meanness and injustice" in so doing. But the same writer on the same page (Vol. XII. p. 778) has no word of encomium for those heroic Jews, who he says presented their breasts to the sword rather than violate their conscience; nor for those high-minded Jewish maidens and wives, who fastened stones to their bodies and sought refuge in the river from the polluting touch of Christian soldiers. In one of our best periodicals, while I am writing these paragraphs, I read an impatient paragraph, complaining of the "obstinacy" of the Russian Jews in avoiding agriculture and sticking to petty traffic. As if, in all the empire of Russia, until very recently, an Israelite could own an acre of land, or till a farm to advantage, while forced to observe the numerous festivals of the Greek Church!

The Jews are, in truth, singularly adapted by natural disposition to agriculture, their skill in which once made Palestine a garden. At the present moment the attention of benevolent and public-spirited Jews is directed to the return of their people to agricultural pursuits, and the scene of the first experiment is Palestine itself. There are now thirteen thousand Israelites in that country, nine thousand of whom live in or near Jerusalem; and there is no reason in the laws or customs of the land why they should not cultivate the soil. But hardly a Jew in the world knows how to plough and reap, and the Jews in Palestine — pilgrims and descendants of pilgrims — have been steadily demoralized by the alms sent to them from orthodox synagogues in every part of the world. M. Netter, the agent of the Israelitish Alliance, who was sent to Palestine to inquire into the condition of the Israelites there, reports that this unwise, sentimental almsgiving paralyzes the arms and corrupts the hearts of his people. "As the elders," he remarks, "get a double portion of the alms, and as they themselves distribute whatever little may be left of it, the indigent and lowly get but a very small portion of it. We therefore see parents allowing their children to marry early, in order that the offspring of these marriages may share in these charities and increase the resources of the family. Children are also made to study the Talmud, a knowledge of which brings in an additional income. The weak and powerless are held in abject subjection by their superiors, and frequently seek relief from the English missionaries, who are always ready in such cases."

Here is another example of the pernicious consequences of ill-directed benevolence, from which the future is to suffer so much. The remedy M. Netter suggests is agriculture; although at present not a Jew in Palestine cultivates the soil. A few of them have tried gardening, and failed, as Christian amateurs generally fail, from ignorance. An agricultural school and experimental farm, in aid of which money has been subscribed in New York and other capitals, is about to be started in Palestine. All things must have a beginning, and the disuse of eighteen centuries cannot be overcome in a year or two, but there is reason to believe that the people who once made their land a proverb for its abundant harvests are about to recover their skill in the cultivation of the soil. In reading Jewish periodicals and in conversing with enlightened Jews, I perceive an impulse in this direction which will produce results where Sunday laws do not hinder.

Who can estimate the reparation which Christendom owes this interesting and unoffending people? How abundant, how untiring, should be our charity in judging the faults of character which our own superstition has created or developed!

Of the giant wrongs to which they have been subjected for the last ten centuries, — the huge Andersonville outrages, — few readers need to be reminded. In the slaughter of the Jews of Seville, in 1391, thirty-five hundred *families* were murdered. In 1492, under Ferdinand and Isabella, three hundred thousand heroic Israelites preferred exile to apostasy. Many of them found a resting-place only in the grave or in the depths of the sea; for neither Portugal nor Italy nor Mohammedan Morocco would tolerate the presence of a people who would not comply with their superstitions, and who, by their frugality, continence, temperance, and industry, absorbed the wealth of every country in which they lived. Those who remained in the Peninsula suffered baptism, and were obliged to conform to the outward observances of the reigning church. Far more enviable was the lot of those who had accepted banishment. The favorite office of the Spanish Inquisition for two centuries was to "question" the sincerity of those two hundred thousand Jewish converts; and the national amusement was to witness the burning of Jewish Rabbis and Jewish maidens. Similar atrocities were committed, as we all know, in England, Germany, and France.

Nor can we claim that Protestants have been guiltless toward them. Since I have been interested in this subject, I have found nothing more savage against the Jews than a passage from Martin Luther in which he offers for the consideration of the Christian public seven propositions: 1. "That we should set fire to their synagogues and schools, and what cannot be burnt should be covered over with earth, that no man may ever discover a stone or brick of it; we are to do this for the glory of our Lord and Christianity." 2. Burn all their houses, and lodge them in stables like gypsies, "in order that they may know they are not lords in this land, but in captivity and misery." 3. Burn all their prayer-books and Talmuds. 4. Forbid the Rabbis, under pain of death, to give instruction. 5. Deny Jews the right of protection on the highways; "for they have no business with the land." 6. "Being neither lords, farmers, nor merchants, nor anything of the kind, they are to remain at home." "You lords shall not, and cannot, protect them, unless you would take part in their abominations." 7. Put a flail, axe, mattock, or spindle into the hands of every "young and strong Jew and Jewess," and compel them to manual labor. This was Luther's idea of the treatment due to the only body of religious people in Europe who could be in sympathy with him in his struggle with superstition. But Luther himself was only half emancipated: for he clung to that fatal, fatal root of bitterness, the belief that human souls can be eternally lost by erroneous opinions.

But we have done worse to these people than murder and torture them. Wrongs like these are occasional; the rack palls at last; and the most infuriate mob of Christians that ever hunted down an innocent people grows weary of massacre at last, and a long period of peace usually succeeds. In our own day I have seen Protestants in Philadelphia pursuing in blind fury harmless Catholics, burning their churches, and insulting their priests; and I have seen, in New York, Catholics rioting in the massacre of the most inoffensive laboring people in the world. In three days the fit passes; reason returns; and the very men who inflicted the wounds are ready to assist in healing them. But there is a wrong which all Christians, for many hundreds of years, have done to all Jews, all the time, — *we have despised them.* Having excluded them from the occupations most favorable to the development of human nature's better side, we have added to this giant wrong the crueller sting of despising them for not having their better side developed. Having kept them styed in Ghettos and in Jews' streets age after age, we loathe them because they are not all clean.

Human beings are so constituted and related, that among the most precious possessions any of us can have is the respect and good-will of our community. Happily, few are aware of this truth, because, like good digestion, the value of such a possession is not known until it is lost. Those quadroon and octoroon gentlemen of New Orleans knew it, who said to General Butler with so much passion: "We care not on which side we fight; we will fight as long as we can, and spend all we have, if only our boys may stand in the street equal to white boys when the war is over!" If the reader has ever happened to have his eye upon the face of a well-dressed person at the moment a policeman touched his arm, and he felt that he was *arrested*, no longer one of the passing throng, no longer a member of the community, no longer a man among men, but a detected thief, whom any boy might make faces at, a thing abhorred and despised, upon whom no countenance could cast a benignant nor even an indifferent look, — if the reader has ever noted the awful shadow that falls upon a human countenance at such a moment, he can perhaps form some idea of what it must be to feel always the contempt of men. Or, still better, if the reader can look back to his school-days and call to mind moments or hours when, for some peculiarity of dress, person, or conduct, he was the object of general derision, either in schoolroom or play-ground, and can feel still the scorch of the old blush in his cheeks, he cannot be quite ignorant of the value of that unexpressed good-will which usually invests us like the air we unconsciously breathe.

And the Jews were never allowed to forget that they were a despised people. Contempt of the Israelite was embedded in law and exhibited in daily custom. In Protestant Holland, down nearly to the days of Louis Bonaparte, Jewish paupers were compelled to say their prayers bareheaded, and to work all day Saturday, although they begged the privilege of doing in five days their whole week's work. It was not till 1790 that this poor boon was granted them. Some of the watering-places in Germany could show, among their chartered privileges, the right to exclude Jews. At Strasburg, within the recollection of living persons, a Jew had to pay three francs a day merely for the privilege of staying in the town. In Switzerland, as late as 1851, the contemptuous law was re-enacted, imposing a fine of three hundred francs upon every Christian who gave a Jew employment. In Russia, at the present hour, the government presumes to prescribe what shall be the garb of a Jew. In New York, London, Paris, and other cities there is an alliance, or society for the sole object of promoting the emancipation of the Jews from the remaining disabilities which the aversion of Christendom has imposed. Without troubling the reader with a catalogue of similar facts, I can convey some idea of the scorn in which Jews were once held in a more convenient manner by showing how they are now treated in the city of Rome, — Rome being a fragment of the Past preserved, like an Elgin marble, for the inspection of the moderns. In 1860, when there was talk of a congress of European powers for the settlement of international questions, the Jews of Rome prepared a petition for presentation to it, in which some of their grievances were stated. From this paper we learn that no Jew in Rome can be an artist, nor be a pupil in a school of art, nor frequent a public gallery for practice in art. No college, medical school, law school, or scientific institution can receive a Jewish student. No Jew can exercise a mechanical trade, except cobbling shoes. Cruellest and absurdest of all, no Jew, fond as he is of music, and gifted as his race is in music, can sing in public or play on an instrument. "Woe to the Hebrew," says the petition, "who dares sing or play in public; for the police and the Holy Office immediately pounce upon him and punish the offence with severe penalties." This is the more abominable, because nature has signalized this people, not so much by superiority of understanding, as by talent. The gifted among them are formed to sing, to play, to compose, to carve, to paint, to personate, to excel in all those arts by which human nature is enchanted and exalted by being exhibited to itself.

Edmond About's report of the condition of the Jews in Rome is fresh in the recollection of many. He glances backward at the time, not remote, when every evening at the hour Christians go to the theatre the gates of the Jews' quarter were locked for the night; when on days of holy festival Jews were made to run races for the amusement of Christians; when every year a city official gave them a representative kick, an honor for which they had to pay four thousand francs; when they were compelled to present publicly to every new Pope a Bible; when they were obliged to pay the salary of a Christian priest employed to preach a sermon to them every Saturday, and they could only avoid attending this service by paying a fine; when their Ghetto bred such deadly pestilence, that some of them almost lost the semblance of humanity, and "they might have been mistaken for beasts, if one had not known them to be intelligent beings, apt for business, resigned to their lot, simple in their requirements, kind-hearted, devoted to their families, and irreproachable in their conduct." Such *was* their condition in Rome. M. About tells us what it *is*. The present Pope, he reminds us, has indeed taken away the gates of the Ghetto, so that Jews can go about the city after dark; he has dispensed them from the annual kick and its annual price, and he has closed the church to which they were required to go on Saturdays to be converted.

But the author adds: "I secretly questioned two well-known inhabitants of the Ghetto. When they understood why I concerned myself with their affairs, the poor men exclaimed: 'For Heaven's sake, do not publish that we are wretched; that the Pope *actively* regrets his concessions of 1847; that doors invisible, but impassable, close the Ghetto, and that our condition is worse than ever. All that you might say in our behalf would be visited upon us, and instead of benefiting you would injure us.'" The inquirer visited the Ghetto, in the low ground near the Tiber, and found it "the most horrible and neglected quarter of the town," in which not the humblest of the thousand prelates about Rome would set his foot, any more than an Indian Brahmin would cross the threshold of a Pariah's hovel. "I learned," says this author, "that the most humble employment in the most humble office would as soon be given to a beast as to a Jew; that for a child of Israel to ask in Rome to be employed as a commissary, would be more absurd than for the giraffe of the Jardin des Plantes to ask for an under-prefectship in Paris." No Jew can own a foot of land in the papal dominions, nor cultivate one, unless in the name of a Christian; and if a Jew, using this artifice, ventures to cultivate a garden or a farm, his harvest is safe from pillage only so long as the legal device remains a secret. Let but the Christians around learn that the harvest is the property of an Israelite, and "a rage for plunder" seizes them, which leaves the hapless proprietor with desolated fields.

This is the testimony of a witness who is prejudiced, as all modernized minds are prejudiced, against government by priests. Let me summon another witness, a Christian who writes to *L'Ami d'Israel* an account of his visit to the Roman Ghetto: "It is situated on the borders of the Tiber, in a place subject to inundations; the population is confined in narrow, dirty streets; and although the Jews are much too numerous for this small quarter, they are not allowed to take up their abode beyond the limits of the Ghetto. The closing of the gates is discontinued, but the prohibition as to residence remains the same. I was struck with the activity and industry of the Jews; for while one sees a great many idlers and crowds of beggars in Rome itself, in the Ghetto every one is at work, and there is not a beggar visible." The struggle for life, this writer remarks, is so severe, that out of a population of more than four thousand, two thousand five hundred are extremely poor, and in part dependent upon the charity of their neighbors.

As Israelites are now looked upon and treated in Rome, so were they once regarded and treated in every capital of Europe; and their partial emancipation is a thing too recent to have more than begun to obliterate the effects of fifteen centuries of outrage and contempt. For the faults which we see in them, and which clearly result from the contracted Ghetto and the exclusion from the broadening employments, we should blame ourselves, not them; and when a Jew plays upon us a scurvy trick, let us go out straightway and kick a Christian for it.

In conversing upon this subject with the enlightened and accomplished Israelites now to be found in all our cities, I am amazed at the absence of everything like rancor and fury from their hearts when they dwell upon the wrongs of their race. A decent Christian boils with anger as he reads of the indignities they have suffered; but they, the victims of our insensate aversion, speak of these indignities with such calmness and good temper, that I have been ready to exclaim: The Jews are the only Christians! And certainly, if the peculiar virtue of Christianity *is* the patient endurance of outrage, then we must admit that they have excelled all known people in practising the religion which Christians have preached. But of course the patient endurance of outrage is *not* the great Christian virtue, nor is it a virtue at all, unless the outrage is irredressible. But that has been precisely their case. Usually a small number in the midst of a hostile population, they have been obliged to endure, or perish; they have had such a training in some portions of the Sermon on the Mount as no other race has ever had.

If a Christian would know these people aright, that is, if he would know their best, he must observe their home life;

for the great secret of Jewish persistence is the strength of that mingled affection and pride which binds families together. The family, the Sabbath, — in those two words are hidden the secret of Jewish history since their dispersion. Let us accompany a good orthodox Jewish family through their calm and cheerful Sabbath, and see how they keep it and enjoy it. I select an orthodox family, instead of a "Reformed," merely because the orthodox Jew is an historical person; as he keeps his Sabbath, his fathers have kept it for many centuries.

The Jewish Sabbath begins on Friday evening half an hour before sunset, and ends on Saturday evening half an hour after sunset, or when a star is visible in the sky. On Friday, the day of preparation, the women and girls of the family are busy in providing for the morrow the best food of the week; for whatever is eaten or drank during the joyous sacred hours must be the very best the family can afford. Poor Jews will pinch all the week in order that their wives and children may have something delicious to eat on the Sabbath. But that savory food must be cooked or prepared for cooking before the Sabbath begins; for our Israelitish brethren observe with just strictness the law which gives rest on the Day of Rest to their servants. They shame us in this particular. They will not use even their horses on their Sabbath. On a Sunday, about twelve, M., you may see in front of Dr. Adams's fashionable Presbyterian church in Madison Square, New York, or around Dr. Tyng's fashionable Episcopal church in St. George's Square of the same city, from twenty to forty well-appointed equipages waiting for the last hymn to be finished; but you will never see a vehicle before the superb Temple Immanuel, a Jewish synagogue in the Fifth Avenue, although there are many families within who could ride home, if they would, in their own carriages. I do not say that the Christians are wrong or the Jews right in this. It is no one's business but their own. But if we borrow the Hebrew's word "Sabbath," and adopt, verbally, their Sabbatical law, our practice perhaps ought to conform in some degree to our profession. It probably does not severely tax those coachmen and footmen to show off their gay turn-outs and brilliant liveries on a fine Sunday morning in the Fifth Avenue.

But for the heavy-laden drudges of the boarding-house kitchen, and the maid-of-all-work in average families, I could wish we were all Jews from Saturday night till Monday morning. It is a dastardly shame to compel or permit women, who have faithfully toiled for us from Monday's tub to Saturday's scrub, to work hard all through the best hours of Sunday merely that we may gorge ourselves with dainty food. The Jews avoid this barbarous meanness. Their servants rest on their Sabbath.

As early as possible on Friday afternoon the father comes home. As sunset draws near the family put on their best clothes, and father and sons go to the synagogue for the short Sabbath-eve service. His wife and daughters usually remain at home, where pleasing duties still detain them, though their arduous work is done.

The Jewish religion is a monotone; it is a religion of one idea, and that idea is GOD. Do you wish the most enlightening of all commentaries on the Bible? do you wish to know the original meaning of hackneyed Christian phrases? would you taste the savor and inhale the fragrance of celebrated texts? do you desire to see living descendants of the characters sketched in the New Testament? Then frequent orthodox synagogues, and observe the ways of those who attend them. The Jew "walks with God"; the Jew, "in everything, gives thanks"; the Jew "makes melody in his heart to the Lord"; the Jew "prays without ceasing."

A pious Jew of the old school utters in the course of every twenty-four hours as many as a hundred benedictions, ascriptions, and prayers. On waking in the morning he says: "I thank thee, ever-living, ever-enduring King, that thou hast restored me unto life, through thy great mercy and truth." Whenever he enjoys, whenever he suffers, whenever he gains, whenever he loses, he has a form of Hebrew words ready in his memory in which to call upon his God. If he eats a fine peach he says: "Blessed art thou, O Lord our God, King of the Universe, who hast caused us to be preserved, and permitted us to enjoy this season." But if he were about to eat strawberries, the ascription would slightly vary; as it would also for bread, cakes, melons, vegetables, wine, water, oil. If he enjoys the fragrance of flowers, he will say: "Blessed art thou, O Lord God, King of the Universe, who createst aromatic herbs"; and he has also a form for sweet-scented woods, fruit, gums, spice. On passing a synagogue in ruins, or one flourishing and handsome; on meeting Hebrew sages, and on meeting Gentile sages; when he hears thunder, music, rain, or wind, or sees a rainbow, a fine tree, a mountain, a river, the ocean, a handsome creature; on hearing good news or bad news; at the birth or at the death of a child; upon leaving and returning home;—he utters his short thanksgiving in Hebrew. It is so, Mr. Hepworth Dixon assures us, with the Oriental religions generally; which at the present hour, as three thousand years ago, have a strong family likeness. "An Oriental is a man of prayer," says Mr. Dixon. "If he rises from his couch, a prayer is on his lips; if he sits down to rest, a blessing is in his heart. When he buys and when he sells, when he eats and when he drinks, he remembers that the Holy One is nigh. If poor in purse, he may be rich in grace; his cabin a sanctuary, his craft a service, his daily life an act of prayer." These words describe the pious Jews of our modern capitals. They "walk with God." "God is in all their thought."

The father and his boys enter the synagogue, sometimes pausing in the vestibule, if they have touched uncleanness on the way, to wash their hands, conveniences for which are placed there. As they enter, they are required to bow to the ark containing the scrolls of the Law, and to say: "In the greatness of thy benevolence will I enter thy house: in reverence of thee will I bow down toward the temple of thy holiness." The "ark" is a closet at the eastern end of the synagogue, usually made of costly woods, closed with sliding doors, and approached by stairs. Within are scrolls of parchment, each of which contains one book of the Pentateuch, written with perfect correctness in Hebrew, by men whose profession it is to write them. One error, no matter how insignificant, condemns a scroll; for the examiners subject it to tests from which no error can escape. The letters of every line, division, and book are counted. In the exact middle of the synagogue is a somewhat spacious platform, raised four or five feet from the floor, and provided with a broad desk and a sofa. Most of the pews face this platform, but there are a few "chief seats of the synagogue," for the trustees and other officers. On the ground floor are men and boys only, all with their hats on; the women and girls being in the gallery. Israelites say that this exclusion of women from the floor of the synagogue — that is, from the synagogue proper — is an homage to their delicacy. Their law requires that, at various periods, women should not enter the sanctuary at all; and the subterfuge of the gallery was invented to avoid the necessity of asking disagreeable questions. In some countries women, for the same reason, assemble in an adjoining apartment, with a door opening into the synagogue, through which the voices of the reader and preacher can be heard.

The Friday-evening service, which lasts an hour and a quarter, consists of the chanting of prayers and psalms in the Hebrew tongue. Sometimes the Rabbi, seated on his sofa, with his hat on, clad in a black silk gown and a white silk tunic over it, intones a portion solo, the people responding with an occasional amen. Then the whole congregation will repeat a psalm; sometimes standing, sometimes sitting, bowing now and then and occasionally bowing very low. At intervals a highly trained choir of men and boys, from a gallery where they cannot be seen, burst into a song or breathe out a most melodious soft chant. No organ smothers the voices; for the orthodox Jew feels that the harp of his people still hangs upon the willow, and must not be heard again till the Temple is rebuilt. But *this* choir (Nineteenth Street, New York) needs no organ; it is itself one beautifully attuned instrument. As the service approaches a conclusion there is more responding and more simultaneous recitation, which sometimes swells into a loud chorus. In less polite congregations than this it is said some of the members become almost vociferous.

When the service is ended, while the men are shaking hands and cheerfully conversing, all the boys crowd upon the platform and gather round the Rabbi, who places his hand upon each little cap, and pronounces a word or two of benediction. To those who have had the profound misfortune of being reared in one of those creeds which repel the young soul, and make it loathe what its elders revere, this sweet spectacle reveals much of the Jewish mystery. They have known how to associate religion with the *pleasing* recollections of childhood.

Upon returning home, after the service, the father and his sons find their abode decked in its brightest attire, the table set in its goodliest array, the ladies in handsome Sabbath costume, and on the mantel-piece of the principal room the two wax-candles lighted, to symbolize the light and warmth shed on Israel by the Sabbath. In some families the old-fashioned "Sabbath lamp," with seven burners, is retained, and lighted only on this joyous evening. The family being now all assembled, the father places his hand upon the heads of each of his children, and invokes upon them the blessing of Jacob. Then they kiss one another, and each wishes the others "Good Sabbath," as we say "Merry Christmas." All join in a Sabbath hymn; after which the father pays honor to his wife by chanting the fine description in Proverbs of a Virtuous Woman, whose price is above rubies, in whom the heart of her husband doth safely trust, who looketh well to the ways of her household and doth not eat the bread of idleness. Next he takes a small silver cup, kept for the purpose, and pours into it some pure home-made wine, of grapes or raisins, and pronounces a blessing on the wine; after which he breaks a piece of bread, and utters the prescribed blessing upon the bread. A formal and longer grace is said for the meal, and then the family take their places at the table.

All this ceremonial, which seems long when it is related, occupies but a few minutes, for the Hebrew is a compact language, and our Israelitish brethren have little conception of what we understand by the word *solemnity*. There is something off-hand in the usual religious acts of the orthodox Jews. When the meal is ended, the family rise and remain standing about the table while a thanksgiving is pronounced and a hymn sung. In many families the father relates to his children on Friday evening some legend of their race, of which the stock is inexhaustible; for there are fifteen centuries of persecution to draw from, without counting the ages during which Israel had a national existence and a recorded history. Hence the collection of Jewish stories, recently republished in New York from the columns of the Jewish Messenger, was happily entitled "Friday Evening." During the Sabbath no musical instrument is heard in the house of an orthodox Jew, nor does he entertain any company beyond the circle of his relations and nearest friends. But this seclusion of families has nothing in common with Sabbatarian gloom and isolation. It is more like a Christmas reunion, when families are happy enough without other friends, than a Sabbatarian withdrawal from cheerful society.

On Saturday morning the service at the orthodox synagogue begins at eight and lasts till twelve. It differs little in character from the service of the evening before, except that toward the close the minister, accompanied by two of the congregation, descends from the platform and walks slowly to the chanting of the choir to the closet where the scrolls of the Law are kept, the doors of which have been previously opened by two of the members. The scroll containing the portion of the Law to be read that day is taken from its place and carried slowly to the platform, where its gay covering is removed and the scroll laid out flat upon the broad desk. After the portion has been read, one of the gentlemen who has assisted in its conveyance from the "ark" lifts it by the ends of its two rollers, and holds it up, open, as high as he can reach, and turns it in various directions, so that all the congregation can see the Hebrew characters written upon it. It was perhaps this holding aloft of the Sacred Object which suggested the elevation of the Host in the celebration of the Mass. Indeed, there is many a rite, ceremony, and usage, of both Protestant and Catholic worship, the idea of which was furnished by the people whom Protestants and Catholics have agreed to revile and torment. Little boys, for example, assist in unrolling and rolling up again the scroll of the Law; and one boy stands upon the platform, in the course of the morning service, and pipes with his shrill tenor a few Hebrew sentences. Doubtless it was this usage of the Israelites, this habit of associating their *boys* with them in every religious act and ceremonial, that suggested the employment of boys in the altars of Christian churches.

The sermon is not regarded by orthodox Jews as a very important part of the Sabbath service. In some synagogues no sermon is preached; in others a short one is delivered in the German language; but it is rare indeed that a sermon in English is heard; for, to the present hour, no Rabbi lives in the United States who was not born and educated on the Continent of Europe.

Four hours seem to us impatient mortals a long time to spend in a religious service; but only a small part of the congregation attends during the first hour; the synagogue does not fill up before ten o'clock; and some leave soon after the service has reached its climax in the elevation of the scroll. A few sturdy old gentlemen are punctually in their places at eight, and go through the whole, — rising and sitting down, responding and reciting, bowing and standing erect, never faltering or shrinking, to the last amen. The secret of this persistence is, that the congregation take an active part in the worship. They do not sit passive more than four or five minutes at a time. At the conclusion of the services the assembly breaks into groups of cheerful talkers, and so drifts down stairs through the vestibule into the street, where there is abundant hand-shaking and friendly merriment. There is a short afternoon service, which is not more numerously attended than that of Christian churches; for after the bountiful Sabbath dinner, our Israelitish brethren are apt to abandon themselves, as we do, to the noble work of digestion.

The Sabbath to the Jews is *wholly* joyous! In all the tales, essays, treatises, catechisms, of this interesting people, which lie heaped up before me at this moment, I can find no hint of that strange institution which the Puritans called Sabbath. To the good Jew the Sabbath means rest, mental improvement, domestic happiness, cheerful conversation, triumphal worship. From a tract recently issued, entitled "The Sabbath, an Appeal to the Israelites of New York," I copy a short passage, to show how pious Jews regard their sacred day, and why they urge its observance.

"The family," says this writer, "in which the Sabbath is a stranger, — as it is, alas! the case with such a large number of our co-religionists, — is bereft of those beautiful ties which make *the Jewish home a paradise to the poorest of its professors*, is a desert with no oasis, an ocean of ever-contending waves, with no haven of shelter. O ye who yet remember the Sabbath eve in the old European home, — and there are many of you, — conjure up before your vision the little chamber with the seven-armed candelabra lit in honor of the Sabbath bride; the table spread, the spotless linen, your father coming home from the synagogue, his eyes beaming with satisfaction, his countenance expressing happiness and contentment, not a ruffle on his forehead which would indicate that care had ever dwelt in that soul, placing his hand on your head, blessing you, and then singing songs of welcome to the regular returning guest, the bride beloved so well! Did ever happiness enter your soul so unmeasured since you gave up all for a heap of gold? Will your children ever feel as happy as you did on that Sabbath eve, will your wife ever know the beatitude your mother felt, when she saw her husband joyous and happy?"

Here we have all that was good in the old Puritan Sunday, without its gloom, restraint, and terror. There is *no* terror in the religion of the Hebrews, no eternal perdition. They are all Universalists. The Puritanism of two hundred years ago, as we find it in the works of the Mathers, was Judaism plus the doctrine of eternal perdition.

That was a happy touch of Mr. Henry Ward Beecher's in his newspaper, The Christian Union, where, after having given the news of the various Christian denominations, he concluded by a few paragraphs, headed thus: —

"OTHER RELIGIONS."

Whether we regard this as a mere stroke of journalism, or as a recognition of the claims of other religions to the regard and respect of Christians, it was worthy of the intelligence of the editor. Nothing is more startling to a student of religions than their likeness to one another, and the similarity of their effects upon the various minds. Men who have lived in the Eastern world, in Japan, Siam, India, China, and in the great islands of the Archipelago, have often remarked that the religions of those lands, however they may differ in name, usages, rites, costumes, traditions, have much more in common than they have of difference; and under them all can be found the same varieties of religious and irreligious character: the sincere and lowly worshipper; the man who expects to be heard for his much speaking; he who affects devotion, and he who affects indifference; the rogue who uses religion as a cloak, and the politician who employs it as capital; the dealer in religious merchandise, who believes in religion as the servants of the Cataract House believe in the sublimity of Niagara; — all these characters, we are assured, can be found under all the religions of the Oriental world.

And, what is more interesting, it seems as if the religions of the world were in the same state of transition, and at about the same stage of progress. They are all anxious, all excited, all in movement. Orthodox, heterodox, ritualists, infidels, — we find them at Calcutta, in Japan, in China, in Barbary, as we do at London, Berlin, Paris, New York, and Boston. English residents in India tell us that in the higher society of Calcutta there are native young men who take precisely the same tone with regard to the Brahmins and the Hindoo sacred books as many of our young pagans do at Paris, Oxford, Cambridge, London, Boston, when the Christian religion is the subject of discourse, — a tone not of contempt, by any means; they are beyond and above that. They speak of the religion of their fathers as the son of an ancient house might descant upon the old family coach, which was excellent in its day, but is now done with, and kept as an interesting relic. Nor are there wanting, in those remoter capitals of the world, young men who surprise their companions, as some of our young ritualists do, by a sedulous imitation or revival of ancient methods and forgotten rites.

Mr. Beecher may well tell us, then, of "Other Religions"; for they are all in a similar critical condition. To the careless looker-on it seems as if they were all dissolving; but, in reality, they are only shedding their non-essentials, which is a painful and demoralizing process. When in the Arctic seas the sun gains power to soften the ice and melt the snows, the first effects upon the ice-bound fleets of fishermen and navigators are disagreeable, if not injurious. Everything is soft, damp, unstable; the snug snow-packing, which had protected and warmed the imprisoned mariners so long, becomes a source of discomfort; and the ice-roads which had borne them stiffly up are safe no longer. But the thaw is about to set them FREE, and send them careering over the boundless deep.

Our Israelitish brethren, besides sharing in the influences which are mitigating all creeds and liberalizing all minds, are now subjected to a trial peculiar to themselves. From being persecuted everywhere, they are beginning to be honored and sought. The grand example of the youngest of the nations in protecting all religions equally, while recognizing none, has had its effect in improving the condition of the Jews throughout the greater part of Christendom and beyond Christendom. Within the recollection of men still young, Jews have been admitted to the British Parliament, where, I am informed by a distinguished Rabbi, who gloried in the fact, no Jew has ever sided with the party of reaction, except one, and he a renegade. The Jews to-day in the House of Commons vote on important measures with John Bright. The professor of Hebrew in the London University *is* a Hebrew; and among the Jewish students last year at Oxford and Cambridge, one was a senior wrangler and another the crack oarsman of his college. In London one of the noted clubs is Jewish, and there are so many Jews in the city government that they may almost be said to have the controlling influence. Happily, the Jews are not proselyters, and can be aldermen without using their office to get a sly advantage for their synagogue. Among the seventy-five thousand Jews in London, there are many business men who, despite the double Sunday, hold their own against Christian competitors, to say nothing of the much greater number who have no Sunday at all. There is one Jewish clothing-house in London that has thirteen stores and employs eleven thousand people.

In France the Jews are fortunate in the free Sunday permitted both by law and custom; and as a consequence there is less poverty among them than elsewhere. The Rabbis are paid from the public treasury, as the ministers of the various Christian denominations are, and the government courts their good-will. The Jewish newspaper in Paris describes in glowing words the manner in which "the Emperor's fête" was celebrated at the principal synagogue. A detachment of chasseurs, commanded by an officer, was stationed in the temple opposite the choir, and while the

"Halel" was chanted the edifice resounded with the blast of trumpets from a military band. At the moment when the scroll of the Law was taken out of its sacred enclosure the troops presented arms, the trumpets sounded, and the organ pealed its melodious thunder. Thus the host is saluted on festive days at Notre Dame. In Paris, among a large number of other charitable organizations of Israelites, I find two designed to aid parents who desire to apprentice their children to trades. These are societies for paying the premiums required in Europe when apprentices are taken.

Throughout Germany Jews at length stand upon an equality before the law with Christians, — even in Austria, so long the citadel of conservatism. Austria has abolished all Sunday laws that would prevent Jews from cultivating land, and the Emperor has sought to compliment his Israelitish subjects by appointing two young Hebrew gentlemen to positions on his personal staff. This in Austria, where until 1860 a Jew could not exercise many of the most usual avocations, — could not be a farmer, miller, apothecary, brewer; and in some wide regions and populous places of the empire could not reside at all! In Frankfort, where the Rothschilds originated, the Jews are masters of everything. Those great bankers, as all the world knows, live in luxury more than regal; but all the world does not know that several members of this family are persons of genuine liberality of mind as well as bountifully liberal in charitable gifts. It is a pity the head of so conspicuous a house should not set a better example to Christians, by living more simply.* But all things in their time. When the time comes for general reaction against the burdensome and immoral splendors of modern life, — such as are described in Lothair, — the Jews will not be the last to adopt a style of elegant and rational simplicity.

* "Not far from Ferney one of the Rothschilds has his magnificent palace, in sight of the lake and Mont Blanc. This chateau, and that of the king of Prussia at Babelsberg, are the finest that I have yet seen in Europe: yet the banker's is more costly and imperial than the king's, without, however, the least dash of vulgar extravagance in its splendor. I was assured that the interior is in keeping with the charming grounds; and a lady who was a frequent guest there told me that crowned heads were sometimes at the table, and the banquet was as stately as the company, so much so that the different courses were served by different bands of servants, each band with its own dress.

Spain, wonderful to relate, joins the nations in restoring to the Jews the rights of man, of which she despoiled them four centuries ago. The Israelites of the world are now joining in a dollar subscription to build in Madrid a temple, worthy by its magnitude and splendor to commemorate the abrogation of the edict of 1492, which silenced Hebrew worship throughout Spain, and dismantled every synagogue. Within these few weeks Sweden has swept from her law books every remaining statute which made a distinction between Jews and Christians; and now, except in Russia and the Papal States, there is, I believe, no part of Europe where an Israelite has not the essential rights of a citizen, so far as they are enjoyed by the rest of the people.

If any one desires to revive his detestation of caste, the oppression of class by class, of color by color, of race by race, let him mark in the history of this people how *uniformly* they rise and expand and ennoble when the stigma is removed and the repressive laws are abolished. Always complying with the fundamental conditions of prosperous existence, that is, being always as a people chaste, temperate, industrious, and frugal, they have only needed a fair chance to develop more shining qualities. Americans need not recur to history to learn this. We need only to walk down Broadway as far as Castle Garden (where all the histories of all the nations come to a focus and show their net results), and compare Israelites fresh from the countries where they have been oppressed and despised for many centuries with Israelites who have lived in the United States for one or two generations. America can boast no better citizens, nor more refined circles, than the good Jewish families of New York, Cincinnati, St. Louis, Philadelphia.

Not that the repression of ages can be overcome in a few

"I got a different impression of another branch of the Rothschild family from travelling awhile with some of them in Switzerland, and having considerable conversation with the ladies. They were accomplished, elegant, and unpretending, with no outward mark of station but attendant servants; and I was not a little surprised and instructed to find that the courtly mother was at once so zealous a daughter of Israel as to change her plans of journeying in order to keep some of the great days of the synagogue, and at the same time so much of a liberal as to delight greatly in the writings of Theodore Parker."—*Rev. Samuel Osgood, in New York Evening Post.*

years. We must expect that many Jews will long continue to exhibit unpleasing traits peculiar to themselves; and in some instances we shall observe that those traits, subdued in a parent, will reappear in his children. We have a highly interesting example in the author of Lothair. The elder Disraeli, though descended from a line of moneyed men, was curiously devoid of the commercial spirit, caring for nothing but his books and his collections of literary curiosities, — a guileless, unaspiring student. His gifted son revels in the external. After fifty years of familiarity with the sumptuous life of very rich people, he writes of jewels in the manner of a dealer, and of nobles in the spirit of a footman.

One of the happy effects of light and liberty upon a religious body is to divide it. It is only people who do not think at all that value themselves upon thinking alike. Black night is uniform: daylight shows a thousand hues. Ignorance is a unit: knowledge is manifold. As long as the Jews were persecuted, they clung to ancient usage and doctrine with thoughtless tenacity; their whole strength being employed in the mere clutch. But when the repressive and restrictive laws were relaxed, the *mind* of the Jews resumed its office; divisions arose among them; and the world began to hear of the Orthodox and the Reformed. Women, for example, are profoundly honored by the men of Israel, as they are by all the chaste races (and by no others); yet they retained in their morning service that insulting thanksgiving: "Blessed art thou, O Lord our God, King of the Universe, who hast not made me a heathen; who hast not made me a slave; who hast not made me a WOMAN!" While the men were uttering these offensive words, the women were required to accept their hard destiny by thanking God for having "made them according to his will," and imploring him to deliver them from "impudent faces," "a bad man," "an evil eye," "an oppressive lawsuit," "an implacable opponent," and other evils. All this had become unsuitable, but it was retained. Then, in ancient times when almanacs were not, the festivals (all regulated by the moon) were required to be kept for two days, instead of one, lest the time of the new moon should not have been exactly ascertained. This inconvenient custom was maintained in rigor, although the moment of the birth of the new moon was known to every family. In Palestine the eating of shell-fish and pork was forbidden, because in that country those articles were thought to induce leprosy; and so in New York and London not a Jew would eat an oyster or a sausage. For similar reasons, minute directions were given by the ancient lawgivers respecting the mode of killing animals, all of which were, doubtless, necessary or humane at the time; and down to a recent period every Jewish community had its butcher, and no man would kill a chicken except in the authorized way. The service of four hours on the Sabbath was much too long; but on high days the pious Israelites were engaged in public worship for eight hours without a pause. Veritable rams' horns were blown in the temple; and every Jew who built a house left some visible part of it unfinished, to denote that the Temple was still in ruins. All life was overlaid with minute observances, and religion was to many families almost as much a burden as a solace.

In one of the stories published in "Friday Evening," there is a scene which illustrates the ruthless tyranny of ancient custom when it has acquired the sanction of religion. A poor family of Jews had just seated themselves at the table to enjoy the Sabbath dinner, for which the father, in the midst of cruel misfortunes, had ventured to provide a fine, fat goose. The eagerly expected moment arrives; the children gaze breathless as the majestic bird is placed upon the table; and the happy father, with beaming countenance, begins to use the carving-knife.

"The goose was at length completely carved, and still rested in delicious morsels on the plate before him, when, suddenly, little Schimmele cried out: 'Look, look, there is a nail driven in the goose!'

"'Where? where?' demanded at the same time both father and mother. The child pointed to the place, and there, indeed, the nail was revealed.

"The knife dropped quickly from our Anschel's hand, who stood transfixed, his face paler than the cloth before him on the table. Esther at once removed the bird, and ordered Schimmele to hasten to the Rabbi's house, and inquire of him if it were unclean or not. The boy seized the dish, covered it with a napkin, and staggered away under his tempting load as fast as legs could bear him.

"Meanwhile, gloomy and melancholy silence reigned throughout the house. The children gazed on, with an expression of disappointment and dismay. Anschel lowered his eyes, whilst Esther sat immovably in her seat without uttering a word.

"A few minutes afterwards Schimmele returned, but his countenance foreboded no good; tears were in his eyes.

"'Well?' demanded Esther, as he stood irresolutely on the threshold.

"'The goose — the goose is unclean,' replied the boy, after a desperate effort, sobbing."

It was all over with the Sabbath banquet! No one thought of eating a morsel of the goose.

I have before me a curious narrative of a young Jewish lady in Southern Russia, venturing to carry a parasol in the streets on the Sabbath. Her mother, reproached by the stricter Israelites for allowing her daughter thus to transgress traditional law, forbade the young lady ever again on the sacred day to interpose a human invention between her fair countenance and the sun's rays. The daughter, offended, refused to go out at all on the Sabbath, and after four months the mother relented, saying: "I am not so strict as my mother is, and you will not be so strict as I am. You may, therefore, just as well begin now to practise your laxer principles; it is of no use trying to make you what I am myself." The grandmother, in fact, was a pilgrim in the Holy Land, whither she had gone to end her days; the mother was merely a good orthodox Jewess; the daughter was willing to carry a parasol on Saturday!

The recent movement among our Israelitish brethren toward Reform is merely the revolt of emancipated intelligence against the rites, usages, and doctrines which had become unsuitable and obstructive. It is a reassertion of the supreme authority of human reason. The reformers, while clinging with the tenacity of their race to the two essentials, — God and the Sabbath, — demand and concede in all minor matters perfect liberty! Nor do they adhere to the weekly day of rest so much because it is commanded, as because it is best. The most advanced statement of the reformed ideas is a little work published a few weeks ago, "What is Judaism?" by Rev. Rafael D. C. Lewin of New York. Mr. Lewin, in discoursing upon the laws and rites ordained by Moses, asserts that they are obligatory only so long as they answer the end intended. "As soon," he remarks, "as reason has decided that the time for their observance has passed, that they no longer effect their purpose, that according to the age in which we live the religious Idea, if requiring an outer covering at all, needs one of different materials, then the observance of them has forever passed, and a continuance of them is but a violation of those grand eternal principles which constitute pure Judaism."

Sacrifices, according to this bold writer, were permitted only in condescension to the barbarism of primitive tribes, and he ventures upon the tremendous audacity of saying, that even the venerated rite of circumcision must give way before advancing intelligence! He evidently regards it as the merest relic of barbarism, and speaks of the coming abrogation of all such usages as "a glorious event." Again and again he holds language like this: "Judaism is religion, and religion is life, spirit; it is neither letter nor law. The Bible is the word of God only when it is construed from its spiritual signification. There is nothing supernatural about the Bible. It is not a revelation of God's will imparted to any certain man under mysterious circumstances, nor is it a direct communication from God to man. It is a book, and only a book; a book written by mortal hands, a book containing ideas, sentiments, and doctrines emanating from the brain of man." But, he adds, although the Bible is man's work, wherever in it the true spirit of religion is expressed, there, but only there, is it "the true inspired word of God."

Few of our Israelitish brethren are yet prepared to receive such advanced heresy as this. Perhaps one third of all the Jews in the United States are still orthodox; another third neglect religion except on the greatest days of the religious year, and are indifferent on the disputed questions; another third are in various stages of Reform, a few even going beyond Mr. Lewin. A very small number, both in Germany and America, are prepared, for reasons of convenience, to adopt the first day of the week instead of their Sabbath. They say truly that the essential thing is to rescue *a* day from business for the higher interests of man; and, that great boon being secured, the only other point of importance is, that we should all have the same day. This idea, however, is held in aversion by a vast majority of the Jewish people, and it will be many years in making its way to general acceptance. Meanwhile they employ our Sunday in holding their religious schools and in transacting the business of synagogue and charity.

The difference of opinion between the Orthodox and the Reformed does not create visible division among them, because the Jews are congregationalists. Each synagogue is independent in all respects. There is no ecclesiastical body nor Chief Rabbi in the United States, to interfere in the concerns, to criticise the ritual, or censure the belief of any congregation. If a congregation is in need of a minister, a preacher, a reader, a sexton, it simply advertises for one, stating the salary to be given, and usually whether the congregation is Orthodox or Reformed. In almost any of our Jewish papers we can find a long string of advertisements like the following: —

WANTED. — The Cong. *Anshe Chesed*, of this city, desire to engage a minister for the term of five years from August next, at the yearly salary of three thousand dollars. He is expected to deliver sermons in German, and to superintend the congregational school.

Applications and testimonials to be handed in before the 8th of April next.

THE Congregation *Anshe Chesed*, of Vicksburg, Miss., desire to engage a gentleman to take charge of their new temple. It is requisite that he be able to lecture in the English as well as in the German language, and perform the functions of Chazan, leader and instructor of a choir.

A salary of $ 3,000 per annum will be paid.

Competent men are invited to correspond with the undersigned on the subject, and enclose references and testimonials.

TO CONGREGATIONS. — A gentleman, who has for a number of years filled the position of Chazan, Baal Korah, and teacher of Hebrew and German in a rather large congregation, but on account of religious principles has given up his situation, is anxious to meet with a similar position in an Orthodox congregation, in either city or country. He is a well-qualified Shochet and practical Mohel,* and, though not a professional preacher, able to lecture in both German and English languages.

The best of references can be given.

* Circumciser.

WANTED. — A CHAZAN and SHOCHET (Orthodox) by Congregation K. Keneseth Israel, of Richmond, Va., within sixty days from date. Salary, $1,000. Applicants must have the best of recommendations, and must be able to deliver a discourse. No travelling expenses allowed.

WANTED. — A SHOCHET and CHAZAN (Orthodox) by the Congregation Beth Ee, of Buffalo, N. Y. Election to take place Sunday in Chalamood Pesach (April). Applicants must have the best of recommendations. No travelling expenses allowed.

In every congregation there is, of course, a party inclined to reform, and a party of sticklers for "the good old ways of our fathers." The occasional election of a minister furnishes an opportunity for measuring the strength of the two; and each member has always the resource of joining another congregation more in accord with his own disposition. Nor can there be very bitter contentions in a religious body that never thinks of winning proselytes, and has only a faint and vague belief in retribution beyond the grave. Among the thirty-two congregations in New York, the two most conspicuous represent the extremes of Orthodoxy and Reform, but there appears to be good-will between them, and they unite in the support of charitable institutions.

The most costly and picturesque edifice in the Fifth Avenue, New York, if we except the unfinished Roman Catholic cathedral, is the new Temple Immanuel, belonging to a reformed congregation. The interior, which is bright with gilding and many-hued fresco, is arranged so much like one of our churches that no one would suspect its Oriental character. Men and women sit together; the men are uncovered and wear no scarf; there is an organ; the Saturday morning service lasts but two hours; some of the prayers are read in English, others in German, others in Hebrew; the scroll of the Law is solemnly taken from the ark, laid upon the desk and a portion read, but it is not elevated; and there is always a sermon, one week by the minister, Dr. Adler, in German, and the next, by the English preacher, Dr. Gutheim, in English. The service, in general, is extremely like that of the Episcopal church when the prayers are intoned and the psalms and responses are chanted. A stranger coming in by chance, and seeing the reader, the minister, and the English preacher dressed in ample gowns of black silk and wearing university caps, might suppose he had strayed into an Episcopal church where three professors from Oxford were conducting the service in a style recently introduced in England, but not yet known in America.

The Sunday school of this spacious and magnificent temple exhibits two novelties worthy of consideration: 1. Every class has its own room; 2. The teachers are *paid* at the rate of five dollars for each Sunday. Instead, therefore, of the Sunday school presenting a scene of chaos with Babel accompaniment, it is as quiet, efficient, and orderly as a well-arranged week-day school. At ten, the pupils assemble in a large room in the basement of the temple. The stroke of a bell calls them to order; one of the pupils — perhaps a little girl — is called to the platform, and the school rises and remains standing, while she says a very short prayer; all responding with a loud AMEN! When the school is seated again, another child is invited to the piano, and, as she plays a lively march, the classes, each in its turn, march to their rooms, where they remain two hours under instruction; at noon they march back to the music of the piano, into the large apartment, where another little prayer is said by one of the children, a hymn is sung, and the school is dismissed.

To an outside barbarian it is sorrowful to see such bright young intelligences fed upon lists of ancient kings, Hebrew roots, and innutritious catechism; but we have to steel ourselves against emotions of that kind whenever we look upon such a gathering. The world is full of minds whose growth was early arrested by mere lack of nutrition.

In all New York there is no ecclesiastical establishment more vigorously alive than this Temple Immanuel. Free from debt, and even possessing a handsome surplus in the form of unsold pews, it expends annually about forty thousand dollars in salaries, repairs, and insurance, and gives away an average of thirty thousand dollars in charity. On one occasion recently it raised sixteen thousand dollars for a hospital, to which patients of all religions or of none are equally welcome. In this congregation, as in all others, there are societies for ministering to the sick, burying the dead, assisting the poor, and aiding oppressed Israelites in other lands. The ancient festivals are not neglected; but if you converse much with the fathers and mothers, you will suspect that the day of the year which really interests and kindles the people most is the one on which, in the presence of the greatest congregation of the year, the children are confirmed.

The Jews are happy in the United States. There are now two hundred congregations of them here, half of whom have arrived within the last twelve years. They are good citizens, firmly attached to those liberal principles to which they owe their deliverance from degrading and oppressive laws, and are rising in the esteem of the people among whom they dwell. Their attachment to the system of universal education is hereditary; it dates back three thousand years; and though their religious feelings are wounded by the opening exercises of many public schools, they would not for that reason destroy them. They prefer rather to rally warmly to their support, trusting to the magnanimity and growing good sense of their fellow-citizens to spare their children, at length, the pain of taking part in exercises which they regard as idolatrous. For this they are willing to wait. They hope, also, to see the day when the thanksgiving proclamations of governors and presidents will be so worded that they, too, can comply with them; though of late they have viewed with needless alarm the attempts, on the part of a few well-intentioned persons, to break the silence of the Constitution respecting religion.

Our Israelitish brethren object, and with reason, to a thoughtless habit of some reporters in speaking of a person arrested for an infamous crime as "a Jew." They say that, before the law, Jews are citizens merely; the word *Jew* being now descriptive, not of their nationality, but of their religion. Why not, they ask, report that Patrick O'Mulligan, a Roman Catholic, was arrested for drunkenness, or John Smith, a Presbyterian, was tried for forgery?

But nothing irritates this good-tempered people so much as the societies maintained for the purpose of converting them to the faith which for so many centuries made their lives shameful and bitter. Amiable as they are, they really resent this effort with some warmth. They point with derision to the fact that the society in London expends fifty thousand pounds sterling per annum in converting a dozen or two poverty-stricken wretches, and sending abroad, on highly interesting tours, a few plausible renegades. The very organ of this society confesses that poor Jews in London are morally superior to poor Christians. "As to their moral qualities," says the editor of Jewish Intelligence, in the number for November, 1862, "the evidence seems to show that the lower class of Jews are *decidedly superior* to the same class among ourselves. They are far less given to drinking; their religious customs enforce a certain amount of cleanliness, both personal and in their dwellings; and two families are never found inhabiting the same apartment!" We can hardly be surprised at the Jews for regarding the maintenance of such societies as a standing menace and insult. Fifty thousand pounds a year, drawn from the limited benevolence fund of Christendom, is too much to waste upon such missionaries as write the reports in the magazine of the London Society for converting the Jews.

Our Israelitish brethren in the United States have their own battle to fight. It is substantially the same as ours. They, too, have to deal with overwhelming masses of ignorance and poverty, just able to get across the ocean, and arriving helpless at Castle Garden. They, too, have to save morality, decency, civilization, while the old bondage of doctrine and habit is gradually loosened. In this struggle Jews and Christians should be allies; and allies are equals.

THE CORRESPONDENCE OF NAPOLEON BONAPARTE.*

MR. BENJAMIN DISRAELI won many friends, and softened the animosity of some enemies, by a sentence in the Preface to his edition of his father's writings: "My father was wont to say, that the best monument to an author was a good edition of his works; it is my purpose that he should possess this memorial." The pious intention was worthily executed, and the edition will remain, as long as men care for curious odds and ends of knowledge, a monument both to father and son.

The Bonapartes owed such a tribute to the memory of the head of their family; for, however the account may finally stand between Napoleon Bonaparte and mankind, no one can deny that to him his relations owe the whole of their importance in the world. He was ever mindful of what is due to kindred; he was fatally generous to his family; and it was not for them to regard his fame merely as part of *their* inheritance, to be expended or husbanded according to their convenience or caprice. Moreover, a good and complete edition of the writings of Napoleon Bonaparte — who was at least the consummate specimen of his kind of man, and as such worthy of attentive study — would have been a boon so precious and interesting, that it would have atoned for much which his present representatives have done amiss. The work would have been dearly purchased, but it would have remained a solid addition to our means of knowing one another.

In the issue of costly works there is usually, in these times, a publisher and an editor; and few literary workmen

* Correspondance de Napoléon 1er, publiée par Ordre de l'Empereur Napoléon III. Paris. 1858–1869.

have been so blessed in their career as not to know what it is to have, in the back office, veiled from the general view, a timid or an embarrassed publisher, who shrinks from liberal expenditure and trembles when one subscriber writes a fault-finding letter. The editor of this collection is Prince Jerome, who was aided by a corps of assistants. These gentlemen appear to have done their work with fidelity, giving the text with exactness, and avoiding all elucidation except such as they alone possessed the means of affording. The copy before us, which was sent for in the ordinary way, contains a large number of minute corrections with the pen, and there are many other indications, too trifling for mention, tending to show that the editors have done their duty as well as they were permitted to do it.

But they had a publisher, that "half-scared literary man," who is called Napoleon III. He appears to have bothered the zealous but irresponsible editors extremely. *They* had no throne to lose, no necks in danger of the guillotine. The issue of the letters, which was begun in 1858, came to an abrupt conclusion in 1869, with the publication of volume twenty-eighth, which is only half as thick as the others. The twenty-seventh volume fell short a hundred and twenty pages, but the twenty-eighth is so thin as to destroy the uniformity of the set, and gives a rather ridiculous dwindling appearance to it, not without significance to the minds of the Irreconcilables. The last utterance of Napoleon given in this collection is the famous Protest, dated August 4, 1815, written on board the Bellerophon, against his detention as a captive by the British government. But we learn from a "Report to the Emperor," prefixed to volume twentieth, that as late as 1867 Prince Jerome expected and intended to include the letters and documents dictated at St. Helena. He had calculated that the productions of the Emperor in exile "would form only three or four volumes," which would be given to the world by the end of the year 1869. But they did not appear. After a pause of some months, a New Series is announced, to consist only of the letters written in exile, and these volumes are now issuing.* We shall not wait for them, however; for, besides the fact that we do not need more material for our purpose, there is no knowing what

* June, 1870.

other change of plan may occur in the councils of a family now more than "half-scared."

The publisher has unmercifully scrimped the editors in point of expenditure; for not only is the paper cheap and fluffy, but the publication has been continually retarded by want of money. "If," explains Prince Jerome, "our task has not proceeded more rapidly, it is because we believed it our duty to institute researches in the archives of Germany, England, Spain, Italy, Portugal. These researches, little as they have cost, have so lessened the fund at our disposal, that we have found it out of our power to bear the expense of printing a greater number of volumes without going beyond our allowance. . . . . The time afforded us by the slenderness of our resources we have turned to account in examining documents beyond the period reached in the volumes given to the printer, thus diminishing our general expenditures." One toilet the less in a week for Eugénie would have relieved the editor's embarrassment.

In all these volumes, though they average more than six hundred pages each, and contain twenty-two thousand and sixty-seven letters and documents, there is revealed no fact so remarkable as the one intimated in the passage just quoted, namely, that the letters of Napoleon Bonaparte, published by his family half a century after his death, in twenty-eight volumes, sold at seven francs a volume, did not pay expenses! Little as our grandfathers, who saw him at the summit of his power, the terror of the world and the delirium of France, may have believed in the duration of his throne, few among them would have hazarded the prediction that the mere curiosity of the world with regard to him would have so nearly died out in fifty years. These volumes, whatever their defects and omissions may be, do really admit the reader behind the scenes of the most startling, rapid, and tremendous melodrama ever played with real fire and real cannon, real kings and real emperors' daughters; and yet they do not sell, and we find the custodians of some of our most important libraries hesitating whether it is worth while to add them to their store. This is the more strange from the evident intention of the persons interested to publish the work on strict business principles. It is cheaply edited; it is sold at a fair booksellers' price; and the public are twice notified in each volume that the rights of translation and of republication are reserved, or that every one infringing will be prosecuted. Carlyle has lived to see his prediction of forty years ago fulfilled in good part: "The time may come when Napoleon himself will be better known for his laws than for his battles, and the victory of Waterloo prove less momentous than the opening of the first Mechanics' Institute." This was a bold remark to utter in 1829, under the very nose of Wellington. How commonplace it seems in 1870! The prophecy would have been already fulfilled to the letter, if it had read thus: "The time may come when Napoleon himself will be more esteemed for his laws than for his battles, and the victory of Waterloo prove less momentous than the founding of the first Workingmen's Protective Union."

There is, very naturally, a distrust of this publication in France. Frenchmen know very well who the publisher in the back office is; what he is; what his motive was in issuing the work; and whether he would be likely to give the world a sight of a document calculated to weaken the spell of Napoleon's name in France. People of our race, we think, need not share this distrust: for the family concerned in publishing the correspondence of Napoleon, much as they might wish and intend to make his fame subservient to their interests, would not know how to present him in the most favorable light to the outside world. They would be as likely to suppress passages honorable to him as passages dishonorable. They would be likely to glory in some letters that would offend an American, English, or German reader. When a whole family have been eating garlic, they may gather after dinner about the head of the house, and the children may climb into his lap, and hug him close around the neck, and none of them will be able to discover anything wrong in his breath. To *us* these volumes exhibit the man, Napoleon Bonaparte. *We* may believe Prince Jerome when he says: "Let your Majesty be pleased to remark to what a proof we submit the memory of Napoleon I. We place in the clearest light all the acts of his government; we reveal the secret of his inmost thoughts. . . . . We have faith in the public reason." Doubtless the editor felt himself justified in commending the work to "the judgment of enlightened men" as a "loyal publication."

Certainly there is enough of detail and minutiæ to satisfy the most ravenous collector. Letter No. 8089, addressed to Berthier, is to this effect : "My cousin, the words of my writing which you cannot make out are *bataillon d'élite suisse.*" No. 20093, to the Empress Marie Louise, is : "Madame and dear Friend, I have received the letter in which you say that you received the Archchancellor in bed. It is my desire that, in no circumstances and under no pretext, you receive any one in bed, whosoever he may be. It is not permitted to a woman under thirty." No. 21591, written at Elba, to an officer of the household : "I think it will be necessary for all the books asked for Leghorn to be rebound. Order that, if possible, an N shall be put upon each." There are hundreds of notes as brief and trivial as these, as well as a vast number of the answers scrawled upon the notes of ministers submitting minor questions of administration to the master. Napoleon Bonaparte is within the covers of these volumes, and he can be extracted from them by those who will take the trouble.

Upon turning over the first volume, — which begins with the siege of Toulon and includes the conquest of Italy, — we are struck at once with the maturity of mind and character exhibited by the artillery officer of twenty-four. He seems to have been completely formed before he had held a command. He never equalled, as Emperor, the exploits of the young general. We see in his earliest letters every trait that distinguished him afterwards, and we see him also employing the methods and devices which marked his policy when he gave laws to a continent. These first letters give the impression that at twenty-four he could have fought Austerlitz as well as he did at thirty-five, and Waterloo better than at forty-six. The *young* man is betrayed, here and there, by a tendency to moralize, and a habit of uttering neat generalities, such as: "It is artillery that takes places, — infantry can only help"; or, "Three fourths of men occupy themselves with necessary things only when they feel the need of them"; or, "In artillery, the most difficult operation is the formation of a siege-train." But, generally speaking, the mature Napoleon is exhibited, and the whole of his career is foreshadowed in the few letters relating to his capture of Toulon in 1793. We see in them, what we see in all his military achievements, first, that the sure way of doing the thing was revealed to him at a glance; that that sure way was so simple that, when pointed out, every man not an absolute fool saw it as plainly as he did, and wondered why no one had thought of it before; that then he executed his plan with the precision of mathematics; and, finally, that he knew how to relate what he had done so as to intoxicate Frenchmen, and concentrate their admiration on himself. He had no sooner surveyed the situation at Toulon, than he perceived a point from which a few pieces of cannon could force the English fleet from the roads. But there were no cannon at command. Then he writes clear, masterly letters to the government, begging cannon. After two months of letter-writing and intense effort in camp, the cannon are placed in position, and all falls out exactly as the young officer had predicted.

From that time, by the mere natural ascendency of genius over ordinary mortals, Napoleon Bonaparte was the ruling mind of the French Republic. Sitting quietly at his desk in a government office in Paris, he evidently provided the Committee of Public Safety with whatever they had of continental policy and administrative skill. He suggested their plans; he wrote their important letters; he gave away some of their good places. Already he had acquired the habit of surveying the whole scene of European politics, and of seeking vulnerable points in the enemies' line at a great distance from the actual seat of war. Just as the Emperor fought England in Spain and Russia, so now the officer of artillery proposed to make a diversion in favor of beleaguered France by going to Constantinople and rousing Turkey to arms against allied Russia and Austria. Before he had suppressed the riots in Paris in 1795, before he had held an independent command of any kind, before his name was generally known in France, he could write to his brother Joseph: "I am attached at this moment to the Topographical Bureau of the Committee of Public Safety. . . . . If I ask it, I shall be despatched to Turkey as General of Artillery, sent by the government to organize the artillery of the Grand Seigneur, with a handsome allowance and a very flattering title of envoy. I shall name you consul, and Villeneuve engineer, to go with me." And in the same note, he tells his brother that he is charged by the committee with the direction of the armies and the formation of plans of campaign. Who governs a country in time of war, if not he who suggests its foreign policy and devises its plans of campaign?

These letters, written before his fame existed, show him to us in a light wholly amiable and admirable. He is in love with Josephine, and tells Joseph that it is not impossible "the folly may seize him to marry," and asks his brother's advice. The following passage, written to Joseph in September, 1795, a month before the "whiff of grapeshot" from General Bonaparte's field guns terminated the Revolution, is a pleasing specimen of his family epistles of the time. He is looking out for a good post for Joseph: "I shall remain in Paris specially for your affair. You ought not, whatever happens, to fear for me. I have for friends all the people of worth, of whatever party or opinion they may be. Mariette" (conservative member of the Committee of Safety) "is extremely zealous for me; you know his opinion. Doulcet" (member of the convention of moderate politics) "I am closely allied with. You know my other friends of opposite views. . . . . I am content with (brother) Louis. He fulfils my hope, and the expectation I had formed of him. He is a good fellow; but, at the same time, one after my own heart; warmth, intelligence, health, talent, straightforwardness, good-nature, — all are united in him. You know, my dear brother, that I live only by the pleasure I give my relations. If my hopes are seconded by that good fortune *which never abandons me in my enterprises*, I shall be able to make you happy, and fulfil your desires. . . . . To-morrow I shall have three horses, which will permit me to ride a little in a cab, and enable me to attend to all my affairs. Adieu, my dear fellow; amuse yourself; all goes well; be gay. Think of my affair, for I long to have a house of my own."

All his letters to Joseph at this happy, hopeful time are in the same tone. He appears in them the virtuous young man, distinguished in his profession, honestly in love, and looking forward to the possession of a home, devoted to his brothers and sisters, and striving to benefit them, writing to Joseph his oldest brother every day, the life, stay, and boast of his family. He was a good Republican, too, although of the more conservative wing. "The government," he writes to Joseph, September 12, 1795, "is to be organized at once; a tranquil day dawns upon the destinies of France. *There is a primary assembly which has asked for a king. That has provoked laughter.*" Doubtless he joined in the laughter; for, so far as we can judge from his letters, he heartily accepted the Revolution, and valued himself upon his political orthodoxy. "Passions are inflamed," he wrote a few days after; "the moment appears critical; but the genius of liberty never abandons its defenders. All our armies triumph."

When next he wrote to the head of the family, it was to announce to him the event which put him directly upon the road to his great fortune, — the dispersion of the mob at the Tuileries, October 6, 1795. "At length," he began, "all is finished; my first thought is to give you the news." The brief note ends: "We have disarmed the sections, and all is calm. As usual, I have not a scratch." Five months after, we find him on the same day announcing his marriage to the Directory, and setting off to take command of the French army in the native land of his ancestors, Italy.

Persons who remain during long periods of time the idols of a multitude usually possess, along with other gifts, a keen eye for effect, a histrionic talent which enables them, in a pleasing and striking manner, to exhibit and exaggerate their own good qualities. This wonderful being was not a hypocrite: nor, at this part of his career, was he, in any vulgar sense, an actor; but he possessed naturally an acute sense of the decorous and the becoming; and now, on his way to Italy, he gave a proof of it. The earliest letter of his which we have seen in print is one written to his mother, when he was a boy of sixteen; and it is signed, "Napoleone di Buonaparte." Just before leaving Paris for Italy he signed his marriage contract with Josephine, in the presence of a notary, thus: "Napolione Buonaparte"; and his previous letters in this collection are all signed in the Italian form, "Buonaparte." But now, being at Toulon within a few miles of the beautiful land of his fathers, which he was about to overrun and pillage, he appears to have awakened to the impropriety of spoiling Italy while bearing an Italian name. At Toulon, for the first time in his public career, he spells his name "Bonaparte"; a form from which he never after departed. It is significant, that the very page which shows this new spelling contains the proclamation offering fair Italy to the hunger and rapacity of French troops: "Soldiers: You are naked, ill-fed. The government owes you much, it can give you nothing. The patience, the courage you have shown in the midst of these rocks are admirable; but they procure you no glory: no lustre from them is reflected upon you. I desire to lead you into the most fertile plains of the world. Wealthy provinces, great cities, will be in your power. You will find in them honor, glory, riches. Soldiers of Italy, will you be wanting in courage or in constancy?" Certainly we must approve the taste of a man of Italian lineage in Frenchifying his name a little before issuing such a proclamation.

With regard to those Italian campaigns, to which the first three volumes of this work are chiefly devoted, the correspondence of the commanding general confirms what military men have often remarked, that they were Napoleon's greatest. The dash, the brilliancy, the rapidity of his operations are less apparent when the mind is detained by fifteen hundred pages of orders, letters, and documents; but we see more clearly than ever what a master of his art he was. In fifteen days after setting foot upon Italian soil he had given the world assurance of a general. There was then in Europe no general but himself, and nothing remained but for him to continue his method until the continent was his own. A great artist is not apt to talk much about the processes by which he produces his great effects, and, accordingly, there are not many passages in these letters upon the art of winning victories. The reader can see Napoleon winning them; but it is only at long intervals that we meet a sentence that betrays the master's method. One such as this: "The enemy, in the Austrian manner, will make three attacks; by the Levante, by Novi, and by Montenotte: refuse two of those attacks, and direct all your forces upon the third." This is another: "In military operations, hours decide success and campaigns." This is another: "One bad general is better than two good ones. War, like government, is an affair of tact." And this another: "If the English attack you, and you experience vicissitudes, always bear in mind these three things: reunion of forces, activity, and firm resolution to perish with glory. These are the three great principles of the military art which have rendered fortune favorable to me in all my operations. Death is nothing; but to live vanquished and without glory is to die every day." In the spirit of this last passage his Italian campaigns were conducted; especially when, after a long series of triumphs, his lines were broken and his hold upon Italy endangered. The celerity with which his scattered forces were reunited and hurled upon the enemy, and the personal daring of the young general, restored his fortunes before the news of his disaster had crossed the Alps. For the benefit of young soldiers, however, who may think that victories can be won by following maxims, we must add one of Napoleon's own comments upon the general opposed to him in Italy: "He has the audacity of fury, not that of genius."

It was in Italy that General Bonaparte exhibited his talents and revealed his moral defects. We have seen that he roused his ragged and hungry soldiers by appealing to their vanity, appetite, and avarice. They took him at his word. No sooner had he given them victory in the wealthy provinces of Italy, and possession of some of its rich towns, than they proceeded to do precisely what he had invited them to do. "The soldier without bread," he writes, a few days after entering Italy, "yields to such excesses of fury as make me blush to be a man. . . . . I am going to make some terrible examples. I shall restore order, or I shall cease to command these brigands. . . . . To-morrow we shoot some soldiers and a corporal who stole vases from a church." When next he addressed his soldiers, he began by recounting to them, that in fifteen days they had won six victories, taken twenty-one flags and fifty-five cannons, conquered the best part of Piedmont, captured fifteen thousand prisoners, and killed or wounded ten thousand men; but he ended by saying: "I shall not permit brigands to soil our laurels. . . . . Pillagers shall be shot without mercy; several have been already." And he assured the people of Italy, in the same proclamation, that the French army had come only to break their chains; that the French were friends of every people; and that their *property*, their religion, and their usages should be respected. "We make war as generous enemies; hostile only to the tyrants who abase you."

All of which signified that General Bonaparte meant to have an army, instead of a horde of robbers, and that he reserved to himself the right to plunder.

Probably no revelation of these volumes will more surprise the general reader than the prodigious extent of his spoliation of the "property" of his countrymen in Italy; especially that portion of their property which the world regards as sacred, and which really was and is most *proper* to that beautiful land, — pictures, statuary, and other treasures of art. That the kingdoms, states, and cities of conquered Italy should be laid under contribution and compelled to disgorge, each its proportion of millions, was to have been expected; at least, might have been forgiven. But the reader of the correspondence feels that in that wholesale picture-stealing Bonaparte fell far below the natural level of his character. It might have been pardoned in a Masséna, but it was infinitely beneath Napoleon Bonaparte, — the man of intellect and breeding, whose ancestors had contributed something to what constitutes the sole glory of modern Italy, its art and literature. He knew better; for at Milan the young conqueror had written to an astronomer of the university: "The sciences which honor the human mind, the arts that embellish life and transmit great deeds to posterity, ought to be especially honored by free governments. All men of genius, all those who have obtained an eminent rank in the republic of letters, *are Frenchmen*, in whatever country they may have been born." When these brave words were penned he had already sent to Paris for a corps of artists to come and select the works of art best worth stealing.

From the mass of letters relating to the systematic plunder of Italy we select a few sentences showing how General Bonaparte squeezed the Pope. We copy from the Armistice of June 6, 1796, only premising that the Pope fared no worse than his neighbors: "Art. 8. The Pope will deliver to the French Republic one hundred pictures, vases, or statues, to be chosen by the commissioners who will be sent to Rome; among which will be comprised, for certain, the bronze bust of Junius Brutus and the one in marble of Marcus Brutus, both from the Capitol; and five hundred manuscripts, at the choice of the commissioners. Art. 9. The Pope will pay to the French Republic twenty-one millions of francs, ... independent of the contributions which will be raised in Bologna, Ferrara, and Faenza." This large sum was to be all paid in three months. Nor did the conqueror remain content with the hundred works of art demanded in the Armistice. We find at the end of volume third of the correspondence a catalogue, drawn up in form and signed by the French commissioners, of the works of art selected by them at Rome, and sent to Paris "in the year VI. of the French Republic one and indivisible," which we style 1797. The list comprises about eight hundred objects; among which are six colossal statues and six groups of statuary. The rest are statues, busts, fragments, bronzes, medallions, and vases. The readers of this interesting catalogue may be excused for not comprehending what such spoliation of Roman churches and galleries had in common with delivering Italy from its tyrants. The tyrants were squeezed and left; it was the works of art from which Italy was delivered.

At a later period of the negotiations we observe that the insatiable conqueror demanded more of the precious manuscripts of the Vatican than the number named in the Article. In recounting to the Directory the treasures extracted from the Papal dominions he remarks: "The Papal commissioners yielded with a good grace everything except the manuscripts, which they were unwilling to give up; and we have had to reduce our demand from two or three thousand to five hundred." His letter to the Directory (No. 685, Vol. I. p. 431), in which he exults over the plunder of the Pope, is more bandit-like than any other in the collection. We learn from it that, besides the works of art already mentioned, and besides retaining some of the Pope's best provinces, he obtained from him in all thirty-four million seven hundred thousand francs. He also informs the Directory that he would have wrung from him a few millions more, if he had not been interfered with by *their* commissioners. "I am *consoled*," he adds, "by the fact that what we have got surpasses the terms of your instructions."

Was there ever such a godsend to an unpopular government as this young general was to the Directory of 1796? Victory alone would have sufficed, but here was a general, who, besides sending home the most thrilling bulletins, kept consigning to a drained treasury whole wagon-trains of wealth. "Twenty-four wagon-loads," he wrote from Bologna in July, 1796, "of hemp and silk set out to-day for Nice. .... I am getting together at Tortona all the silver plate and jewels, which I shall send to Paris by Chambéry. I hope that convoy alone will be worth five or six millions. I shall add as much in money." But what should he do with the plunder of Rome? "The statues can only be transported by sea, and it would be imprudent to trust them that way. We must box them up, then, and leave them at Rome."

The Pope, we repeat, fared no worse than the other princes of Italy. From Milan an amazing booty was sent to Paris; the first instalment being, as the General remarked, "twenty superb pictures, chief of which is the celebrated St. Jerome of Correggio, which has been sold, they tell me, for two hundred thousand francs." Another item — again to translate from the General's joyous despatch — was "two millions in jewelry and ingots, the proceeds of different contributions." Other letters announce to the Directory the coming of rare plants from the public gardens of Italy, of a fine collection of serpents from a museum, and other natural curiosities. He is so considerate as to send them "a hundred of the finest carriage horses of Lombardy," to replace "the ordinary horses that draw your carriages." But enough of larceny, grand and petit. Let us come to the volumes which show how kingdoms were stolen, and how poor France was kept reeling drunk while her life-blood was drained.

At St. Helena, in conversation with the companions of his exile, Napoleon designated the moment when he first felt the stirrings of lawless ambition. "It was not till after Lodi," he said, "that I was struck with the possibility of my becoming a decided actor on the scene of political events.

Then was enkindled the first spark of a lofty ambition." Having a lively recollection of this sentence, which we read long ago in Mr. Abbott's entertaining volume upon Napoleon at St. Helena, we had the curiosity to turn to the letters written by General Bonaparte at the time, to see if there was anything in them to confirm his statement. Yes: just after Lodi, for the first time he begins to protest and swear that his only ambition is to serve France in any capacity which the Directory may be pleased to assign him. Five days after his troops had given him, at the bridge of Lodi, that surprising proof of devotion, he writes to his patron, Carnot: "Whether I make war here or elsewhere is indifferent to me. To serve my country, to deserve from posterity one leaf of our history, to give the government proofs of my attachment and devotion, — this is all my ambition." It is a touch worthy of Shakespeare. Thus might the great dramatist have indicated the birth of an ambition.

It was after Lodi, too, that he showed his eager promptitude to reward those who served him, and his tact in adapting the reward to the nature of the case. The battle of Lodi was won by the column that rushed across the bridge in the face of thirty pieces of cannon and the fire of infantry. The General caused a printed list of the names of the men composing the column to be posted in every district of France where any one of them resided! Could any reward have been more thrilling to the men or more promotive of the next conscription? At a later day it became a custom with him to have such lists posted upon the parish churches of the soldiers whom he desired to honor. But when once a priest presumed to read the list to his parishioners *in* the church, the master wrote from Vienna to the minister of police to forbid the repetition of the act; because, said he, in substance, if priests may announce victories, they may comment upon them, and if bad news should arrive, they may comment upon that. "Priests must be used with civility, but not made too much of."

From Italy the young conqueror, after a short interval of busy preparation at Paris, betakes himself to Egypt, in pursuance of his policy of striking England through her dependencies and allies. No one, with this correspondence before him, can say that he was *sent* to Egypt by the Directory, in order to get him out of the way. It was his own conception. He was master of France almost as much in 1798 as he was in 1805; and the tone of his letters in 1798 is as much the tone of the master as in 1805. The very order assigning him to the command of the army destined for Egypt was penned by himself; and in preparing the expedition, the Directory did nothing but sign what he dictated. His object was to dispossess the English of their Indian empire, using Egypt as a base of operations; and he spoke of the enterprise, in a confidential letter, as "the greatest ever executed among men." Only it was not "executed!" Nelson destroyed the French fleet at the battle of the Nile, and blockaded Egypt with such sleepless vigilance that General Bonaparte and his army were, in effect, prisoners of war. The General himself informed the Directory that, during the eighteen months of his residence in Egypt, he only heard from Paris once; and then he received part of his despatches, snatched by the courier from his grounded boat a moment before his English pursuers clutched it. It was an error to land a French army in Egypt while the English were masters of the sea; but it is evident from the correspondence that General Bonaparte really believed the French fleet a match for the English. He was not aware that in Horatio Nelson the English possessed an admiral who trebled the force of every fleet that he commanded.

The correspondence, reticent as it is concerning whatever tends to exhibit Napoleon vulnerable, shows plainly enough that it was Nelson who destroyed him. Nelson hit him two blows, — Nile and Trafalgar. By the battle of the Nile he penned him in Egypt, killed his Indian projects, and reduced him to absolute paralysis for a year and a half. By Trafalgar he again destroyed the French naval power, made invasion of England impossible, and compelled Napoleon to continue his policy of fighting England upon the territories of her allies. In other words, he penned him in the continent of Europe. This led to that prodigious extension of his operations, until he had vast armies in Spain, Italy, Prussia, Russia, and France, and had so distended his "empire," that ten cold nights in

Russia at the time when his power seemed greatest caused his ruin. This was Nelson's work, and well Napoleon knew it; for there is not in all these volumes one allusion to the battle of Trafalgar. It is a telltale silence. Amid the bulletins of Austerlitz, few except the master knew what had happened upon the ocean; and except himself perhaps no one comprehended its importance.

But to glean a trait or two from the Egyptian letters. The mighty man of war, it seems, was subject to sea-sickness. "Have a good bed prepared for me," he writes to Admiral Brueys before leaving Paris, "as for a man who will be sick during the whole passage." In Egypt, where he was absolute master, he had an opportunity to rehearse the drama of the French Empire, and he displayed all the devices of the emperor which the scene admitted. Despising all religions, he showed that he could flatter, use, and laugh at any religion that chanced to be available for his purpose. At Malta, on his way to Egypt, wishing to employ the bishop to conciliate the people of the island, he wrote to him: "I know of no character more respectable or more worthy of the veneration of men, than a priest who, full of the true spirit of the Gospel, is persuaded that it is his duty to obey the temporal power, and to maintain peace, tranquillity, and union in the midst of his diocese." A few days after he issued to his troops the proclamation in which he enjoined them to pay respect to "the Egyptian Muftis and Imams, as you have to rabbis and bishops." He continued thus: "Show the same tolerance for the ceremonies prescribed by the Koran as you have for convents, for synagogues, for the religion of Moses and of Jesus Christ. The Roman legions protected all religions." He went himself far beyond the letter of this order; for he celebrated the religious festivals of the Mohammedans with all the emphasis and splendor possible in the circumstances. From Cairo he wrote to one of his generals: "We celebrated here the feast of the Prophet with a pomp and fervor which have almost merited for me the title of Saint"; and he ordered commanders of ports and garrisons to do the same.

In Egypt, as in Italy, he would permit no one to plunder but himself; and it was here that he put in practice the only device for preventing pillage which has ever answered its purpose. It consisted in holding each division of an army responsible for the misconduct of the individuals composing it. A theft or an act of violence having been committed, the perpetrators, if discovered, were to make good the damage, or pay the forfeit with their lives. If they were not discovered, then their company was assessed to make up the amount. If the company could not be ascertained, then the regiment, brigade, or division. This was a masterly device, and it has become part of the military code of nations. But the plunder of Egypt, on system, by the orders of the General commanding, was great and continuous; for the French army, severed from the world without, had no resource but to subsist upon the fertile province upon which it had descended. It will not exalt the world's opinion of the Commanding General to discover, in his correspondence, such notes as the following: "Citizen Poussielgue, General Dumas" (father of the novelist) "knows the house of a bey where there is a buried treasure. Arrange with him for the digging necessary to find it." Another engaging epistle begins thus: "You did well, citizen general, in having the five villagers shot who revolted. I desire much to learn that you have mounted your cavalry. The shortest way, I believe, will be this: Order each village to furnish you two good horses. Do not accept any bad ones; and make the villages which do not furnish theirs in five days pay a fine of one thousand talari. This is an infallible means of having the six hundred horses you require. . . . . Demand bridles and saddles as well."

He found leisure to establish an Institute in Egypt, on the model of that of France. At the first sitting the Commanding General proposed the following questions: Are our army bread-ovens susceptible of improvement? Is there any substitute in Egypt for the hop in making beer? How is the water of the Nile cleared and kept cool? Which is best for us at Cairo, to construct water-mills or wind-mills? Can gunpowder be made in Egypt? What is the condition in Egypt of jurisprudence, the judiciary, and education, and what improvements in either are possible, and desired by the people of the country? He was making himself very much at home in Egypt, evidently meant to stay there, had sent to Paris for a troop of comedians, and was meditating vast plans for the improvement of the country.

But in August, 1799, a package of English newspapers, of which the most recent was nine weeks old, fell into the General's hands, and gave him information that made him willing to risk capture in order to get to France: Italy lost! The French beaten in Germany in two pitched battles, and compelled to recross the Rhine! The Russians marching to join the coalition! The English blockading every port, and lording it on every sea! The Directory distrusted, inactive, imbecile! France beleaguered on every side, and threatened with dissolution! His mind was made up on the instant. In eleven days he was ready to go. His paper of secret instructions to Kleber, whom he left in command, betrays his perfect satisfaction with what he had done in Egypt, his entire conviction of the *right* of the French to possess and hold the country. "Accustomed," he says, "to look for the reward of my pains and labors in the opinion of posterity, I abandon Egypt with the keenest regret." Another sentence is significant: "You will find subjoined a cipher for your correspondence with the government, and *another for your correspondence with me.*"

In three months General Bonaparte and the "government" were one and the same. The very company of comedians which he had written for as General Bonaparte he sent to Egypt as First Consul. He was absolute master of France, a fact which he announced to the people in the following neat and epigrammatic manner: "Citizens, the Revolution is fixed in the principles that began it. IT IS FINISHED." Yes; it was finished, and it was General Bonaparte who gave it the finishing blow. Whether he could have *saved* it can never be known, because he did not try; and his talents were so prodigious that it is impossible to say what he might or might not have done, if he had had the "lofty ambition" to help the French govern themselves. There was so much that was large and generous in this man, that we cannot always resist the impression that he was capable of something much better than the tawdry rôle into which he lapsed. But human nature is so limited a thing, that there is not room in an individual for more than one decided talent; and that talent, when it is eminent, is apt to bewilder, mislead, and dominate the possessor of it. The successes of this sublime adventurer, besides being rapid and immense, were of the very kind that most dazzle and mislead. He found France impoverished, misgoverned, anarchic, without an ally, defeated, discouraged, with powerful foes on every side, on land and sea. In two years what a change! Internal tranquillity, universal joy and exultation, enemies signally beaten, territories enlarged, the treasury replenished, and peace restored! In 1799 he might have risen to the height of the great citizen; he might have fought in the service of France, and when he had delivered her from her enemies, he might have lent his great administrative abilities to the restoration of internal peace and prosperity, without despoiling her of that hope of liberty cherished through so many years of suffering and blood. This was possible in 1799, but not in 1801.

But how marvellously well he enacted the part of the ruler of a free people! How adroitly this foreigner flattered the amiable and generous people whom he had subjugated! In announcing the peace of 1801, he played upon their vanity and their patriotism with singular skill, throwing upon *them* all the glory of his achievements in the field: "Frenchmen, you enjoy at length that entire peace which you have merited by efforts so long continued and so generous. The world contains for you only friendly nations, and upon every sea hospitable ports are open to your ships. . . . . Let us perfect, but, above all, let us teach the rising generation to cherish, our institutions and our laws. Let them grow up to promote civil equality, public liberty, national prosperity. Let us carry into the workshop, the farm, the studio, that ardor, that constancy, that patience, which have astonished Europe in all our difficulties. . . . . Let us be the support and example of the peoples who surround us. Let the foreigner, whom curiosity draws into our midst, linger among us attached by the charm of our manners, the spectacle of our union, the attraction of our pleasures; let him return to his country more friendly to us than he came, a wiser and a better man." Soon after appeared the first of his annual messages, his *Exposé de la Situation de la République*, modelled closely (as to the form only) upon the messages of our

Presidents, although longer than those of Washington, Adams, or Jefferson; — a message without a legislature which could act upon it! "It is with sweet satisfaction that the government offers to the nation a view of public affairs during the year that has passed." The government was a general of the French army, and his message was ingenious, intoxicating flattery of the most susceptible people in the world.

Was all this mere coarse, conscious hypocrisy on the part of General Bonaparte? We think not. Great histrionic personages, like Napoleon Bonaparte, appear sometimes to dazzle and deceive themselves. Men familiar with Brigham Young tell us that that stupendous American Turk is one tenth sincere; and it is the fraction of sincerity which gives him his power over his followers. There are pages in these volumes that exhibit Napoleon to us in the threefold character of hero, actor, and spectator; as though David Garrick should play Richard III., be Richard III., and see Richard III., all on the same evening; himself lost in the marvels of the scene, deceived by his own acting, and dazzled by his own exploits. We cannot believe that this delirious *Exposé* was a thing contrived to deceive and captivate the French people. He had seen such striking things done at the word of command, that he seems to have supposed all things possible to a great soldier. He appears to have thought that national institutions, industries, lyceums, colleges, universities, durable alliances, and national welfare could be summoned into being at the tap of the drum. "Thirty lyceums," said he, "wisely distributed over the territory of the Republic, will embrace all its extent by their influence, will shed upon every part of it the lustre of their acquisitions and their triumphs, will strike foreigners with admiration, and will be for them what some celebrated schools of Germany and England once were for us, what some famous universities were which, seen from a distance, commanded the admiration and respect of Europe." The whole message is in this taste. Poor man! Poor France!

The great question of the reign of Napoleon is: Which was to blame for breaking the peace of Amiens, the English government or the French? This correspondence confirms the constant assertion of French historians, that the responsibility is to be laid at England's door. Bonaparte wanted peace: that is plain. Peace was his interest: that is undeniable. England had agreed to evacuate Malta, and when the time came refused to give it up: that also is certain. England should have frankly accepted Napoleon as head of the French government, and forborne to give a pretext for breaking the peace to a man so exquisitely skilled in the use of deadly weapons. On the other hand, what absurdity more complete than for *France* to go to war with Great Britain for a little distant island in which neither of them had any rights? We cannot dwell upon this point, although there is no volume of the correspondence in which Napoleon's talents are more brilliantly exhibited than in the one which contains his letters and instructions previous to the declaration of war in 1802. He had the advantage of being technically in the right; and England labored under the disadvantage of putting forward a pretext, instead of the real grievance. Napoleon's matchless skill in the use of deadly weapons was the real grievance. The peace was broken, coalitions were formed and renewed, because four crowned persons in Europe felt that they were not safe while such a man controlled the resources and commanded the armies of France.

Behold him now at the summit of his power. The volumes devoted to this part of his career are precious to the French people at the present moment, when they are preparing to expel the Bonaparte intruders from their territory. If, on the one hand, they show him a very great general, on the other, they reveal so clearly the essential littleness of the man, and expose so fully the artifices by which he ruled, that the spell conjured up in France by his very bones twenty years ago can never be conjured up again. This publication kills Napoleonism past resurrection. It shows to an attentive reader that Napoleon's personal ambition was not "lofty," as he termed it, but personal, i. e. low and small; and that the means by which he gratified it were often base, often despicable, often ridiculous. The desire of this man's heart was to be admitted to the circle of European kings, and then to be the most powerful of them all. We could only make this clear to the reader by going carefully over the whole of his dealings with the reigning families of Europe, which would more than exhaust our space. The truth shines out in hundreds of passages, and it excludes him forever from the rank of the great, whose ambition is to become eminent by serving their kind. He was so little superior in moral discernment to the ordinary mortal, that he thought it grander to be the Frederick William of a country than its Bismarck; to be a George III. than a Nelson or a Chatham. So little had he reflected upon men and governments, that he did not know the proper place of a man of great talent; which is not at the head of a nation, but in a place subordinate.

The proper head of a nation is a sound average man,—one whom the average citizen can recognize as a man and a brother; one who will keep the brilliant minister, the great general, always in mind of the homely material with which governments have to deal; one who will embody and represent the *vis inertiæ* of things. Bismarck, firmly astride of Prussia, would ride that great kingdom to the Devil; as Bonaparte did France; as Hamilton might the United States, if average human nature had not stood in his way, represented in the august person of George Washington. It is *mankind* whom the head of a government should represent. The exceptionally gifted individual who serves under him needs his restraining slowness and caution, as much as the chief needs the light and help of minds specially endowed.

Of all this Napoleon knew nothing. His poor ambition was to *reign*. "For the Pope," said he, "I am Charlemagne, because I reunite the crown of France to that of the Lombards"; and he told his brother Joseph, when he put him up as king of Naples, that he wished his "blood" to reign in Naples as long as in France, for "the kingdom of Naples was necessary to him." It is at once ludicrous and affecting to see such a man so infatuated with the part he was playing, to read in his letters to kings, emperors, and popes such expressions as, "my house," "the princes of my house," "my capital" (meaning Paris), "my good city of Lyons," "my armies," "my fleet," "my peoples," "my empire," "my kingdom of Italy"; and to read elaborate papers rearranging states and nations in which everything was considered, except the will of the people inhabiting them.

Nothing will astound the reader of these volumes more than the bulletins, dictated by Napoleon on the field, and published in the *Moniteur* by his command. It was those bulletins that kept France in a state of delirium, and drew to distant fields of carnage the flower of her youth and the annual harvest of her educated talent. He was accustomed to send every day or two from the seat of war, when anything extraordinary had occurred, chatty, anecdotical bulletins, designed chiefly to keep up the martial frenzy of the French; but he inserted also many paragraphs intended to sow dissension among his enemies; knowing well that these documents would be closely scanned at every court, club, and head-quarters in Europe. Those anecdotes of the devotion of the troops to the Emperor, which figure in so many biographies and histories, here they are, where they originated, in the bulletins *dictated by Napoleon's mouth, corrected by his hand, and published by his command* in the official newspaper of his empire, and now given to the world as part of his *correspondence* by the head of his family! The following are passages from the Austerlitz bulletins:—

"On the 10th" (the day before the battle), "the Emperor, from the height of his bivouac, perceived, with joy unutterable, the Russians beginning, at two cannon fires' distance from his advanced posts, a flank movement to turn his right. Then was it that he saw to what a point presumption and ignorance of the art of war had led astray the counsels of that brave army. Several times the Emperor said: 'Before to-morrow night that army is mine.'"

"In the evening he wished to visit on foot and incognito all the bivouacs; but scarcely had he gone a few steps than he was recognized. It would be impossible to depict the enthusiasm of the soldiers when they saw him. In an instant bundles of straw were placed at the end of thousands of poles, and eighty thousand men presented themselves before the Emperor, saluting him with acclamations; some complimenting him on the anniversary of his coronation; others saying that the army would present its bouquet to the Emperor to-morrow."

To any one who ever saw an army of even ten thousand men in the field, the entire and absolute falsehood of all this will be apparent. The imperial reporter proceeds: —

"One of the oldest grenadiers approached him, and said: 'You will have no need to expose yourself. I promise you, in the name of the grenadiers of the army, that you will have to fight only with your eyes, and that we will bring you to-morrow the flags and artillery of the Russian army by way of celebrating the anniversary of your coronation.' The Emperor said, upon entering his bivouac, which consisted of a sorry straw cabin without a roof, which his grenadiers had made for him: 'This is the most beautiful evening of my life; but it saddens me to think that I shall lose a good number of those brave fellows. I become sensible, from the grief which this reflection causes me, that they are truly my children; and, indeed, I sometimes reproach myself for indulging this sentiment, fearing it will render me at last unskilful in making war.'

"At the moment of sunrise the orders were given, and each marshal rejoined his command at full gallop. While passing along the front of several regiments, the Emperor said: 'Soldiers, we must end this campaign by a thunderbolt which will confound the pride of our enemies'; and immediately, hats at the end of bayonets and cries of *Vive l'Empereur!* were the veritable signal of battle!"

"This day will cost tears of blood at St. Petersburg. May it cause them to throw back with indignation the gold of England, and may that young prince, whom so many virtues call to be the father of his subjects, snatch himself from the influence of those thirty coxcombs whom England artfully seduces into her services, and whose impertinences obscure his good intentions, lose him the love of his soldiers, and throw him into operations the most erroneous. Nature, in endowing him with great qualities, called him to be the consoler of Europe. . . . . Never was there a more horrible field of battle. . . . . May so much bloodshed, may so many miseries, fall at length upon the perfidious islanders who are the cause of them! May the base oligarchs of London bear the anguish of so many calamities!"

"The Emperor of Germany" (in his interview with the Emperor) "did not conceal the contempt which the conduct of England had given both himself and the Emperor of Russia. 'They are shop-keepers,' he said more than once, 'who set the Continent in flames in order to secure for themselves the commerce of the world.' . . . . Several times the Emperor of Germany repeated: 'There is no doubt that France is in the right in her quarrel with England.' . . . . They say that the Emperor said to the Emperor of Germany, as he invited him to come nearer the fire of his bivouac: 'I receive you in the only palace I have inhabited these two months.' To this the Emperor of Germany replied, laughing: 'You turn habitations of this kind to such good account that they ought to please you.' *At least, this is what those present thought they overheard. The numerous suite of the two princes was not so far off that they could not hear several things!*

"The corpses have been counted. The totals are, eighteen thousand Russians killed, six hundred Austrians, and nine hundred French. Seven thousand wounded Russians are on our hands. All told, we have three thousand French wounded. General Roger Valhubert is dead of his wounds. An hour before he breathed his last he wrote to the Emperor: 'I could have wished to do more for you. I die in an hour. The loss of my life I do not regret, since I have participated in a victory which assures you a happy reign. As often as you shall think of the brave men who were devoted to you, remember me. It is sufficient for me merely to tell you that I have a family; I need not recommend them to your care.'"

From the whole of the bulletins we could gather, perhaps, two hundred anecdotes similar in character and purpose to those we have given; and we do not believe that ten of them are the exact statements of fact. They were fictions coined to make France willing to bleed. Interspersed with the bulletins are quiet, business-like notes to the Minister of War and others, the burden of which is: *Conscripts, conscripts, conscripts; send me conscripts; armed or unarmed, in uniform or in peasants' rags, no matter; send forward conscripts!*

Appended to the bulletins are decrees giving pensions to the widows of every man who fell in the last battle, — six thousand francs to a general's widow, and two hundred to a private's. After Austerlitz, a decree was published which was as captivating to delirious France as it was unjust to the army in general: "We adopt all the children of the generals, officers, and soldiers who fell at the battle of Austerlitz. They will be maintained and reared at our expense, — the boys at our imperial palace of Rambouillet, and the girls at our imperial palace of Saint Germain. The boys will be placed in situations, and the girls dowered, by us. To their baptismal and family names they will have the right to add that of Napoleon." No man ever displayed such art in rousing a nation to frenzy, and silencing its reason. If space allowed, we could give a catalogue of at least one hundred different devices of his fertile mind to reward and signalize soldiers who served him with conspicuous devotion. Many of these — such as orders, medals, flattering mention, and inscribing the names of fallen soldiers upon Pompey's pillar — were of a costless and sentimental nature. Others — such as gifts of money, pensions, promotion — were of a solid and practical character. Sometimes he would order a picture painted of a feat of arms, and decree that the uniform of the soldiers depicted should be that of the corps which performed the act. Nor was he lavish of rewards and honors; but in this, as in all things relating to war, he acted upon system, and preserved perfect coolness of judgment.

And while by these various arts this Corsican kept average France in delirium, the superior mind and judgment of France were denied all utterance. We have marked dozens of passages in the correspondence showing this. While he had writers in England in his pay for the purpose of embarrassing the Ministry and making friends for himself by their articles in English newspapers, he would not permit so much as a woman to live in France whom he suspected of having escaped the prevailing madness. Three times he orders back Madame de Staël, — "that bird of evil omen," as he styles her, — when he heard she had approached or crossed the frontiers. "It is the intention of the government," he wrote in 1803, "that this intriguing *foreigner* shall not remain in France, where her family has done harm enough." Again, in 1807, he speaks of her with contemptuous fury, as a "crow" whose approach foreboded mischief, and repeats his command that she be kept from the soil of France. Nor was she the only lady whom he feared and exiled, because he saw her sane in the midst of lunatics. As to the press, not a paragraph was allowed to appear calculated to recall Frenchmen to themselves; and not a line escaped his vigilant distrust, if it provoked Frenchmen to ask why their countrymen should be slaughtered by thousands in Poland, in Spain, in Russia, in Austria, in Prussia, for a quarrel about Malta, — an island of no interest to France, except as the source of Maltese cats.

For military men we must find room for a curious order addressed to Marshal Berthier at Boulogne, in 1805, just as Napoleon was about to begin that swift, silent march across Europe which ended at Austerlitz. It shows how little magic there was in his proceedings, and by what homely, plodding labors the most brilliant results are produced. "My cousin" (he called all his marshals cousin), "I desire you to have two portable boxes made, with compartments; one for me and the other for yourself. The compartments will be arranged in such a way that, with the aid of written cards, we can know at a glance the movements of all the Austrian troops, regiment by regiment, battalion by battalion, even to detachments of any considerable magnitude. You will divide the compartments into as many divisions as there are Austrian armies, and you will reserve some pigeon-holes for the troops which the Emperor of Germany has in Hungary, in Bohemia, and in the interior of his states. Every fifteen days you will send me a statement of the changes that have taken place during the preceding fifteen days; availing yourself for this purpose, not only of the German and Italian newspapers, but of all the information which my minister for foreign affairs may send you; with whom you will correspond for this object. Employ the same individual to change the cards and to draw up the statement of the situation of the Austrian armies every fifteen days. P. S. You must intrust this business to a man who will have nothing else to do, who knows German well, and who will take all the German and Italian papers, and make the changes which they indicate."

Before leaving the volumes, which exhibit him in the

plenitude of his power and glory, we offer for the reader's amusement the most characteristic letter, perhaps, of the whole collection; one written in 1807, to that good Louis whom young General Bonaparte had so cordially praised a few years before as a lad after his own heart. Louis was now called King of Holland; and trouble enough he had between his own amiable dream of being a good to Holland and the determination of his brother to regard Holland only in the light of so much war material. Was ever a *monarch* so lectured, bullied, berated, and insulted as poor Louis was in this epistle?

"I have received your letter of the 24th of March. You say that you have twenty thousand men at the Grand Army. *You do not believe it yourself;* there are not ten thousand; and what men! It is not marshals, chevaliers, and counts that we want; we want soldiers. If you go on so, you will render me ridiculous in Holland.

"You govern that nation too much like a capuchin. The goodness of a king ought always to be majestic, and not that of a monk. Nothing is worse than that great number of journeys which you make to the Hague, unless it be the contribution made by your order in your kingdom. A king commands, and asks nothing of any one; he is deemed to be the source of all power, and to have no need to recur to the purse of others. These niceties, you feel them not.

"Some notions occur to me concerning the re-establishment of your nobility, upon which I wait to be enlightened. Have you lost your senses to that point, and would you forget to such a degree what you owe me? You speak always in your letters of respect and obedience; but it is deeds, not words, that I require. Respect and obedience consist in not precipitating measures so important; for Europe cannot imagine you to be so wanting in a sense of duty as to do certain things without my consent. I shall be obliged to disavow you. I have asked for the document relating to the re-establishment of the nobility. Prepare yourself for a public mark of my excessive dissatisfaction.

"Despatch no maritime expedition; the season is passed. Raise national guards to defend your country. Pay my troops. Raise plenty of national conscripts. A prince who, the first year of his reign, is thought to be so good, is a prince who will be ridiculed in the second. The love which kings inspire ought to be a masculine love, mingled with a respectful fear and a great opinion of their merit. When people say of a king that he is a good man, his reign is a failure. How can a merely good man, or a good father, if you please, sustain the charges of the throne, suppress the malevolent, and conduct affairs so that the passions of men shall be hushed, or march in the direction he wishes? The first thing you ought to have done, and I advised you to do it, was to establish the conscription. What can be done without an army? For, can one call a mass of deserters an army? How could you avoid feeling (the condition of your army being what it is) that the creation of marshals was a thing unsuitable and ridiculous? The king of Naples has none. I have none in my kingdom of Italy. Do you believe that if forty French vessels should be united to five or six Dutch barks, that Admiral Ver Huell, for example, in his quality of marshal, could command them? There are no marshals in the minor kingdoms; there are none in Bavaria, in Sweden. You overwhelm men with honors who have not merited them. You go too fast and without advice; I have offered you mine; you respond by fine compliments, and you continue to commit follies.

"Your quarrels with the queen reach the public ear. Have at home that paternal and effeminate character which you exhibit in the government, and in public affairs practise that rigor which you show in domestic matters. You treat a young wife as one would lead a regiment. Distrust the persons who surround you; you are only surrounded by nobles. The opinion of those people is always diametrically opposite to that of the public. Beware of them; you begin to be no longer popular either at Rotterdam or Amsterdam. The Catholics begin to be afraid of you. Why do you employ none of them? Ought you not to protect your religion? All that shows little force of character. You pay court too much to a part of your nation: you offend the rest. What have the chevaliers done to whom you have given decorations? Where are the wounds which they have received for their country, the distinguished talents which recommend them, I do not say of all, but of three fourths of them? Many of them have done service to the English party, and are the cause of the misfortunes of their country. Was it necessary to ill treat them? No, but to conciliate all. I also have some *émigrés* in office; but I do not let them go too far, and when they think they are near carrying a point, they are further from it than when they were in a foreign country: because I govern by system, and not by weakness.

"You have the best and the most virtuous of wives, and you render her unhappy. Let her dance as much as she wishes; it belongs to her time of life. I have a wife forty years old; from the battle-field I write to her to go to balls; and do you wish that a wife of twenty years, who sees her life passing, who has all of life's illusions, should live in a cloister? should be like a nurse, always washing her baby? You attend too much to your domestic affairs, and not enough to your administration. I should not say all this to you, but for the interest I take in your welfare. Make the mother of your children happy. You have only one means of doing so; it is to show her much esteem and confidence Unfortunately, you have a too virtuous wife. If you had a coquette, she would lead you by the end of the nose. But you have a wife who respects herself, whom the mere idea that you could have a bad opinion of her revolts and afflicts. You should have had a wife like some I know of in Paris. She would have played you false, and kept you at her knees. It is not my fault, for I have often said as much to your wife.

"For the rest, you can commit follies in your own kingdom; very well; but I shall see to it that you commit none in mine. You offer your decorations to everybody; many persons have written to me who have no title to them. I am sorry that you did not feel that you were wanting in proper consideration towards me. I am resolved that no one shall wear those decorations near me, being determined not to wear them myself. If you ask me the reason, I shall reply, that you have as yet done nothing to merit that men should wear your portrait; that, besides, you have instituted the order without my permission; and that, finally, you give them away too lavishly. And what have all those people done who surround you to whom you give them?"

This it was to be one of Napoleon's kings! He lectures Joseph, Jerome, Lucien, his sisters, and even his uncle, Cardinal Fesch; not always with such severity, but always in the tone of the master. To Cardinal Fesch, his ambassador of Rome, he once wrote: "I find all your reflections upon Cardinal Ruffo small and puerile. You are in Rome like a woman. . . . . Don't meddle in affairs you don't understand." *This* it was to be a cardinal of Napoleon's making.

The suddenness of the collapse of this showy mockery of an empire is exhibited in the correspondence in a manner truly affecting. It was the freezing to death of thirty thousand horses that destroyed the "Grand Army," and tumbled the empire into chaos. Burnt out of Moscow on the 14th of September, 1812, the Emperor was inconvenienced certainly, but felt still so much at ease, that he sent a note, sixteen days after, to his librarian at Paris, scolding him for not keeping him better supplied with the new publications; and he continued for another month to direct even the police of Paris from the vicinity of the burnt capital. A bulletin written on the homeward march, October 23, is all glowing with victory, and recounts the burning of Moscow only as a disaster and shame to *Russia!* It ends thus: "The people of Russia do not remember such weather as we have had here during the last twenty days. We enjoy the sun of the beautiful days of our excursions to Fontainebleau. The army is in a country extremely rich, which can compare with the best provinces of France and Germany."

This was written on the 23d of October, and published in Paris November 16th. As late as November 3d, still the Emperor wrote to one of his ministers: "The weather continues to be very fine; a circumstance extremely favorable to us." Three days after, namely, November 6, 1812, the icy blast swept down from the North and chilled the army to the marrow. Ten nights of sudden, premature cold killed or disabled nearly all the horses; which compelled the abandonment or destruction of all the provisions that the men could not carry. Clouds of Cossacks hovered about the track of the gaunt and weary troops. Napoleon was twenty days without hearing from Paris. The Grand Army perished, and the empire was no more!

He died game. He was himself to the last. As soon as he had reached a point from which a courier could be safely despatched to Paris, he sent an aide-de-camp and a bulletin to break the news to Europe. He would not trust any one to write the paragraph which he ordered the aid to have inserted in German journals on his way to Paris, but gave it to him written by his own hand. On the 2d of December, from the midst of the wreck and ruin of his army, with ghastly pallor and rigid death on every side, this great histrionic genius wrote the following orders to the aide-de-camp charged with his despatches :—

"He will announce everywhere the arrival of ten thousand Russian prisoners, and the victory won upon the Beresina in which we took six thousand Russian prisoners, eight flags, and twelve pieces of cannon. . . . . He will cause to be inserted everywhere in the Gazettes : 'M. de Montesquiou, aide-de-camp, etc., has passed through, bearing the news of the victory of Beresina won by the Emperor over the united armies of Admiral Tchitchakof and General Wittgenstein. He carries to Paris eight flags taken in that battle, at which also six thousand prisoners were captured and twelve pieces of cannon. When this officer left, the Emperor's health was excellent.' M. de Montesquiou will see to it that this paragraph is published in the Mayence journal. The Duc de Bassano will cause it to be put into the Vilna papers and will write in the same strain to Vienna. M. de Montesquiou will travel with the utmost speed in order to contradict everywhere the false reports which may have been spread abroad. He will explain that those two (Russian) corps meant to cut our line in two, but that the army routed them utterly, and has arrived at Vilna, where it finds numerous depots, which will at once end the sufferings which it has experienced."

This was for Prussia, Austria, England. But it would not do for France, which must instantly supply new armies. This same aide-de-camp carried a bulletin for the *Moniteur*, — long, detailed, artful, — which, with mitigations, acquainted the French people that "a frightful calamity" had befallen them. They rallied gallantly to the support of the man who had flattered them with such transcendent ability, and they fought for him with much of the old courage and devotion. It did not suffice. Elba, the Hundred Days, Waterloo, the Bellerophon, complete the story. The last line of his published correspondence charges England with having extended to a fallen foe a hospitable hand, and then, when he had given himself up in good faith, "she immolated him," — *elle l'immola!* But in 1806, when he dethroned the king of Naples, he wrote thus to his brother Joseph: "The king of Naples will never ascend his throne again. You will explain that this is necessary to the repose of the Continent; since he has twice disturbed it."

THE GOVERNMENT OF THE CITY OF NEW YORK.*

ON certain conditions, a very large proportion of the whole human race will steal. The opportunity must be good, of course, and the chance of detection small; the stealing must easily admit of being called by another name; and, above all, the theft must be of such a nature that the thief does not witness the pain which the loss of the stolen property occasions. On these conditions, almost all children and other immature persons, as well as a great number of average honest men and women, will steal. One proof of the civilizing power which the late Horace Mann exercised over the pupils of Antioch College in Ohio was, that no depredations were committed by those raw lads upon the orchards and gardens of the neighborhood. Mrs. Mann is justified in mentioning this fact as one that does honor to the memory of her husband; for the boy who steals apples from an orchard usually has an excellent opportunity and seldom has the slightest sense of doing an injury to the owner. He takes a handkerchief full from an unseen person, who has whole acres strewn with fruit and trees bending with the weight of it, and who will never know that particular loss. If the stolen property presented itself in its ultimate form, — a piece of bread and butter going into the mouth of one of the farmer's little children, — not one boy in ten thousand would steal a crumb of it; but so long as it is mere apples lying in an orchard, all boys will steal it without compunction, unless they have been exceptionally well bred or taught.

Well-informed persons, who have been officially obliged to consider the matter, assure us that a majority of car-

* This article was written in 1866.

conductors, omnibus-drivers, and all other takers of unrecorded and untraceable money, are habitual thieves in all countries. It is the constant study of able managers to arrange a system that shall remove a temptation which ex perience has shown to be generally irresistible. Our fair readers, if we are so happy as to have any for so repulsive a subject, are acquainted with a class of active little mortals, — the cash-boys of our large dry-goods stores. Cash-boys had never appeared on earth if clerks had never stolen. But we need not multiply examples. The self-knowledge of the most honest men suffices. Who has not observed the unwillingness of persons of tried and punctilious integrity to put themselves in the way of temptation? It is because those know most of the moral weakness of men who have converted that weakness into strength. How often have we admired the exquisite modesty of Benjamin Franklin in that passage, written when he was an old man, in which he attributes the honesty of his early life to the fact that his trade brought him in such "plentiful supplies" of money that he had little temptation to do wrong. This was not a confession in the "high-toned" style, but that is the way honest men feel who know themselves.

We have undertaken to write something about the government of the city of New York, and yet we have fallen into a discourse upon stealing. The reason is, that, after having spent several weeks in investigating our subject, we find that we have been employed in nothing else but discovering in how many ways, and under what a variety of names and pretexts, immature and greedy men steal from that fruitful and ill-fenced orchard, the city treasury.

That the government of the city of New York has had, for several years past, an exceedingly bad name in the world, is probably known to all our readers. It has fallen into complete contempt. It is a dishonor to belong to it. Persons of good repute do not willingly associate with the rulers of the city, unless they are known to be of the small number who hold their offices for the purpose of frustrating iniquitous schemes. When it was found, last winter, that the Aldermen and Councilmen of the city must necessarily attend the ball of the Seventh Regiment at the Academy of Music, many respectable persons who had bought tickets sold them again, rather than jostle those magnates. The Rev. Henry Ward Beecher recently said, in the pulpit, that perhaps the government of the city of New York did more moral harm to the people of New York than all the churches together did good. Nevertheless, since we are all disposed to exaggerate evils vaguely known, and since the cry of corruption is habitually raised by corrupt men for purposes of intimidation or revenge, we entered upon our task fully prepared to find the affairs of the city less corruptly administered than they are supposed to be. It is an old remark, that good people are not quite as good, nor bad people as bad, as popular rumor gives them out.

It occurred to us that perhaps the best way of beginning an investigation of the city government would be to go down to the City Hall and look at it. It proved not to be there. To keep the whole city from falling a prey to the monster, it has been gradually cut to pieces, and scattered over the island; but, like the reptiles whose severed fragments become each a perfect creature, with maw as spacious and appetite as keen as the original worm, so each portion of the divided system is now a self-operating and independent apparatus. In the City Hall, however, the legislature of the city still assembles. It consists of two honorable bodies, — the Board of Aldermen, seventeen in number, elected for two years, and the Board of Councilmen, twenty-four in number, elected for one year, — each member of both boards receiving a salary of two thousand dollars a year. Considering that they meet but twice a week, always in the afternoon, and that the session averages one hour's duration, these gentlemen cannot be said to be ill paid. They are compensated for their valuable services at twice the rate at which the labors of the Chief Justice of the Supreme Court of the United States are rewarded. But then it costs those city legislators something to be elected. The legitimate expenses of an election to either of the boards amount to about three hundred dollars; but many a candidate expends a thousand dollars of his own money and several hundred dollars of other people's.

It is to the Chamber of the Board of Councilmen that we beg first to invite the courteous reader. This apartment being in the second story of the building, we pass many open doors on our way to it, through which we see idle men with their feet upon tables, smoking cigars. There are few buildings in the world, probably, wherein the consumption of tobacco in all its forms goes on more vigorously during business hours than the City Hall of New York. Smoke comes in clouds from many rooms, and the vessel which Mr. Thackeray used to call the "expectoratoon" is everywhere seen. If we enter the Councilmen's Chamber a few minutes before the time of beginning the session, we observe many members smoking; and as soon as there is a prospect of an adjournment, the same gentlemen begin to fondle their cigars, to hand them about, or even toss them to one another, so that when the adjournment does take place not a moment may be lost. Twice we have seen a member light his cigar before an adjournment was carried. The very clerks of this "honorable body" write out their notes of the proceedings smoking cigars of a flavor beyond that which the pursuit of literature allows.

The Councilmen's Chamber, a lofty and spacious room, provided by the liberal forethought of honest and public-spirited men sixty years ago, is furnished with preposterous magnificence; *not* "regardless of expense," however, as some have inconsiderately alleged. On the contrary, expense was evidently the first object sought by the persons who had the work in charge; and, accordingly, wherever a thousand-dollar thing could be put, there you behold it. The apartment is arranged on the plan of the Representatives' Chamber in the Capitol at Washington. The President sits aloft, in a richly canopied recess; below him are four clerks in a row; the members sit in two semicircles, in chairs of the most massive mahogany, at desks of solid elegance. The windows are shaded by curtains heavy with expense, and the carpet is thick with it. In case the session, which begins at 2 P. M., should chance to prolong itself to the evening, there is a chandelier of the most elaborate and ramified description, such as would rejoice the heart of any contractor to furnish. To remind members, who all have gold watches, of the passage of time, there is a clock of vast size, splendid with gilt and carving. Four staring, full-length portraits of Fillmore, Clay, Young, and Hamilton Fish disfigure the walls, and the Father of his Country looks coldly down upon the scene in marble. *He* never had such furniture either at Mount Vernon or at Philadelphia, nor did he ever see such at Independence Hall. The ceiling is frescoed, and a great gilt eagle spreads his wings over the President's canopy. Besides this gorgeous apartment, the Councilmen have a large and handsomely furnished room for their clerks and books, and a private room, densely carpeted, for themselves, where there is a wardrobe for each member's overcoat and umbrella. These wardrobes are very properly provided with lock and key.

To assist this "honorable body" in the business of legislation, there is a "chief clerk," whose salary is $ 3,000 a year; there is a "deputy clerk," at $ 2,000 a year; there is a "first assistant clerk," at $ 1,500 a year; there is a "second assistant clerk," at the same; there is a "general clerk," at $ 1,200 a year; there is an "engrossing clerk," at $ 1,250 a year; there is a "sergeant-at-arms," at $ 1,200 a year; there is a "reader," at the same; there is a "door-keeper," at $ 750 a year; there is a "messenger," at $ 1,200 a year; and there is an "assistant messenger," at $ 1,100 a year. In short, there is not a legislative body in the world more completely provided with all external aids and appliances for the work in hand than the Honorable the Board of Councilmen of the City of New York. To the salaries of these officers the Councilmen add, in the form of gifts for "extra services," six or seven thousand dollars more; and they bestow upon the reporters of seventeen newspapers, for not reporting their proceedings, two hundred dollars a year each. Perhaps the clerks also are paid for not doing their duty, — if any duty can be found for so many, — for we were present in the chamber, last June, when a communication from the Mayor was read, in which he complained that bills came to him for approval so badly written that he could scarcely read them, and declaring that hereafter he would pay no attention to acts not properly engrossed.

The twenty-four Councilmen who have provided themselves with such ample assistance and such costly accommodation are mostly very young men, — the majority appear to be under thirty. Does the reader remember the pleasant description given by Mr. Hawthorne of the sprightly young bar-keeper who rainbows the glittering drink so dexterously from one tumbler to another? That sprightly young bar-keeper might stand as the type of the young men composing this board. There are respectable men in the body. There are six who have never knowingly cast an improper vote. There is one respectable physician, three lawyers, ten mechanics, and only four who acknowledge to being dealers in liquors. But there is a certain air about most of these young Councilmen which, in the eyes of a New-Yorker, stamps them as belonging to what has been styled of late years "our ruling class," — butcher-boys who have got into politics, bar-keepers who have taken a leading part in primary ward meetings, and young fellows who hang about engine-houses and billiard-rooms. A stranger would naturally expect to find in such a board men who have shown ability and acquired distinction in private business. We say, again, that there *are* honest and estimable men in the body; but we also assert that there is not an individual in it who has attained any considerable rank in the vocation which he professes. If we were to print the list here, not a name would be generally recognized. Honest Christopher Pullman, for example, who leads the honest minority of six that vainly oppose every scheme of plunder, is a young man of twenty-seven, just beginning business as a cabinet-maker. Honest William B. White, another of the six, is the manager of a printing-office. Honest Stephen Roberts is a sturdy smith, who has a shop near a wharf for repairing the iron-work of ships. Morris A. Tyng, another of the honest six, is a young lawyer getting into practice. We make no remark upon these facts, being only desirous to show the business standing of the men to whom the citizens of New York have confided the spending of sundry millions per annum. The majority of this board are about equal, in point of experience and ability, to the management of an oyster-stand in a market. Such expressions as "them laws," "sot the table," "71st rigment," and "them arguments is played out," may be heard on almost any Monday or Thursday afternoon, between two and three o'clock, in this sumptuous chamber.

But what most strikes and puzzles the stranger is the crowd of spectators outside the railing. It is the rogues' gallery come to life, with here and there an honest-looking laborer wearing the garments of his calling. We attended six sessions of this "honorable body," and on every occasion there was the same kind of crowd looking on, who sat the session out. Frequently we observed looks and words of recognition pass between the members and this curious audience; and, once, we saw a member gayly toss a paper of tobacco to one of them, who caught it with pleasing dexterity. We are unable to explain the regular presence of this great number of the unornamental portion of our fellow-beings, since we could never see any indications that any of the crowd had an *interest* in the proceedings. As the debates are never reported by any one of the seventeen reporters who are paid two hundred dollars a year for not doing it, and as the educated portion of the community never attend the sessions, this board sits, practically, with closed doors. Their schemes are both conceived and executed in secrecy, though the door is open to all who wish to enter. This is the more surprising, because almost every session of the board furnishes the material for a report, which an able and public-spirited journalist would gladly buy at the highest price paid for such work in any city.

Debates is a ludicrous word to apply to the proceedings of the Councilmen. Most of the business done by them is pushed through without the slightest discussion, and is of such a nature that members cannot be prepared to discuss it. The most reckless haste marks every part of the performance. A member proposes that certain lots be provided with curbstones; another, that a free drinking-hydrant be placed on a certain corner five miles up town; and another, that certain blocks of a distant street be paved with Belgian pavement. Respecting the utility of these works, members generally know nothing and can say nothing; nor are they proper objects of legislation. The resolutions are adopted, usually, without a word of explanation, and at a speed that must be seen to be appreciated. The first and last impression made upon a disinterested spectator is, that this most expensive body, even if every member were an honest man, would be absolutely useless. A competent street inspector, properly aided by the police, could do all the real work that is left to them to do; for such has been the flagrant abuse of their power, that, by degrees, they have been deprived by the State Legislature of a great part of the authority they once possessed; but the power to do mischief remains. This "honorable body" can still waste, give away, and steal the money of their constituents.

The only way in which we can convey to the reader's mind a lively idea of the character of the city legislature is to relate, as simply as possible, a few of their acts of last summer, which we witnessed ourselves and recorded on the day of their perpetration. There is no "mystery of iniquity" in the business; to understand the game which the majority of this body are playing, it is only necessary to sit out two or three of their ordinary sessions. We own it is a trial to the patience. There will be moments when a person of a vivacious turn of mind will feel an almost irresistible impulse to throw something at the head of those insolent young bar-keepers, who have contrived to get their hands into the public pocket, and are scattering wide the hard-earned money of good citizens and faithful fathers of families.

At almost every session we witnessed scenes like the following. A member proposed to lease a certain building for a city court at two thousand dollars a year for ten years. Honest Christopher Pullman, a faithful and laborious public servant, objected on one or two grounds: first, rents being unnaturally high, owing to several well-known and temporary causes, it would be unjust to the city to fix the rent at present rates for so long a period; secondly, he had been himself to see the building, had taken pains to inform himself as to its value, and was prepared to prove that twelve hundred dollars a year was a proper rent for it, even at the inflated rates. He made this statement with excellent brevity, moderation, and good temper, and concluded by moving that the term be two instead of ten years. A robust young man with a bull-neck and of ungrammatical habits said, in a tone expressive of impatient disdain, that the landlord of the building had "refused" fifteen hundred dollars a year for it. "Question!" "Question!" shouted half a dozen angry voices. The question was instantly put, when a perfect roar of *noes* voted down Mr. Pullman's amendment. Another hearty chorus of *ayes* consummated the iniquity. In all such affairs, the visitor notices a kind of ungovernable propensity to vote for spending money, and a prompt disgust at any obstacle raised or objection made. The bull-necked Councilman of uncertain grammar evidently felt that Mr. Pullman's modest interference on behalf of the tax-payer was a most gross impertinence. He felt himself an injured being, and his companions shared his indignation.

We proceed to another and better specimen. A resolution was introduced, appropriating four thousand dollars for the purpose of presenting stands of colors to five regiments of city militia, which were named, each stand to cost eight hundred dollars. Mr. Pullman, as usual, objected, and we beg the reader to mark his objections. He said that he was a member of the committee which had reported the resolution, but he had never heard of it till that moment; the scheme had been "sprung" upon him. The chairman of the committee replied to this, that, since the other regiments had had colors given them by the city, he did not suppose that any one could object to these remaining five receiving the same compliment, and therefore he had not thought it worth while to summon the gentleman. "Besides," said he, "it is a small matter anyhow"; — by which he evidently meant to intimate that the objector was a very small person. To this last remark, a member replied, that he did not consider four thousand dollars so very small a matter. "Anyhow," he added, "we oughter save the city every dollar we kin." Mr. Pullman resumed. He stated that the Legislature of the State, several months before, had voted a stand of colors to each infantry regiment in the State; that the distribution of these colors had already begun; that the five regiments would soon receive them; and that, consequently, there was no need of their having the colors which it was now proposed to give them. A member roughly replied, that the colors voted by the State Legislature were mere painted banners, "of no account." Mr. Pullman denied this. "I am," said he, "captain in one of our city regiments. Two weeks ago we received our colors. I have seen, felt, examined, and marched under them; and I can testify that they are of great beauty, and excellent quality, made by Tiffany and Company, a firm of the first standing in the city." He proceeded to describe the colors as being made of the best silk, and decorated in the most elegant manner. He further objected to the price proposed to be given for the colors. He declared that, from his connection with the militia, he had become acquainted with the value of such articles, and he could procure colors of the best kind ever used in the service for three hundred and seventy-five dollars. The price named in the resolution was, therefore, most excessive. Upon this, another member rose and said, in a peculiarly offensive manner, that it would be two years before Tiffany and Company had made all the colors, and some of the regiments would have to wait all that time. "The other regiments," said he, "have had colors presented by the city, and I don't see why we should show partiality." Whereupon Mr. Pullman informed the board that the *city* regiments would all be supplied in a few weeks; and, even if they did have to wait awhile, it was of no consequence, for they all had very good colors already. Honest Stephen Roberts then rose, and said that this was a subject with which he was not acquainted, but that if no one could refute what Mr. Pullman had said, he should be obliged to vote against the resolution.

Then there was a pause. The cry of "Question!" was heard. The ayes and noes were called. The resolution was carried by eighteen to five. The learned suppose that one half of this stolen four thousand dollars was expended upon the colors, and the other half divided among about forty persons. It is conjectured that each member of the Councilmen's Ring, which consists of thirteen, received about forty dollars for his vote on this occasion. This sum added to his pay, which is twenty dollars per session, made a tolerable afternoon's work.

Any one witnessing this scene would certainly have supposed that *now* the militia regiments of the city of New York were provided with colors. What was our surprise to hear, a few days after, a member gravely propose to appropriate eight hundred dollars for the purpose of presenting the Ninth Regiment of New York Infantry with a stand of colors. Mr. Pullman repeated his objections, and recounted anew the generosity of the State Legislature.

The eighteen, without a word of reply, voted for the grant as before. It so chanced that, on our way up Broadway, an hour after, we met that very regiment marching down with its colors flying; and we observed that those colors were nearly new. Indeed, there is such a propensity in the public to present colors to popular regiments, that some of them have as many as five stands, of various degrees of splendor. There is nothing about which Councilmen need feel so little anxiety as a deficiency in the supply of regimental colors. When, at last, these extravagant banners voted by the Corporation are presented to the regiments, a new scene of plunder is exhibited. The officers of the favored regiment are invited to a room in the basement of the City Hall, where city officials assist them to consume three hundred dollars' worth of champagne, sandwiches, and cold chicken, — paid for out of the city treasury, — while the privates of the regiment await the return of their officers in the unshaded portion of the adjacent park.

It is a favorite trick with these Councilmen, as of all politicians, to devise measures the passage of which will gratify large *bodies* of voters. This is one of the advantages proposed to be gained by the presentation of colors to regiments, and the same system is pursued with regard to churches and societies. At every one of the six sessions of the Councilmen which we attended, resolutions were introduced to give away the people's money to wealthy organizations. A church, for example, is assessed a thousand dollars for the construction of a sewer, which enhances the value of the church property by at least the amount of the assessment. Straightway a member from that neighborhood proposes to console the stricken church with a "donation" of a thousand dollars to enable it to pay the assessment; and as this is a proposition to vote money, it is carried as a matter of course. We select from our notes only one of these donating scenes. A member proposed to give two thousand dollars to a certain industrial school, — the favorite charity of the present time, to which all the benevolent most willingly subscribe. Vigilant Christopher Pullman reminded the board that it was now unlawful for the Corporation to vote money for any object not specified in the tax levy, as finally sanctioned by the Legislature.

He read the section of the act which forbade it. He further showed, from a statement by the Comptroller, that there was no money left at their disposal for any *miscellaneous* objects, since the appropriation for "City contingencies" was exhausted. The only reply to his remarks was the instant passage of the resolution by eighteen to five. By what artifice the law is likely to be evaded in such cases, we may show further on. In all probability, the industrial school, in the course of the year, will receive a fraction of this money, perhaps even so large a fraction as one half. It may be that, erenow, some obliging person about the City Hall has offered to buy the claim for a thousand dollars, and take the risk of the hocus-pocus necessary for getting it, — which to *him* is no risk at all.

It was proposed, on another occasion, to raise the fees of the inspectors of weights and measures, who received fifty cents for inspecting a pair of platform scales, and smaller sums for scales and measures of less importance. Here was a subject upon which honest Stephen Roberts, whose shop is in a street where scales and measures abound, was entirely at home. He showed, in his sturdy and strenuous manner, that, at the rates then established, an active man could make two hundred dollars a day. "Why," said he, "a man can inspect, and does inspect, fifty platform scales in an hour." The cry of "Question!" arose. The question was put, and the usual loud chorus of *ayes* followed.

As it requires a three-fourths vote to grant money, — i. e. eighteen members, — it is sometimes impossible for the Ring to get that number together. There is a mode of preventing the absence or the opposition of members from defeating favorite schemes. It is by way of "reconsideration." The time was, when a measure distinctly voted down by a lawful majority was dead; but by this expedient the voting down of a measure is only equivalent to its postponement to a more favorable occasion. The moment the chairman pronounces a resolution lost, the member who has it in charge moves a reconsideration; and, as a reconsideration only requires the vote of a majority, *this* is invariably carried. By a rule of the Board, a reconsideration carries a measure over to a future meeting, — to any future meeting which may afford a prospect to its passage. The member who is engineering it watches his chance, labors with faltering members out of doors, and as often as he thinks he can carry it, calls it up again until at last the requisite eighteen are obtained. It has frequently happened that a member has kept a measure in a state of reconsideration for months at a time, waiting for the happy moment to arrive. There was a robust young Councilman who had a benevolent project in charge, of paying nine hundred dollars for a hackney-coach and two horses which a drunken driver drove over the dock into the river one cold night last winter. There was some disagreement in the Ring on this measure, and the robust youth was compelled to move for many reconsiderations. So, also, it was long before the wires could be all arranged to admit of the appointment of a "messenger" to the City Librarian, who has perhaps less to do than any man in New York who is paid eighteen hundred dollars a year; but perseverance meets its reward. We hear that this messenger is now smoking in the City Hall at a salary of fifteen hundred dollars.

There is a manœuvre also for preventing the attendance of obnoxious, obstructive members, like the honest six, which is ingenious and effective. A "special meeting" is called. The law declares that notice of a special meeting must be left at the residence *or* the place of business of every member. Mr. Roberts's residence and Mr. Roberts's place of business are eight miles apart, and he leaves his home for the day before nine in the morning. If Mr. Roberts's presence at a special meeting at 2 P. M. is desired, the notice is left at his shop in the morning. If it is not desired, the notice is sent to his house in Harlem, after he has left it. Mr. Pullman, cabinet-maker, leaves his shop at noon, goes home to dinner, and returns soon after one. If his presence at the special meeting at 2 P. M. is desired, the notice is left at his house the evening before, or at his shop in the morning. If his presence is not desired, the notice is left at his shop a few minutes after twelve, or at his house a few minutes past one. In either case, he receives the notice too late to reach the City Hall in time. We were present in the Councilmen's Chamber when Mr. Pullman stated this *inconvenience*, assuming that it was accidental, and offered an amendment to the rule, requiring notice to be left five hours before the time named for the meeting. Mr. Roberts also gave his experience in the matter of notices, and both gentlemen spoke with perfect moderation and good temper. We wish we could convey to our readers an idea of the brutal insolence with which Mr. Pullman, on this occasion, was snubbed and defrauded by a young bar-keeper who chanced to be in the chair. But this would be impossible without relating the scene at very great length. The amendment proposed was voted down with that peculiar roar of *noes* which is always heard in that chamber when some honest man attempts to put an obstacle in the way of the free plunder of his fellow-citizens.

These half-fledged legislators are acquainted with the device known by the name of the "previous question." We witnessed a striking proof of this. One of the most audacious and insolent of the Ring introduced a resolution, vaguely worded, the object of which was to annul an old paving contract that would not pay at the present cost of labor and materials, and to authorize a new contract at higher rates. Before the clerk had finished reading the resolution, honest Stephen Roberts sprang to his feet, and, unrolling a remonstrance with several yards of signatures appended to it, stood, with his eye upon the chairman, ready to present it the moment the reading was concluded. This remonstrance, be it observed, was signed by a majority of the property-owners interested, — the men who would be assessed to pay for one half of the proposed pavement. Fancy the impetuous Roberts with the document held aloft, the yards of signatures streaming down to his feet and flowing far under his desk, awaiting the time when it would be in order for him to cry out, "Mr. President." The reading ceased. Two voices were heard, shouting, "Mr. President." It was not to Mr. Roberts that an impartial chairman could assign the floor. The member who introduced the resolution was the one who "caught the speaker's eye," and that member, forewarned of Mr. Roberts's intention, moved the previous question. It was in vain that Mr. Roberts shouted, "Mr. President." It was in vain that he fluttered and rattled his streaming ribbon of blotted paper. The President could not hear a word of any kind until a vote had been taken upon the question whether the main question should be now put. That question was carried in the affirmative by a chorus of *ayes*, so exactly timed that it was like the voice of one man. Then the main question *was* put, and it was carried by another emphatic and simultaneous shout.

We have spoken of the headlong precipitation with which all business is done in this board. Measures involving an expenditure of millions, and designed to bind the city for a great number of years, are hurried through both boards in less time than *paterfamilias* expends in buying his Sunday dinner in the market; and, frequently such measures are so mysteriously worded that no one outside of the Ring can understand their real object. We happened to be present when a resolution was brought directly from the Board of Aldermen (who had passed it without debate), directing the Street Commissioner to make a contract with the lowest bidder for lighting the whole island for twenty years with gas, — the price to be fixed *now*, when coal and labor are twice their usual price. No such simple words, however, as *twenty years* were to be found in the resolution; which merely said, that the contract should be for "the same number of years as the contract last made and executed with the Manhattan Gas Company." A member, bewildered by the furiously rapid reading of this long and vague resolution, timidly inquired how many years that was. No one seemed to know. After a pause, some one said that he believed it was ten years. Whereupon, Councilman White, a faithful and intelligent member of the honest minority, proposed that the term of the contract be two years, which Mr. Pullman supported. The amendment was instantly voted down, and the original resolution was carried by the usual eighteen votes. The Mayor promptly vetoed the scheme. The Tribune thundered against it; but the veto message had no sooner been read, than it was passed over the veto by the Aldermen; then taken to the Councilmen's Chamber, where the requisite eighteen votes were immediately cast for it. This resolution, as we were afterwards informen, was merely one of a long series of measures designed to tap the lamp-posts of the city, like so many sugar-maples, and make them run gold into the troughs of a few notorious politicians.

We are lingering too long in the Councilmen's Chamber, and must abruptly leave it. Nor can we remain more than a moment with the Aldermen. It is not necessary, for there is not a pin to choose between the two bodies. We observe in their chamber the same lavishness of furniture and decoration; pictures as numerous and as bad as those which hang in the chamber opposite; the same wild profusion of clerks, assistant clerks, readers, engrossers, messengers, and assistant messengers; the same crowd of unwashed and ugly spectators outside the railing. Except that the Aldermen are a little older and somewhat better dressed than the Councilmen, we could discern no difference between them. Whatever dubious scheme is hurried through one body is rushed through the other. Sometimes the Councilmen point the game, and the Aldermen bring it down; and sometimes it is the Aldermen that start up the covey, and the Councilmen that fire. As with the Councilmen, so with the Aldermen, there is a sure three-fourths vote for every scheme which has the sanction of the interior circle who control the entire politics of the city. And, as among the Councilmen, so among the Aldermen there are a few honest and public-spirited men who vainly protest against iniquity, or silently cast their votes against it. If one such body is one too many, how shall we express the enormous superfluity of two? It is impossible.

But there is a third legislative board sitting in the City Hall. The island upon which New York is built is a county, and that county has its board of twelve Supervisors, who have the spending of seventeen millions of dollars per annum. The city and the county cover the same territory. Each creature in the island of Manhattan lives both in the county and in the city of New York. The existence, therefore, of a separate legislature for each is a complete absurdity; and, if both were honest, there would be constant danger of clashing between them. They do not often clash, because both have in view the same object, and pursue that object under the direction of a central gang, — the masters of both. It is the Board of Supervisors who, being authorized, eight years ago, to build a court-house at an expense not to exceed two hundred and fifty thousand dollars, have expended upon it two millions and a half; and there it stands to-day just half done. It is computed, by architects professionally employed, that for every dollar spent upon this unfinished edifice another dollar has gone elsewhere.

Our principal object in this article is not to present the reader with a startling catalogue of iniquities, but to endeavor to contribute our little towards discovering a mode of expelling the thieves, keeping them expelled, and getting a few honest men in the place of that great multitude of plunderers. Before entering upon that part of our subject, however, we must show to readers remote from the scene, that the corruption exists, that it taints nearly every branch of the public service, that it is an evil of gigantic and menacing proportions, and that the numerous expedients devised for holding it in check have failed. Hitherto we have related what we have ourselves seen and heard: we now proceed to glean a few of the more striking facts from our notes of what others have told us and from printed testimony.

The volume entitled "The Manual of the Common Council" is itself a curious specimen of the artifices resorted to by these official plunderers of the public purse. In the year 1841, a zealous assistant clerk to the Common Council conceived the idea of publishing a little volume, which should be a kind of city almanac; containing, besides what an almanac usually presents, a list of all the persons connected with the city government, their places of business and residence, and a map of the city. A neat, small volume of 180 pages was the result of his labors. Even this was unnecessary, because the most useful part of the information which it gave respecting the members of the government had already appeared in the City Directory, and an almanac could be had of pill-venders for nothing. No good reason could be given why even so inexpensive a work as that should be paid for out of the public treasury. But see to what proportions this trifling imposition has since grown. The next year, our zealous assistant clerk added to his catalogue of city officials a list of all previous members of the Corporation, from the earliest period of the city's existence, and a picture of New York as it was two hundred years ago. This year the volume swelled from 180 to 253 pages. The picture was interesting, and caused the work to be much spoken of and sought after, which was only another proof how unnecessary it was that it should be published at the expense of the city. The next issue, besides the list of names and residences, contained extensive extracts from ancient city records, which increased the number of pages to 312. Every year the Manual increased in bulk, in the quantity of superfluous matter, in the number and costliness of the pictures, until it has now become a manual of folly, extravagance, and dishonesty. Let us glance at the Manual for 1865; for, to add to the exquisiteness of the art employed in its preparation, the book is not published until the year is nearly expired, and a new set of officers are about to be chosen, so that the volume for 1866 had not appeared when these lines were written. The Manual for 1865 is a most superb and lavishly illustrated duodecimo volume of 879 pages. It contains one hundred and forty-one pictures, of all degrees of expensiveness, — steel-plate, woodcut, plain lithograph, and colored lithograph. The large colored map of the city, at the beginning, cost as much money as a map of that kind could any way be made to cost. Next comes a steel portrait of the person who, for twenty-five years, has hired people to compile the annual volume, and whose name has always appeared on the title-page as its editor, and who is supposed to be liberally remunerated for his editorial labors. Next appears a very elegant colored title-page, containing six finely executed pictures.

Before proceeding with the list, we remind the reader that the ingenuity of the compilers of this work has been severely taxed for many years to devise and discover subjects for illustration. Subjects that could be called legitimate, or that approached the legitimate, having been long ago exhausted, the editor this year appears to have been in the direst straits to supply his lithographers and engravers with the regular quantity of work.

Accordingly, the next illustration is a plan of the Aldermen's Chamber, designed to show where each member sat in 1865; and the next is a four-paged, folding lithograph, containing — O precious gift to posterity! — a fac-simile of each Alderman's signature. In the next two plates posterity is blessed with the signatures of the Councilmen for 1865, and the means of ascertaining the precise arm-chair occupied by each. The following are the subjects of a few of the costly colored lithographs: the "fur store" established in 1820 by the father of the Mayor of the city in 1865; the "old frame-house" in which the editor of the Manual "passed his youth"; "Mr. Stewart's house in Fifty-Fourth Street"; "a grocery and tea store" of the year 1826; the house in North Moore Street in which Speaker Colfax was born; "twin frame-houses in Lexington Avenue"; Tammany Hall in 1830; a billiard saloon in the Fifth Avenue; Harlem Lane, with fast horses travelling thereon; the "Audubon Estate" on the Hudson; the upper end of the Central Park drive. Besides these, there are pictures, not colored, of a prodigious number of public and private buildings, and portraits of undistinguished persons. The number of pages occupied by extracts from old records, newspapers, and memories is 423!

Such is the book which the tax-payers of the city are called upon every year to pay for, in order to swell the income of sundry printers, lithographers, politicians, and the compiler. But this is not all. The number of copies annually ordered to be printed is ten thousand! The number paid for is ten thousand. The number actually printed, we are positively assured by men who are in a position to know, is about three thousand. Of this number, about fifteen hundred are distributed gratis about the City Hall, and the rest are sold by, and for the benefit of, the compiler. A considerable number find their way into the second-hand bookstores which make Nassau Street so fascinating to poor students and rich collectors. We bought our copy there, and its price was three dollars. The bookseller informed us that he laid in his supply of the Manual for 1865 at two dollars per copy, which is three dollars and thirty-six cents less than a copy costs the city. Nor have we yet got to the bottom of this enormous "job." We have said that the city pays for ten thousand copies of the preposterous volume. It pays for nearly twice that number. The items of the Manual account rendered for 1865 were these: —

Bill of engraving	$4,353.10
Bill of engraving and printing	733.00
Bill of drawing and printing	5,150.00
Bill of lithographing and printing	3,185.00
Bill of printing 10,000 copies	27,951.20
Bill of corrections and alterations	300.00
Bill of paper for title-pages	600.00
Bill of thirty reams tissue paper	150.00
Bill of papering 10,000 copies	100.00
Bill of ten reams wrapping paper	150.00
Bill of binding 5,000 copies in cloth	5,000.00
Bill of binding 4,000 copies in muslin	4,000.00
Bill of binding 1,000 copies in morocco	2,000.00
Total	$53,672.30
D. T. Valentine, for compiling	3.500.00
Total	$57,172.30

This shameful account being brought to the notice of the present Mayor of the city, Mr. John T. Hoffman, he did himself the honor to veto the resolution authorizing a similar expenditure for 1866. He told the men who passed that resolution, that he had made inquiries of such publishing houses as the Appletons and the Harpers, and had ascertained that ten thousand copies of the work could be manufactured for $30,000, instead of $53,672; although a new publisher would not have the benefit of the large amount of stereotyped matter which appears in the Manual from year to year, with little alteration. The truth is, that the book actually costs the compiler about $15,000 per annum; and the difference between that sum and the amount charged is taken from the pockets of the New York tax-payers by a process which we leave our readers to characterize with the proper term.

The most usual manner of stealing is to receive money for awarding or procuring contracts, appointments, donations, or increase of salaries, which money, of course, the favored person gets back, if he can, from the public treasury; and he usually can. The President of the Board of Health, last spring, when New York was threatened with the cholera, had occasion to remonstrate with a person who held the contract for removing dead animals from the streets, and threatened him with the breaking of the contract if its conditions were not better complied with.

"That would be rather hard, Mr. Schultz," replied the man, "for that contract cost me $60,000." And well it might; for the city pays $25,000 a year for getting rid of a commodity every pound of which ought to yield the city a revenue. A dead horse, worth twenty dollars, the city pays for having carted off to where it can be conveniently converted into twenty dollars. Another contractor receives $21,000 a year for removing night-soil, which could be sold for enough to pay the cost of its removal. By various extra charges, the holders of this contract have continued to swell their gains incredibly. Mr. Jackson Schultz, the energetic and capable President of the Board of Health, has recently published his conviction, that the "total swindle under this contract is $111,000," and we have had the advantage of hearing him demonstrate the fact. The story, however, is too long for our very limited space.

Does any one need evidence that the men who award such contracts, in the teeth of opposition and elucidation, receive a large share of the plunder? The fact is as certain as though ten witnesses swore to having seen the money to them in hand paid. Three years ago a contract was awarded for sweeping the streets for ten years, at $495,000 a year. Since the accession to power of the new Board of Health, responsible men have handed in a written offer to buy the remainder of the contract for a quarter of a million dollars, i. e. to clean the city for seven years at $495,000 a year, and give the city a quarter of a million dollars for the privilege. There are those about the city offices who know, or think they know, how the plunder of this contract is divided. We believe we are not violating any confidence, expressed or implied, when we say, that it is the conviction of the Board of Health that $100,000 per annum of the proceeds of this contract are divided among certain politicians; that a certain lawyer, who engineered the project, and stands ready to defend it, receives a salary of $25,000 per annum as "counsel to the contract"; and that the men in whose name the contract is held are "dummies," who get $6,000 a year for the use of their names and for their labor in superintending the work. The contract is further burdened with the support of several hundred cripples, old men, and idle men, all of whom are voters, who are put in the street-cleaning force by Aldermen and Councilmen who want their votes and the votes of their relatives, thus kindly relieved of maintaining aged grandfathers, lame uncles, and lazy good-for-nothings. These statements, we are aware, cannot be proved. Such compacts are not trusted to paper; and a witness driven to bay can always balk his assailants by refusing to criminate himself. The reader, therefore, may decline to believe these details. One thing remains, and is certain, that the workingmen of New York are annually plundered of two hundred thousand dollars per annum by this single contract.

How the work so munificently paid for is *done* is sufficiently well known. Into that foul subject we cannot enter, except to notice the blind devotion of the great mass of poor men who annually vote to keep in power the people who steal their earnings and poison their children. New York boasts a *Democratic* majority of more than thirty thousand votes, and the government of the city is always in the hands of the party so named. Is it, then, the rich men's streets that are unswept, and the poor men's crowded avenues and lanes that are clean? Are the small parks and squares where thousands of poor children play better kept than those to which scores of rich men's children are carried? Is the Bowery cleaner than Broadway, and Tomkins Square more inviting than Union? In the spring, when the March thaw has unlocked the accumulated dirt of the winter, and the whole city is deep in mire, which are the streets that a Democratic contractor first throws himself upon? Does he first remove the festering mounds of pollution that block the poor man's path to his home, and make that home loathsome to him, and *then* betake himself to the coating of mud that soils the rich man's boots? Or does he leave reeking with abomination the crammed thoroughfares where Democratic voters live, half a hundred in a house, until every shovelful of dirt has been removed from the places where rich men reside, seven voters to a block? But why ask idle questions? It is the law of this world that the strong shall rule it. In a commercial city, the strong men are rich. Label your government what you will, it is the strong men in a community who have their way; and therefore, under all governments, the streets where rich men live are clean.

The plunder of the persons who are so unfortunate as to serve the public, and of those who aspire to serve the public, is systematic, and nearly universal. Our inquiries into this branch of the subject lead us to conclude that there are very few salaries paid from the city or county treasury which do not yield an annual percentage to some one of the "head-centres" of corruption. The manner in which this kind of spoliation is sometimes effected may be gathered from a narrative which we received from the lips of one of the few learned and estimable men whom the system of electing judges by the people has left upon the bench in the city of New York. Four years ago, when the inflation of the currency had so enhanced the price of all commodities that there was, of necessity, a general increase of salaries, public and private, there was talk of raising the salaries of the fourteen judges, who were most absurdly underpaid even when a dollar in paper and a dollar in gold were the same thing. Some of the judges were severely pinched in attempting to make six thousand half-dollars do the work which six thousand whole ones had accomplished with difficulty; and none, perhaps, more severely than the excellent and hospitable judge whose experience we are about to relate. A person known by him to be in the confidence of leading men about the City Hall called upon him one day, and informed him that it was in contemplation to raise the salaries of all the judges $2,000 per annum. The judge observed, that he was much relieved to hear it, for he had gone so deeply into the Sanitary Commission and other projects for promoting the war, and had made so many expensive journeys to Washington in furtherance of such projects, that he did not see how he could get through the year if the inflation continued. "Well, Judge," said the person, "if the judges are disposed to be reasonable, the thing can be done." "What do you mean by *reasonable?*" asked the judge. The reply was brief and to the point: "Twenty-five per cent of the increase for one year." The judge said no. If his salary could not be raised without that, he must rub on, as best he could, on his present income. The person was evidently much surprised, and said: "I am sorry you have such old-fashioned notions. Why, Judge, everybody does it here." Nothing more was heard of increasing the judges' salaries for a whole year, during which the inflation itself had become inflated, and every door-keeper and copyist had had his stipend increased. At length the spoilers deemed it best, for purposes of their own, to consent that the salaries of the judges should be increased $ 1,000; and, a year after that, the other $ 1,000 was permitted to be added.

It was recently proved, in the presence of the Governor of the State, that the appointment of the office of Corporation Attorney was sold to one incumbent for the round sum of $ 10,000. This is bad enough, but worse remains to be told. Sworn testimony (from thirty-six witnesses), taken by a committee of investigation, establishes the appalling fact, that appointments to places in the public schools are systematically sold in some of the wards, — the wards where the public schools are almost the sole civilizing power, and where it is of unspeakable importance that the schools should be in the hands of the best men and women. One young lady, who had just buried her father and had a helpless mother to support, applied for a situation as teacher, and was told, as usual, that she must pay for it. She replied that she could not raise the sum demanded, the funeral expenses having exhausted the family store. She was then informed that she could pay "the tax" in instalments. Another poor girl came on the witness-stand on crutches, and testified that she had paid $ 75 for a situation of $ 300 a year. Another lady went to a member of the Ring, and told him, with tears, that she saw no way of procuring the sum required, nor even of saving it from the slender salary of the place. The man was moved by her anguish, took compassion upon her, and said he would remit *his share* of "the tax." It was shown, too, that the agent of all this foul iniquity was no other than the principal of one of the schools. It was he who received and paid over the money wrung from the terror and necessities of underpaid and overworked teachers. We learn from the report of the committee that the Ring in this ward was originally formed for the express purpose of giving the situations in a new and handsome school "to the highest bidder"; and, as the opening of the new school involved the discharge of a small number of teachers employed in the old schools, the Ring had both the fear and the ambition of the teachers to work upon. "There was a perfect reign of terror in the ward," says the report of the investigating committee. "The agent performed his duty with alacrity and with a heartlessness worthy of the employers. It appears that he not only summoned the teachers to come to him, but that he called on their parents and friends as to the amount they should pay for their appointments, — the sums varying from $ 50 to $ 600, according to the position sought."

And who were the Ring that perpetrated this infamy? They were a majority of the Trustees elected by the people, and the School Commissioner elected by the people, — six poor creatures, selected from the grog-shop and the wharf, and intrusted with the most sacred interest of a republic, the education of its children. It was known before that in some of the wards the school trustees were drunkards; it was known before that little children were piled up, like flower-pots in a green-house, in small, ill-ventilated rooms; but no one supposed, before this investigation in 1864, that men could be elected to office who were capable of such revolting meanness as this.

When appointments are sold, appointments are likely to be numerous. Some of our readers, doubtless, have smiled at the ridiculous catalogue of offices created to relieve the pecuniary straits of Louis XIV., and given by Voltaire in his history of the reign of that expensive monarch. In Paris, in the year 1710, men holding the rank of counsellors of the king held such posts as hog-inspectors, inspectors of calves, of wigs, and of slaughter-houses, inventory-drawers, measurers of fire-wood, deputy measurers of fire-wood, pilers of fire-wood, unloaders of fire-wood, comptrollers of timber, markers of timber, charcoal-measurers, grain-sifters, comptrollers of poultry, barrel-gaugers, barrel-rollers, butter-testers, beer-testers, brandy-testers, linen-measurers, unloaders of hay, and removers of boarding. Not that counsellors to the king performed any of these labors. That was done by underlings; the counsellors to the king merely pocketing the greater part of the fees. But how mild and trivial was this abuse of kingly power, compared with the hoards of superfluous officers that swarm in the public buildings of the city of New York! In the office of the

City Comptroller there are one hundred and thirty-one clerks. The Street Commissioner employs sixty. In the precious Manual described above, the reader, amazed at the interminable list of persons employed by the city, is every now and then puzzled by such items as these: twelve "manure-inspectors," at $ 3 a day each; twenty-two "health-wardens," twenty-two "assistant health-wardens," twenty-two "street-inspectors," all at $ 3 a day each; seven "assistant inspectors of meat, at $ 900 per annum each; seven "inspectors of encumbrances," at $1,250 each; twenty-two "distributors of corporation ordinances," at $ 2 each per day. We have not space to continue the catalogue. Who has ever seen any of these wardens and inspectors? A gentleman connected with the Citizens' Association, had the public spirit to sally forth, Manual in hand, in quest of the twenty-two health-wardens and twenty-two assistants; for neither he nor the writer of these lines, nor any of their acquaintances, had ever so much as heard of the existence of such officers. Long and painful was the search. He found that those guardians of the public health were bar-keepers, low ward politicians, nameless hangers-on of saloons, who absolutely performed no official duty whatever except to draw the salary attached to their places. They were the merest creatures of the worthless man who appointed them, — the man who sold or gave away *blank interment-permits, signed,* to favored undertakers, "to save them the trouble of coming down town every time they had a funeral." * For the benefit of those gentlemen of leisure in New York, who excuse their want of public spirit by saying that the city government is so corrupt that it is of "no use to try" to reform it, we will mention that, very much through the exertions of the warden-hunter referred to above, those three twenty-two's were abolished a few months ago, as well as the entire department to which they belonged. To that single item of reform we owe it that the city was not desolated by the cholera during the past summer.

The reader has, perhaps, heard something respecting the

* This was the reason given by the undertakers when they were questioned on the subject by members of the new Board of Health. The possession of blank permits did not, however, prevent them from charging for the permits in their bills.

cost of "opening" new streets in the city of New York. Under cover of those innocent-looking words, incredible sums of money are stolen from the owners of real estate. In the year 1811, the entire island, except a small strip at its northern extremity, was surveyed; the sites of all the future streets and avenues were settled, marked with stone pillars, and laid down on maps; so that, ever since that time, all land has been bought, sold, held, and improved with reference to the streets that were one day to run through it, by it, or near it. The work was so well done that those maps, and no others, are still used by assessors of taxes, and for all other official purposes. Copies of them are to be found for reference in one of the rooms of the building whereto all the world repairs every November to be taxed. Bearing these facts in mind, the reader will easily comprehend the audacity of the theft to which his attention is now directed.

A new street is ordered to be "opened," and the judges of the Supreme Court appoint three commissioners to perform the work, at four dollars per day each. To "open" a street, in the legal sense, is not to go to work with shovel and pickaxe and convert a strip of meadow into a street, but merely to buy the strip from the owners, transfer the title to the Corporation, and then formally declare the street "opened." Since the surveys are already done, and the maps already made, and since the expense of the whole transaction is borne by the owners of land upon the street, who bought that land *because* the street would one day exist, this legal opening is the merest form. The commissioners buy the land required at the rate of one dollar for each lot taken, which is one among many proofs of the pure formality of the business. We will now state, first, what the three commissioners actually do who are so lucky as to have a street to open; and then we will show what is charged for the arduous work.

They meet in a room in the third story of a building in Nassau Street, which is from five to eight miles from the street about to be opened. They hire the room for the meetings of the commissioners. True, it is already occupied, and no change in it is made by the occupant; but they hire it, nevertheless. They appoint a surveyor, a clerk, an assistant clerk, and sometimes, we believe, a messenger. These appointments cost them three minutes of their valuable time; for there are people who have acquired, in some way, a claim to those appointments, and are appointed as a matter of course. There is not, there cannot be, a doubt that the "understanding" between the judges, the commissioners, the surveyors, and the clerks is complete before the first step is taken. The clerk is the ruling mind of the affair. It is he who lets the room; it is he who draws up the final report; it is he who divides the spoil, and takes, probably, the largest single share. He conceives, arranges, starts, and conducts the operation, and he does it at his ease in his own hired room. The officers being appointed, the commissioners have earned their four dollars each, and adjourn.

Every day, between the hours of twelve and two, they visit the apartment, inquire after the health of their clerk, perhaps take a cigar with him, see that their names are entered as having attended, which entitles them to four dollars, and then return, refreshed, to their private business. Meanwhile sundry advertisements are published, announcing to parties interested what is going on. The surveyor may or may not take a car and ride up to the street, or walk over the part to be opened. Perhaps there is a house, built before 1811, which extends over the line of the street; and if so, the owner is entitled to compensation. Usually, however, there is nothing of the kind; and usually the surveyor, an old hand at the business, knows whether there is or not without going up to see. A draughtsman, meanwhile, has been copying a map of the street from the maps of 1811; and the clerk writes along the border of it (from the tax-books) the names of the owners of the lots on each side of the street. Sundry other advertisements are then published, calling upon parties interested to come and see what has been done, and state objections, if any there are. The clerk then draws up a report, and the thing is done. None of these operations are hurried. Care is taken of the interests of the commissioners. It is not until they have paid their noontide respects to the clerk for a prodigious number of days that the street is pronounced "open."

Then the bill is presented. The surveyor charges as

though he had made original surveys and drawn original maps. The clerk charges as though his report were the result of original searches and researches. The commissioners charge as though the opening had been the tardy fruit of actual negotiations. The rent of the room is charged as though it had been occupied wholly by the commissioners. And all of these charges are the very highest which any one, in his most lavish mood, could even think of in connection with the work supposed to be done. When we add, that half a dozen of these openings are frequently going on at the same time, in the same snug upper room, and conducted by the same individuals, the reader will not be surprised to learn that the net result of the business to the master spirit, for the year ending June, 1866, was $ 25,466, of which sum $ 4,433 was charged for the rent of the room, which he hires for about $ 300 per annum, and $ 950 was charged for "disbursements and postage-stamps." One surveyor's bill for the same year was $ 54,000. It has been ascertained, after a laborious examination of the public records, that the total cost of "opening" twenty-five streets, or parts of streets, averaging less than half a mile each in length, was $ 257,192.12. The public is indebted for this information to Mr. William H. Whitbeck, president of an association of property-owners recently formed to protect themselves against further spoliation of the same nature.

The Executive Council of the Citizens' Association has recently given publicity to a large number of facts relating to the same iniquity. We will select one of them :—

"In opening 124th Street, the Commissioners awarded to the owner of a house standing in the northwest angle of 124th Street and Second Avenue some $ 4,500 for the damage to his building by the opening of the street. If this house had stood in the middle of the street, and had been entirely destroyed by the opening, he should not have received one cent, inasmuch as the house was built subsequent to 1811, when the map of the city was planned. The fact is, that, in 1811, a monument was planted at the intersection of 124th Street and Second Avenue, and the person who built the house built it in the angle of the street, and facing the country road. The owner knew well where the street was to be, and *so avoided building upon it.* As the house was built facing the angle, the two ends of its rectangular piazza extended about six feet over the line, the one end over the line of Second Avenue, and the other end over the line of 124th Street. Now, if the owner built his house encroaching upon the street, he should not have been paid for the damage caused by his own negligence. It appears, however, that the piazza has been rounded so as not to extend over the line; and for this rounding of the piazza, which could have been done at an expense of certainly not more than $ 1,000, the owner has been allowed the enormous sum of $ 4,500. The house stands there as good as it ever was. Need we say that the owner is a prominent politician?"

We have since conversed with the gentleman who was charged with the investigation of this case. He assures us that the rounding of the piazza cost, in reality, about $ 250; and that he placed it at $ 1,000 in his report, because, being ignorant of carpentry, he deemed it best to mention a sum much in excess of the probable cost.

Our lessening space warns us to forbear, though we have scarcely made an impression upon the mass of facts before us. We cannot dwell upon the favoritism practised toward the real constituents of the spoilers, — the liquor-dealers, — who actually paid a less sum per annum for licenses, and contributed a smaller amount to the Inebriate Asylum, than the liquor-dealers of Albany. We must pass by such enormous frauds as that known by the name of the Gansevoort swindle, in the course of which a tract of land was bought from the city at half its value, kept in costly litigation for several years, then bought back by the city for twice its value, and all the taxes remitted for the intervening period. Nor can we give details of the manner in which mean men steal from the price of the school-children's copy-books and slate-pencils, nor open up the enormous and complicated cheat which is covered by the word "stationery." How the hard-earned claims of poor laborers are "shaved," under pretence that there is no money to pay them in the Treasury; by what means a clerk of a market enjoys an income as large as that of the President of the United States; how the funerals of eminent men, the celebration of national festivals, and the return of scarred veterans from the seat of war have been made the occasion, first, of drunken revelry, and afterwards of wholesale plunder; how the delicate wines provided for the sick in the public institutions are poured down the filthy gullets of many whose natural drink is distilled molasses; how the most valuable ferry leases, wharf privileges, and railroad charters are given away or sold for a tenth of their value to "dummies" who represent the very men who grant them; how many men hold two or more offices at once; and fifty other scandals into which we have looked, — we must pass by with this brief indication of their nature. It would be amusing to show the process by which (until honest Christopher Pullman stopped it last spring) the city was made to pay $ 87 every time the Corporation granted permission to an old woman to keep a peanut-stand on a corner, for which she paid one dollar. As a portion of the "proceedings" of the two boards, the "resolution" had to be published in seventeen newspapers, and paid for in each, which cost the sum just mentioned. The same worthy gentleman has proved, by personal inquiry, that every rocket or firework discharged on the Fourth of July by order of the Corporation costs the city exactly twice as much as a private citizen pays for the same articles.

The result of all this plunder is, that in thirty-six years the rate of taxation in the city and county of New York has increased from two dollars and a half to forty dollars per inhabitant! In 1830, the city was governed for half a million dollars. In 1865, the entire government of the island, including assessments on private property for public improvements, cost more than forty millions of dollars. In 1830, the population of the city was a little more than two hundred thousand. It is now about one million. Thus, while the population of the county is five times greater than it was in 1830, the cost of governing it is sixteen times greater. And yet such is the value of the productive property owned by the city, — so numerous are the sources of revenue from that property, — that able men of business are of the deliberate opinion that a private company could govern, clean, sprinkle, and teach the city by contract, taking as compensation only the fair revenue to be derived from its property. Take one item as an illustration: under the old excise system, the liquor licenses yielded twelve thousand dollars per annum; under the new, they yield one million and a quarter. Take another: the Corporation own more than twenty miles of wharves and water-front, the revenue from which does not keep the wharves in repair; under a proper system, they would yield a million dollars above the cost of repairs.

We trust no reader of this article — not one — needs

to be reminded that the money stolen by the thieves into whose hands the city has fallen is the smallest item of the mighty sum of evil resulting from the system. A person, however, must intimately know New York to realize what a welling fount of moral pollution it is. Those within the circle of corruption, and all with whom they continue to have dealings, lose at length all sense of honor and shame, all power to distinguish between right and wrong, and, finally, all knowledge that there *is* any difference between them. It is a most insidious thing. Many a good young man has been drawn into the system so insensibly that he has become an habitual stealer of the public money, almost without knowing it. Others are conscious thieves, but not yet hardened beyond remorse. Some of these are, as it were, imprisoned in the system, and know not how to escape. A very large number are morally non-existent, and have no other thought or occupation except to devise and execute schemes of spoliation. And we do believe that *no* man who serves, sells to, or buys from the city, and no man who tries to serve, sell to, or buy from the city, does entirely escape contamination. What a tale we could tell of one notorious, but not naturally bad man, who, from a respectable though humble employment on the wharves, was lured into the low politics of his ward, and drank himself into such favor that he obtained, at length, the means of buying the privilege to steal as head of one of the departments, — and now, his place being abolished, and all his ill-gotten gains squandered in vice and ambitious schemes, slinks out of view, fatally diseased, and bereft of hope! But this part of our subject we leave to our readers' own reflections, and we rejoice to know that it will fare better there than it could in these pages; for, truly, the moral harm which this system is now doing in New York, and to the country through New York, is something which baffles and eludes written language.

The question now occurs, How was it that a city containing so many public-spirited and honorable men fell into the control of a gang of thieves?

It has all come about in one generation. Within the memory of men still living, the affairs both of the city and the State of New York were so well managed that other

States and cities were glad to copy their methods of doing public business. The time was when men, after a brilliant career in Congress, regarded it as promotion to be Mayor of the city; when a seat in the city legislature was the coveted reward of a lifetime of honest dealing in private business; when a seat in the State Legislature was the usual first step to the highest places in the national government; when the very ward committees were composed of eminent merchants and lawyers; and when even to serve as secretary to a ward committee was a feather in the cap of a bank-teller or head book-keeper in a great house of business. In other words, the time was when the city was governed by its natural chiefs, — the men who had a divine right to govern it. Nay, more: it was once a distinction to be a voter, — since none could vote who were not householders. None could vote who had not given their fellow-citizens *some* evidence of an ability to vote understandingly, and *some* indication of a disposition to vote correctly. The particular test selected we do not admire; and all we can say in favor of it is that it was better than none. It did exclude the great mass of ignorance and vice; it did admit the great mass of intelligence and virtue; it did answer the purpose in a respectable degree.

This system was changed by the Constitutional Convention of 1821, which abolished the household restriction, and admitted to the polls all citizens, native and foreign, except convicted criminals and madmen. Among those who opposed this fatal change was Martin Van Buren; and all the dire consequences of it which he predicted have come upon the city. He said it would utterly corrupt the politics of New York, by giving it over into the hands of ten thousand ignorant or vicious men, whose votes could not be overcome. It would "drive from the polls all sober-minded people," from mere despair of effecting any good by voting. It would take away one powerful motive to virtue by abolishing the distinction between voters and non-voters. To be a voter, said Mr. Van Buren, is now "the proudest and most invaluable attribute of freemen." It was one of the rewards of industry and self-control. A proud day it was to a young mechanic, when he left his new home and his newly married wife, and walked, for the first time, to the polls to deposit his vote. It stamped him a respectable man. He was thenceforth a full-fledged citizen, one of the masters of the city, the rulers of which were his servants; and they knew it, and treated him accordingly. Mr. Van Buren's remonstrances were not heeded, and the old system was abolished.

The evil consequences did not immediately appear, because the habit of selecting respectable men for the public service survived the system which had created that habit. The reign of Andrew Jackson, which debauched the national government, developed rapidly all the tendencies to corruption latent in the government of the city. A lower grade of men were elected to office, and a grade still lower worked the machinery by which they were elected. Still, there was no *system* of stealing. A defalcation occasionally occurred; aldermen sometimes pocketed bundles of cigars from the "tea-room"; others contrived to convey their families to evening parties at the expense of the city; others may sometimes have cribbed an odd half-ream of paper or a box of pens; and, doubtless, there was some jobbery, and much favoritism, as there is in all governments. Honesty, however, continued to be the rule in the public service. We mean, that, although the politics of the city were debased, and the men elected were always depreciating, there was no thought among them of using their places as conveniences for plundering their constituents. As late even as 1850 an alderman or chief of a department would have actually lost standing with his fellows if suspected of taking a bribe or of having a concealed interest in a contract. Yes, even in 1850, but sixteen years ago, it was a disgrace to steal the people's money on any pretext. If any one had then foretold that the time was at hand when the only men in the city government despised and snubbed by their equals would be the few who did *not* steal, no man could have believed the wild prediction.

About the year 1850, when it began to be perceived that omnibuses could no longer convey the morning and evening multitudes of people, and when street railroads in many avenues were projected, the Corporation conceived the fancy that they had the right to grant the privilege of laying rails in the public streets to private companies. In fact, it was taken for granted on all hands that this was their right; and it was in connection with those railroad grants that the corruption, on a great scale, began. It was then that the low, immature, ignorant, unprincipled, irresponsible, untaxed persons who formed the majority of the city legislature discovered that an alderman could, by a judicious use of his opportunities, not merely get a good deal of money, but make his fortune, during a single term of service. "Rings" were then first formed; "agents" were then first employed, — the mysterious go-betweens who have to be "seen" before anything can be done. The necessity for this machinery was soon perceived; for, at first, some sad mistakes occurred, which threatened for a time to spoil the game. One company, for example, distributed forty thousand dollars among the Aldermen, but were outbid, and the grant was given to another company. Naturally enough, they demanded their money back; but many of the poor creatures had already squandered their shares, and were totally unable to refund. One of the defrauded men, as it chanced, was a member of the grand jury, and he announced his determination to bring the matter before that body. Means were found to satisfy his claim; about one half the whole sum was given up, and the rest was paid in promises that have never been fulfilled. New-Yorkers remember the ancient, familiar firm of Kipp and Brown, formerly blazoned on the gorgeous sides of countless omnibuses. Mr. Solomon Kipp, the head of that firm, used to say that he personally expended fifty thousand dollars in "getting through" the two comparatively unimportant railroad grants in which he was interested. We have the affidavits of other parties before us, which justify the conclusion that, from this single source, the Corporation corruptly gained a round million in about ten years.

Thus the system of spoliation began. Thus was the cupidity of the politicians inflamed. From that time to this, the ordinary New York politician has regarded public office in no other light than as a chance to steal without the risk of the penitentiary. It is not that the city government, so far as controlled by politicians, sometimes steals. We do not make that charge. We say it does nothing *but* steal; for even the most useful or necessary public work is sanctioned by it only so far as it affords promise of gain to politicians.

At the present time, as we are informed by one whose opportunities of knowledge are unequalled, all the political concerns of the city are controlled by about seven men, — heads of city departments and others. In most of the wards, a nomination to office by the party which is ludicrously styled Democratic insures an election by the people; and it is these seven men who work the machinery by which Democratic nominations are ground out. They are the power behind the ballot-box, greater than the ballot-box itself. Candidates for Congress, for the State Legislature, for the numerous boards of city legislators, must pass the ordeal of their inspection, and pay their price, before their names can go upon the "slate"; and such is the absoluteness of their power over ignorant voters, that they have caused to be elected to Congress by Irish votes a man who, as editor of a "Know-Nothing" newspaper, had been employed for seven years in vilifying Irishmen and their religion. They have taken up a man who commanded one of the companies of artillery that marched from the field of Bull Run because their "time was up," and, while the whole civilized world was pointing at him the finger of scorn, elected him to one of the most lucrative offices in the United States. Of late years, these lords of the town have had the deep cunning to give a few of their best appointments and several minor offices to Republicans, as part of their system of preventing investigation. This was a master stroke. Most of the publishers of newspapers were already bribed to silence by the Corporation advertising, and all the reporters were hired not to report anything disagreeable by the annual gift of two hundred dollars. This letting in of a few Republicans to share the spoils completed the system of repressing inquiry. They have known, too, how to turn to account the feud between two Republican leaders, which, after distracting the politics of the State of New York for many years, has transferred the battle-ground to Washington, and now threatens to snatch from the nation the fruits of its victory over rebellion, or at least to postpone its enjoyment of them.

Such are some of the consequences that have resulted

from admitting to the polls unqualified and untaxed men, in a city which catches and retains the worst of the foreign emigration, and where there are seven foreign-born voters to every five native. In New York, we actually see the state of things contemplated by Daniel Webster in his Pittsburg speech, when he asked, "Who would be safe in any community where political power is in the hands of the many, and property in the hands of the few?" Such an unnatural state of things, he added, could nowhere long exist. Political power in the city of New York is in the hands of seventy-seven thousand foreign voters and fifty-two thousand native voters; while the great bulk of the property of the city is owned by about fifteen thousand persons. Political power in New York simply means the power to steal with impunity the property of those fifteen thousand persons. This stealing does not take the form of open and indiscriminate spoliation, because it can be more conveniently done, and longer done, through the machinery of politics.

Having now stated as fully as our limits permit the condition of the government of the city, it remains for us to do what little we can towards pointing out the remedy. In considering this part of our subject, modesty and hesitation would become the wisest and ablest of men. It is no time to dogmatize and declaim, when the dearest interests of civilization are to be rescued from imminent and deadly peril. Next year, we trust, there will be a convention assembled to revise the Constitution of the State of New York, and upon the action of that body we hang all our hope of speedy and radical reform. If any one, therefore, has so much as a single well-weighed suggestion to offer toward a practicable plan, now is the time for him to offer it. On this great and most difficult problem every person in the State of New York who is so happy as to have a thinking head upon his shoulders should now habitually meditate and converse.

Patchwork will not answer. That has been tried, and found insufficient. While the ship is still on the ocean, it is well to stop the leak with anything that will even slightly diminish the risk of death. But the thing now in order is to go into dock, and overhaul the hull from keel to taffrail, or perhaps to abandon the vessel and build a new one. It is so exceedingly important for us all to understand this, that we will pause here a moment to mention a few of the expedients for checking thievery which have signally failed. *All* mere expedients have failed, or are failing. Nothing will ever stop it but some system, the natural working of which will put into office a controlling number of honest men.

The total failure of the contract system is a case in point. To check jobbery and favoritism, it was enacted several years ago that all work done for the city, and all commodities supplied to the city, greater in value than $ 600, should be the subject of contracts, to be awarded, after due notice, to the lowest bidder. The contract system, so far from putting an obstacle in the way of corruption, has furnished facilities for it. We have the sworn testimony before us, that it is common for fictitious bids to be sent in, for genuine ones to be bought off, and for parties who are best prepared to do the work required to be kept in ignorance of the proposals. Large iron contracts, for example, have been awarded before any one of the great iron firms have been aware that such contracts were in the market; and they have been awarded to men who never melted a pound of iron nor had any means whatever of doing the work. To a pork-butcher was assigned the contract for building a very costly bridge over a wide river; and the difficult work of grading an avenue, hilly and rocky, has been awarded to a politician ignorant of the most rudimental engineering. We have before us a successful bid for supplying the city offices with stationery, in which we find the bidder offering to supply "blue folio post" at *one cent* per ream; "magnum bonum pens," at one cent per gross; "lead pencils," at one cent per dozen; "English sealing-wax," at one cent per pound; and eighty-three other articles of stationery, at the uniform price of one cent for the usual parcel. This was the "lowest bid," and it was, of course, the one accepted. It appeared, however, when the bill was presented for payment, that the particular kind of paper styled "blue folio post" had never been called for, nor any considerable quantity of the other articles proposed to be supplied for one cent. No one, strange to say, had ever wanted "magnum bonum" pens at one cent a gross, but in all the offices the cry had been for "Perry's extra fine," at three dollars. Scarcely any one had used "envelopes letter-size" at one cent per hundred, but there had been countless calls for "envelopes note-size" at one cent each. Between the paper called "blue folio post," at one cent per ream, and the paper called "foolscap extra ruled," at five dollars and a half, the difference was too slight to be perceived; but every one had used the foolscap. Of what avail are contracts, when the officials who award them, and the other officials who pay the bill, are in league with the contractor to steal the public money?

To prevent one of the most common kinds of theft, it was enacted that every person who presented a bill to the city should take an oath, before receiving his money, that he had not paid, and would not pay, any part of it to any one for getting him the work. This law is shamelessly evaded every day. A school commissioner orders work of a printer, telling him to be sure to charge a good round price. The work is done, the bill presented, the oath taken, the money paid. A few days after, that commissioner or his friend has some printing of his own to be done, which the printer does, and sends with the work a receipted bill. We can produce a printer who has upon his books $10,000 worth of work done *gratis*, in recompense for services rendered in procuring him city jobs. When the procurer of the work has no occasion for printing, it is usual for him to *borrow* sums of money of the printer, which, like Dr. Johnson's sixpence, are "*not* to be repaid." Many of these petty politicians are, in fact, universal "dead-heads," and prey on all the town. One remark which we chanced to hear from one of them was exceedingly suggestive. "Pullman," said a young Councilman to our honest friend Christopher, "what did you want that Harlem Railroad grant rescinded for?" He alluded to the grant of the privilege to lay rails and run cattle trains through the handsomest street in the upper part of the island, in the teeth of the most vehement opposition on the part of the residents. "For my part," continued the virtuous youth, "there is no company I would sooner give my vote to than the Harlem. If I ask 'em to take on a hand or give a place to a friend, they 're sure to do it. There 's not a more obliging company in New York than the Harlem." The Harlem Railroad Company, reader, is Mr. Cornelius Vanderbilt, one of the ablest men of business now living. The Councilman whose words we have quoted would not be employed by him in any post requiring average skill and honesty. And yet, behold the great, strong man courting the favor of the weak, little one! Do we blame either of these men? We arraign only the system which puts them in false and corrupting relations with each other and with their fellow-citizens.

It was lately enacted, that a three-fourths vote of both boards — the Aldermen and Councilmen — should be requisite to pass any bill granting or paying money. This was done because there was always a Democratic majority in both boards, and that majority was always corrupt. But it did not even retard the profuse voting of money. It merely required the Ring to buy up or bully a few more members, which was done in a week, and the work went on as bravely as before. The present board of Councilmen began their term of service with thirteen Republicans and twelve Democrats, owing to special exertions on the part of reformers. Those thirteen Republicans were elected, at great expense, for the sole purpose of outvoting the thieves, and they were all solemnly pledged so to do. But the system repels men of strong and tried honesty, and consequently seven of the thirteen speedily fell into the toils. Some were purchased, others were intimidated, others were persuaded, but all yielded alike to the behests of the Ring. And, really, we cannot wonder at it. The six faithful members of the board are useless to their constituents. The most just, the most necessary measure proposed by *them* is voted down as a matter of course. A young, inexperienced Councilman sees, on the one hand, the favor of his colleagues, the smiles of the City Hall, the freedom of the city's stores and shops, places for his friends, and $ 7,000 a year; and, on the other, the frowns and surly opposition of his colleagues to everything he asks or proposes, a warfare against nefarious schemes which he knows to be useless, and which the public neither applaud nor hear of. For *his* brother, no easy clerkship is created; for *his* second-cousin's benefit, no great man discovers that he is in need of a fourth assistant messenger; and if a carman in *his* ward loses a horse through a hole in a wharf, and justly calls upon the neglectful city government to buy him another, it is enough for him to introduce the bill for it to be voted down. Can we wonder that so many immature persons yield to a temptation so insidious, and which addresses itself to so many of the weak places in human nature at once?

Another well-meant expedient has completely failed. Owing to the lavish expenditures, it invariably happens that many of the sums appropriated for specific objects are exhausted long before the end of the year. For example, in 1865, the comptroller estimated the cost of printing and stationery at $ 145,000, and the Legislature of the State granted $ 160,000. But the amount expended in that year was $ 310,324. This excess would have presented difficulties to ordinary financiers, but none to those who control the finances of New York. Formerly, the deficit was supplied by "transferring" the money appropriated to other objects. "Transfer, the wise it call." But this device having been forbidden by legislative enactment, parties interested sued the city for the amount of their claims; and, having obtained judgment against the unfortunate city, went through the form of seizing the portraits and furniture of the Governor's room in the City Hall. Then a judicial decision was obtained, which declared that judgments against the city "must be paid"; and, sheltered by this decision, the city treasurer paid them. In the year 1864, the amount of the judgments paid from the public treasury was $ 1,262,398. Last winter, a new expedient was devised to prevent this impudent evasion of a most proper and necessary law. It was enacted that no amount in excess of a specific appropriation should be recoverable by judgment. By what audacious trick this enactment will be set at naught has not yet appeared; but that it *will* be set at naught we have little doubt. If it is not, it will be only owing to the vigilance and tact of the public-spirited lawyers who are lending the aid of their talents to the Citizens' Association.

As these minor expedients have failed of their object, so, we believe, the grand expedient of all — the transfer of the control of the city government to the State Legislature — is not to be relied on for the future. That expedient, false in principle, was justified only by the urgent necessity of the case. To that temporary transfer of power from a completely corrupt to an incompletely corrupt organization, we owe it that the city of New York is still, in some degree, inhabitable. For ten years past, nothing has stood between the city and universal spoliation, except the Governor of the State and a small number of intelligent, incorruptible members of the Legislature. To them we owe the rescue of the police from the control of city politicians; and to the police, thus rendered efficient, we owe the deliverance of the city from rapine during the riots of 1863. For twenty-four hours, until adequate assistance arrived, they kept the mob in check by their discipline, courage, and rapidity. No one can tell what would have occurred, or what would not, if we had then had for policemen creatures appointed to serve the mean purposes of the mean men whose character we have been exhibiting, and who were in the fullest sympathy with brother savages torturing our prisoners captured in war. To the Legislature, also, we are indebted for a tolerable administration of the affairs of the Central Park, of the Health Board, and of some other departments now controlled by honest men appointed at Albany.

On the other hand, the interference of the Legislature has, at length, reduced the city government to a condition of political chaos. The Mayor has been deprived of all controlling power. The Board of Aldermen, seventeen in number, the Board of twenty-four Councilmen, the twelve Supervisors, the twenty-one members of the Board of Education, are so many independent legislative bodies, elected by the people. The police are governed by four Commissioners, appointed by the Governor for eight years. The charitable and reformatory institutions of the city are in charge of four Commissioners whom the City Comptroller appoints for five years. The Commissioners of the Central Park, eight in number, are appointed by the Governor for five years. Four Commissioners, appointed by the Governor for eight years, manage the Fire Department. There are also five Commissioners of Pilots, two appointed by the Board of Underwriters and three by the Chamber of Commerce. The finances of the city are in charge of the Comptroller, whom the *people* elect for four years. The street department has at its head one Commissioner, who is appointed by the Mayor for four years. Three Commissioners, appointed by the Mayor, manage the Croton Aqueduct department. The law officer of the city, called the Corporation Counsel, is elected by the *people* for three years! Six Commissioners, appointed by the Governor for six years, attend to the emigration from foreign countries. To these has been recently added a Board of Health, the members of which are appointed by the Governor. Was there ever such a hodge-podge of a government before in the world? And nowhere is there any adequate provision for holding these several powers to their responsibility. Consequently, although the system of plunder has now been in operation for sixteen years, during which the public thieves have stolen not less than fifty millions of dollars, not one man of them has ever been punished, nor even made to disgorge.

There is a still more terrible objection to governing the city of New York at a city one hundred and sixty miles distant from it. The Legislature itself is corrupt. The same seven men who control the politics of the city nominate the city members of the Legislature; and these, reinforced by corrupt men from other cities, control one branch of the Legislature and are powerful in the other. Sometimes the city leaders cause themselves to be elected to the Legislature; but usually they select, from the clerks in the public offices, their own creatures, — mindless, dependent men, whose only virtue is a cur-like fidelity to their masters. No language can overstate the hopeless incapacity of these men for the business of legislation. They can only vote as they are ordered; and if you wish to buy their votes, you must arrange the price, not with them, but their owners in New York. To elect such men to the Legislature is only to transfer power from the Legislature to the lobby. There at Albany we see, within the rails of the Assembly, a crowd of poor, ignorant, irresponsible clerks; and in the lobby we find men representing Cornelius Vanderbilt, the Central Railroad, the Erie Railroad, the Astor estate, and many other men and companies controlling vast resources and carrying great prestige. Moreover, the agents representing these strong men and powerful organizations are persons of skill and audacity. When such a reversal of the natural order of things exists, and when the members of the Legislature are paid by the State a less sum per diem than their board costs, — to say nothing of drink and billiards, — what *must* be the result? We need not say.

A very able lobby agent, who has been in the business many years, has given us an inkling of the mode of procedure. "When we get to Albany," said he, "we make out our lists, and, after studying them and comparing notes, we *classify* members, and make an estimate of what it is going to cost to get our bills through. We find out about how much each man expects, and who is running him. Then we arrange the thing in New York with certain people, whose consent is necessary. The price for a vote ranges from fifty dollars to five hundred, unless it is that of the chairman of a committee. *He* wants more, because he has to appear on the record as originating the measure."

It was probably one of these originating gentlemen who could explain the testimony given recently in an Albany corruption case by a lady who proved herself a true helpmeet to her husband. She testified that a lobby agent called at her house one Sunday afternoon, when there was "some conversation" respecting the accused Senator, which the court "ruled out." She continued thus: "The next morning I put $ 2,500 in greenbacks into a yellow envelope, and gave it to my only son, eleven years old. The boy got into the wagon with his father. *I never saw the money again.*"

If there is in this world a man who can be truly said to *know* anything, Mr. Thurlow Weed knows the Legislature of the State of New York. His testimony respecting the corruption in that Legislature, as given in the "Daily Times," a few months ago, is as follows: —

"Formerly the *suspicion* of corruption in a member would have put him 'into Coventry,' while *knowledge* of such an offence would have insured the expulsion of the offender. Now 'bribery and corruption' prevail to an extent greater than existed in the worst days of the Parliament of England, where, happily for England, the practice, has been reformed, as it must be here, or corruption will undermine the government. No measure, however meritorious, escapes the attention of 'strikers.' Venal members openly solicit appointment on paying committees. In the better days of legislation, when no unlawful motive existed, it was considered *indelicate* in a member to indicate to the Speaker any preference about committees. The evil has been growing, each year being worse than the preceding, until reform is sternly demanded. Could the secret history of the present Legislature be exposed to the public gaze, popular indignation would be awakened to a degree heretofore unknown. In the Assembly everything was struck at. Not even a religious charity found exemption. The source of rapacious corruption were the Assembly Railroad Committee, and the Committee on Cities and Villages. I say this upon reliable authority, to correct the 'Tribune' and the 'Times,' in both of which journals this Legislature is commended for its integrity. That there were honest and honorable members in both Houses, by whose integrity and firmness much bad legislation was arrested, is true. The Senate, fortunately, presents an inflexible majority of upright members; while in the House, the Ring was formidable enough to put through whatever paid or promised to pay liberally, in defiance and derision of the efforts of an honest minority."

Mr. Weed says, that not even a religious charity found exemption. We can confirm that assertion. A committee of benevolent ladies went to Albany last winter, and asked the Legislature to give them $ 20,000 in aid of an institution for the nurture and education of children who lost their fathers in the war. They said in their petition, that, after having been compelled to refuse admission to two hundred children of slain soldiers and sailors, who had no one left on earth to care for them, they had resolved to try and erect a larger building, for which purpose they proposed to raise $ 20,000, and asked the Legislature to double the sum. Even this holy charity the shameless villains "struck at." An agent of the Ring called upon the ladies, and said, in the plainest English, "Pay me $ 2,000, and you can have half the sum you petition for; pay me $ 5,000, and you have the whole." The poor ladies, confronted for the first time in their lives with the extreme of human depravity, knew not what to think of this proposal, nor what to say to the man who made it. Anxious for their orphans, and far from their natural advisers, they were on the point of yielding, when the husband of one of them came to the rescue, and urged them not to taint their infant enterprise with the leprosy of corruption. They were reluctant to give up the aid so urgently needed, but they did so at last. Later in the session, the Ring, finding that nothing could be got from them, allowed the honest minority to carry a bill giving them $5,000. This narrative we received from the lips of the estimable and distinguished lady who headed the deputation.

It is such facts as these which convince us that the Legislature, as now elected, cannot be trusted for the future government of the city. The reform must be radical. It must begin at the bottom, with the voters, and work its way up. The Citizens' Association — a body of eminent merchants, lawyers, and men of leisure, united for the sole object of reforming the government of the city — have proved, by most costly and laborious experiment, that the majority, long controlled by the plunderers, cannot be shaken from their devotion to them. By needless interference with the Sunday usages of the Germans, as well as by some wise and just restrictions upon the selling of liquor, the friends of reform have rendered the great grog-shop interest a unit for the corruptionists, and that interest can send to the polls twenty-five thousand votes. By very great exertions, an honest man can be chosen Mayor; for there is still in New York a small majority of the whole number of voters who will vote as they ought, if the issue is clear between honesty and corruption. But in the wards and districts inhabited chiefly by ignorant foreigners and vicious natives, the case is hopeless. Printed matter cannot reach them. They are untrained in the duties of citizenship. A prodigious number of them have some small interest in maintaining the system of plunder; for from the stolen millions flow numberless rills of lawless or excessive gain; so that the city is like an Italian farm irrigated by the dirty waters of a pestilential stream. They pay no tax. Since their share of the taxation is paid by them in the form of rent, it is the "extortionate landlord" whom they blame when their rent rises, in five years, from six dollars to twelve dollars a month, for two little rooms. They never think of going round to Councilman O'Rafferty's grog-shop, or Assemblyman Tooley's desk in the Comptroller's Office, or Supervisor McShaughnessy's market-stand, and berating *them* for cutting down their children's allowance of fresh meat and Christmas toys. It has been found impossible to make them see any connection between their pinching rents and the reckless votes of a man who has promised one of their relatives the place of seventh assistant door-keeper to the scavenger's office. The thing has been faithfully tried, and found *impossible*. What honest men print they cannot read, what honest men say they will not hear.

In view of the expected Constitutional Convention, we beg to offer for consideration the following suggestions.

No man should be deprived of the right of suffrage who now legally possesses it. The State must fulfil its compact to the end, cost what it may.

But no man, native or foreign, should henceforth be admitted to the suffrage who cannot read English composition of medium difficulty. More than that the State has no right to demand. Its right to exclude persons who cannot read arises from the fact that such persons are dependent upon others for the information without which an intelligent vote cannot be cast. Such a rule, applied to the city of New York, would exclude not less than fifteen thousand votes; and this alone would give the city back to its legitimate owners, the virtuous and industrious portion of its inhabitants. This alone would do it!

No man should be allowed to vote at any city or State election who has not paid a direct tax; and that tax should vary with the whole amount to be raised. It would cost about twenty millions a year, for many years to come, to govern, tame, and teach Manhattan Island. Suppose the voters' tax were thirty cents per million dollars of the levy. Then, if the city were honestly governed, a workingman's tax would be $ 6 a year. But if stealing should raise the levy to forty millions, it would be $ 12. Now, the difference between $ 6 and $ 12 to a man who earns $ 15 a week is such that he would be very likely to ask his representatives what it meant, which is the very result to be desired.

The system of governing the city of New York at Albany should be abandoned as soon as it can be safely done. If the city cannot govern itself, it must learn how to do it; and there is no way of learning how to do a thing except by doing it.

No officers should be elected by the people except the

Mayor and the members of the city legislature. The people are puzzled and confounded on election days by long lists of candidates, whose names they never heard before. To ask the mass of voters to select a corporation counsel, a sheriff, a comptroller, a judge, is self-evident absurdity.

The distinction between the city of New York and the county of New York, with all its costly train of consequences, should be abolished.

Longer terms of service for Mayor, Aldermen, and Councilmen would, perhaps, be desirable. The appointments to all minor offices should be permanent. No creature should be intrusted with the unlimited power of removal. If the city would be well served, it must treat its servants so that men of honor and capacity will be found to serve it. A man of honor and capacity will not hold his livelihood at the mere mercy of another man.

There must be a decided increase of many salaries. Men capable of managing the finances of a great city, men fit to control any of the departments, cannot be induced to forego their chance of fortune in private business by salaries no greater than those paid to bank-tellers and book-keepers. A rich man of respectable talents *may* occasionally be induced to serve as Secretary of the United States Treasury for a sum per annum less than modest housekeeping costs in Washington. It is insanity to pay him such a salary, it is true; but then the honor counts for something. In a commercial city, business is done on business principles; and if a $ 20,000 man is wanted, $ 20,000 must be paid for him. It is not just salaries that burden any people; it is stealing that does that. On the other hand, an officer who holds his office until proved to have misbehaved in it need not be paid the salary justly due to one whom a breath unmakes.

Somewhere in the system of city government there must be a power, a court, a something, independent and disinterested, before which an officer accused of misconduct or incapacity can be arraigned promptly and fairly tried.

It might be well that the Board of Aldermen should be composed of men who pay a tax upon $ 5,000 worth of real or personal estate. With a taxed and restricted suffrage, this safeguard against profusion might not be necessary;

but if the suffrage remains unrestricted and untaxed, some provision of this kind will have to be adopted.

These are some of the ideas which have occurred to us, and we offer them for consideration, with sincere deference to those who are versed in the art of governing. It is an arduous task which the people of New York have before them, and it will task both their wisdom and their patience to the uttermost. It will be difficult to dislodge the public thieves. It was difficult to take Richmond. But the taking of Richmond and the capture of the Rebel army were not more essential to the triumph of the United States over its enemies, than the reform of the government of New York is to the credit and spread of free institutions throughout the world. We have all heard of revivals of religion. Why may we not look for a great and glorious revival of public spirit? There are, indeed, indications that such a revival has begun. We hear of several instances of men of leisure who are awakening to the truth that there is a nobler way of using the gift of leisure than in looking out of a club window, or in collecting valueless rarities, or in printing exactly one hundred copies of antiquated trash upon "large paper." The existence of an organization so respectable and determined as the Citizens' Association is a sign of promise, and we hope to see its efforts seconded by other societies. Dr. Franklin mentions that, several months before the meeting of the Constitutional Convention of 1787, clubs and societies were formed for the purpose of exchanging opinions and gathering knowledge relating to the science of government. One of them met weekly at his own house, when papers were read and discussed, and questions were proposed for consideration during the week. Why not have a dozen such in every ward this winter ready to co-operate with the Citizens' Association? The "Tribune," which has honorably distinguished itself by giving unrelenting publicity to schemes of spoliation, and the "Times," which has exposed much of the interior working of the system, and holds no parley with the thieves, — both, we are assured, are ready to lend their columns to the work of reform. Whatever any club may be able to expose or suggest, that is of the requisite brevity and importance, will find ready access to the public through those great journals.

We have been obliged in this article to limit ourselves to a single feature of the misgovernment of New York, — the stealing of the public money. There are departments of the system into which we shrink from casting a glance. To some of these corrupt men are intrusted the pauper, the sick, the criminal, the insane. It is their duty to guard the myriads of the virtuous poor against the rapacity which builds for them habitations that are unsafe and pestilential. Think what the government of such a city might be and do, what noble institutions it might found, what grand experiments undertake, what beautiful edifices construct, what merit employ and reward! The legislature of the city, composed of men eminent in business, in science, and in benevolence, — the men first in their several spheres, — would rank high among the great parliaments of the world, and contribute powerfully to its advancing civilization. The city of New York abounds in able and honest gentlemen, in every sphere of life. On just conditions they can be won to the public service. Why can we not have them?

And let no one suppose that this is a subject which concerns the people of New York only. It concerns us all. Not only has every American citizen an interest in the welfare and honor of his country's chief city, but the evils under which New York suffers exist, to some degree, in many other towns, and threaten *all* of them. New York, as we have said, is a sieve which lets through the best of the emigration that comes to our shores, but catches and retains the worst; and therefore it is in that city that the system of unqualified suffrage has been *first* put to a test under which it has broken down completely and hopelessly. But in all our large cities there is of necessity an assemblage of ignorant, irresponsible, and thoughtless men, totally incapable of performing the duties of citizenship. We accordingly find in Brooklyn, Philadelphia, Boston, New Orleans, San Francisco, Chicago, Albany, Rochester, Buffalo, St. Louis, and many other cities, the insidious beginnings of that misgovernment which has made New York the by-word and despair of the nation.* New York, too, is suffer-

* During the prevalence of the cholera, an appalling glimpse was given the public of the interior of a jail in the city of Brooklyn. An eye-witness wrote: "The cholera there resulted from overcrowding the cells. The ventilation is bad, the air offensive, the food, pork, beans, bread, and mo-

ing vicariously for her sister cities. As it has been her destiny to suffer most from the evils of ignorant and untaxed suffrage, so it is her duty to wrestle first with those evils, and apply a remedy which shall be radical, final, and universally imitable. She will perform that duty. She is performing it. No city of equal size on earth contains so great a mass of public spirit and administrative capacity, and we feel persuaded that the time is near at hand when those great qualities will be successfully exerted in rescuing the metropolis from the hands of the spoilers who have stolen into possession of it.

It looks now as though one half of civilized mankind were going henceforth to live in towns; and it appears to us that in the laying out, the decoration, and government of towns America has shown a particular talent. How full of all pleasantness are the villages of New England, with their gardens and lawns, their tidy fences and spotless houses, their ample streets, and their mighty elms waving over all. What other land can show towns so vigorous and handsome as Nashville, Cleveland, Detroit, Buffalo, Rochester, and fifty others that will occur to the reader? What a spirited thing it was in Vermont to commission young Larkin Mead to adorn her Capitol with a statue of Ethan Allen; and in Cleveland, to commemorate Perry's victory by one of the finest out-of-door monuments in the world; and in Tennes-

lasses; and when the late intensely hot and debilitating weather is taken into account, it should be a matter of wonder that every one was not stricken down. The criminal courts adjourned from June until October, and to my knowledge there are many there too poor and friendless to get bail, that will be able to prove their entire innocence when put on trial. To keep these persons in overcrowded cells with broken-down drunkards, whose systems were fitted by long habit for disease, would be little better than murder. . . . . A panic existed that no imagination can conceive. Terror was in every face. In one cell, an Englishman in collapse, rising up and falling down convulsively, his cell-mates running round almost distracted; in another, a corpse about to be removed. Two little boys, waiting to go to the House of Refuge, were screaming at the top of their voices from fear; a drunken man singing a maudlin song in a corridor; men in the halls, with their faces to the gratings, trying to breathe fresh air, for fear of inhaling contagion. Several others, with symptoms of approaching cholera, were expecting death. If all the prisoners could be kept in the jail until they dropped off one by one, there might be some sense in it, apart from its inhumanity. But the jail supplies the almshouse, the penitentiary, the workhouse, and, in many instances, the lunatic asylum, with inmates. Prisoners are first usually taken there before being sent to those institutions."

see, to crown the heights of Nashville with a State House of unequalled elegance and solidity; and in marvellous Chicago, three times to raise the entire city for the sake of better drainage, and to bore far out under Lake Michigan for pure water! How good it was in great Boston to put it within the reach of all her boys and girls to learn how to swim, and of all her men and women to practise the art! This was one of those fine details of civilization which are only reached after the great essentials have been realized and become habitual. New York, too, might boast, even amid her blushes. The Central Park was a noble gift to posterity; the Croton Aqueduct was a truly Roman thought; and all the islands, — are they not covered with public institutions, nobly planned? We can truly say, that the people of the United States have shown an aptitude for orderly and elegant arrangement. They know how to make their towns and cities fit abodes for civilized beings, and they mean to make them such.

But the spoiler must be expelled, or he will spoil all. Honest men possess all the true, trustworthy intelligence there is in the world. Villains of talent there may be, but no wise villain, still less a villain of public spirit. The thieves must be driven out, if it costs a bloody war; and it *will* cost a bloody war if they are not.

THE END.

Cambridge: Electrotyped and Printed by Welch, Bigelow, & Co.

www.ingramcontent.com/pod-product-compliance
Lightning Source LLC
LaVergne TN
LVHW020111110826
845151LV00001B/126

* 9 7 8 1 4 2 5 5 4 3 5 8 7 *